ANNIE LENNOX

The Biography

ANNIE LENNOX
The Biography

Bryony Sutherland and Lucy Ellis

OMNIBUS PRESS
LONDON · NEW YORK · SYDNEY

Copyright © 2001 Omnibus Press
(A Division of Book Sales Limited)

Jacket designed by Phil Gambrill
Picture research by Nikki Lloyd

ISBN: 0.7119.7986.3
Order No: OP48174

Exclusive Distributors
Book Sales Limited,
8/9 Frith Street,
London W1D 3JB, UK.

Music Sales Corporation,
257 Park Avenue South,
New York, NY 10010, USA.

The Five Mile Press,
22 Summit Road,
Noble Park,
Victoria 3174, Australia.

To the Music Trade only:
Music Sales Limited,
8/9 Frith Street,
London W1D 3JB, UK.

Every effort has been made to trace the copyright holders
of the photographs in this book but one or two were unreachable.
We would be grateful if the photographers concerned would contact us.

Printed by MPG Books Ltd, Bodmin, Cornwall
Typeset by Galleon Typesetting, Ipswich

A catalogue record for this book is available from the British Library.

www.omnibuspress.com

In loving memory of
Dorothy Marshall & Dorothy McPherson

Contents

Acknowledgements

The very first person we contacted with regard to this biography was Annie Lennox herself. As a very private lady with a natural wariness of examination into her personal and professional life, she declined to speak to us. We are therefore grateful to have maintained an open and friendly relationship with her representatives, 19 Management.

Nevertheless, an up-to-date biography of Annie Lennox is long overdue, and well-deserved. In unravelling the myths surrounding this most enigmatic figure, we were fortunate to be able to speak to the following people, from all facets of her life: Peter Ashworth, Joe Bangay, Marilyn Beattie, Ron Bryans, Irene Burnett, Chris Charlesworth, Barry Dransfield, Anne Dudley, George Duncan, Mickey Gallagher, Dean Garcia, Wendy Godfrey, Rob Gold, Colleen Gray-Taylor, Geoff Hannington, Derek Honner, Margaret Hubicki, Judd Lander, Sandra MacKAY, Barry Maguire, Hugh Megarrell, Neil Meldrum, John Murray, Jean Oates, Keith Peacock, John Pooley, Claire Powell, Michael Radford, Pat Reid, Ray Russell, June Smith, Patricia Smith, Jack Steven, John Turnbull, Lawrence Wess, Dave Whitson, Norma Whitson, Elaine Williams and Olav Wyper.

Certain interviewees requested anonymity, and we have respected their wishes.

Unfortunately, Annie's reluctance to become involved was conveyed to a few friends and colleagues who declined interview requests. Most of these worked with Annie during her solo career in the Nineties. Intriguingly, those involved before this time were willing to help in any way they could.

Additional research for this book was undertaken by Keith Badman, Andree Buchler, Ruth Byrchmore (Royal Academy of Music), Clare Ellis, Edward Ellis, Donna Evleth, Janet Snowman (Royal Academy of Music) and Catherine Taylor (Aberdeen Central Library).

Lucy O'Brien's excellent *Sweet Dreams Are Made Of This* and *Sweet Dreams – The Definitive Biography Of Eurythmics* by Johnny Waller and Steve Rapport provided a sound starting block and are to be highly recommended to all discerning Eurythmics fans. Likewise, certain articles have proved invaluable, including interviews in *The Face* by Max Bell and Elissa Von Poznak, in *Rolling Stone* by Brant Mewborn and various others by Alan Jackson. A comprehensive list of all books and articles used is to be found in the bibliography.

At Omnibus Press we would like to thank Chris Charlesworth, Lucy Hawes, Nikki Lloyd, Hilary Power and Melissa Whitelaw.

Thanks also to Richard Balls, Ruth Brown, Diane Cheung (Henry's House), Helen Donlon, Gary Gilbert, Camilla Howarth (19 Management), Tim James, Laura Lutostanska (19 Management), Peter Misson, Simon Robinson, Leila Stacey (Isobel Griffiths) and Chris Stein. A special mention should go to the Onelist/e-groups community, whose views are frequently perceptive and thought-provoking. Nice One Says Cherie.

Special thanks must go to Peter Ashworth and Rob Gold for their extreme patience and generosity with both their time and address books. As always we send our love and gratitude to Frankie Sutherland, Elton Thrussell and our families for their ceaseless support.

Bryony Sutherland & Lucy Ellis
September 2000

Prologue

I WANT IT ALL

"I feel I cannot be put into a box of just one concept. I think that everyone is a whole mixture of personalities, and I feel that's particularly true of myself."
– Annie Lennox

Wild eyes askew behind the mask, a trace of a sneer on her immaculately drawn lips, her tanned limbs flexing and forming a threatening fist, Annie Lennox glares at the photographer with a mutinous air of challenge. She is an android, or an androgyny; her 'razor blade smile' simultaneously beckoning and discarding criticism. But she sings like an angel.

Few have missed that most memorable visual image of the early Eighties. Nearly two decades later, the photographer's subject still patiently shrugs off the 'androgynous' tag which has clung to her since she reigned supreme as a gender-bending queen.

She has exacted an art form of keeping her private life just that; frequently denouncing glossy magazines as an "invasion" and sighing, "Personally, I don't see that talking about myself is interesting to people." Yet, presenting the perfect dichotomy, the poor Scots lass made good freely concedes, "Everything I write is about myself."

Few lives could be catalogued as intriguingly as in the searing words and musical mastery of hits such as 'Sweet Dreams (Are Made Of This)', 'Who's That Girl?', 'Here Comes The Rain Again', 'Beethoven (I Love To Listen To)', 'You Have Placed A Chill In My Heart' or 'Why'. Each of these tracks, and countless others, crystallises not just a genre of music but also an era, bringing back into focus periods of dramatic social and political change. Not necessarily consciously, fans of this esoteric mother-of-two have witnessed an ongoing autobiography of depression and joy, heartbreak and desire, and an unrivalled perfectionist's viewpoint on life.

The ability to balance a formal education at the prestigious Royal Academy of Music with an assertive need to rebel, a highly individual voice, multi-layered songwriting skills and a strong sense of visual presentation has become her trademark. Rarely has her music appeared anodyne or mundane. Always she has experimented to the extreme, along the way unpredictably blurring the lines between male and female, love and obsession, security and danger.

Her creative development was immeasurably amplified on meeting Dave Stewart; four years her lover and now recently reunited collaborator. Theirs has been a relationship of dependency, cruelty and devotion, producing almost as a by-product musical masterpieces that amply charted a decade.

All too frequently Stewart is deemed a mad professor of the recording studio, yet alongside co-writing songs with over 70 other major artists, he has successfully branched out into photography and film directing. Like his female counterpart, his work for charity is faultless, and tireless.

The two presented a united front through Annie's rise from Joni Mitchell-styled singer/songwriter, to three minutes of plastic-clad fame in power pop group The Tourists, before securing a place in history as the enigmatic frontwoman of Eurythmics. For the first half of Eurythmics' career it was assumed Annie was merely a voice for Dave Stewart's compositions. Even when she achieved recognition as a gifted lyricist in her own right, critics, often more preoccupied with beating her strong views to a pulp, maintained it was only Dave's manic wizardry that kept the hit machine afloat. How wrong they were proven when Annie embarked on a hugely successful solo career, outselling umpteen Eurythmics records with her debut offering, *Diva*.

The accolades Annie Lennox has earned within her profession speak volumes about the sheer impact she has made on the music world over the last two decades. The millennium edition of the *Guinness Book Of World Records* lists her as the artist who has won the most BRIT Awards since the ceremony's conception: an unprecedented seven in total for both solo and group work. The most poignant BRIT distinction has since been added; the 'Outstanding Contribution To British Music' award, which Eurythmics accepted in February 1999.

Of course, this last major achievement was a significant catalyst in propelling Annie and Dave into admitting that a decade apart was quite long enough. Their reunion was officially announced shortly after and the resulting album, *Peace*, surpassed all expectations; soaring on the back of a triumphant world tour – the profits of which went directly to charity without so much as touching the inner lining of the stars' pockets.

Naturally Annie's success is not just measured in her home country, and she has collected a handful of Grammys, as well as being frequently honoured by the likes of MTV and VH1 for her phenomenal onscreen performances as much as her musical output. As a solo artiste, Annie was from the outset exceptionally well received, but it is perhaps the prolific pop of Eurythmics that is best remembered; selling tens of millions of albums and spending well over 200 weeks in the singles charts, let alone nine cumulative years in the album charts.

"I'm just trying to do something interesting," she told *Record Mirror* in the late Eighties. "Life as I've experienced it has been a very complex affair. It's not always been easy, there are tensions going on between moments when you're calm and at ease with yourself and other times when it's not like that at all and it's all very threatening. As I said in *Savage*, 'everything is fiction, all cynic to the bone', and I feel like that sometimes."

Annie has not led a charmed life by any means and has fought tooth and nail to retain both her sanity and integrity in the face of on-going criticism and speculation. Her chosen career has presented a minefield of obstacles; as she herself once permitted, "If you want to be in a pop group, you either become completely debauched and die of a drug overdose after a couple of years, or else you renounce everything and live like a nun. I think I've straddled them both."

Her dual personality continues to inform her every action. The need for privacy and urge to be confrontational exist side by side. In the earlier stages of her career she took delight in mocking the very industry that exalted her by arriving at events provocatively dressed and prepared for battle. Yet she still readily admits that she yearns for the attention, and continues to return to it after uneven periods of 'retirement'.

"When I was a child I had a lot of fantasies, this is like living in them," she said excitably at the height of her first taste of Eurythmic fame. "The wigs, the videos with flash cars, even seeing myself on magazine covers – it's like a dream in many ways."

Despite being mistaken for a drag queen by narrow-minded MTV executives when first seen removing her prostitute's wig in the ground-breaking 'Love Is A Stranger' video, Annie has become an unlikely heroine for feminists, gays and traditionalists alike. "I took a lot of risks in my personal life," she states. "I always lived in a very full way, I can't do anything half-heartedly. I'm not grey, I'm either black or white. I always ran the risk of getting badly hurt through my experiences and destroying myself. I think that's common to a lot of women."

Indeed, Annie successfully pre-empted a whole generation of Nineties female talent and an altered perception of womankind by at least a decade, as former colleague Jack Steven stresses, "She was the pioneer of girl power, that's one of the things that made it so special. But also that she's smart, intellectual and creative."

Dave Stewart himself is perhaps best placed to offer the truest insight into the personality behind the myth. "Her strength is her intensity," he says, "she's not a person who messes around or does things for a laugh . . . which can also be her weakness as well because she gets too intensive . . ."

At the dawn of a new millennium, Annie shows no sign of discarding her performer's garb. Yet age has mellowed her. Always the first to self-deprecate, this self-made diva once proclaimed, "I'm not hanging on to success. If I've no right to be up there singing then I won't be. As soon as you start to be a has-been you should get out and find yourself a piece of pride and some fresh pastures. You don't do anyone any favours by hanging around."

Should the time ever arrive when Annie Lennox departs the spotlight for good, she will certainly be sorely missed, in any of her numerous incarnations.

1

WHO'S THAT GIRL?

"I see life as a very, very temporary thing: you're born, you grow up, you grow old, you die."

– AL

On Christmas Day 1954, just nine months and two weeks after their registry office wedding, Thomas Allison Lennox and Dorothy Farquharson Lennox (née Ferguson) were blessed with a daughter. They chose to call her Ann, a name popularly characterised by elements of creativity alongside practicality, countered by anxiety. As Ann herself later conceded, these were also attributes in keeping with her star sign. "I'm a Capricorn. I was born on Christmas Day with my Sagittarius rising. I definitely have the traits. Very determined, serious, tend to be disciplined, earthbound in that sense, feet on the ground. Goatish determination – that's the main thing."

Such tenacity she inherited in spades from her father. Tom Lennox was a 29-year-old boilermaker working at Hall Russell's Yard on the bitterly cold docks of Footdee in his native city of Aberdeen, on the north-east coast of Scotland. He was an active communist, his left-wing politics having been instilled in him by his proudly working-class parents, Archibald and Jeannie Lennox.

One of four siblings including an adopted brother, Tom had worked in the yard since the age of 14, following in the hard-working footsteps of his own father. A thoughtful and dedicated man, he started out as a ship's plater, then steadily climbed the ladder, becoming a boilermaker by the time his child was born. Eventually he would be promoted to foreman.

In his late twenties Tom met and courted Dorothy, daughter of William and Dora Ferguson, who was five years his junior. Dorothy's middle name was passed down from her mother's side and boasted truly noble origins; the Farquharson clan were considered among the most loyal and faithful supporters of the 17th century House of Stuart. They upheld their motto, *Fide et Fortitudine*, with pride and over the years amassed an estate encompassing approximately 200,000 acres of forest and moors in the Grampian region of Aberdeenshire. Dorothy herself was an only child and was raised in the scenic countryside of Aberlour, at their family home, 'Grantlands'. As family friend June Smith recalls, "Dorothy came from the country, but they're still very close. The whole clan is very supportive of each other. They're great ones for getting together."

By the time she met Tom, Dorothy had grown into an attractive, friendly young woman who had come to work in Aberdeen as a school cook. After their marriage on March 13, 1954 at 162 Union Street and an uneventful pregnancy, she was only too happy to leave work for a while to care for her cherished daughter Ann.

"Her mum's incredible," says Ann's later friend and colleague, Barry Maguire. "Beautiful for a start – a most stunning woman; tall and graceful, moves like an angel, gentle, with ivory pink skin. She always wears her hair up, it's always perfectly in place, but she doesn't come across as fussy. She's a very caring mother, wanting Ann to do the right thing." Dorothy's country accent, statuesque figure and habit of pinning up her long blonde hair in a bun set her apart from the average Aberdeen mum whose hair hung loosely in a curly crop.

Little Ann made her expectant parents wait until the very last 50 minutes of Christmas night 1954 before she made her debut at the clinically unfestive surroundings of the small three-storey Fonthill Road maternity hospital. It was just a short walk away from her parents' first home at 109 Gairn Terrace, a modest semi-detached house situated opposite a bus station in a quiet residential street. The Lennoxes lodged with the Middletons and for their rent they received a large living room incorporating a sink and kitchen area, and a loft upstairs for their sleeping quarters. Money was stretched to the limit, particularly with an extra mouth to feed, and could well have been a contributing factor in their decision to have just one child. But this only made the tiny family closer.

"They were a lovely couple," says June Smith. "I think they were quite strict parents. They only had Ann and she was a very special person to them. They were very proud parents." The fact that Ann lacked brothers and sisters meant that she benefited in kind. "They were a working-class family, but she was an only child so she probably got more than families with five kids."

"It's always a bit tough being an only child," admitted the child in question years later. "You tend to be under the illusion that the whole world revolves around you. It might have been nice to have an older brother or sister to take the attention away from me." Although she had no siblings, Ann had plenty of cousins to play with on her father's side, whilst on her mother's side she was later to form a close relationship with her grandparents.

"They were very quiet, very self-assured people," says June of the Lennox clan as a whole. "People from the north-east tend to be very close, they don't say a lot, they keep themselves to themselves, and that's how Tom and Dorothy were."

In stark contrast to this warm, loving and tight-knit background, Ann's physical surroundings were cold, impersonal and grey. Quite literally carved in stone, Aberdeen is known as the 'Granite City' because so many of its buildings are constructed from the pale granite quarried nearby. Most of the oppressive solid structures that line Union Street, the town's main thoroughfare, date from the 19th century. However beautiful some of the architecture and cobbled streets of old Aberdeen to the north of the city may be, there is no escaping the monotony of its greyness. When the city was relocated from the historic college environs 300 years ago to its present position closer to the docks, the colour didn't change.

"You have the North Sea where I come from," Ann later mused. "It's a very dangerous, dark ocean. It can change its mood a lot. It's not the blue Mediterranean. And it's cold when you step into that water and I think that that must have come into my sensibility somewhere down the line." Situated on the bracing North Sea coast, with the River Don to the north, the Dee to the south, and the brown quartz of the Cairngorm Mountains to the west, Aberdeen's primary industries during the first half of the 20th century were shipbuilding, fishing and granite. Although it was the chief commercial and fishing seaport of northern Scotland, in the early Fifties the city was relatively poor compared to Glasgow or Edinburgh, and due to its raw, remote location, remained extremely isolated.

This secluded nature led to the town becoming dominated by a few clans who were either large or important, as were the Lennoxes and Farquharsons respectively. Aberdeen's socio-economic detachment from the more cosmopolitan Scottish cities meant that the more spirited individuals within the town were able to get their voices heard, and because its citizens were predominantly working-class, the opinions voiced were generally left-wing.

"Her father was a member of the Communist party with my father," explains June. "And her grandfather, her uncle, in fact the whole family were in the socialist movement at that time. Her father was in my father's ward, he was in charge of a particular area." Ann's father and uncles inherited their strong political leanings from their parents' generation, notably Ann's great uncle Robert who became Lord Provost of Aberdeen, and her father who was a proud, card-carrying member of the Communist party. For a little girl this manifested itself in enjoyable social occasions like children's parties and picnics, but in private Tom's brooding on politics would make him increasingly strict and authoritarian in his ways, a trait which in time would sow the seeds of disquiet between father and daughter.

★ ★ ★

When Ann was just a baby the Lennox family moved from one council property, 109 Gairn Terrace, to another; 140 Hutcheon Street, on the north side of town. Their new home was a granite end-of-terrace tenement building located opposite, and consequently in the shadow of, an imposing canvas factory, with a tall chimney pouring out smoke.[1] The factory workers virtually took over the area, filling the street at break times, and it was the scene of the first female pay strike in Britain.

Tom, Dorothy and Ann found themselves in a run-down and unfurnished two-bedroom flat in a three-storey house with one communal toilet. This they shared with five other families with nine children between them. As she grew older Ann would be amazed on visiting her friends' houses to discover that they often had their very own bedroom; already social status was setting her apart from her peers. "Hutcheon Street was never what you could call grand," says June Smith. "Hutcheon Street is where they used to have the slaughter house, and just across the road was the only factory in the whole of Aberdeen city, a great big brick thing. They've kept the gates to the slaughter house, and the pub on the corner called The Butcher's Arms is still there, as it was when the slaughter house was there."

In this rather unromantic setting the toddler began to demonstrate musical leanings. Tom Lennox had long been a keen bagpipe player with a penchant for Jimmy Shand and his band, and secretly hoped that his young daughter would share his love for music. He had always enjoyed hearing Ann singing along to Gaelic folk songs and so one day brought her home a toy piano. Before long he was delighted to hear the three-year-old picking out tunes from the television on the tiny instrument. Tom and Dorothy were impressed with their child's instant aptitude for music, and encouraged her wholeheartedly.

But it wasn't just in musical terms that Ann was advanced for her age. At four-and-a-half years old she continued to please her parents by being accepted into the prestigious Aberdeen High School for Girls, near the

---

[1] Coincidentally, the narrow street running down the side of the factory facing their front window was called Ann Street.

centre of town. This was no mean feat, as June remembers, "It was a very selective process to get in."

The High School was originally founded in 1874 in Little Belmont Street. Due to its popularity as a grammar school of exceptional standard, the pupil intake expanded, necessitating a move in 1893 to its present location in a low, elongated granite building at 18–20 Albyn Place. This transition entailed amalgamating the school with Mrs Emslie's girls' orphanage which had been *in situ* since 1846.[2]

Colleen Gray-Taylor (née Sweeney) joined the High School along with Ann in 1959 and the two were friends until their late teens. "There were three girls' schools in Aberdeen, two were fee-paying and the High School wasn't, but you had to pass a test to get in," she says. "A very mixed bag of girls went there. There were certainly girls who came from affluent families, but there were other girls who had a 'normal' family life.

"It was a very strict school insofar as you had a strict uniform code. In the third term you took a letter home to say it was now summer, and you could wear your blazer and white Panama hat." Alternatively the winter uniform consisted of a black velour hat, navy tunic, white blouse and co-ordinating tie. "It was very polite," Colleen continues. "If a teacher came into the room, you all stood up and curtseyed. There was a great deal of emphasis on 'being a lady'. The school motto was 'By Learning And Courtesy' and it was certainly that!" The High School even boasted its own crest to complement the motto: a shield divided by a white strip at the top, displaying a book, two turrets and a white tulip. The strong sense of tradition was reinforced further with the adopted customs of many schools of this era. "There was an assembly with prayers every morning," says Colleen. "The whole primary school was together for assembly and when you moved up to the senior school, then *they* would all be together."

The girls went to their classes under the watchful eye of the head-mistress, Miss Margaretta McNab; a prim, tidy and respectable lady with horn-rimmed spectacles who was to serve the school for nearly 20 years. Colleen remembers: "Miss McNab was the overall head teacher, and in the primary school it was a Miss Clarke. She was nice, I liked her. She would come round and speak to everybody, she was a 'hands-on' head teacher." But for Ann, who soon earned the nickname 'goldilocks' on account of her long blonde hair, which was usually held back with an Alice band, the primary school wasn't always as friendly as outward appearances would suggest.

---

[2] When Ann left in 1972, the Aberdeen High School for Girls was renamed Harlaw Academy as it became co-educational.

She has often been quoted on her first academic experience as saying rather sweetly that she "learnt how to curtsey, point my toes, sit nicely at table and to stand up for old age pensioners on the buses." However, being suddenly uprooted from the protective cocoon of a devoted family and placed in one of two classes of around 30 clever pupils her age, was to prove a rapid learning curve for the sheltered apple of her parents' eye. "I wasn't at all academic, although the school was supposed to be for bright kids," she says. "I was bright enough, but I was labelled as a daydreamer because I lacked the ability to concentrate. I was always a 'nice' kid though . . . I tended to identify with people who I felt were hard done by."

While Ann struggled to keep up with the other children in the more scientific classes, there was no doubt as to her obvious artistic talents. She excelled at music and art and had a strong appreciation of English literature, although it was to be a while before the full extent of her musical ability was to shine through. Ann was a sensitive and thoughtful child who earned praise from those teachers honing her creative leanings, but these very qualities seemed at times to attract negative attention from teachers in other fields. This only served to confuse Ann even more, as she explains, "Teachers at school would praise me for my 'talent' on the one hand, and then on the other they'd be really cruel and sarcastic because I wasn't any good at maths. I developed a kind of dual superiority/inferiority personality complex."

This early criticism from her elders and being constantly under the scrutiny of her father, who was adamant that his only daughter should succeed academically, placed a pressure on the young girl's shoulders which was compounded by a further feeling of inadequacy in her neighbourhood.

"I was made aware of class differences as soon as I enrolled," she says. "Attending the school alienated me from the working-class people around me. These people were intelligent, but they were people who were never given the opportunity to develop." At such a young age, Ann had thus far been made aware of any cultural differences between her and other children only when she went round to her friends' houses and discovered she was at a financial disadvantage. The majority of the intake of Aberdeen's High School for Girls was from privileged middle-class families. Suddenly Ann was uncertain of her standing.

"There's a weird perverted snobbishness about the working class," she later observed. "I was born in a tenement and my father worked in the shipyards, but you don't go round shouting about it." Now conscious of this social contrast to her peers, Ann began ascending the academic ranks as a quieter, more introspective character than she might have been had she not felt quite so 'different' from the outset. Fortunately, music is an entity that traditionally cuts across all social barriers and she would make firm friends with the musical elite, such as Jennifer Brown and Rhonda Shand, both of whom were later to make names for themselves alongside Ann in the school orchestra.

At home Ann continued to develop her interests in the creative arts and, to her mother's enchantment, by the age of five she was writing poetry, drawing and painting pictures as well as singing and playing her toy piano. As Dorothy Lennox confirmed to previous biographer Johnny Waller, "Oh, aye, she was always drawing, she would take her drawing up to bed and draw there. I always thought she was musical, and I encouraged her, but sometimes it was difficult . . ."

The gifted young child soon became known for her inventive ideas after school and at weekends, and she began 'performing' regularly around Hutcheon Street. "All the kids from the neighbouring tenement houses used to play together out on the street or in the backyards," she smiles. "We could keep ourselves blissfully amused for hours with a wide variety of invented games – occasionally somebody would get the idea to put on a concert in someone's backyard. All the mothers were invited and they would erect a makeshift 'stage curtain' by hanging an old sheet over a washing line and all the kids would do a little 'turn' – everybody loved it!" In addition to this theatrical outing, Ann would wholeheartedly take part in traditional children's activities such as dressing up and going 'trick-or-treating' at Hallowe'en. Despite this evident willingness to play, another friend notes that even out of school, "Ann was a serious person – I never saw her double up or really giggle . . ."

At the tender age of six, Ann was considered old enough to leave her parents for a few days to spend time with her maternal grandparents, William and Dora Ferguson, in their home town of Aberlour. This quietly beautiful and historic village is to be found in Speyside, situated in north-east Scotland with Inverness and the Highlands to the west, and Aberdeen to the east. It is known mainly for its salmon fishing, Walkers shortbread and malt whisky, made with the water which originates from St. Drostan's well. William Ferguson, a gamekeeper, was supposedly one of the village's best advocates of said whisky.

Dora was delighted to introduce their grandchild to the classics she kept in her library, and to take the little girl for long walks in the wooded country-side surrounding Aberlour. Like her own daughter, Dora also encouraged Ann in her poetry-writing exercises and fuelled the child's imagination with stories and intelligent conversation, speaking to her as an equal. These happy times were to provide some of Ann's fondest childhood memories.

Back at school, at the age of seven, Ann made her first public appearance that did not require her to jump out from behind a neighbouring mother's washing. Her debut was at the grandly titled Aberdeen and North-East of Scotland Music Festival in 1962, where she sang a traditional Scottish song that included the immortal line, 'My banty hen has laid an egg, I'm having it for tea!' Neil Meldrum, a music teacher at the High School during Ann's time there explains today, "The Festival is organised by an independent council of people, both school and private music teachers, but not under the auspices of the school. It's for all ages from wee ones right up to adults. It's just like a standard competitive music festival, and is mainly a solo competition." Ann did not win the contest, though she provided the adults with a thoroughly memorable and spirited performance.

At this time she was also being instructed in Eurhythmics, a form of dance and mime derived from an ancient Greek format of teaching children musical rhythm by graceful movements. It had been devised in 1905 by the Swiss composer and teacher Émile Jaques-Dalcroze, who had intuitively recognised that young children in upper-class establishments were being taught music in a manner too intellectual for their age. The system had made sufficient impact in the early 20th century to have been used in a character-building scene by D. H. Lawrence in his novel, *Women In Love*.

Ann first learned of this theory of harmony in music and physical movement as part of the school curriculum when she was just one of dozens of girls obliged to take part in a weekly lesson. Her teacher was Marguerite Feltges, a vivacious and voluptuous lady whom Ann later described as "an eccentric dance mistress".

"Mrs Feltges taught Greek dancing," recalls Irene Burnett, herself a former pupil who had become the school secretary by the time Ann was in attendance. "It taught you deportment and that kind of thing. The Greek dancing was sort of floating about barefoot, a bit ballet-ish but not so regimented. It was all individual, but you would be in a circle and make patterns. It was very free; a freestyle of dancing." Adds Colleen Gray-Taylor: "We had to wear these short, sky blue, almost tunic-type things, with splits up the side. It was just like moving to the rhythm of the music."

"At the end of term there would be concerts in front of the school and parents," continues Irene. "Mrs Feltges was small, think of Margot Fonteyn, but a lot more 'proper'. She always walked like a ballerina, with her toes pointed and her feet turned out. Her hair was dark with streaks of grey. She was an extrovert." Marguerite herself harboured fond and rather telling memories of the young Ann Lennox. "She was a charming child. I taught her mime and movement, and I remember when 'Waltzing

Matilda' first came out . . . my pianist was playing it and all the children were dancing in a circle while I stood with my arms outstretched. And Ann was the child who took my hands and danced with me."

★   ★   ★

Still aged seven, Ann experienced another milestone in her musical development. Having spent many hours playing with her toy piano, she now showed an interest in her grandmother's full sized version. Fortuitously, tuition in the instrument then became available at the school. Ann would have welcomed ballet, Highland dance or piano lessons, but her parents could afford only one of the three and chose the latter. Although disappointed that she was unable to take dance classes, Ann began taking piano lessons with Mrs Murray, a conscientious, if a little old-fashioned teacher. Ann immediately showed an aptitude for the instrument and over the years was to prove and develop her skill by taking the recommended examinations faced by all budding pianists: "I took all the grades, one to eight and passed," she confirms. "It was the usual thing; Bach, Beethoven, Mozart, all of that."

The reasons behind Tom and Dorothy's inability to pay for more than one extra-curricular activity for their daughter were rooted in worrying and unhappy circumstances. Tom had changed jobs when Ann was small, and was now working on the railways as the wages were higher. But in 1963, when Ann had just turned eight years old, Dr Beeching, the then chairman of the British Railways Board, produced the controversial *Beeching Report*. This advocated concentrating resources on inter-city passenger traffic and freight, at the cost of closing many rural and branch lines. In short, Tom's post was no longer necessary and he was made redundant.

As Ann explains, her father had little choice in his next move. "He had to go back to the yards again. That was tough because he wasn't getting any younger and it's physical work in all kinds of conditions." Always a stern and somewhat distant fellow, the enforced change only served to make Tom tougher and more reserved, as he no doubt viewed a resumption of his old work as a bit of a 'step down'.

He returned to the shipyard in Footdee which, although once a tiny village with a community of its own, had now become a rather violent place where local gangs of disenchanted youths would hang around threatening to prevent entry into the area. Workers at the yard resigned themselves to toiling 10-hour days for overtime and bonuses, their tasks resembling a factory assembly line where a whole ship would be built every four-and-a-half days. This period saw the introduction of the welding technique, a revolution in ship-building. According to George

Duncan, a local resident whose father also used to work at the yard, the hapless employees weren't properly trained in the intricate procedure, and many ships built during this period of fast turnover sank as a result.

Meanwhile Ann continued to flourish at the High School, occasionally even taking time off her studies to represent her school in music festivals. She was now also a keen singer, having joined the school choir. The atmosphere could sometimes border on the competitive, as school friend Pat Reid remembers, "Aberdeen was such a musical hothouse at that time, and they were all of such a good standard, that it really did push you."

The Head of the Music Department at the High School in those days was Mr Cutbush. "He was a small, very bright little man," elaborates Irene Burnett today. "You had to be 'just so' with Mr Cutbush, you didn't step out of line. He was a very good musician. At one point he was the only man on the staff, but the girls wouldn't take a shine to him. He was quite strict, not *that* sort of chap." A man as fastidious in his mark book as in his teaching, it seems Mr Cutbush was perhaps more respected by the anxious parents than the wary students.

In 1964, when Ann was nine, she earned her first accolade for her developing abilities; winning second prize in a talent contest during a rare and well-deserved family holiday at Butlins. She performed the old Scottish song 'Marie's Wedding' and far outshone the majority of the young entrants.[3] But in May that year, any hope of further immediate appearances was quashed.

One year after the town of Zermatt in Switzerland had suffered an outbreak of typhoid, Aberdeen was struck by the same infectious disease caused by ingesting drinking water or food contaminated with the bacterium *Salmonella typhi*. In this case a mere 7lb tin of Argentinean corned beef was the culprit, as between May 5 and 10 it was sliced and sold in small quantities to customers of a local supermarket. Within a fortnight it had caused an epidemic.

Suddenly hundreds of Aberdonians were suffering the initial symptoms of chronic headaches, weakness, fatigue, abdominal pain and intestinal upset. As the illness progresses a fever develops, red spots appear on the chest, the stomach swells and the spleen enlarges. Without treatment using the relevant antibiotics, severe complications such as intestinal bleeding, urinary tract infection, renal failure or peritonitis may occur.

[3] In July 2000, ITV's *Find A Fortune* uncovered a unique 7″ made cheaply by Ann and a school chum in a Woolworths' recording booth. The pop song, which consisted mainly of the girls' giggling, was valued at £1,000 – a true collector's item.

"Aberdeen is now a beleaguered city!" proclaimed the city's chief medical officer, Dr Ian MacQueen, in Aberdeen's *Evening Express* on May 30, 1964. "Don't leave the city if you are an Aberdonian. Don't come to Aberdeen unless it's absolutely necessary." Following his advice schools, ballrooms, cinemas, youth clubs and swimming pools were closed. Even where public places were allowed to remain open, any canteen facilities therein were suspended.

For Ann and her peers this meant an enforced quarantine until the epidemic could be beaten. For the three weeks approaching the school summer holidays, she had to remain indoors, out of contact with anyone else and unable to attend the High School for lessons, let alone any of the scheduled music festivals. Aberdeen was officially given the 'all clear' on June 17, 1964, after some 444 people had been hospitalised. It was quite enough excitement for Ann, who was longing to get out for the summer and resolved to make the most of her school holidays that year.

She was back at the Aberdeen and North-East of Scotland Music Festival a year or so later, when once again she received second prize for her singing, this time in the juvenile girls category. For this honour she was rewarded with her picture appearing in the local paper. However, it was shortly after reaching her 11th birthday on December 25, 1965 that she finally found her musical calling.

"There was a flute made available in the school orchestra," she remembers with fond amusement. "It was a really old one with elastic bands fitted instead of springs and it was falling to bits – I called it Flora. In those days, I used to personalise everything, and my flute was called Flora. So, 11 years old, pigtailed and precocious, the envy of all the potential Shirley Temples of Aberdeen, I started to learn the flute and went to play in military bands and symphony orchestras."

Ann attended the Music Centre situated on nearby Loch Street, which was overlooked by a large soap factory and granite tenements similar to her home. "It used to be a school and was a very old-fashioned, but lovely building," Pat Reid, then also a budding musician, explains. "There were lots of different floors. Orchestra was held as you came in, in this huge hall, and then you went up this wonderful staircase to the military band which was held on the first level." Unlike the choice between piano and ballet a few years earlier, there was no financial reason why the Lennox family should object to Ann's attendance. "All the instruments were free and the tuition, if it wasn't free, was very cheap," says Pat. Ann embraced her new place of learning with glee.

Every Saturday morning she would get up early and walk to the Music Centre, her first appointment being to sing in Miss Auchinauchie's choir at half past ten. Described as "quite a character" by Irene Burnett, Miss Auchinauchie was solely in charge of the energetic youngsters and was a good friend of Marguerite Feltges, the Eurhythmics teacher. Ann's friend Patricia Smith remembers that, "You just had to be able to sing in tune – Miss Auchinauchie used to go round the schools and listen to the girls. She was an old, strict lady, but very kind as well; you had to do what she told you."

After a bout of enthusiastic singing Ann would climb upstairs to the hall where military band rehearsals were held. "The military band was a bit daunting because the conductor always liked to shout at us and everybody was a bit scared of him. We made an awful racket though – I'm not surprised he used to go mad!" Ann laughs today. Despite her initial wariness of the conductor, she truly seemed to have found an early passion at these rehearsals, as she later confessed in another interview, "I really loved it. I envisaged myself playing in a small chamber ensemble."

While Mrs Murray laboured the finer points of piano arpeggios and theory, the military band leader Bill Spittle undertook the task of teaching Ann to play the flute. Lessons would take place once a week either at the High School or at the Music Centre.

"Bill came from Newcastle and moved up to Aberdeen after the war," says Sandra MacKAY, a friend of Ann's and fellow member of both the school and military band. "He became the peripatetic woodwind teacher at a number of schools in Aberdeen. He was very influenced by American military bands which had woodwind as well as brass in them. His ambition had always been to start a military band for the schools on a Saturday morning, and because he taught at the schools he knew that people would come." Pat Reid continues, "He was a very strict man, he was a great disciplinarian – he had very high standards. If you were not a good timekeeper he would move you down the ranks. I think Ann was one of his favourites."

In actual fact, Ann herself has since admitted to being a little lazy and not studying quite as hard as she should, but nonetheless Bill's enthusiasm was infectious and she was altogether swept away by the beginning of this new social chapter in her life. "Bill loved all the razzmatazz, he'd come on in a white tuxedo – how embarrassing!" laughs Sandra. "He was an inspiration and was very encouraging. If he thought you had talent, he would make sure you had lessons once a month from someone from the Scottish National Orchestra."

"Bill's the one who really had a major influence on Ann, obviously being her flute teacher," explains Neil Meldrum. "It was strange in some ways because he was a very old-fashioned traditionalist as well, but I think he was perhaps a little more flexible than Mr Cutbush, realising the talent and ability that she had."

Not everyone was able to recognise Bill's softer side though, and perhaps being one of his acknowledged 'favourites' helped, as June Smith offers: "He was very strict, he was a contentious old sod! Ann got on well with him, but of course she *was* one of his best pupils."

Bill originated from a different background to most of the music teachers around at the time, having worked with more modern light orchestral material. He also made quite a startling physical impression, according to Pat: "He had a Friar Tuck haircut, and he had obviously had reddish hair, there was a hint of that showing. He had a lovely polished bald head with freckles on it and wore glasses and a moustache. He was also a little bit flashy in his own way too; he used to wear tweed suits, he was always immaculately dressed. I remember him being dapper, with shiny shoes." Such a character was bound to attract Ann's interest, and she soon became one of his most promising students, which by all accounts was no mean feat. "At that time the musical scene in Aberdeen was a competitive thing," says June, "and only the best from the city were allowed to play in the schools' orchestra and the military band – you were selected."

Sadly Bill passed away in the mid-Nineties, but he was able to give Lucy O'Brien, author of *Sweet Dreams Are Made Of This*, an informative interview about his time with one of his most devoted pupils. "She was a very promising young musician and showed flair from the start," he said. "She was a useful pianist and a proper singer . . . She wasn't swell-headed or inclined to think herself better than the others, but she didn't lack confidence. She had a zest to do well. Her *ability* gave her self-confidence." Even more importantly, Ann astutely seemed to recognise who was boss with this most abrupt, to-the-point and charismatic teacher: "She was wise enough that if she disagreed with me she wouldn't let us fall out. I wasn't an easy teacher, but I've had some good results . . ."

The overall portrait painted by the former members of Bill's military band is that children didn't just attend the rehearsals, concerts and even mini-tours because they were instructed to by their parents; they went to further their musical ambitions and because it was *fun*, pure and simple. "They would play the usual marches and overtures, but Bill Spittle also had a penchant for Latin American music, and he used to wiggle his bottom to it!" chuckles current music teacher Neil Meldrum, and both Sandra and Pat confirm that most of the music they played under the exacting beat of the self-possessed conductor was American marches, several light years away from the staid hymns they would be singing in school assembly. Colleen Gray-Taylor recalls that, "At prize-giving every year they had a big leaving ceremony on the very last day of school before the summer holidays and the school orchestra would always play at that." In addition, once a year the Saturday morning band would perform an eagerly awaited concert in the Music Hall on Union Street, which as Sandra recollects, "would be packed because everyone's mum would come!"

Interspersed with the weekly meetings of the school choir and the military band were the rehearsals of the schools' orchestra, of which Ann and Co were also members. "You got in through a recommendation from the school or music teachers. There was an audition for the orchestra," says Pat.

"The orchestra was taken by a local violin teacher called William 'Peddie' Willox, he was marvellous," explains Sandra. "We always did a Rossini overture, one of us would play a concerto and then we'd finish off with something like Sibelius' *Karelia* suite." Pat continues, "Peddie was a very thin man, always looking worried. He had a grey type of personality, not colourful like Bill. He was a bit wishy-washy."

Ann was now flourishing under guidance from her new tutors, and stood out from her contemporaries as being one of the better players, if a little quiet with it. "She was one of a group of girls who were very good musicians," remembers Neil Meldrum on the academic side. "The school was very well known for producing a lot of musical girls. Because it was a selective school these kids were obviously very intelligent anyway.

"She was a fine musician and a lovely flautist. There is a concerto for flute which was written for her by Louis Fussell, who was the string teacher in the school at that point and did quite a lot of composing. She was a good player and obviously made an impression on Louis." Nobody seems sure why this particular teacher should have taken such a shine to the young player, and to have an entire concerto written 'in her honour' was indeed worthy praise.

★   ★   ★

While Ann ensconced herself in the rigours of the Aberdeen music scene, the Lennox family uprooted once again, this time to the western outskirts of the city. Ann's new neighbourhood was Mastrick Land, a housing scheme set up by Clement Attlee's Labour Government after the Second World War. By the Fifties granite was no longer used in the construction of local buildings as the industry was fading fast, so a dash of colour was added to the young girl's life in the form of sandstone yellow. She lived in the only skyscraper in that particular area – in fact one of the first built in Aberdeen – its name simply 'Mastrick'. The tower block, which still stands today, is 13 storeys high and during their stay there the Lennoxes occupied a two-bedroom flat on the top floor offering a spectacular view over the city. It was a drastic change of lifestyle for the pre-pubescent girl.

"The city was smaller then," says local resident George Duncan. "This place, Mastrick, was miles out of town and you didn't have cars in those days. There was a bus service, but it used to take an hour-and-a-quarter to get there from the city, so the women didn't like it. But the houses had all the mod cons that we never had before, like a bathroom or a kitchen." While the Lennoxes also benefited from a local pub and a small parade of shops, the location entailed a major upheaval for Ann's daily travel to school.

She had now progressed into the senior division of the High School, having passed her 11-plus examinations in 1966. She was taught by history teacher Neil Kooney, head of French, Miss Middleton and head of music, Mr Cutbush among others. Mr Cutbush and Mr Kooney were the exceptions to the rule, as Marilyn Beattie who joined the senior school when Ann moved up laughs, "There were a lot of Misses at that school!"

The attitude of the High School had not changed from Ann's primary years; if anything it became increasingly scholastic and strict for the older girls. "It was very academic," Marilyn continues. "You didn't get any office skills, or typing lessons like other schools. You had to do a foreign language even then. In fact the top classes did Latin as well.

"Everything had to be just so. We used to have to wear berets at all times. If you were going down Union Street and you hadn't got your beret on, the prefects would tap you on the back, and even when you were out of school you would be reported for not wearing your hat. Even when I was nearly home I daren't take it off!"

Fellow pupil Colleen elaborates, "You had to wear a uniform but you adapted it. In the winter you had to wear a trench coat and you had to have the beret – it was very fashionable to put the beret right on the back of your head so that nobody saw that you had one. You weren't allowed to have your skirts really short, so as the mini skirts came in you'd have it a normal length for school and then roll it up as you left." The main uniform of the secondary school comprised a black blazer with the High School badge and motto, v-neck pullover, a blouse and a tie – a blue band was worn on the blazer to distinguish the sixth formers. "I remember at the time that we used to wear knee-high socks over the tights, but you used to get told off for that. And there was another phase when people used to have these tights with holes all the way up the sides!" cringes Marilyn.

Every academic year was divided into six houses, each with its own badge, primarily for sporting competitions. The annual school sports day was a tedious trial for the less athletic girls. "On sports day you would have to parade around the gym in your sports knickers with your house ribbon sewn on the side," Marilyn sighs. "It was awful, but you couldn't get out of it."

Miss McNab's reign of terror prevailed throughout the majority of Ann's time at the secondary school. "She could be very strict. You weren't allowed to go past the headmistress's room – that corridor was out of bounds," says Irene Burnett, adding that along with having to wear the beret at all times travelling to and from school, "you weren't allowed to eat in the streets". Marilyn remembers that even mealtimes were a bone of contention. "School lunches were provided, but not many people took them. Most girls had packed lunches. But there was a carry-on about that, because people weren't eating properly. Miss McNab would insist that you ate a hot meal, and if you took packed lunches you had to take a note from your parents to say that you would have a hot meal in the evening."

She recalls that most of the girls were fairly strait-laced: "There were very few who would stretch the boat a little bit, but you didn't really rebel." With specific regard to Ann, Neil Meldrum surmises, "From what I can gather, her time at the school was not altogether the happiest period of her life. The school was a selective single sex school and everyone con-formed, and Ann didn't really fit into that category."

2

WIDE EYED GIRL

"I had a very strong sense of alienation from everything around me. I wanted very much to fit in with one particular thing, but there never was one particular thing to suit me. So as a result I always found myself expressing certain aspects of my personality in order to accommodate, in order to seem as if everything was fine."

– AL

As Ann hit her teens at the end of 1967 she began to realise the extent of her isolation from any one social scene. Having already breached the boundaries of working-class origins and upper-middle-class education, she was even unsure in which dialect to speak as her mother retained her country vowels while her father spoke the brusque tongue of the docks.

The fact that she had no brothers or sisters began to have an increasing effect on her behaviour. "I was an isolated kid, writing poetry and imagining things a lot," she later admitted. "I was usually labelled a daydreamer because I lacked the ability to concentrate at school."

There were so many images and feelings flooding her brain, her anguish no doubt fuelled by hyperactive adolescent hormones, that Ann felt she had to give vent to her emotions in some form or other. Initially she chose writing. *The Visitor*, an early poem about an elderly person's disassociation with a young relative, was printed in the school magazine when she was 13, and gave a strong indication of her empathy with an outsider looking in:

> "And now, I lie here, still and old,
> And watch you flit by, here and there,
> I see the thoughts in you I thought myself,
> And wonder why you never seem to have the time."[4]

---

[4] *The Visitor* was published in full in Johnny Waller and Steve Rapport's 1985 book, *Sweet Dreams*.

Although Ann could be quite gregarious if she wanted, she often found it difficult to relate to intimidating large gangs of girls, and so preferred to share her thoughts with just one special friend her age. If she squabbled with this girl, as is inevitable with teenagers, soon enough she would find another companion and start afresh. "I'm very much a one-to-one person," she reveals. "I don't hang with the group, I never did. I always had one friend that I felt very close to." But as these relationships failed, she seemed happy enough to make do with her own company. "I'd drift off into my own private dream world instead. My self-image was always of a tortured soul who nobody really understood, wandering around in an empty school corridor with my music case and pigtails."

Seemingly unaware that she was already turning heads, the Lennox lass was blossoming into an attractive teenager. "Ann was a pretty girl," describes Irene Burnett. "Pretty teeth and a nice smile. She was quite tall and very slim. She had a nice bone structure." Colleen Gray-Taylor elaborates, "She had long, blonde hair and nine times out of 10 it was in pigtails, plaits." June Smith attributes Ann's good looks to her genes: "Ann is a striking person to look at, and in many ways she has the Lennox look – they're all quite striking."

At 13 Ann began to think more about her outward appearance and started to develop a unique style of her own. The shy young girl made regular visits to Aberdeen's second-hand shops and experimented with the hippy fashions that were filtering through after the 1967 'Summer Of Love'. Her mother was initially happy to let her daughter test the new trends, although sometimes the line had to be drawn. "When the two schools combined, and I was at the annexe, the orchestra came down and Ann was not allowed to play because she was wearing fishnet tights!" laughs Neil Meldrum today.

With this new image came a reappraisal of the opposite sex and the first stirrings of a proper social life, spurred on by a growing interest in pop music. This was a far cry from the childish saccharine of the *Mary Poppins* soundtrack which Ann had enjoyed five years before. Ann found new popularity in 1969 when she arrived at a school disco armed with her second, more hip record – Procol Harum's quasi-mystical 1967 recording of 'A Whiter Shade Of Pale'.

"I remember the first party with *boys* – I abstained from a kissing game while my copy of 'A Whiter Shade Of Pale' grew steadily more warped on the turntable as we played it over and over again . . . They played it continually. In fact, they didn't play anything else! And I remember I felt very hippyish, I'd just bought myself a blue paisley tent-dress and a little bell!"

Ann's early attempts to come out of her shell were met with serious misgivings by her father, who sought constantly to keep her away from such perceived bad influences.

"I definitely changed very radically when I became 14," Ann later acknowledged. "I developed my own ideas and opinions and they tended to clash with my parents'." Tom Lennox was a difficult person to please, especially after his demotion from the railways back to the docks. "I used to feel very angry for my father," Ann continued. "He built ships and was exploited and abused. He was tired all the time and got old suddenly. I feel very angry about that."

It seemed that Tom's resentment of his new situation affected the manner in which he raised his wayward daughter. "She didn't get away with anything as far as her parents were concerned," said her flute teacher, Bill Spittle. "I wouldn't say she was spoiled, they were kind to her, but thought enough of her to keep her on a tight rein – not like some who let their children go like scarecrows."

Although as Ann recalls, "there were loads of arguments and doors slammed," rarely was there a genuine reason for her parents to worry excessively. June Smith supports the view that Ann's well-reported spats with her father have been prone to exaggeration: "I've read various reports in the press about Ann, and her supposed break with her parents, but I think she was just a typical teenager. They were very supportive all the way through her various struggles."

However, many years later Ann was to divulge to *Q* magazine at least one incident beyond her control that marred her relationship with her father. One afternoon she arrived home from school to find her mother in tears. "My father's face was grey. I thought somebody must have died, but it was that the headmistress had called and said she wanted to see me.

"What had happened was the police had gone to all the schools in Aberdeen asking the prefects to write down all the people they thought might be on drugs. My name was on the top of the list.

"It wasn't true. A girl who was a bit jealous of me did it, I found out later. The headmistress said, 'People are talking about you. There are dark shadows under your eyes, your work is suffering, you won't pass your exams, you'll get kicked out of school!'

"I felt *betrayed*. As if there were enemies around me. And they went straight to my parents. I had no one to talk to. I was depressed all the time."

This was the beginning of a disturbing change in Ann's personality, which was to manifest itself in increasing bouts of self-doubt. "My childhood was relatively happy, sort of normal, nothing traumatic," she told *Musician* magazine in November 1985. "But at the age of 13 or 14, everything changed. I became very moody, very easily depressed, a bit withdrawn. Although I seemed to be an extrovert, in my own inner world I was much more withdrawn, watching the world, trying to cope with who I was and really very confused about it."

★　★　★

While Ann fought her inner emotional turmoil, somehow she continued to be a committed student. In addition to being an established and accomplished member of the school orchestra from her early teens, Ann's other scholastic achievements included attaining a Burns Poetry Reading certificate and playing for the British Youth Wind Orchestra. She was still a keen singer, taking part in the Aberdeen Schools Choir as well as being a willing participant in obligatory smaller scale vocal activities. "At Christmas time we used to go to the church at Union junction for the service, and we were all taught to sing 'O Come All Ye Faithful' in Latin ('*Adeste Fideles*')," remembers school friend Marilyn Beattie. "One of the first things you did when you went to the High School was to write the lyrics on the inside cover of your hymn book. We used to sing French carols as well."

In 1970 the inevitable happened. Despite her father's best efforts to curtail her social life, Ann started dating. Her first boyfriend was Clifton Collier, a public schoolboy whose father worked in advertising. Despite the excitement of a few dates, their teenage affair was sadly short-lived as Clifton unceremoniously dumped his pretty blonde girlfriend with no apparent warning.

"There was a boy I was mad about for ages called Clifton Collier," Ann later confessed. "I remember holding hands with him after school and meeting him at the local bowling alley when I was 15 – all very innocent. He told me to get lost and I was heartbroken. I didn't get over him for a long time. He's probably got a big paunch and three kids living in a nice suburban house with a dog and a mortgage by now – who knows?" It remains to be seen whether Clifton developed the paunch, but he later emerged as a successful businessman in the city.

Ann did her best to recover from this early heartbreak by throwing herself into the lively teenage scene that revolved around a couple of Aberdeen's ballrooms. A fervent desire to rebel against her father's strictness abruptly forced her out of her shell, and before long she found herself able to mix more easily with people her own age. At first Ann was allowed out only once a week, on a Friday night, so as not to disrupt her schooling, but although she was set a stringent curfew of 10.30 p.m. she managed to let her hair down in some style.

"The Beach Ballroom was down at the beach, obviously!" says Marilyn. "It hasn't changed much. It's got a tremendous floor – it springs. It was built for ballroom dancing, so the floor actually gives with the dancers. If you were all dancing close to the centre, you could actually feel it bend. The dance floor is a big circle, and you can go upstairs to the balcony and look down. The girls would put their handbags in the middle and dance round them. The boys would mostly walk round the side and when they saw a girl they fancied dancing with, they'd just tap her on the shoulder."

Situated on the seafront, just off Beach Boulevard and quite far away from any form of civilisation save a golf course, the Beach Ballroom soon became Ann's home from home. It is still there today, a grand white building resembling a pavilion with a red tiled roof and a little old-fashioned in appearance. Occasionally pop bands such as Pickettywitch and Scotland's own Marmalade would visit, but mainly the entertainment was the disco in the centre of the building which pumped out the decidedly un-hippyish sounds of Stax and Motown, and well-established UK favourites like The Beatles, The Rolling Stones and The Kinks.

Ann would keep up with these latest trends by listening to BBC Radio 1 on a transistor radio on her bedside table. Her favourite pop music was undeniably the black soul coming over from America. "I loved all the Tamla Motown artists and I think soul was the music I most related to – they used to play The Temptations, The Supremes, The Four Tops, Marvin Gaye, Stevie Wonder . . . That was what we used to dance to and I used to come home from that and sing songs I'd heard that night – because I never had a hi-fi. I couldn't afford it."

Other favoured haunts included the Royal Hotel, the Music Hall (which attracted big names like Seventies heavy rockers Deep Purple), and also the university students' union bar, situated beside the Marischal College on Broad Street. The teenagers experimented with alcoholic drinks like 'snakebites' or a notably brave student variation of "three nips of Tia Maria, cider and lager". Striving to appear older, some of the crowd started smoking, which Ann herself admits to doing while at school.

But this was still Aberdeen, and the young ladies of the High School were expected to carry themselves with decorum. "There was Madam's in Kenndry Hall and you used to have to dance properly there, the Gay Gordons etc.," Marilyn recalls. "And you would get your Coca-Cola and crisps at half-time. There used to be a lady who would go about and if you were too close to your partner she would tap you on the shoulder."

Although Ann had fully embraced the contemporary pop music scene, particularly citing the white British soul singer Dusty Springfield as an early heroine, she was still devoted to classical music and continued her

keen attendance at all the local orchestras. Flora the flute was in dire need
of replacement and Ann diligently saved up her pocket money in the hope
of one day affording a new instrument. On June 4, 1970 she took part in
the Aberdeen and North-East of Scotland Music Festival, which was held
at Cowdray Hall, Aberdeen, and she was listed in the *Aberdeen Press And
Journal* as winning the "Under 18 Woodwind Instruments Prize" for her
flute playing. Ann was only 15 years old and was delighted to come first,
beating many older entrants.

Summer 1970 also saw Ann sit her 'O' Level exams. Her studying paid
off and she passed her fifth year subjects in French, Art, Mathematics,
History, Music, Biology and English Language. Looking back over Mr
Cutbush's mark book, Neil Meldrum comments, "She did her 'O' Grade
Music in 1970 and Miss Lennox got a band four which gave her an A-plus,
and then she went on two years later in 1972 to do her Highers."

There was no doubt in anyone's mind that Ann's gift for music was quite
extraordinary, and after gaining such successful grades, she decided to concentrate on Music, Art and English for her 'Highers', the Scottish exams
taken in either the fifth or sixth year. Although it now seemed that music
was set to define her life, Ann continued to nurture her love of literature,
identifying with the often disturbing, confessional poetry of Sylvia Plath as
well as the beat poet Allen Ginsberg. In 1971 a younger headmaster called
Alexander Chalmers took over from Miss McNab, and this amiable-
looking, grey-haired man was to oversee the rest of Ann's education at the
High School.

Despite her growing love of dancing and pop music, Ann was still
searching for her niche. Although it seemed to her that her life might
revolve solely around music, she had no fear of the traditional aspiration of
becoming, in her own words, a "wife and mother". This was not surprising, given her unexceptional Scottish upbringing and the fact that feminist
career ideals took longer to reach Aberdeen. "I started to hang out with
people a lot older than me when I was 16, but I was too young to feel
completely at ease with them and the kids my own age just bored me. So
there was always a lot of polarisation going on, with me somewhere in the
middle struggling to find out who I was," she later divulged.

There was one aspect to her personality of which Ann was certain: she
was what she describes today as "boy crazy". Aberdeen's youth had
formed its own teenage custom, namely "doing the matt", a local phrase
meaning parading the length of Union Street, and hanging out in the
"monkey house" eyeing up members of the opposite sex. The monkey
house was to be found at the crossroads of Union Street and Union
Terrace. Now a branch of the CGU insurance company, it was then a

bank and acquired its unusual nickname from the two columns outside the entrance, akin to bars on a cage. Presently there are iron gates to prevent the young folk from convening inside, but in Ann's time this was *the* place to be.

"We used to meet our dates in the monkey house, when I was about 16," she chuckles today. "That was really exciting, standing on the steps, just as it was getting dark and the streetlights were coming on, all dressed up to go dancing at the Beach Ballroom." It was around this time that Ann started seeing an older student, a somewhat intense young man named Bob Morroco. They dated loosely for a while before going their separate ways.[5]

With this latest surge of confidence came more explorations into the world of fashion. "I was always a little experimental, to say the least," Ann recollected of this new hobby to journalist Tony Jasper. "I used to go to the local thrift shops and pore through these old clothes. I would come back with great parcels of second-hand clothes and with high delight used to show my mother all these clothes. I'd spread them over the floor. She used to literally pass out and say, 'I'm not walking down the street with you wearing those things,' or, 'Oh, God, no,' a pained look used to cross her face . . ."

★   ★   ★

If Ann often gave her parents cause for concern, she also provided them ample opportunity to beam with pride. The sixth formers at the High School traditionally put on a play each Christmas and Ann's year was no exception, choosing *Peter Pan* for their production in December 1971. Alongside their adaptation of the well-known story, the pupils would add humorous references to their teachers, emphasising recognisable mannerisms and personal habits.

But it wasn't just the script that was under their control. "There were a lot of girls who would meet and come up with ideas whenever they had spare time," recalls Colleen Gray-Taylor. "All the outfits were made by the girls. The sixth year did the whole thing, all in their free time. Everybody had a part." If any one of the teenagers was not interested in performing then she could be involved behind the scenes, but Ann excelled herself, stealing the show in the lead role of Peter Pan.

"Playing Peter Pan in the school pantomime was my first *big* starring role. Typically I hogged all the limelight. I loved it. It was such fun to be let loose on stage, really exciting," says Ann, still fond of the memory years

---

[5] Bob Morroco is now a taxi driver working near Aberdeen airport.

later. She also left a lasting impression on her classmates, as Colleen remembers, "Ann really was very, very good. Even then you could see that she had something a bit different from the rest of us who were in the chorus."

The show was performed twice, once for the pupils and then again for family and friends who were seated on a raised, wooden tier, facing the small stage in the school's dark, imposing main hall. Marilyn Beattie describes the unforgettable climax of the show – the first time Ann was to experience resounding audience appreciation for her singing. "The show was mainly verse, but there was also quite a lot of music in it. Ann was superb as Peter Pan, she came to life on stage. She sang 'My Way' at the end of the pantomime. It wasn't so much when we did it for the school, because the children didn't really know 'My Way', but when we did it for the parents, I remember that applause; it was deafening."

In the meantime Ann and her contemporaries had witnessed considerable change in Aberdeen. During that same month, December 1971, there was a demonstration involving 2,500 students who marched down Union Street in support of government reform for the financing of further education. While the youth action hit the local headlines, the Reverend James W. Tyrrell, minister of Mastrick Parish Church, wrote an article for his Christmas edition of the parish magazine declaring that the present generation of teenagers was the finest yet. He opined that families in the Seventies were encountering an "unbridgeable gap" between parents and children which was partly due to modern society as mothers were returning to work. This in turn meant that the area was increasingly affluent with teenagers receiving an allowance of more than £2 per week, sufficient to purchase a brand new LP by their favourite pop star.

Indeed, Aberdeen in general was enjoying a financial boost as the North Sea oil boom in the early Seventies enabled the granite city to become the hub of the industry and a major supply centre for the offshore oil rigs. With this economic growth the city improved and expanded, providing better housing, new offices, schools, and industrial development in chemicals, fertilisers, the manufacture of machinery and the curing and canning of the abundant fish catch. School friend Frances Penny astutely recognised the effect this change had on the town's youth. "In the pre-oil days Aberdeen was a lot smaller, more parochial and old-fashioned. If you went downtown on a Saturday afternoon you always saw people you knew. After the oil boom it became a lot bigger, with a lot more incomers, a turnover of people and more cosmopolitan wine bars and nightclubs. Within one or two years everything changed very quickly, and there was suddenly more money."

With Aberdeen blossoming as a city, it came as a complete surprise when Ann announced to Tom and Dorothy her brave decision to leave behind all that was familiar in favour of the bright lights of London. Having toyed with the idea of going to art college she realised that her true vocation lay in classical music. Although she loved the trendy pop and soul played in the ballrooms, at home Ann had a treasured suitcase full of her favourite composers; among them Mozart, Telemann, Bach and Debussy.

Aberdeen boasted a most respectable university dating back over half a century, which had in fact kept the more historic parts of the town together when the beautiful old buildings were threatened with demolition. There was also an excellent university in Edinburgh and a specialist music college in Glasgow, but Ann was resolute. London was the path to her future.

She was not alone in her decision to further her musical education – nearly 30 students from the High School were to follow that route from the four or five academic years around Ann's age. Many of these were later to teach music themselves. However, Ann had an additional reason for wanting to move out of town, and has since hinted that her parents' increasing over-protectiveness was a major contributing factor.

"I wanted to be a music student desperately," she told journalist Elissa Van Poznak in January 1985. "I considered the Glasgow Academy of Music too provincial for me and really wanted to go to the Royal College."

The Royal College of Music is among England's finest musical establishments, based in Knightsbridge, in up-market London SW7. For Ann this entailed a 400-mile trip to participate in a rigorous series of auditions, testing her flute, keyboard, vocal and theoretical abilities in the early part of 1972. In the event Ann's future did not lie at this College, and there was a piquant lesson to be learnt from her unsuccessful audition.

"Actually, here's an interesting bit of sexual discrimination for you," she continued to Van Poznak. "I was told that the one remaining place on the performer's course was down to me and this boy and they said, 'Wouldn't you rather become a teacher, we think it's more realistic, your being a girl?' I said, 'No, I don't want to be a teacher, I want to play the flute.' The boy got the place."

Dismayed by the College's old-fashioned attitude, Ann persevered with auditions at the remaining specialist institutes in London. On April 18, 1972 she attended an interview and a day's worth of tests at the Royal Academy of Music. Those teachers holding the auditions immediately noted her high intelligence in addition to her technical proficiency on the flute. She was offered a place on the proviso that she attained good grades in her Highers, which were to be held in two month's time, and without hesitation she accepted.

Once the serious-minded student set her sights on achieving a goal there was no stopping her, and in June 1972 Ann passed her examinations in Art, Music and English with flying colours. Her last ever school report from nearly 13 years at the High School contained the comment, "Undoubted talent in music!" and legend has it that she ripped her detested school beret in two on the day she left.

★   ★   ★

Ann's acceptance into the Royal Academy of Music spelled a dramatic change in lifestyle for which nobody was quite prepared. She was, after all, still only 17 years old, and a wrenching move all the way down to London posed very real questions of maturity, safety and independence. June Smith proved to be a source of great support at this most important junction in Ann's life.

"I remember when she first got in to the Academy we had a baked potato in Aberdeen's first baked potato house and she talked about her fears of going to college; should she do it, or should she not," June recalls. "It was a big thing for people to go away, not just to Glasgow or Edinburgh, but to actually take yourself into a different culture, away from your parents. She was quite concerned about how she would cope if she didn't like it. There was possibly the doubt in her own mind whether the Academy was the right place for her, but I think that's something that everybody goes through.

"Tom and Dorothy were as concerned as any other parents, but I think they were very proud of the fact that Ann had succeeded in getting into the Academy. In fact, the whole family were proud that she had decided to make music her career, and to be able to pursue it at this level. To make the break to want to go to London, and then to actually get in to music college was really quite a feat from up here." Contrary to popular belief, although Ann was a talented musician she would not attend the Academy on a scholarship, but as Sandra MacKAY recalls, "Money would not have been a problem, she would have got a good grant for rent and spending money. The fees would have been paid by Scotland." Indeed, Ann would have received support by the Scottish Education Department, which was standard for all Scottish students.

Nevertheless, any student travelling to the notoriously expensive capital of England was well aware that hard cash was one of the necessities of university life, and over the summer of 1972 Ann took on a temporary job to save some money to help her on her way. The local Findus Fish factory thus became the first establishment to benefit from the labours of Ann Lennox, and although she was determined to profit financially from this somewhat smelly engagement, it didn't make the work any easier to bear.

"I used to wrap my work clothes in a plastic bag each night and fall flat on my face when I opened it the next morning," she told Johnny Waller. "Working on the plaice-filleting machine made me want to throw up all the time. Yet, looking back, I suppose it was beneficial in discovering exactly what I *never* wanted to do again. I was paid a basic wage of £9.50 for a 40 hour week! I saved all the money I could to supplement my grant." When she left the job at the end of three long months, Ann swore that she would never again set foot in a fish factory. It was clear that manual employment was not something for which this particular young Aberdonian was cut out.

3

REGRETS

"Although I'm not embarrassed about my past it's, well, past *me."*

– AL

At the age of 17 Ann faced the daunting prospect of leaving all she had ever known behind and heading for the 'big smoke'. "I suppose it sounds rather clichéd, but there was always something missing for me up in Aberdeen, but I never quite knew what it was. And I came down to London, I suppose expecting that I would find what was missing up there," she later explained in *NME*.

Ann's acceptance into the Royal Academy of Music was not just a matter of pride for herself and her family; the High School had also adopted her ambitions. But her self-admitted naïvety belied the fact that her parents were particularly concerned about their daughter's safety. "To think that you're coming from a fairly close family, a one-child household and all of a sudden you're uprooted into the big bad world," says June Smith. "To some extent you were sheltered in Aberdeen, certainly if you went to the Girls' High. And even though her grandparents, her father, aunties and uncles all involved in the Communist Party, it was still a very sheltered upbringing. Suddenly to be thrust into London must have been quite a culture shock." For Ann, this also meant leaving behind her small circle of friends.

Ann looks back on her arrival at the Academy in September 1972 with the hindsight of regret, although she was well aware at the time that it represented her only chance to escape provincial Aberdeen, which she had over time grown to resent. "On the very first day, when I arrived with an old trunk and two suitcases, I was terribly disappointed and knew already that I was going to hate the place – it was an antiquated wreck. It was so uninspiring and I was really miserable," she complains.

On first impressions it is true that the Academy can seem more than a little daunting to a newcomer. Founded in 1822 under the direct patronage of

King George IV, the institution's royal charter of 1830 proclaimed its virtu-
ous intention to implement "the cultivation of the science of music and the
facilities for attaining perfection." Situated on Marylebone Road, with the
grand and well-cultivated expanse of Regent's Park lying directly behind,
the imposing red brick Edwardian building looked after the interests of some
850 future musicians in the early Seventies.[6]

The first day for any student involves countless queues to register for
each module, having a photograph taken for an ID card (reinforcing the
myth that one has truly entered the world of the elite), and a series of
welcome meetings where freshers struggle frantically to decipher the maze
of practice rooms, studios, concert halls and classrooms that make up the
substantial five storey building. A single elevator accommodating all of
three people and one double bass is the only alternative to the grandly
sweeping central staircase stretching up for the first three floors; the site
where over the years numerous budding opera singers have loudly tested
the echoing quality of the spacious acoustics, much to the chagrin of all the
other students, including Ann.

The newest flautist was to be in the same year as future pop star Joe
Jackson, who enrolled under his real name of David Ian Jackson, and a
year below the intense and committed young conductor, Simon Rattle.
Ann signed up for flute lessons as her principal study to be taught by Derek
Honner, choosing piano as her second study. She would also be instructed
in theory, harmony and music history among other subjects, and her lec-
turers were to include Christopher Reagan as the Director of Studies and
Margaret 'Peggy' Hubicki, who was both a harmony teacher and Ann's
personal tutor.

The issue of Ann's accommodation had been high on her parents' list of
safety concerns, and they accompanied her on her moving-in day to the
recently refurbished (and unfinished) academic halls of residence at the
Ethel Kennedy Jacobs House in Camberwell. The building was to be
found opposite Kings College Hostel at 23 Champion Hill, off Denmark
Hill, SE5. It was an old listed building with extensive gardens at the front
and back, and the students delighted in visiting the popular pub on the
corner, the Fox On The Hill.

Ann had relished rather idyllic preconceived ideas about life in London,
somewhat misleadingly inspired by her choice of television viewing.
"There was a series on the TV called *Take Three Girls* about these girls
living in 'Swinging London' and sharing a flat together," she later

---

[6] In 2000 these numbers had dwindled to around 600, with a large portion of the students
coming from overseas.

chuckled. "I thought it would all be just like that . . . boyfriends with little white sports cars, wine bars, Kensington sophistication, parties, good times. Was I ever wrong!"

Elaine Williams, a singer and pianist, was also present on the day Ann moved in. "I remember her standing with her relatives in what was then being used as the dining hall, where we kept our food in cardboard boxes," she recalls. "We all had a cardboard box each. And I remember Ann standing there; a fresh-faced Scottish lass, fair-haired with a page boy hairstyle, very feminine, a bit unsure of herself. Peaches and cream complexion, hardly any make-up (if any at all), and a simple mini dress."

Brass player Wendy Godfrey was another student living in the halls at the time, and remembers vividly just how basic the accommodation was. "It was a large house that was refurbished for the students – it was the first year that it was open," she says today. "It wasn't finished, the kitchens weren't finished and there were about 60 of us there with a warden. All the rooms were different sizes, some students had individual rooms, and some shared." In the quest to feel 'at home' in these unfamiliar surroundings, the pupils would swap around and change room-mates until they felt comfortable. Quite by chance after a short time in the city, Ann met Claire Powell, a mezzo soprano from Cornwall, on the tube.

"You come up to London and everybody's a new face," remembers Claire. "It turned out our journey into the Academy was similar, on the Circle Line. We got chatting and that's how we got friendly." The two were to become firm friends for the first year or so of their studies, and soon managed to move around so that they could lodge together. They were decidedly underwhelmed by their shared abode.

"The room was minute, cramped. We had a basin and two beds in a room you couldn't swing a cat in. We just used to sit there and wonder how the heck we were going to get out. We were both miserable as sin there." The pair planned to move to somewhere more salubrious together in the future, but eventually went their separate ways although retaining their friendship for some time, both becoming members of the third orchestra during the rest of the first year.

It wasn't long before Ann came to realise the extent of her disappointment with Academy life. Having expected a place dedicated to music and its performance, she found instead a displeasing downside to this commitment; an atmosphere of extreme competitiveness encouraged by the shortage of places in the available orchestras and the one-sighted natures of certain musicians.

"I wanted to be in a chamber music ensemble or an orchestra because I was a fairly good flautist," she said in 1983. "After a bit I hated it.

Everyone was competing with each other and there was so much banal jealousy. I suppose we were all immature but the students just seemed like extensions of their instruments. They suppressed their own characters."

Hugh Megarrell, a trumpet player of the same year, confirms today, "Quite a number of people would have gone through Academy life without actually having the experience of playing in a big orchestra, the competition for places was quite fierce." Claire, too, offers a possible insight into Ann's disenchanted state of mind: "One had to very much fight one's corner . . . I always got the impression that she went on to fight her dragons from outside an institution like that, but I decided to battle on from within."

Ann particularly disliked what she saw as a 'closed vision' of her subject, in that her fellow students seemed unable to appreciate other genres of music, and certainly not the pop she herself had grown to love while dancing at the Beach Ballroom. "When you go to music college it's actually quite hard to find any broad-based people. There were talented violinists and pianists, but they're so single-minded," says Claire. "I think what was obvious about Ann from the start was how broad-based she was."

The flautist's growing resentment began to manifest itself in little outbursts, and one day she showed up for an orchestral rehearsal without her instrument. She had been hoping to keep a low profile, but her secret was discovered when there was a deathly silence in place of her small solo. Naturally the conductor was not best pleased and Ann shouted back defiantly, before being thrown out of the concert hall in disgrace.

★   ★   ★

Lessons at the Academy are structured so that the majority of rehearsals and teaching time can be incorporated into just one or two days, depending on the individual student's depth of involvement. Consequently the pupils find they have ample spare time in which they are supposed to practise their first study for five to seven hours a day, and their second for a couple of hours less. Halls of residence are quite understandably notorious for prohibiting instrument practise on site, and so students tend to drift back to the Academy to find themselves a spare room to occupy for as long as necessary. As a result, although there are relatively few lessons, pupils congregate most of the time at the Academy; in the canteen, the bar or the student common room. Along with the few nearby pubs on Marylebone Road and High Street, these become the main locations for the students' budding social lives.

"Because of the cost of living in central London most of us lived in flats and most of the flats were either in North London or somewhere south of the river," explains Hugh. "So the journey to the Academy was quite a lengthy one, and when you got in you tended to stay in."

"You never saw Ann that much," says trumpeter John Pooley. "I got to know her basically by sitting in the common room – there were never that many places to practise. If you wanted to practise you would have to sit in the common room and wait. Eventually one of the porters would come in and say, 'Who's the next person waiting for a room?' and then give you the key. So we would all have to sit there for ages – it was a bit of a social thing in a way. And that's how I got to know Ann. We'd have a chat about how things were going; your social life and so on."

It was in this setting that Ann became familiar with the composers and conductors studying at the Academy. Their constant search for players willing to perform their pieces for the price of a beer drove them to mix with anybody and everybody who has ever laid hands on an instrument. "Simon Rattle was heavily into contemporary music and sometimes he would be doing pieces composed by people at the Academy, or sometimes it would be contemporary composers," John continues, "and he would hold lunchtime rehearsals. I played with Ann in a few things, mostly small ensemble things. They weren't the proper traditional concerts set up by the Academy, just things that Simon set up. I remember thinking then that Ann was a very good player."

As a flautist participating in wind band, Ann would find herself socialising with the brass players in her year and although she still preferred one-on-one friendships, was happy now to mix in a bigger group. Norma Whitson played trumpet and remembers Ann as, "very, very quiet, but she was a strikingly beautiful girl. She did hang around with the brass players for the first year or so, so we got to know her a bit." However, players such as John were aware that Ann was uncomfortable with her new set-up. "She never really got into the Academy way of life. I don't think she was really socially orientated to the Academy . . . It was very separate in many ways. If you went down to the canteen the singers always sat on the same table all by themselves. The woodwind players were also like that, and I don't think Ann was."

Ann continued her friendship with the two girls with whom she shared a room for separate periods, Elaine Williams and Claire Powell. "Ann was quite a demanding friend – if you could fulfil it, you got it back in spades," says Claire today. "We used to talk an awful lot. Having both come from extremes of the country to London, to *the* Royal Academy of Music, *la crème de la crème*, we discussed how disappointing certain aspects were. I think the thing about the Academy was you could fit all your lessons into one day if you wanted, but unless you managed to find friends, it could be a very, very lonely place. She was very eclectic in the choice of people she got to know. She didn't just stick with the instrumentalists, she mixed with composers, conductors, all sorts of people. She was very inquisitive and had a great thirst for knowledge."

"The impression that I had of Ann was that she tried to fit in, she wasn't unpopular, but she just wasn't 'one of the group'," says Elaine. "I think she had difficulty finding a comfortable group to be with. She had a boyfriend and I felt she was more comfortable on a one-to-one basis with him.

"I remember him vaguely, he was slightly older than us, he seemed to appear in suits rather than in jeans and T-shirts. He wasn't at the Academy. She seemed quite keen on him, but I think it was a bit on and off. I felt he was a little bit smarmy, he came on to me one time! I didn't know whether that was because he was trying to make her jealous because they'd had a bust-up, but I didn't really get too involved."

Ann's arresting good looks continued to attract plenty of attention from the opposite sex, but to those who remember her, appearances proved to be quite deceptive. "When you see her now it would be quite hard to reconcile the two, because I can remember she would wear a pale pastel blue skirt and a pastel blue fluffy twin set," Claire reminisces. "It was very soft and very feminine. She had ethereally white skin; beautiful, incredible white skin. And she was exceptionally blonde, with enormous blue eyes. She looked quite demure. But there was certainly no demureness in the personality."

"The thing about Ann was she *looked* all 'peaches and cream', but she was a tough cookie underneath," agrees Elaine. "I always felt there was something quite hard about her. She had this soft Scottish accent, but what came out of her mouth was as if the words were made of steel, rather than a softer, more feminine person." Claire, as one of Ann's few confidantes, grew to understand some of the reasons behind this 'steeliness' – it appeared that the loner from Aberdeen was battling with numerous conflicting issues from the moment she set foot in London.

"Ann had a core of steel, but the counter-side of her was an extremely emotional girl, very sensitive, someone who felt things very deeply. But it was counterbalanced by a steely, angry side. I always remember her saying that she found it hard when she went to grammar school because she'd got the 11-plus and she said that where she lived in Aberdeen, people didn't go to grammar school. And she learned to be tough quite early on."

Another indication that events in the young flautist's past made her a force to be reckoned with comes from Elaine. "Ann said to me one night that she had been followed when she was walking through Camberwell on her own. This man was following her and rather than running off, she turned round and confronted him.

"She was scared, but stood her ground and just uttered verbal abuse at him and scared the living daylights out of him. He just scarpered!" It was becoming increasingly apparent that Ann felt no one should stand in her way, even if that meant taking risks or rebelling against the norm.

Accordingly, the impression made by Ann on her closest friends was very deep and remains firm to this day. "She was just someone who was bursting with talent, but it wasn't this incredibly specific single-minded talent like a future solo violinist or a future concert pianist," continues Claire. "There was talent of various kinds bursting out of her, whether it was artistic design, or musical composition, or whatever. I don't think she needed *fun*. My memory of what Ann needed was a lot of intellectual stimulation. Although I can remember we used to have a laugh and knock back the beer or wine, or whatever it was we drank in those days.

"She was a serious, intense person. Very interesting, stimulating company, but I wouldn't put her down as someone who was first in line for student rag week. She had quite an aloofness about her. I think Ann was very clear about what she wanted; she wanted knowledge and intellectual stimulation, and to be with people who could give her all that."

On one occasion, Ann's quest for intellectual stimulation stretched a little further than was comfortable for her fellow lodgers. "One night at the halls there were a number of us girls up very late, and we were in this large room where we held a séance," remembers Elaine. "It was about midnight and I remember certain people there; there was Hilary, Kate, Helen, Ann and Moira." The girls hastily constructed a handmade Ouija board and began to summon the spirits. "We were moving the glass around – well, *we* weren't moving the glass around, it was moving itself!

"Anyway Ann decided, no one else did, that *she* wanted to call up 'Lucifer X', and a number of us in the group thought, 'Oh no! What is she doing?' But she wanted to, and then things went haywire . . . the glass started to go bananas and I left at this point." Still, a number of Ann's classmates bravely remained in the room to see what would happen.

"The following day I heard that things went really badly wrong. Moira, who was sitting back from these goings-on, imagined that she was in her room looking down into the garden, and she saw two men having a duel, in period clothes. Then she suddenly felt as if she was being strangled and she couldn't get her breath. Helen later said to me that she didn't know what to do, so she just called out 'Jesus Christ' and things from the Bible. She was very scared. I remember after that that Moira was a bag of nerves. She had to go and see a priest about it . . ."

★   ★   ★

34

Ann's bravado was perhaps a direct reaction to the inflexible method of teaching, although by all accounts it appears that certain tutors would bend to accommodate this unpredictable and often moody teenager. Ann has never hesitated in interviews to stress how much she loathed the ways of the Academy, with oft-quoted statements like, "I hated the place, the boys were all gay and the girls all thought they were Maria Callas." She spoke of her experiences further in *Musician* magazine in 1983: "I'd been taught that there was a perfect phrasing, a perfect sound, a perfect dynamic. But there is no perfect. The most perfecting thing is to express yourself, totally, but nobody teaches you that. I think for most trained musicians, it's just a job. I learned that there and it was horrible."

In contrast to Ann's perception of the tutors, her flute teacher Derek Honner explains that he usually forged a friendly relationship with his students, whereby they would be able to chat to him as a peer rather than an elder. With Ann however, he found it difficult to penetrate her strong reserve. "She was not the sort of person who opened up to you very easily. She was not that forthcoming. She tended to be a bit of a loner in a way. She didn't gush over you, or come in with apparently great expectations. She was rather, maybe, a bit austere."

Sadly lacking this personal touch their lessons continued nonetheless, and he taught her the traditional selection of studies including Bach, Handel and some of the more modern French composers. While she had previously excelled at the High School back in Aberdeen, at the Academy Ann was less noticeable for her talent.

"Her flute playing was pretty average. It wasn't anything exceptional. She progressed quite well," Derek sums up. "It was my way of doing things to encourage people to get up and play, make them prepare for concerts. It was my way of developing them as performers. But we never got round to actually doing a public performance. Whether this was due to any uncertainty in her mind, I don't know."

If he was unable to persuade Ann to participate in any concerts at the Academy, Derek apparently bent over backwards to help her out in other ways, constantly trying to ease her journey through the archaic institution. "Lessons as far as I remember were strictly to do with what we were supposed to be doing at the time and any conversations were out. Until it came to the time when she suddenly said to me that she wanted to know what I felt about things. She had been going out and playing country and western, and she felt a leaning towards that, and what should she do? I said, 'Well if that's where your interest lies, then you must do that.'"

Because she had finally broken her spell of silence and expressed a personal interest in *something*, albeit a passing fad for country and western – not quite Derek's cup of tea – he was only too happy to accommodate her. "It did involve her being a bit irregular in her attendance because she would have to go overnight for one of these performances. So I said, 'Well, I'm quite willing to adjust my timetable every week so that you can do these things and you don't miss out on your flute lessons.' And she accepted that and did it. She didn't ever tell me what sort of progress she'd made and partly it wasn't a sort of world I knew anything about."

Sadly, despite his best efforts, Derek was unable to entice the begrudging flautist any further out of her shell. While he was one of the younger and more trendy tutors, who himself experienced altercations with the antiquated system and its professors, he recognises that her other teachers were not so sprightly. Derek recalls a certain piano tutor of Ann's. "I can't remember his name, but he was a very elderly man, very slow. Certainly not up to her standards. He was well, well past it. I just wondered how she put up with it – it would have depressed anybody! She had a moan to me about him."

If Derek failed to become Ann's regular confidant, then Margaret Hubicki was the most obvious choice, being her personal tutor. "I taught her theory and at that time there was a system for one of the professors to be tutors, which meant that there were a number of things that were your responsibility if they had a problem," explains Margaret. "So our relationship was that she was my harmony pupil but she did also need help in the personal side." Margaret, like Derek, says she tried to help Ann overcome her differences with the Academy, particularly as she could see her student's dormant potential. She continues, "I got the overall impression of her as a vibrant personality, in a quiet way. In my mind she had very appealing qualities. She was very sensitive. She wasn't an enormously, deeply involved theoretical student. That was where a lot of her problems came in."

Alongside the emotional problems Ann may have been suffering, Margaret targeted the technical difficulties her pupil was experiencing in her harmony classes, which clearly weren't Ann's primary concern. "When you go to the Academy, part of the year's curriculum was also understanding the more theoretical side. For her it wasn't something that was a number one priority at all, and she got into trouble because there were certain demands made of the theoretical aspect, that is to say, examinations. There were certain things you have to do for the exams which were 'right' and 'wrong'. There were problems for her where her commitment didn't really meet what was required.

"But I also talked to her about music in a general way and it was more obvious then that she was deeply committed to it. I was able to give her an idea of the wide way in which she could make use of her music. She was able to give a practical value to what I told her, and this was something she wished to discuss." Overall Margaret found that teaching Ann was quite a challenge. "I had to play her lessons by ear because quite often harmony was something she didn't do an awful lot of work on. It could have been a disastrous thing if I had lost my temper!"

Margaret persevered with Ann because she could see past the lack of interest in harmony through to a pleasant student with strong convictions. "I got the impression of her as a colourful, delightful personality. She somehow gave a sense of light when she came into the room. There was a sort of vibrancy about her. One was very conscious of her need for encouragement and felt inadequate that one didn't do more for her."

Nevertheless, it seemed that Ann really wasn't very interested in what the teachers had to offer. "I learned a lot more because I rejected my teachers so much," she says herself. "That was the point of my main development. I had to reappraise all the things I'd been taught. People who are taught things can just copy it pat and think, 'If I do this perfectly I'm going to be famous', but I think that's rubbish. I was never in this for success in the public eye."

Evidently the Academy failed to live up to Ann's unrealistic expectations, and she has since described her time there as "possibly the biggest disappointment of my life". For her the atmosphere was claustrophobic and she gradually realised that classical music was no longer a career she cared for. "I discovered I had the whole vision out of proportion," she says. "That the sort of existence I had in store for me [classical music, chamber orchestra etc.] I didn't really identify with."

She has since spoken many times of the lack of "personal expression" she felt she was allowed and how this was so inherently wrong for her as a strong "individualist". But most of all, it appeared to be the music itself she resented so much. "I spent three dreadful years there trying to figure a way out. I worked so hard to fit in, to understand my colleagues and tutors, but I felt they were so stifling, so rigid, so uninspiring . . . I found that classical music, despite its elements of emotion – which I loved – was so inflexible, too redundant and too restrictive in its formalism."

Although this reaction was a tremendous surprise to her family and friends who had shared in her original enthusiasm to study in London, June Smith had an inkling of the potential clash. "Coming from the kind of background she did, where her family were involved in the Socialist movement, the Academy music scene was very conservative. People that came from our kind of background weren't really allowed to become involved in classical music. I think it was quite astonishing for her to realise that she didn't quite mix, especially at the Academy where you're talking about a long tradition of conservative background. It was quite a culture shock."

Despite Ann's strong feelings of hostility towards her new lifestyle, she tended not to share her concerns with her friends, or even those teachers for whom she had a modicum of respect. Claire Powell was aware that Ann felt she was not being stretched, saying, "She had a very good brain and the Academy didn't offer her enough with that brain," but was denied any further insight into her friend's unhappiness.

Derek Honner could see that Ann was struggling, but had never quite achieved a bond with his pupil that gave him an opportunity to help out. "I think her way of behaving was this bubbling up of what she had inside her, and the rather contemptuous idea she had about the general running of the Academy – which a lot of us had as professors anyway," he adds on reflection. "It was a hard thing if you'd got a good point to make, to actually get it through, because you were coming up against prejudices and very old-fashioned views."

The only time Ann really opened up to her flute teacher was to tell him her feelings on a section of the students, which, with the benefit of hindsight, could be seen as a subtle indication of jealousy. "The one thing she said that she couldn't stand about the Academy was the singers," Derek recalls of this common complaint. "She really got into a bit of a twist over the fact that they would wander around the corridors trilling at the top of their voices. I think she regarded this as a form of showing off. I think she regarded them as rather shallow. Which compared with her was true – she wasn't shallow."

As Ann slowly changed musical direction, the Academy, some 19 years before the introduction of their first Commercial & Media Music course, was unable to bend with her. This was not to stop students with contemporary leanings continuing their all-round development whilst still at the Academy; indeed, besides Joe Jackson, former pupils of the establishment include Elton John and Jethro Tull's occasional arranger David Palmer. But the flautist felt stunted and began to long for the pop music that had provided the soundtrack to her teenage years. Surprisingly, the obvious progression did not occur.

"I never heard her sing then," says Derek. "I had known her to sit down and accompany people on the piano, and very, very well. I don't know what she was like as a solo pianist, but she had all the flair to accompany someone and follow them." Claire recalls that, "She had a very nice, folky voice; but I never had her down as a raunchy rock singer! One thing I do remember is she had the most beautiful speaking voice, a really, really soft Aberdonian accent."

★　　★　　★

After the customary visit to see her parents in Aberdeen over Christmas 1972, Ann returned unhappily to London, now aged 18 and no more enamoured with her situation. Periodically she would telephone her mother and confide her problems at the Academy, but while Dorothy Lennox offered as much encouragement as the long distance phone bill would allow, Ann was aware that both parents viewed a degree at the Academy as their daughter's best hope of being able to support herself properly from her musical talent.

In spring 1973 Ann was to find a welcome diversion from her gloomy state of mind when she hooked up with a bass trombone player and friend of John Pooley, forming a relationship that was to last for the rest of the first academic year and beginning of the second. Her new boyfriend was a year older than her, and was called Ron Bryans, known affectionately as Ronnie.

"She was basically a very sweet, very charming, well-adjusted and intelligent person," Ron recalls today. "She was a well-built girl, statuesque. She had wonderful teeth and a wonderful smile. A very friendly, open face. And the lilting Scottish accent . . ."

As typically poverty-stricken students, Ron and Ann had little money to go out on dates, although it seems that Ann wasn't that way inclined anyway. "We never went to any music venues, or concerts. She wasn't particularly a *bon viveur*, she was quite introverted in many ways."

Instead the couple would amuse themselves by sightseeing for free around the English capital. "She had come from Aberdeen and I had come from Belfast, so London was an extremely exciting place just to see. And we did actually do quite a lot of walking around and just looking at fantastic, touristy sights, like Trafalgar Square, Downing Street, the Houses of Parliament."

According to Ron, Ann was basically a home-loving girl, who would rather cook a meal, curl up on the sofa and watch old movies than gad about town. By the time she became involved with Ron, Ann had made a brave independent statement and moved out of the Ethel Kennedy Jacobs House. Unhappy with the image of student life and all its related preconceptions, her aim was to disassociate herself totally from that lifestyle outside the Academy.

"She had her own little bedsit, in Ladbroke Grove kind of way," he remembers. "The actual place was quite OK in terms of space, but it was pretty grubby. It wasn't a studenty place to stay; it was more artisan, bohemian. I felt it was semi-exotic. The buildings were neo-Georgian, the area was fine and Portobello Road market was just round the corner."

Ron was aware of and sympathised with Ann's dejection, and the pair would often commiserate with each other. "There was an undercurrent of students who were incredibly upset with the attitude of the Academy. I certainly felt dissatisfied with the structure of the course and I knew she felt very much the same." Sadly, despite this shared alliance and an enjoyable summer, the romance fizzled out as Ann became increasingly convinced of her vocational change of heart. Shortly before her 19th birthday, the lovers split up.

"Our relationship was just shorter than a year," Ron says today. "The change came about when she realised that to be a flute player among others maybe wasn't the best career, and she wanted to go elsewhere and leave behind the usual classical player's role. She did definitely realise that this career wasn't for her and that she wanted something else, before her course ran its natural longevity."

During her second year as a student, Ann's conviction that the Academy was not for her prompted her to speak to the tutors and inform them of her decision to leave. Countless soul-searching conversations with her anxious parents served to change her mind, and in June 1974 she wrote a brief letter to the Academy, explaining that she would be rejoining them for the third and final year of her degree after all.

She returned in September for the start of her final year, determined to make an effort and show some enthusiasm for her studies. One change that she consciously made was to drop piano as her second study and take up harpsichord. To this day she cherishes fond memories of these lessons, overseen by the late Geraint Jones. "I actually took up the harpsichord because I enjoyed it – it's a beautiful instrument," she smiles today.

★   ★   ★

At the age of 20, Ann stood poised to take her finals, complete her degree and at last leave the institution she had so disliked with at least a semblance of pride. Then, as May turned into June 1975, something went terribly wrong. Sick with stress and unconvinced of her examination potential, Ann left the Academy just three days before she was due to sit her tests. Was there a plan behind this seemingly panicked move?

"I realise that quitting was a very cowardly thing to do," she admitted many years later, "but at the time it seemed like an extremely dramatic and positive action and I was determined to make an impact." Ann had come to realise that she would have felt fraudulent taking exams that she no longer deemed of any worth. Despite her sudden resolve, the "impact" she had so desired immediately reflected less on the Academy, and more on those she loved, who had been anxiously crossing their fingers for her back in Aberdeen.

"My parents were totally stunned," she later explained to author Tony Jasper. "I really dropped them in it. I rang them up in the week of my final exams at the Academy and said, 'Look, I'm giving up the Academy. I can't take the exams. I can't face it. I've been here for three years but I think it would be hypocritical in a way to sit those exams because I don't believe in them.' They were very stunned. They said, 'What are you going to do?'"

The answer to this wasn't something that Ann had ever considered before, but suddenly it seemed so clear that she felt her parents should be the first to know.

"I said I thought I wanted to sing, write songs and of course all this caused a lot of pain and tears, from their point of view. I thought I could do what I had now decided. But they could see I had a straight direction and was convinced I could do it. So they had to shrug their shoulders and say, 'Well, try!'"

"It was quite a shock," recalls June Smith of this sudden change of heart, "but at the same time, although her parents might have been annoyed or upset, they were supportive of Ann. I can't see Tom and Dorothy being anything but supportive. Perhaps a little bit disappointed at the beginning because they wouldn't have been the kind of sights they had set for their daughter."

And what of those who had spent nearly three years honing her talents? According to Ann, "The teachers couldn't have cared less. There was not one person I was in tune with. I felt very lost." In the whirl of high emotion and fervent self-belief, Ann neglected to say goodbye to any of her friends, or even the staff.

"I found out because somebody picked up a piece of music of mine off the library floor, which was a piece I had lent Ann that she never returned," recalls Derek Honner ruefully. "She never came to see me, she must have been in all frames of mind when she left. I think she must have been working herself up to it for some time. She didn't tell me anything about it – it came to me via somebody else who told me that she had walked out, she was in a high temper about it."

"Her big break came when she walked out of the Academy," he continues after a moment's consideration. "I think that's when she asserted herself as a person. It was all there, but it came to the surface and boiled over which made her snap out of it."

The last word on the cathartic matter should go to Ann herself. "Much to everyone's disappointment and my relief I have the Academy to thank for giving me the opportunity to rebel against it so violently, because it led me to what I actually wanted to do," she retorted. "If I hadn't spent all those years practising and playing music then I don't think I would have ever had the ability and conviction to go in for a career in rock."

4

LEGEND IN MY LIVING ROOM

"When we're younger we don't have the benefit of hindsight and experience, we're so eager to go out there and get burned."

– AL

Having made the enormous decision to leave the Academy without any qualifications, Ann faced an even more daunting task: creating a new life for herself. Determined to stick it out in England's capital she discovered she was alone, hundreds of miles away from her family with very few friends for emotional or financial support. Resignedly returning to menial employment for sheer survival over the summer of 1975, Ann tried her hand at a succession of casual waitressing and sales posts. It was a depressing period with little direction and near-squalid living conditions. "I spent the next few years in 'bedsit land', which means you earn a few pounds doing boring jobs and live in a box with a bed in one corner and a cooker in the other," Ann later explained.

A position working in a bookshop was the unlikely catalyst to rekindle her passion for pop music as she moved into a flat with one of her colleagues, Steve Tomlin. Ann benefited in many ways from the arrangement as it not only offered shared living costs, but Steve also owned a stereo and a respectably modern record collection. Among the vinyl Ann unearthed Motown singer/songwriter Stevie Wonder's outstanding 1972 album *Talking Book*, containing such classics as 'You Are The Sunshine Of My Life' and 'Superstition'.

"One night I was on my own listening to *Talking Book* by Stevie Wonder and I had a revelation," Ann recounted of her magical awakening to *The Face* in 1983. "Those songs struck a response within me that I had never experienced at the Academy. Years before I had sung Tamla Motown songs at the Beach Ballroom in Aberdeen where the kids went to dance, but I wasn't aware of what I was doing. Stevie Wonder seemed to have a new definition of perfection, instead of the precision with the flute that the school drilled into me. It touched me – the joy, the freedom, the form of expression. It made me realise that the person I was turning into liked *that* kind of music, not Hector Berlioz concerts."

It was the album's closing number, 'I Believe (When I Fall In Love It Will Be Forever)' that particularly moved Ann. The lyrics eloquently explore the anguish and loneliness endured in the painful quest for true love, but as it is placed at the end of an otherwise pop/funk orientated album the track showed Ann that contemporary music can possess the intellectual and artistic content she believed were confined to classical music.

Ann frequently cites this night as the turning point for her. Future colleague Dave Stewart told *Musician* magazine: "It was Stevie Wonder who actually turned her on to singing. She was totally into being a flute player in a classical orchestra until she heard that album for the first time. Somebody put headphones on her head and played her *Talking Book*."

Ann elaborated on the stimulating night in the same interview, "It was such a revelation to me to listen with very heightened senses to that record. It was an extraordinary experience to me at the time. I held that very dear, as something that had touched me, made a profound impact on me. It was something that in the future I wanted to aspire to, that kind of depth of subtlety and profound statement through music. You use your instinct and you also use your intellect."

Music had always been her greatest passion, but since playing classical pieces on the flute was strangely unfulfilling, Ann reasoned that she might be more suited expressing herself as a singer. She began by covering those songs she had grown to love from Steve's record collection and was amazed to find that she possessed a startling voice.

"It was not just a realisation, it was a revelation to me! Because all of a sudden there was this kind of birth of this *thing*!" Ironically, never having received vocal tuition seemed to inspire Ann further. "I enjoyed singing so much because I hadn't been taught anything about it. Nobody was telling me, 'This is the way you have to do it.' "

But it wasn't until Ann discovered the powerful messages Joni Mitchell exudes in her 1970 album *Ladies Of The Canyon* that she felt compelled to write her own music. "I heard a woman writing articulate songs, realising the power of words – I thought she was incredible," Ann later enthused. "I started looking for alternatives and found the most important thing I had to offer was my own response to music, which was very spontaneous. So I started to write songs and sing them to friends – and suddenly I discovered that I could silence a room and have people almost moved to tears."

Drawing from her personal background of Sixties soul music and

Mitchell's unique style Ann wrote voraciously and even took voice lessons. She came across an Australian tutor who explained the dynamics of projection and introduced the idea of singing with real emotion. "I didn't know about octaves and all that stuff," she once claimed somewhat incredulously in view of her three years study at the Royal Academy of Music. "Everyone thinks I must know about all the female singers, like Bessie Smith or Lena Horne, but I don't. This tutor taught me how to sing with soul, with abandonment. *Thinking* about singing gets in the way of communication." The teacher told her equivocally to "sing like a black nigger", but fortunately realised that Ann needed to "loosen up" in order to prepare mentally. Ann cancelled her tuition after just a few lessons, realising that greater satisfaction came from performing purely for herself: "I sing for my stability and happiness, for expression."

Fuelled by the frustration of wasted years, Ann quit her job at the bookstore for temporary work with more flexible hours, which allowed her to concentrate on music. She moved around London earning money wherever possible, waitressing at a health food restaurant on Tottenham Court Road, and a wine bar in Kensington. She then found weekend work on a second-hand clothes stall with a friend called Margo in the perpetually hip Camden market that sprawls alongside the Regents Canal. Now able to stand on her own two feet, Ann moved out of Steve's flat and into a small bedsit in Camden, NW1.

Gaining confidence in herself, she found she could make friends more easily than in the past. Carol Semaine also ran a clothes stall on the market, designing stage wear for punk bands such as The Vibrators and Generation X, and the two built up a good rapport. As they were both interested in fashion Ann and Carol often discussed the latest trends, but however daring she was to become, at this point in her life Ann's clothes tended to reflect her prudish upbringing. "When I knew her she was very, very anti showing any part of her body for effect," said Carol in Lucy O'Brien's 1991 biography *Sweet Dreams Are Made Of This*. "She had this strict Scottish attitude, and certainly didn't approve of flaunting yourself – no matter what the reasons were behind you doing it . . . I don't think she realised at first how stunning-looking she was. Either she didn't realise or she knew but couldn't handle it. That went hand in hand with her not wanting to flaunt her body. You'd *never* see her in a low–cut dress. If she was whistled at in the street, it'd really make her hackles rise."

This personal reserve also filtered into her music as Ann spent more and more time alone, practising her original compositions privately in her small bedsit. She had bought an old harmonium; a small pump organ resembling an upright piano, through which air is driven by two foot-operated bellows. Not only is it difficult to master, but it is rather an anti-quated machine for an aspiring pop singer. Like Flora, her first flute, Ann became very attached to it and even recalled its fate to *The Face* in 1985. "Oh it's a tremendous instrument . . . The knee-swells are going! It's a sad tale . . . Somebody stole it from me. They were moving house at the time and this girl sold it to the removal man without my permission. When it came back it was all messed up. I never forgave her for that!"

In the summer of 1975 Ann met Margo's boyfriend Paul Jacobs, who owned a neighbouring record stall on Camden market. As the three friends spent time together Ann and Paul found that they were kindred spirits. Paul remembers their connection, "We seemed to have a lot in common. In a way we were both very lonely people."

Although not a musician himself, Paul adored the whole image sur-rounding bands and devoted his life to the world of pop. In tandem with his stall on the market, Paul owned a record shop in the heart of Crouch End called Spanish Moon.[7] Barry Dransfield, a cellist involved in the Crouch End musical set, describes his friend's obsession, "He was a real sycophant! He thought that anybody who could play music was a god and used to hang around musicians. But he was very nice. He dressed like a bass player – three days' growth, long hair and dirty, scruffy jeans, the whole thing."

It was hardly surprising therefore that when Ann mentioned she was a singer and had started writing her own songs, Paul expressed a keen interest. Managing to overcome her usual shyness, Ann gave in and invited him to her cramped bedsit where she played around 30 of her compositions on the harmonium that dominated the room. Paul was in awe throughout the performance and gushed that he believed she truly had innate talent. Their friendship blossomed and he proved to be a tre-mendous source of encouragement for the usually reticent singer. His support eventually extended to providing Ann with a room above his shop, rent free in return for keeping the place tidy and cooking him meals from time to time.

During this period Ann acquired a boyfriend of Greek Cypriot origin who was living near Holloway Road. For a while she became quite serious with her new lover. "I was very close to it [marriage] at one point," she groans. "Mind you, fortunately he got rid of me which broke my heart but I'm grateful to him in hindsight . . . His name was Agis . . . He broke my

---

[7] Spanish Moon, the title of a song by Little Feat, is now a hairdresser's, opposite the clock tower.

heart in 17 places. I met him again as one does some time after and didn't even recognise him. I thought, 'Good grief, was that what I was so upset about?' "

★ ★ ★

In 1976 Ann was 21 and eager to progress as a pop musician. She spent many hopeful hours scanning the classified adverts in *Melody Maker*, traditionally the place where bands advertise for members. She started by contacting groups who were looking for a singer and was one day given an audition after cheekily boasting about her uncanny vocal resemblance to Joni Mitchell. Despite her confidence on the telephone, Ann was unsure which musical genre she would best suit and so tried out for the position of lead singer for a folk/rock band called Dragon's Playground. Ann's inbred talent for Scottish folk singing secured her the place over some 250 eager applicants.

A bizarre debut with the band proved an omen for things to come. "My first gig was in a pub in South London on a revolving stage and I was absolutely petrified," recounts Ann. "I was singing to people who couldn't care less whether I was on the stage or not. I've never been so frightened."

The situation deteriorated further since Dragon's Playground could obtain bookings only in working men's clubs, playing between bingo callers and stand-up comedians. Although she gained invaluable experience learning how to sing with a microphone, in front of a band and to a crowd, Ann soon became frustrated by indifferent audiences more interested in drinking than watching an unknown group.

"When we're younger we don't have the benefit of hindsight and experience, we're so eager to go out there and get burned. Experience *means* getting burned, going right to the bottom, getting your teeth kicked in and having the guts to stand up, admit you made a terrible mistake and get on with it again. People get destroyed through that. It depends on how many risks you're prepared to take," Ann said more recently of this difficult period.

Disheartened but not defeated, Ann left Dragon's Playground and tried her luck with a more established outfit, a left-leaning jazz/rock fusion orchestra called Red Brass, which suited her Communist upbringing even if the music was out of her line. The band had already released an album called *Silence Is Consent* and were able to command occasional gigs at London's famed 100 Club. The latest member undertook a multi-faceted role in this 10-strong group, primarily as vocalist but also playing on her beloved flute and occasional percussion.

Her experiences with Red Brass even included a British tour which incorporated a welcome return to Aberdeen. Unfortunately, although the band offered an opportunity to build a rapport with an attentive audience, they failed to ignite a spark strong enough to hold Ann's interest.

Alone again, Ann turned once more to the classified section at the back of the music papers. She responded to an advert in *The Stage* and found herself auditioning for a small-time agent alongside another female singer, Joy Dey. He liked both their styles and sold them on the idea of working together as an unaccompanied duo under his management.[8] "She had a really nice voice," said Ann of her one-time colleague, "so we thought we could try singing together. But it was doomed from the beginning."

The partnership was never likely to reach the giddy heights of stardom, not least because Ann and Joy naïvely agreed to be christened the Stocking Tops. Obviously open to interpretation, Ann admits that the name "really made me cringe, but I didn't know enough to refuse!" True to his word their somewhat shady manager found some work for the pair, albeit in some of the shoddiest pubs in South London. Ann recalls, "He got us some pub work as the Stocking Tops and dressed us accordingly . . ."

To be fair, the duo gave the Stocking Tops their best shot, struggling bravely around the country in Joy's decrepit Ford. "Joy had a little Anglia car which always had to be started with the assistance of the gentlemen from the AA," laughs Ann. "She drove and I navigated. After a couple of weeks, we packed it in as it seemed to be pointless!"

Aware that they had few contacts and the only performance of any note was a one-off event for the troops, Ann and Joy called a swift halt to what was rapidly becoming a farce.[9] Ann remains more than a little embarrassed by these adventures. "Oh God, I wish I'd never mentioned that," she told an interviewer after she became famous. "I was very young, didn't know anything. It seemed the only way to get started."

As 1976 dragged on Ann was increasingly conscious her career as a pop singer was resolutely refusing to start. Feeling the onset of depression, she sought solace on the telephone to her parents hundreds of miles away in Aberdeen, just as she had done back at the Royal Academy of Music. "The early days in London were really difficult, and my parents have had to answer quite a few anxious telephone calls from me when things got rough. They've been a really great help to me in everything I've tried," she recalls gratefully.

Providing endless support for their daughter must have been difficult for Tom and Dorothy Lennox. As respectable members of their small

[8] During her search Ann almost also shared management with the Bay City Rollers.
[9] Joy Dey released a solo single some time later called 'Can I Touch You?'

community, it cannot have been easy to trust their 21-year-old only child to look after herself in what they surely imagined to be a wildly hedonistic London music scene.

"They were aware, so was I," says Ann of the entertainment industry debauchery from which she had no doubt made a lucky escape when the Stocking Tops disbanded. "But my parents knew my motivations and goals, my morals and they are very high. Along the way I've seen the corruption in the music business but it's not only there. We all live in a corrupt society . . . I won't let people exploit me – I felt that at the beginning and I've always thought that way. If I thought or found I was being exploited, I would put a stop to it."

In order to support herself while singing remained unprofitable, Ann drifted restlessly into another waitressing job, this time in a health food restaurant called Pippins in Hampstead. Her part-time wage did little to ease the expense of living alone in the room above Spanish Moon. Salvation, though, was just around the corner.

★   ★   ★

In the autumn of 1976 Ann's landlord, Paul Jacobs, became reacquainted with an old friend who used to sell him records for his Camden stall. Running his own record shop called Small Mercies in Kilburn, this friend was, predictably, a musician and songwriter in a local band, playing unimaginatively under the same name as his shop. His name was Dave Stewart.

Paul was busy redecorating his own store in Crouch End one day when, as he says, "all of a sudden I saw this *thing* float past the window in a big floppy hat and a flower – and it was Dave! I had half a bottle of Jack Daniels which we demolished while catching up on each other's news."

"Paul knew I was looking for someone to write songs with," nods Dave, who at the time was a hippyish, bedraggled looking fellow living in a squat. "He said to me, 'You've got to meet this incredible singer. She sings and you get goosebumps . . .'"

When the hangover cleared, Paul told Ann about Dave. Rumour had it, he informed her, that Dave was extremely experienced in the music field and might be able to help her out with advice about a business proposition that was bothering her. "I had a contract that someone had offered me and I was dubious about the whole thing," Ann recalls. "I wanted to talk to somebody who knew about contracts and my friend Paul said he knew this guy."

The propitious introduction occurred at Pippins during one of Ann's shifts. Much to the dismay of the manager, Paul arrived accompanied by his scruffy friend. "I hope you don't know those two," muttered the manager to his flustered waitress, evidently appalled at their state. "They look like a couple of drug addicts." Dave was dressed in a big overcoat trimmed with a fur collar and plastic children's sunglasses from inside a cereal packet. "Kellogg's Frosties glasses! They're like sunglasses with Tony The Tiger at each end," he offered by way of an explanation.

Ann was not overly impressed. "He had all these plastic carrier bags and he was a real mess. Blood dripping down the front of his overcoat because he'd just had his ear pierced." The unfortunate lancing had been done that very afternoon by an inebriated 'expert' who, in his ineptitude, had missed Dave's ear. But, as first impressions go, Dave Stewart was not quite finished.

"The first words Dave said were, 'Will you marry me?' " Ann recalls in amazement. "I thought he was a serious nutter!"

Paul's work was done. "He put Dave and Ann together and Paul wanted desperately to put something together that was auspicious artistically," says his friend Barry Dransfield. "And that was the closest he ever got. But perhaps without him, it might never have happened!"

5

SPIRITUAL COWBOY

"I'm more like Woody Allen . . . a caricature."
– Dave Stewart

Born September 9, 1952 in Sunderland, Tyne & Wear, David Allan Stewart[10] was never destined to lead a normal life. According to biographer Johnny Waller, David, always shortened to Dave, was distantly related to the Duke of Northumberland on his maternal grandmother's side and to a pirate on his maternal great-grandfather's. From early on his middle-class parents, both fully trained in accountancy, were determined that their children should live exceptionally liberated lives.

"I came from a well-off family, and a totally different kind of background from Ann," says Dave. "Our family was regarded as being a bit mad in Sunderland." Situated in north-east England, some 75 miles from the Scottish border and 150 miles by sea from Aberdeen, Sunderland was a proudly working-class town, and the Stewarts were from the start natural outcasts. "I always wanted to play with the working-class kids, but they'd always call me 'richie' and whack me on the head with cricket bats and things," Dave has since relayed.

His parents were extremely devoted to their children, and their strong influence on Dave and his elder brother John is still obvious today. Their father, also called John, but nicknamed 'Jack', was a keen harmonica player and belied his strait-laced accountancy background by his avid dedication to music of all types. He invested in the latest hi-tech stereo system and wired it up to every room in the house, so that each morning Dave and John would wake to the sound of his eclectic record collection blaring through the house.

Jack and his wife Sadie shared a strong interest in child psychology, and together they would experiment with numerous broad-minded ways of

---

[10] His middle name was inherited from his mother's maiden name.

raising their young family. "I'd read a lot of psychology and I was fasci-nated by children – I always tried to give them an insight to life," Sadie explained to Johnny Waller. "We must encourage children to cope with frustration in a practical way. In the summer we let them sleep in the garden in a wigwam I made out of old sugar sacks and they'd dress up like Red Indians and cook barbecues."

The couple favoured culinary trial and error as an interesting study of development for their two sons. "Every Wednesday I cooked a meal from a different foreign country out of this big cook book – just to widen their horizons," Sadie continued. "I didn't want them to be put off by appear-ances. I also used to make little figures out of mashed potato! I wasn't trying to be different, it was just fun." Famously, Jack also added his own creative touches in the kitchen, offering Dave and John a selection of staple meals enhanced with various food colourings. They both remember being presented with blue porridge and green potatoes just so that their father could observe the effect of hue on their appetite.

But it was the energetic and irrepressible Sadie who took the lead in indulging her children, much to the delight of Dave in particular.

"My mum was great," he enthuses. "She had the idea that children should be allowed to follow their imagination to the full. We weren't spoiled but we could do a lot of things that other kids weren't allowed to do." Sadie herself possessed an especially fertile mind, as can be demon-strated by one of Dave's clearest childhood memories. "When I brought some friends round to see *Scott Of The Antarctic* on television, she covered the whole room in white sheets, and pulled out some rucksacks and left the window open so it was bitterly cold," he recalls with glee. "I just got used to that sort of thing, and felt totally secure within it."

It was hardly surprising, therefore, that Dave developed a somewhat eccentric personality. "I was always obsessed with something," he says. "I'd have to know all there was to know. I'd buy books and become a walking encyclopaedia on whatever took my fancy." One such early fix-ation was, prophetically, with a small tape recorder. "When I was about nine, I was fascinated by the tape recorder," he chuckles. "I had this miniature reel recorder and I made myself a badge which said 'The Junior Candid Camera Team' and I'd go into local shops and ask people silly questions – like a reporter. Then I'd go home and nearly wet myself listening to them."

Dave's aim was to shock as many people as possible, and it didn't matter if they were strangers, family or friends. "I'd go and swim in the goldfish pond in a rubber suit with a harpoon gun. Then I'd measure the harpoon cord. If it was 14' long I'd get a friend to stand 14' 7" away with an apple on his head. Then I'd fire it at him. I felt like a misfit all my life," he said bizarrely to *Music Maker* in 1991.

Accompanied by his black Labrador named 'Solo', after the character Napoleon Solo from popular Sixties television spy series, *The Man From U.N.C.L.E.*, Dave would set out on many adventures. Perhaps this was a direct reaction to a nasty spate of bullying he endured for a while as a pupil at the Bede Grammar School For Boys, as well as his mother's encouragement to be independent.

"The boys had a lot of freedom," Sadie explains, "but they knew that someone was always at home waiting for them, so we didn't worry as long as we knew where they were and who they were with." From the rather delicate age of eight, Dave would frequently disappear and catch a train to whichever destination took his fancy at the time, only calling his parents later to inform them of his whereabouts.

As he grew older Dave's focus switched towards sport, at which he excelled, much to the annoyance of the school bullies. But one day, when he was 12 years old, a chance injury in a football match altered the course of his life forever. Lying in hospital with a broken leg, the normally hyperactive Dave fretted over what could possibly keep his buzzing mind occupied during his recuperation.

"I got so fidgety with nothing to do that someone lent me a guitar, which of course was near fatal," he laughs today. "As I couldn't walk, I started learning it. Then somebody else brought me a leather jacket, and I hung it at the foot of the bed. I used to look at this leather jacket and play the guitar and wish I could get out of the hospital."

Finally returning home with the fire of his latest obsession burning bright, his first stop was his elder brother John's bedroom. By this point Dave idolised his brother, as not only had he played first a banjo and then a guitar, but he was also the proud owner of an extensive record collection. This was what the would-be guitarist fixed his sights on. "As soon as I got home, I pinched all my brother's Mississippi John Hurt and Robert Johnson albums and branched out into the world of blues, which I dearly love, and taught myself blues guitar," he recalls fondly. "I had the Stefan Grossman *How To Play Blues Guitar* LP with booklet and, of course, the Bert Weedon book as well. I was also a big fan of all the Stax stuff."

Dave locked himself in the garage with his brother's guitar in the few precious hours he had before John returned home. Meticulously he picked out the contents of John's record collection, note for note. After working his way through the blues LPs, he progressed diligently to the early folk records of Bob Dylan, and later the glam rock of T.Rex. Soon enough he had set his goals even higher than becoming a guitarist.

"I was so crazy to be a pop star, I used to phone up the local radio station and sing down the phone, not realising I was only singing to the receptionist – I think she used to like it, mind!" he told one interviewer. "Then I'd dial a random number in France and try to get them to say something so I could tape a French voice, but they never could understand what I was asking, so I'd say, 'Never mind, here's a song' and I'd sing them something . . . No wonder my dad used to complain about his phone bill!"

Amid his adolescent pranks, when he was 14, Dave's parents split up. His life changed domestically, and he channelled all his confusion, anger and energy into achieving his dream of being a pop star. It became the main focus of his life. He began to attend live performances by local rock bands, and became so fascinated by the performance of English folk rockers Amazing Blondel that he hid himself in their van after a gig in Newcastle. Dave later recounted the fantastic string of events that followed.

"I stowed away in the back of their van and they didn't discover me 'till we arrived in Scunthorpe. They rang the police and my parents, who came to collect me." At that point most parents would have given their errant son a piece of their mind, especially as it was by then four o'clock in the morning, but not so the recently separated Stewarts. "My mum and dad had a chat with Blondel, who agreed that I could travel with them sometimes and learn about roadieing and playing. That adventure gave me my first taste of being in a band."

For the next six weeks (which conveniently tied in with Dave's school holidays) he toured with Amazing Blondel, sharing the back of the van with their pet Great Dane and earning his keep as a roadie. The members of the group indulged his eagerness by teaching him pavanes and galliardes on the lute, and by the end of the trip he was allowed to open the set for them with the odd solo guitar performance.

This unexpected exposure gained him a small following in the north of England, and he even appeared on local radio and TV shows, opening for recording acts such as Ralph McTell. At one stage, implausible as it may seem, he was approached by Bell Records who imagined him as the next child star, along the same lines as teen heartthrob, David Cassidy. Dave turned this particular offer down on the grounds that he wanted to make his name as a 'serious musician'.

Dave was not slow to realise that he was not going to achieve this goal by staying in Sunderland, and at the tender age of 16 he left school and headed for London. First he moved into a flat with an artist called Eric Scott and Eric's girlfriend Ann, but before long he upped sticks to live with his best mate Eddie Fenwick, and thoroughly revelled in having his very own space.

"It was a den of . . . iniquity?" he recalls, unsure of the idiom, " . . . it was mad. It was one of the best times of my life. It was like being in a holiday camp with no rules, like being the bad boy in *Pinocchio* – where they all start smoking cigars and go green." By this point it was evident that Dave would have to begin earning money on a regular basis to make ends meet. He had only ever worked for one day in what could be deemed a 'normal' job, and had failed resoundingly in his role as a porter at the Sunderland Civic Centre, where he was sacked for causing disruption.

Dave decided he could make financial use of his musical talent and put a card in the local newsagent, advertising guitar lessons for 50p. He would also work his way through a bizarre list of part-time jobs, including performing at medieval-style banquets in a castle, dressed as Henry VIII and attracting all kinds of unwanted attention from the opposite sex.

★   ★   ★

The turning point for Dave came when he met up with another singer and guitarist named Brian Harrison. Brian played at a folk club called the George & Dragon, and when he and Dave discovered they shared Sunderland roots they formed a duo under the uninspiring name, Stewart & Harrison. Together they enjoyed moderate success performing live, but they made an incongruous pair: Brian was tall while Dave was short and rather scrawny.

It was 1969 and Dave was 17 years old when north London cellist Barry Dransfield first encountered Stewart & Harrison. Barry was also part of a live duo, alongside his brother Robin. The four musicians found they had much in common.

"I remember going to a Sunderland folk club and there was Dave, ever so young and small, playing this guitar," Barry says today. "He did quite a lot of gigs with this fellow who was with him, Brian Harrison. Dave had a lot of respect for acoustic musicians." As they all lived in close proximity in north London, the friends began to jam together on a regular basis. Barry continues, "I loved playing with Dave because the pair of us used to start and three hours later somebody would be banging the door down – time would just disappear. He was just great at improvising, it was a pleasure." But there was a certain pecuniary downside to associating with Dave, as Barry was soon to find out. "Dave was a bloke who used to borrow money. He was always broke, you'd avoid him in case he borrowed a fiver off you!"

Meanwhile Stewart & Harrison pursued a momentary stab at fame by releasing 100 copies of Dave's first composition, 'Deep December', on the Sunderland-based Multicord record label. It sank without trace, but Dave so enjoyed the benefits of performing with a group that in Autumn 1971 he and Brian expanded into a quartet, teaming up with other occasional contributors Steve Sproxton and Kai Olsson, to form a pop/folk band called Longdancer. The four members played only guitars and bass and made an amusing point of swapping their instruments during their set, cheerfully making up for the lack of a drummer.

Things were moving very quickly for Dave. Still a teenager, and never one for doing things by halves, he had fallen head over heels for a girl named Pamela Wilkinson, and shortly after his 20th birthday they married.

The wedding took place on December 2, 1972 at Sunderland Registry Office, with Dave wearing a ceremonial sword as part of his outfit. Despite this flagrant show of eccentricity, Brian, who was present at the service, recalls: "It wasn't a big showbiz affair or anything and I remember thinking they were both so young, the fools!"

The newlyweds eagerly moved in together, but it wasn't long before their honeymoon period came grinding to a halt. It was the early Seventies, and musicians were inextricably linked with drugs as the heady days of hippyism drew to a close. Pamela Wilkinson, interviewed by Johnny Waller, recalls: "Dave went through a very heavy drug thing. I was a nurse studying for my final exams, so I was having to be really straight, going to bed early . . . and I'd come back from work and find Dave comatose from drugs! I understood what he was going through, but I used to shout at him because I wanted him to stop – so we started fighting."

"I was really naïve about drugs," Dave later admitted to *Record Mirror*. "I thought, 'It doesn't do *me* any harm,' but taking a bit of this and a bit of that eventually does lead to three grams of speed, your heart stopping and getting rushed to hospital." Dave became particularly fond of LSD, taking it every day for a year. The hallucinogenic effects took over his entire personality with Dave alternately convincing himself that aliens were invading his body, he was suffering from imaginary heart attacks and that he was unable to speak. The latter side effect prompted him to invent his own language. "I used to be a complete wreck," he confesses. "I went through a phase of giving my body the worst punishment it could possibly take in the shortest period of time. I had a massive speed habit and got up to all sorts of crazy schemes."

Dave had always been very strong-willed, and his closest family and friends were left feeling helpless, able only to observe in horror as he introduced other hard drugs into his increasingly potent cocktails. Brian was shocked, "He was doing a *lot* of cocaine and I remember thinking, 'He *can't* go on like this.' He was getting really thin and wasted."

It was during this drug-addled state that Dave found his group jumping forwards in leaps and bounds. Kai Olsson's brother Nigel was the drummer for The Elton John Band, and he arranged for Longdancer to meet Lionel Conway, who had previously worked for Elton's manager, the redoubtable Dick James, and was now the head of Island Publishing.

After Conway's invitation for the band to record a demo in London, the boys were thrilled to hear that Elton John himself had heard and enjoyed the tape. Following some negotiation, Longdancer became the first act to be signed to the singer/songwriter's own label, Rocket Records.

"I remember Elton John came down to see us play at the Sundown in Edmonton," Brian recalls. "Once he gave his seal of approval, we signed the contract – but I think it was just a tax loss because they weren't really much of a record company!" Despite Brian's misgivings, the advance given to the northern lads was phenomenal, even in the extravagant days of the early Seventies. Dave, Brian, Kai and Steve were handed £56,000 (around $100,000) on a plate, on the proviso that they recorded a couple of albums and toured Europe as Elton's warm-up act.

After installing themselves in an expensive hotel, Longdancer set about recording their first LP. The result, *If It Was So Simple*, was released on May 4, 1973 to mostly favourable reviews. Their debut single, the title track from the album with the intriguing catalogue number of 'PIG 1', was reviewed by journalist Rosalind Russell as "a beautiful song, well sung, and worthy of a first release. The harmonies are particularly fine; the tune is simple and easy to catch by the end of the first hook. For once an extremely pleasing hit-to-be, I'm sure of it. It's a sad little song, but a memorable one."

After a bout of mildly unsuccessful touring, Longdancer's second and last LP, entitled *Trailer For A Good Life*, was released just over a year later. It too was accompanied by a single, 'Puppet Man', which was reviewed rather eloquently in a trade paper as "A crisp spring melody sung with breezy harmonies. Simple and satisfying. Tasteful music for a warm evening on the back porch, facing the sunset and watching swallows."

Unfortunately, although Longdancer went down well with their critics, actual sales were virtually non-existent, and Rocket Records began to lose interest. It can't have helped that the band had blown their entire advance, much of it on drugs, and were beginning to drift apart musically.

"During this period I was mad about T.Rex," says Dave. "I wanted us to do more over-the-top pop/electric things with more visually stimulating images. But I didn't explain myself very well, so everyone in the group just thought I was mad." Unable to focus their combined talents, by the end of 1974 they agreed to go their separate ways. Barry Dransfield concludes:

"Longdancer nose-dived and I think that was a great disappointment to Dave, because he desperately wanted to be famous."

After the demise of his band and with nothing left from their hefty advance, Dave drifted from one musical outfit to another, each more bizarre than the last. The most notable was the delicately named Sadista Sisters, an all-female cabaret band who had performed a show called *Schoolgirl Slaves Of Soho* the previous year. The introduction was made by Barry.

"I'd got him a gig with the Sadista Sisters. I had been managed by Chris Gilbert for a while, and he said to me, 'Do you know a guitarist, because the Sadista Sisters need somebody to go to Germany with them?'"

Dave's wife Pamela was less than impressed. "While I was studying at night to be a nice little nurse, he was out with this all-girl band . . . I couldn't believe my eyes – those girls were punks before there even *were* punks! They were in leather gear, suspenders, the lot." In his auto-biography *A Cure For Gravity*, Joe Jackson described a typical Sisters act as "a sort of sick S&M magic act" where a planted member of the audience was supposedly dragged on stage, only to have his fingers chopped off as an elaborate joke.

Pam had good reason to be worried. Not long after her husband went to Germany with the Sisters, he became amorously involved with their singer, Jude Alderson. The most extraordinary chain of events followed which, according to Dave, included being held prisoner at gunpoint by a German promoter. In a ridiculously short space of time he was also involved in three separate car crashes, suffering multiple injuries of broken ribs and collapsed lungs as a result. Returning to England for a painful period of hospitalisation, Dave then had to deal with the break-down of his marriage.

This came as no real surprise to Dave's circle of friends. Barry remembers that the impoverished Stewarts had been at romantic odds before the weird and wonderful tour with the Sadista Sisters. "Dave was married to Pam and they were living in a squat towards Finsbury Park. They had no water, particularly hot water. I had this nice little flat in Highgate and they said, 'Is there any chance that we could come round and use your shower?'

"So they'd come round to my house to use the shower, and I think Pam came round a few times without Dave . . . eventually Pam and I got together. Dave was fairly cool about this, of course we were all smoked out of our heads anyway. But he was quite grown up about it, even when I moved in with his wife in another flat . . ."

Dave and Pam were subsequently divorced, both admitting freely that they had married too young. "Really we should have just lived together," says Pam. "I learnt a lot from Dave and I value the time we were together because he was so fantastic to be with and I loved him." The split was amicable and the pair kept in touch in both a friendly and later a business manner.

Still only in his early twenties, Dave was gravely in need of some stability. It eventually arrived in the form of yet another singer/songwriter hailing from Sunderland. Peet Coombes had been writing songs since the age of 14, and after leaving school was unemployed for nearly six years before a short-lived spate in a rock band called Peculiar Star. The two hit it off immediately.

"We would do anything and take anything and go anywhere," Dave remembers fondly. "We were inseparable. We were like Butch Cassidy and the Sundance Kid." Peet seemed to make quite an impression on everyone he met, as Barry recalls: "He was an amazing hippy man with a dog. He had a house full of children and a wife who was a real hippy earth mother, and Peet would sit in the corner with his guitar. He was pretty talented. He had a bit of an attitude, he wanted to be free and didn't want anybody to be messing him around, and his songs were about that. He was so hard up, if you'd have offered him a fiver, he'd have given you all his songs."

Dave and Peet formed their own folk duo and, fuelled by drugs, set off on an ambitious tour around Europe. They stayed for a while in Germany, where, desperate for hard cash, Dave experienced his own personal nadir.

"The worst thing I've ever done, I think, was playing the part of a female game-show host," he said in *Eurythmics* by Paul Roland. "It was called *Beat The Clot* instead of *Beat The Clock*, and we were doing it in these German businessmen's kind of 'orrible clubs. I was playing this game called 'Spit In The Bottle'. I'd get them to hold the bottle and they thought they were doing this really sexy thing, and I used to spit at it and miss and hit them. That was the worst depravation."

The twosome then gravitated to Holland, where they busked in freezing conditions, but that too went badly wrong. Dave: "Yeah, it went right through to being really penniless and addicted to speed . . . without really realising how far you're into something because you think everything's alright, don't you, you go off on a different tangent . . .

"Suddenly it all comes down with a bang – it isn't alright, you're being deported from Holland, you have no money, you've sold your electric guitar to get there in the first place, you've given up your flat and you arrive back in London and you have to start squatting all over again . . ."

Returning to London in 1976, Dave dejectedly admitted defeat and set up a record shop, Small Mercies in Kilburn, still playing occasional gigs with Peet in local pubs and clubs. He was at his lowest state mentally, and felt unable to return to his home town of Sunderland because he thought his old friends wouldn't accept him back after he rejected the town as a teenager in search of a better life. Furthermore, he was still living under the stigma of having jointly squandered an incredible amount of money with a failed band. His health was suffering, and he was desperately in need of a boost of any description that wasn't narcotically enhanced.

★   ★   ★

"Just before I met Dave I had reached a point where I decided I was suffering too much," said Ann Lennox of her own unsuccessful attempts at a career in music throughout 1976. "London can be a cruel, heartless place. I was ready to go home, to become a flute teacher. Then Dave Stewart walked in, and that was the moment that changed my life. He was the first person to take an interest in me . . .

"When we first met I was really keen to write, sing and make records, but I hadn't a clue how to go about it. With Dave I could do all these things." Indeed Dave proved to be the unruly breath of fresh air that Ann needed in her life, and despite her initial misgivings she discovered a side-splittingly funny, talented musician underneath the haywire exterior.

After her shift at Pippins, Paul Jacobs and Dave eagerly followed Ann back to the flat above Spanish Moon, where she performed some of her original compositions on the ancient harmonium. Dave found himself instantly in tune with her work and began to express an expansion of her ideas. High on their shared enthusiasm and the giddy prospects of a creative partnership between Dave and Ann, the trio went out to celebrate. But it wasn't long before Ann and Dave made their excuses to Paul and returned to her flat. They were destined to be more than just musical partners, as Dave coyly reveals, "We decided to go to a club but, within 10 minutes, Ann and I realised that it was more fun in the flat! From that minute on, we lived together for about four years."

Poetic as ever, Ann recollects their instantaneous connection, "We went home and played and sang to each other. It was one of those rare nights of pure magic. We knew we had to work together. I knew Dave was someone special – he'd been married and divorced and was taking a lot of strange drugs – but from that night on we were inseparable."

Their polar pasts simply strengthened the attraction. To Ann, Dave offered a route for her artistic dreams to become reality, while Dave was certain that Ann's high morals and healthy living could only improve his thus far wayward lifestyle.

"She was one of the most radiant and healthiest people I'd met in a long time," he later explained. "She looked completely different to a lot of the people I was involved with who were ashen and grey and lived by night. She had a different attitude. She was fresh and I was immediately knocked out by her. I'd been taking LSD every day for a year. That sounds light-hearted, but when I look back on it I was really lucky not to end up the way most people did. She was really the turning point because she was someone I wanted to be alright *for*. When I met Ann I was about as far off as you could be into orbit. She was my saving grace."

Close friend Barry Dransfield also believed that if anyone could sort Dave out it was Ann. "I met this very straight girl from music college," he says today. "Very nice, and very practical. Whereas Dave and I were always falling about a bit. She thought taking drugs was funny, but she wouldn't have done it herself. She was amused by it, but she used to advise us all the time, 'Stop smoking and don't do this because it will come to no good.'"

Evidently many of Dave's problems, and to some extent, his genius, were triggered by his vast intake of drugs, and Dave himself maintains that he had his new girlfriend to thank for eventually cleaning him up. "I was really into drugs, and by the time I met Ann, I was a real wild man," he admits. "I was into the lot – speed, cocaine, acid – but what I didn't know was that I was going downhill fast. I was thin and wasting away. Within a year of meeting Ann, I was off drugs completely. I know now that they could have killed me."

While Ann was by all accounts a striking-looking woman, Dave was not exactly male model material. "I've always been very insecure about the way I look," he divulges. "I'll make no bones about it. It's one of those classic things – having a beard and hiding behind loads of hair." But Ann could see beyond the shaggy mane and, more importantly for her, knew she had finally found her soulmate. "It wasn't so much attraction at first sight as a question of compatibility with someone you feel totally at ease with," she said in 1984. "We seemed to hit it off straight away. We lived together and everything was terrific. We used to think as one."

Inseparable as they were, Dave quickly moved into the building site that was Ann's flat in Crouch End. "I remember very well the place we lived in," she reminisces in mock horror. "At one point it was almost derelict. I mean there was rubble covering the bathroom floor and we had to climb over that to go to the toilet. It was such a funny picture trying to clamber around in big stiletto shoes." Barry remembers that Ann tried her best to clean up the flat, not to mention her errant boyfriend. "She was really provincial. She did washing up and stuff. I remember her decorating this flat that they were living in, it was disgusting – a scruffy gaff over Paul's record shop. And she sorted it out."

But the common denominator to their mutual attraction undoubtedly lay in music, and once again Paul Jacobs came up with the goods. He had installed a small recording studio in the basement of the building, and by allowing Dave and Ann to use it for a nominal fee, they were able to experiment to their hearts' content.

It wasn't long before Dave persuaded Ann to give up her waitressing job and claim unemployment benefit. That way they could concentrate wholeheartedly on music in the depths of Spanish Moon. "We were a year on the dole," she says. "I hated signing on, I think everyone does. I didn't like the idea of taking money from the State. But you can either do that, or wear yourself out trying to do a part-time job and the band too." This perceived lack of choice left the couple with very little money, just £11 per week between them.

"Our life then was full of adventure and poverty. It was that spirit of adventure that kept us from getting depressed when sometimes terrible things happened," says Ann cheerfully. But the reality was that their standard of living was very low. "We often had no money to buy any food and so we made meals out of scraps – like half an onion, a bit of carrot, half a tin of peas and some rice," Ann later told Ian Birch, while Dave piped up with a different recipe, "I remember once we were starving and she made a meal out of rice, potatoes and one piece of broccoli."

Whatever the hardships, Dave and Ann were making a name for themselves as a quirky couple within their circle of friends. Session guitarist John 'Texas' Turnbull, later to join Ian Dury's Blockheads, remembers how he got involved in the *avant-garde* scene. "I first met Dave when he was living above the record shop Spanish Moon. It was an indie-cum-new age record shop. The people were quite groovy and you'd just get talking. It was mentioned that Dave lived upstairs, and we had lots of things in common so I got friendly with him, and through him Ann. Crouch End was becoming more and more bohemian, the spill over from Hampstead and Highgate."

Somehow, even in this wild culture, Dave was considered the odd one out which troubled the more strait-laced Ann. "It really hurt me because people laughed at him," she told author Paul Roland. "They thought he was mad, wandering around north London with his mad schemes, never getting anywhere. His mum and I sat down in their living room one day and confronted him. We told him he was a complete mess, and he looked shocked, as if he didn't realise."

Those close to Dave were always intrigued by the qualities that separated him from the rest. "Dave's got this air of such quiet confidence," says John. "He's very relaxed. He's like a dreamy academic. You know something's cooking inside his brain and then he might blurt out some bizarre idea. He has this quiet sort of brilliance about him."

Sensing Dave had an underlying plan, the two people closest to him, Ann and Peet, were more than happy to join forces and play as a trio. As Peet was such a prolific writer Ann and Dave held back, opting simply to give voice to his thoughts. "Peet used to write so many songs, maybe three a day. We used to think, 'Why bother?' " said Dave rather defeatistly once. Ann's reasoning was a little more in character as she suddenly found that she had lost her nerve: "I never took myself seriously as a writer, although I did think before I met Dave that that's what I was, but then I was kind of overawed by Peet, because he would write 10 songs in a week."

As 1976 turned into 1977 and Ann passed her 22nd birthday, the threesome began to find their niche and complement each other musically. "Both Dave and Ann were very ambitious, which Peet wasn't," explains Barry about the way in which the group found its natural balance. "The one thing Dave didn't have was a voice, he wasn't a singer. What he needed was two things; he needed some vocals and some glamour. Now Peet Coombes had neither. He wasn't a bad singer, but he had a bit of a speech impediment as I remember. And neither he nor Dave had any signs of glamour!

"As soon as Ann turned up, she could sing *and* she was glamorous, and bang – you got it! Ann really liked the songs. At the time, although she was ambitious, she wasn't thinking of becoming the great star that she was going to be. She took it all very seriously and liked all the good folky based, original stuff."

To fit in with the new image that Dave was slowly moulding for Ann he started calling her 'Annie', and in persuading her to adopt the friendlier name he would repeatedly make fun of her when she attempted to keep the more formal 'Ann'. The Scotswoman was initially reluctant, but eventually gave in on the grounds that if she was working towards an exciting new life, she might as well go the whole nine yards.

Through the winter months Dave, Peet and Annie would meet up with fellow musicians in Crouch End to play, either at a gig or just jamming informally at someone's house. Members of their clique, along with Barry and John, included Steve Sproxton, formerly of Longdancer, and Joe Khoumbas, affectionately known as Mad Joe. "Mad Joe was the Greek who we used to drink a lot with," laughs Barry today. "Joe had a little studio in Crouch End and we went and did something down there a couple of times. He was part of the Crouch End set and a lot of this at the time centred around a pub called The Railway Tavern on Crouch Hill."

The pub, which still exists today, was a favourite meeting point for the group, along with Spanish Moon, and consequently Dave and Annie's flat upstairs. Although Annie did not share the same depth of gigging experience as many of her friends, her classical training meant she lent her own special quality to their circle.

"I had met people from music college before and she had the same musical facility as I'd noticed in those people as well; they could copy anything," Barry illustrates. "They only had to hear it once and they could do anything. Whereas Dave and I were not trained in music at all, so any music you made was by accident! We would just wake up one day and say, 'Oh I wrote this tune, I don't know why, but I did.'

"I remember Annie coming round one day and giving me a cello lesson," he continues. "Although she couldn't play the cello, she showed me a lot of stuff – how to practise in a way that would improve me. She could see what I was doing, and she would say, 'Well, why don't you do this?' and sing a piece. For payment I gave her a very nice jacket with tails, because in those days she looked a bit of a Goth, with a white face and black clothes. A sort of glam type appearance."

Annie compounded her mysterious image by continuing to play the harmonium. "She was individual, there was something about her, something brewing," elaborates John. "We used to hang out upstairs in their flat and I went there one day and she was playing the harmonium. The harmonium's a funny thing to play because you have to pump it yourself, so it's a bit like playing the saxophone, juggling and cooking eggs!

"But her voice sounded so sweet with it. She was singing this song, it was so gorgeous and I just stood there quietly. She sounded like Joni Mitchell, kind of swooping, but saddish, but with a little something in the voice. I said, 'That's great, what is it?' And she said, 'Oh, that's just one of my songs, but I don't play it to anyone.' And I couldn't understand why not, it was so gorgeous."

6

THE FIRST CUT

"It seemed like Dave and Peet didn't realise how special Annie's voice was, because Peet was doing most of the singing."

— Rob Gold

It was not until an old friend of Dave's called Rob Gold reappeared on the scene that Dave, Peet and Annie began to get their collective foot on the ladder. "I met Dave Stewart in about 1974 or 75 when I was at Island Music and he was in a band called Longdancer," Rob says today. "Then I managed him, with a small 'm', in a band called Small Mercies. I left Island Music to join Logo Publishing in 1976 and because I knew Dave from the Island days, we kept in touch."

Logo Records was an independent company based in London's St. Martin's Lane, run by Geoff Hannington and Olav Wyper. Rob ran the sister company, Logo Publishing. There are differing stories surrounding the reformation of a business relationship between Rob and Dave, including help with the lingering management contract hanging over Annie.

Rob describes the chain of events after he heard the trio playing in April 1977: "I went to see them and it seemed like Dave and Peet didn't realise how special Annie's voice was, because Peet was doing most of the singing. He was quite self-effacing in a way. He was almost like a non-singer to me, it was so weird that they had Annie there yet he sung.

"Dave introduced me to Annie and I sensed there was something special there. I was keen to do some demos with them and maybe help get them record deals, and all the rest of it. Fortunately there were about three weeks in the studio that Olav had booked for a blues artist, at Riverside Studios near Acton. That artist couldn't make it so there was a period where the session was booked and I had to think quickly how to make the most of it."

Rob ushered Dave, Annie and Peet into the studio to use up the free time making a demo with which he might secure some interest within the music business. The trio chose a selection of their self-penned songs to record, leaving most of the details to Rob. Barry Dransfield was called on to increase the overall output. "I was brought in by Rob Gold because they wanted as much sound as possible on these demos," he recalls today. "They had Dave's guitar, Peet's guitar, Annie on piano, Annie's vocals, and what they needed on top of that was some colour, so I played some fiddle and cello. And there was a marvellous percussionist, Gaspar Lowell. Gaspar was famous then, well-known on the jazz scene, and I remember Dave going on about him."

With the band's sound augmented by strings and rhythm, Rob turned his attentions to singling out Annie's startling voice. Although Peet was the acknowledged singer in the group, Rob was so impressed with Annie's soft vocals that today he believes he instructed them to take turns singing the songs while only recording her versions.

Unfortunately for Rob, the band members were not all at their peak, as Barry amusingly recalls: "Dave was really out of it and fell over. I was much more together and Annie was very together. We'd all been drinking and smoking and stuff. It was an afternoon that moved into the evening. I remember being quite out of it by the time we left there."

Nevertheless, the demos were completed remarkably smoothly and Rob was pleased with the results. "They were fabulous songs," enthuses Barry, "these songs were brilliant. They were pretty much one-takes and then we did overdubs. Dave knew the stuff backwards, he'd been playing with Peet for years. I think we all thought it was pretty good, wrapped it up and went round to the pub, where Rob bought us all a drink."

In a celebratory mood, and with more alcoholic assistance, the group fantasised about their future. Despite Dave's frame of mind Rob remembers the guitarist's surprising level-headedness: "I remember him saying, 'Don't give me a large advance.' This was after Longdancer, where he'd had quite a large advance which had split the band up. Sometimes a large advance can do more harm than good."

A total of nine songs were recorded on that day in April 1977; two with a full backing band and the remaining seven highlighting Annie as a solo singer/pianist with occasional light percussion. The first composition, 'It's Just The Wind', stands the test of time as one of the strongest tracks, pleasantly folky and immediately establishing Annie as a flighty Joni Mitchell-style vocalist, with elements of Joan Armatrading providing moments of reflective regret. The music featured Dave and Peet on acoustic guitar, Annie on flute, Barry on violin and Gaspar Lowell on congas, with the latter musicians apparently breezing through unfamiliar and unrehearsed territory without a backward glance. Annie sang the lyrics of neighbourhood violence with strikingly high pitched harmonies, flavouring the track with dynamic nostalgia.

The other fully accompanied song was 'Already Strangers', an early indication of future lyrical direction with Annie singing of isolation in common surroundings and increasing anxiety: "I'm standing on the edge of reason." Musically, and especially considering Annie's adopted vocal style, the track is reminiscent of the playful antagonism of Joni Mitchell's 'Big Yellow Taxi', while the featured fiddle part bows to no little Van Morrison influence.

Annie's solo recordings kicked off with a song named 'Tower Of Capricorn'. She accompanied herself on piano, backed by a touch of percussion and a sweetly melodic cello line. The song discussed the rejection of lustful advances, and Annie savoured the opportunity of allowing her voice to sound ugly in parts; extremely artistically encouraging for a girl singer of the time. Kate Bush comparisons are inevitable considering the sexual subject matter, instrumentation and vocal experimentation, although Bush at this point had yet to make the sound her own, her trademark single 'Wuthering Heights' arriving in January 1978.

'Sandboy Samba' was brighter and set in a major key. Tellingly, Annie had found love and was 'as happy as a sandboy' with the recent development. Ironically, here she performed a chiruppy vocal counterpoint of which her Academy tutors would have been proud! 'One Step Nearer The Edge' was, however, a different case altogether. Recorded here with merely dramatic piano chords and sustained cello notes, Annie sang with an intensity that was to be watered down in a future release. Showcasing her bluesy, full voice, this early version allowed Annie to add more poignancy to a song about approaching insanity by *rubato* (bending the tempo) and embracing dynamic phrasing. The abrupt ending of "When I fall I really go down" seemed particularly heartfelt.

'Iceberg Man' broke the spell with a fleeting, busy piano introduction. Simply arranged for piano and vocal, this tale addressing a lover's coldness had some nice chords but came across as a little static on tape, and could have benefited from Dave's imaginative interpretation. 'Space Eyes' housed apocalyptic piano accompaniment, alternately sinister and soulful. Annie's vocal on this track was outstanding as she sang of standing on the margin of society; her articulation of the word "oblivion" drawn out with relish and eventually turning to a seething whisper of "I feel you in the air . . ."

'Song For Joni' held no great secret of its lyrical topic – it was a lazy, brief ode to Annie's heroine in the poetic style of the subject herself: "I see Joni in the picture with a highway running through her/ She sends out like a semaphore into the lonely night". Finally, 'Crow Highway' took the form of a self-indulgent vocal scat, lacking in direction and referring to Annie's past teenage woes. And so finished the brief glimpse into a future talent.

After their exciting day recording with Rob Gold, all went momentarily quiet for the main core of the group. While Rob worked behind the scenes trying to secure interest in the musicians he considered his protégés, over the summer of 1977 Peet, Dave and Annie came into contact with an Australian artiste going by the dubious name of Creepy John Thomas. Creepy John lived in Crouch End, but boasted impressive German connections, specifically with maverick producer, Conrad 'Conny' Plank, whose credits included his pioneering electronic work with Ultravox and German experimental bands, Can and Kraftwerk.

Creepy John had talked his eminent friend into allowing him some free time in Conny's Cologne studio to record a song he had written, called 'Exclusive'. As a favour to his friends Creepy John invited the trio along for the ride, and they contributed musically to the German demo as well as making perhaps their best contact in the business yet.

Captivated by Annie's voice, Conny was tirelessly encouraging and his dedicated genius in the studio equally inspired Dave to take more notice of different recording techniques. Annie and Dave in particular struck up a deep and lasting friendship with Conny and the two musicians frequently cite the producer as a mentor. Annie confirms, "I've learned more from just sitting in Conny Plank's kitchen than from anything else."

★   ★   ★

While Rob Gold was considering his best way forward with the demo he had recorded some months ago, back in London his colleagues Geoff Hannington and Olav Wyper were busy establishing Logo Records. Geoff and Olav both boasted sterling backgrounds in the music business having previously worked in senior positions at Phillips and then RCA, Geoff in particular spending time as marketing manager in America, overseeing RCA's principal artist, David Bowie.

Fancying setting up on his own, after a while Geoff returned from the States, met Olav by chance and together the friends decided to form Logo. Financial backing was secured from a book and magazine publishing company called Marshall Cavendish, and Rob was employed as the head of Logo Publishing. In October 1977 Logo was still in its infancy and had only one significant band on its books, Meal Ticket, whose misfortune was to release their first record on the same day as The Sex Pistols' explosive emergence with 'Anarchy In The UK'.

Nevertheless, Geoff and Olav were determined that their business venture would succeed, and over the summer of 1977 were pursuing negotiation of the purchase of Transatlantic Records from Granada, which would entail inheriting a roster of folk and folk/rock bands. The future seemed bright for the business-like pair.

The three principal Logo associates all harbour slightly different memories of the commencement of their relationship with Dave Stewart, Peet Coombes and Annie Lennox.

"Rob had known Dave in another band," recalls Olav. "Just before we bought Transatlantic, Dave came in to see him with Peet. They had a load of songs that they were touting around and were hoping to use that as the basis of a deal. We listened to them and I said that they needed somebody else to perform the songs, because they were good songs, but they couldn't sing – they were guitar players.

"Dave said that he knew this girl who was a waitress, a classical flautist who had come down from Scotland to make her fame and fortune. He thought she had a great voice and plus she could play the flute on the demos. Rob listened to their material, put it down on tape and gave it to me."

According to Rob, his intention had not been to sign the musicians with Logo. "We did about nine tracks and she sounded like Joni Mitchell," he recalls of the fated demo tape. "I was playing this when I got back to Logo's offices and Geoff Hannington and Olav Wyper heard this voice through the wall. I'd made the tape to impress the record companies, but my idea was not to sign her to Logo Records – more to get her with EMI or a bigger company. So, Geoff and Olav heard this voice and decided they were interested, and as far as I know that was the first time they'd ever heard of Annie."

Geoff remains unsure of any previous connection between the head of his publishing company and Dave Stewart, and simply believes that the introduction was made in the usual, well-trodden manner. "Through the door came a tape one day and we always listened to tapes once a week," he says. "We heard this particular tape which had come from Dave Stewart, and as I recall was a bunch of songs that Dave had written and had got Annie to sing.[11] That was the starter. We said, 'Hey, we've got to meet next week,' because although the songs were crap, the voice was incredibly good."

Either way, before much time had elapsed after Logo's main men had witnessed their first taste of Annie's vocals, the musical trio were summoned in for a meeting at the St. Martin's Lane offices.

"As I recall they were looking for a publisher," Geoff continues. "We

[11] In fact, while Dave may well have had a hand in writing the first two songs on the demo, Annie had actually written the majority of the material.

said, 'Do come in,' and they came in and said, 'We're writers,' and there turned out to be three of them." He concedes, "I think the tape probably did come through Rob as they were looking for a publishing deal." Olav picks up the story, "They came back and they had sort of rehearsed, but it didn't really work. It then turned out that Annie could play piano, so we put her at the piano and she played and sang, and Dave and Peet played guitar."

The effect was instant. "We immediately looked at each other as they sat there and played and said, 'This looks very interesting, so let's give it a try,'" recalls Geoff. "We said to them, 'Let's make some records,' and they weren't quite sure but we said, 'Go on, try!'"

The threesome were torn between their original plan of simply writing songs to be published and performed by other musicians, and Geoff's tantalising promise of fame. Dave especially was itching to try his hand once again at pop stardom, but both Peet and Annie were more reticent, each aware that they had personal problems with being in the spotlight. However, as Olav recalls, time was of the essence and they were soon persuaded to at least explore Logo's invitation. "Geoff said to them, 'If you're going to try and sell yourselves, you have to put something properly down on tape in a studio.'"

Logo presented the group with their desired publishing deal and also a record contract that gave them a small advance of £300 each, simultaneously tying them into a six-album clause with options for future recordings. Dave, Peet and Annie were at this stage extremely hard up, and as Annie states, "They offered us a deal on the spot and we accepted as we were completely broke and needed the cash. We were desperate and couldn't afford a solicitor to check the contract, so we just signed."

"They were very pleased to get a record deal," concludes Olav, "but they felt, I think, that it was only one step in their career – they had to start somewhere and that we were as good a place as any. We were enthusiastic and we had everything to prove in the industry, so we were going to put a hell of a lot into it, which indeed we did."

"Ray Russell was standing outside," Geoff carries on. "He was a musician who wanted to become a producer. Off they went to the studios and put down three or four tracks."

★   ★   ★

Almost immediately there was a discrepancy brewing between the band's plans for the future and Logo's primary interest in their new signing. To the record label Annie appeared the obvious focus of the group, which was tentatively named 'Catch', but the members themselves were each determined to be viewed equally. Says Olav, "We were absolutely entranced by *her*, but we were not at all impressed with the other two. So we suggested that they wrote the songs for her, and that we built a career around her. But she was not in the least bit interested in doing that, and they were deeply offended." Geoff continues, "We thought this girl had a future as a singer, come what may. She had obvious talent. It was something different, it was the voice – it really wasn't the songs, I don't think they were particularly interesting.

"Most tapes you get in the music business you can discount, they're very poor; it's very rare when you think that there's something there. Really it was Annie's voice . . . it was a very average sort of tape in terms of material and I don't think any of the songs that were subsequently used were on that tape."[12]

Annie's reluctance to front the band was clearly rooted not in stage-fright, but in her feelings of loyalty, particularly to the star-struck Dave. As Olav realised, "She was starting a relationship with Dave, so she didn't want to do anything without him, and he wanted to be involved anyway as he had started this whole thing off. So, much against our better judgement we decided that we would try and do this, which pretty much coincided with us buying Transatlantic. So we would then have the financial means to do it ourselves as opposed to going to one of the majors and doing a licensing deal."

The three friends were pleased to have finally secured themselves a record contract, even one with strings attached vis-à-vis the option clause. Although Annie, and certainly Dave, had been naïve in previous contractual dealings, they were still only in their early twenties and had little first-hand knowledge of hard-nosed negotiation. Nonetheless, they were determined not to let outward appearances betray them, and seemed to all at Logo as if they had everything in control. "Once they got into it, Dave and Annie had a very clear idea about what they wanted to do and where they were going," says Olav. "It was not so much that they were headstrong, it was that what they were doing was right for them."

"They were fairly tough kids, Dave and Annie, and to a lesser extent, Peet," continues Geoff. "They might have gone over the top, but they were pretty confident people."

Intriguingly, different members of Logo's staff disagree on who was in charge. Keith Peacock had joined Logo Records in 1977 as a fairly young

---

[12] Annie's piano and vocal composition 'One Step Nearer The Edge' was later recorded for The Tourists' third album, *Luminous Basement*, but by then the musicians and Logo had effectively parted company.

product manager at the age of 23, before swiftly being promoted to marketing manager. His impression was that, "Dave made all the decisions at the time, but you could see that Annie had a steeliness to her which had obviously developed over the years." However, Geoff was convinced otherwise. "I think Annie was really the driving force of most things that happened with the band," he says. "A very perceptive, intelligent woman. I think she had a view and a vision, and Dave was to some extent quite happy to go along with it and play his part."

It wasn't until the late Eighties that, in an interview with Phil Sutcliffe, Annie disclosed her own version of events concerning the Logo situation and her balance of power with Dave.

"Naïve? I'll tell you how green I was when I first got involved in the music industry. The first record company who signed us, Logo, said they would give us £300 each as an advance and I said, 'Oh no, I don't want *that*. I'm not in it for the money.' I felt Dave put his foot on my foot – totally green in every respect."

7

YOUR TIME WILL COME

"I started to feel a little bit of what was missing when I began working with Dave – then I realised that I didn't fit in anywhere, really. And that could be a bonus to me, in a funny sense. I could actually use something that seemed initially to be a negative thing, turn it around and make it positive; a constructive thing."

– AL

Ray Russell was the musician who happened to be standing in the corridor outside the Logo office when the fateful signing of Dave, Annie and Peet occurred. Never one to miss an opportunity to hone his budding production skills, Ray was only too glad to assist in recording the demo which turned out to be Catch's first single.

"Olav asked me to produce Catch, which was a different band. It was mainly Annie back then," he recalls today. In preparation for the sessions, Ray went round to visit Dave and Annie in their flat where he first discovered that Dave too fostered grand ideas of becoming a producer. Very much aware of the old adage that too many cooks spoil the broth Ray was apprehensive, and on the day of recording he countered his misgivings by heartily joining in with the band's narcotic tendencies. "We were pretty out of it. We were all smoking joints; there were so many drugs floating around!" he recalls.

The session took place at Air Studios in central London, where the musicians at the time remember well how the poor quality air conditioning and carpet weren't exactly conducive to recording music. This ensured that virgin bands tried even harder and consequently achieved a certain raw energy. In the case of Catch, however, the three main members were introduced to session players for the first time, which together with Dave's compulsive determination to help out behind the desks and Ray's conflicting brief, put them in a most unband-like position.

"There were different musicians on the tracks who Dave and I picked; Mo Foster playing bass and Peter Van Hooke playing drums," says Ray. Both he and Dave played guitar and, as Logo didn't want to do things by halves, an entire string section was drafted in at the last minute. While this may not have seemed like a big deal to Annie, who had been playing in orchestras all her life, it was almost certainly the first time Dave had encountered classically trained musicians in any great number, and was no doubt left feeling more than a little intimidated, especially as all his ideas were being steadfastly rejected. The producer lends a slight insight to back up this theory: "I think that Dave probably felt that what we were doing might have been too sophisticated. He saw us as sort of 'official musicians'.

"We did several tracks including 'Black Blood' and 'Borderline'. They were writing very prolifically then," continues Ray. "The tracks actually turned out quite well but I don't think the record company wanted to involve Dave that much . . . The record company didn't really like the band, and they didn't think Dave was up to much at the time."

Ray's difficult standing was fortunately alleviated by the singer of the group. "Annie was great. She was always very lively, full of ideas. Dave was a bit disgruntled to have the session taken out of his hands. At the time I was told to produce 'Annie and the band'. I think Dave didn't get what he wanted, but Annie seemed quite pleased."

Confidently they returned to Logo's office and presented Geoff with the fruits of their labour. "They came back with some recordings which weren't going to set the world on fire, but they weren't bad, and said, 'By the way, we're now a band and we call ourselves "Catch".' That's really how it started," says Geoff.

Three tracks were recorded that day, two intended as the A- and B-sides of Catch's debut single. The best song, a solo Lennox composition called 'Borderline', was hailed as the lead title. The track has a strong auto-biographical feel to it, with the inclusion of the lyrics, "Heading over the borderline/ Travelling back to the north east coastline/ Living is lonely in foreign lands/ Going back to the city with the golden sands," suggesting a longed-for return to Annie's home town of Aberdeen. This was quite surprising, considering Annie's sole aim while living in the remote Scottish city had been to escape.

"I started to feel a little bit of what was missing when I began working with Dave – then I realised that I didn't fit in *anywhere*, really," she later told *NME*. "And that could be a bonus to me, in a funny sense. I could actually use something that seemed initially to be a negative thing, kind of turn it around and make it positive, a constructive thing in the sense that I write a lot of songs about that y'know, feeling alienated . . . just to articulate how I feel. So I'm grateful to Aberdeen for that."

Today, the musical arrangement of 'Borderline' stands as gentle and rather elegant in an understated fashion, with the string section adding a certain panache while simultaneously dating it firmly in the disco-strewn late Seventies. The repeated refrain at the end of the chorus is particularly attractive and well-harmonised with Annie singing against male vocals.

The B-side, 'Black Blood', was co-written by Peet and Dave, and was marginally less catchy but musically very similar to 'Borderline'. Listening to the recording over 20 years later, it notably stands the test of time less well than the amiable A-side and is weaker in terms of interest. Annie's voice is not best represented and she sounds untypically harsh as she sings of the "Black blood inside of me".

Catch's first official recording was released as a single on October 14, 1977. The colourful sleeve depicted Dave, Peet and Annie in cheap and cheerful thrift shop outfits, with Annie sporting a recently peroxided crop.[13] Now a rare collector's item, 'Borderline'/'Black Blood' made only the slightest of ripples in its home country. Logo's main promotional angle was to appeal to the local disc jockeys: "At the time the focus was on trying to get radio play, and as I recall, we didn't get much," admits Keith Peacock. It came as a complete surprise to all concerned when the single began to take off overseas.

"We decided to put the record out and test the market," remembers Geoff Hannington. "It became a hit in Holland, curiously enough. It climbed the Dutch charts somehow just on radio play. Our licensee there was EMI and they rang us up and asked if the band could come over, and we said, 'Well, there isn't a band as far as we know!'"

During the few weeks that had passed between the recording session and the single's appearance on the Dutch charts, Annie, Dave and Peet had agreed that the sound and image of Catch was not for them. They informed their record company that they were uncertain of their musical future.

This left Logo in a somewhat challenging position. "They wanted Catch over in Holland to do TV promotion for the single. But Dave and Annie weren't sure. They delayed it and delayed it until I had EMI distributors on the phone saying, 'What's going on?'"

As 1977 came to a close, the ambitious threesome had come to realise that with the growing popularity of punk music, their rather mild brand of light pop was unlikely to make any impact. This left them in a quandary. As Annie, the youngest, passed her 23rd birthday in December they all acknowledged that punk was firmly rooted in the rebellion of teenagers and there seemed to be no obvious opening for those in their twenties.

---

[13] Oddly, on some copies of the 7″ it was revealed on the accompanying promotional insert that Annie's nickname within the band was "Sparky", which was not something any of the interviewees for this book could support!

She maintains she has somehow never been the right age for the current trend. "There was a period when everybody was talking about gurus and going to India. I was too young to be a hippy and too old to be a hardcore punk. Punks were 17, I was 23 already."

Although it was clear that the friends' musical interests lay with a slightly older audience, elements of punk crept into their lives and subtly enhanced their artistic development. This wasn't just about Annie dying a blue streak in her hair.

"When we were first together in the Seventies, we were very influenced by what was going on around us. Because we lived in London, we were really turned on to the whole punk movement, and it really affected us," Annie later revealed. "The basic thing that changed everything for us was the fact that technology had reduced the size of instruments, and computers had come on the scene. That just had an incredible influence on us, Dave in particular."

Dave's interest had begun with the mixing desk, and now that computerised keyboards were evidently the way forward, the seeds of a future obsession were sown. "During the punk movement Annie and I bought a synthesiser," he says today. "We were doing the opposite thing to the punks. We were getting more into sequencers and the mixture of soul feeling with electronics."

Nonetheless, the nameless group's game-plan was at this stage in its infancy, and the majority of the material was still being written by Peet on the guitar. Synthesisers only gradually crept in as Annie began to play them during rehearsals and gigs at which the friends continued to play. The group were delighted with their new format. "We were eager and enthusiastic about the songs," said Annie. "We felt like three gypsies on a mad adventure." The synthesisers made an interesting augmentation to the band's overall sound, but also served to underline the missing musical components.

Logo had not by any means given up on their latest signing, despite the fact that Annie and Co refused to co-operate with any promotion for Catch in Holland or indeed, anywhere else. The record company acknowledged that the occasional pub gigs the trio played around North London were quite successful, but felt they were lacking in any rhythmical support as the mish-mash act consisted of Annie and Peet sharing vocals, Dave and Peet sharing guitar accompaniment, and Annie dabbling in flute and synthesisers. It was suggested that they find a drummer, and perhaps a bass player to assist them for live performances. On Rob Gold's introduction, the group enthusiastically welcomed a drummer from Catford into the band, the poorly nicknamed Jim 'Do It' Toomey.

"At the time, I think I was with Radio Stars," Jim recounted to journalist Mark Diamond in 1979. "I'd been paranoid about contracts and had stayed clear of being committed to anything. I was earning quite a good living but I could see the potential in the band and I got off on the music, so I thought let's do it!" Jim's initial involvement was in the recording of a new demo of Peet's latest material, and for Dave, Peet and Annie it was their first ever experience of playing with a rock drummer, either in any previous incarnation or in their two years together.

"I think we recorded six tracks for the tape, and for the first time in ages I really had a good time," Jim said elsewhere. "I thought they were a bunch of hippies at first, they were real nutcases, but I couldn't believe the strength of Annie's voice through my headphones. I don't think Peet said a word to me throughout. But he smiled a lot." The amiable Londoner made an immediate niche for himself, and soon enough the others wondered how they had ever managed without him. "Jim Toomey always struck me as your classic session player – and a typical drummer," says Keith Peacock. "Nice bloke, good fun – not any huge depth!"

Momentarily drifting away from Logo and unconcerned about the uncertain direction of their recording career, the group busied themselves with establishing their act on the live circuit with their additional weight. For a while bassist Andy Brown and keyboardist Chris Parren[14] were drafted in, and the six-strong band played support acts at various venues including Acklam Hall in Ladbroke Grove, and the Nashville in Earls Court. Later in 1978 they appeared at the Marquee and boldly invited journalist Bev Briggs from *Record Mirror* to attend. She obviously liked what she saw and reviewed them in a positive light, albeit briefly, mentioning that at the time they were without a record contract.

This was not strictly true, as Logo were still waiting patiently behind the scenes for signs of a coherent objective. Keith Peacock for one attended quite a few concerts to see how their music was developing. "I remember going to see them and being staggered at how good they were. Annie was incredibly intense, appearing slightly neurotic with boyish good looks. She and Dave were living in Crouch End and we used to go and see them in a studio up there.

"I got the impression then that she was slightly in awe of Dave - he has always had a kind of Svengali quality, although at the time he seemed a tad too interested in magic mushrooms and other stimulating distractions. I also remember Annie being very concerned about his health – he had had a collapsed lung some time before and wasn't the picture of health that she seemed to be."

[14] Chris Parren was from *Rock Follies*, the group spin-off from the TV series of the same name.

Dave's continuing health worries were an ongoing source of anxiety for his girlfriend, and everyone around noticed the guitarist suffered increasingly as the band gained in momentum. Rob Gold had been present at the start of the worrying recurrence.

"I was having dinner with them in a place called Odette's in Chalk Farm one evening and all of a sudden Dave had to leave, he could hardly breathe," he remembers. "Annie was left sitting there and Dave went off to hospital. It turned out he had a collapsed lung. He was lucky to survive that – it was very touch and go." Ironically it was Dave's poor health that had first tuned him into music as he lay in hospital with a broken leg at the age of 12, and a collapsed lung was not likely to stop him now his prospects seemed promising once more.

★   ★   ★

In early 1978, the band came briefly into contact with the newly formed Radar Records, who had just signed Elvis Costello. Nothing concrete transpired so, unsure of the group's prospects, temporary members Chris Parren and Andy Brown left, to travel and to spend more time with family respectively. Dave, Peet, Annie and now Jim were none too concerned, as Logo had discreetly followed their progress over the last six months. It was high time to name their band and make some important decisions.

Consciously looking for a group identity, one day the musicians were travelling on a bus together when inspiration struck. While briefly toying with the moderately pretentious name, The Spheres Of Celestial Influence, Dave looked up, mid-discussion, and noticed a London Information Centre attracting a substantial queue of people. At that very moment, The Tourists were born.

Brandishing their collective title, the band confidently arrived on Logo's doorstep, ready and raring to continue their recording career. The bare bones of a six-album contract had already been thrashed out the previous year, and it was on this basis that work commenced. However, their lack of a manager prolonged the delay as The Tourists had been unsuccessful in finding someone with whom they were entirely comfortable. On various friends' recommendations they had already approached a couple of agencies, but as yet were unable to inform Logo who was going to manage them.

"It was very difficult because then we had to make a proper deal. But we couldn't make a deal until they had their management sorted out, because we were talking about keeping the band alive for a long time," recaps Geoff Hannington. "We were looking at an entirely different creation to just having a hit single followed by another hit single, perhaps then followed by an album. To invest in an artist you don't normally expect to get your money back immediately, it happens over time. So we renegotiated their deal and it became a five year contract with options."

This corresponded with the expansion of The Tourists who, having bid farewell to Chris and Andy, were sorely missing a bassist. The latest and final addition to the fold came in the form of Malaysian bass player, Eddie Chin, a friend of Jim's. Born in Singapore, Eddie (real name Yung Fook Chin) was in his late twenties when he moved to London. Described many times as 'inscrutable', this strong and silent type looked every inch the Samurai warrior with his mandarin moustache, threatening gaze and ponytail. He fitted in perfectly with the band of misfits.

"I'd been gigging with a band in Europe who'd had a hit single, and when I came back Jim rang me up and said he'd got this band I ought to see," Eddie later told Mark Diamond. "Well, I didn't get to see them and the next thing is he calls me up and says they were looking for a bassist . . . When I arrived Annie was just sitting in the studio writing lyrics, which they were playing. They must have got through nine songs and I was very confused. I went home with my head spinning because the next night we had a gig."

Eddie's confusion did not prevent him from debuting impressively that next night at the Hope & Anchor pub in Islington with a hastily constructed chord sheet at his feet. This was to be the first ever gig by the full and proper line-up of The Tourists.

Although they realised they needed strength in numbers, it was clear that Dave, Peet and Annie were always going to be the dominant members of the group. Keith Peacock continued to observe the shifting dynamics between them. "Interestingly in turn, Dave and Annie both seemed to be totally in awe of Peet Coombes. He was like a Noel Gallagher sort of character. Nice enough, good songwriter – but everyone at the company knew that Annie was the key. She was very obviously a fantastic singer, an incredibly engaging performer and (less obviously at the time) an amazing songwriter.

"I don't think you can downplay Dave Stewart's contribution, though. He was steering the way Annie was developing at this point, and he had an incredible innate rock'n'roll sense . . . I think it was the extreme opposite combination of Dave's penchant for overt rock'n'roll and Annie's purity which made the potent mix."

Partly due to their ages (Annie was the youngest at 23, with the rest ranging up to Jim Toomey, who was then in his mid-thirties), The Tourists agreed that they would have to come up with an alien antidote to punk music to attract an older audience on the live circuit. As they set off on a haphazard tour of pubs and clubs, mainly around London, they slowly formed a contrasting image and sound, leaning more on the side of the power pop that was emanating from across the Atlantic, with bands like Blondie and Talking Heads. This did not necessarily endear them to the current UK scene.

In Britain, punk was all about being young, aggressive and fighting back. The overwhelming message was that, in the style of bands like Malcolm McLaren's Sex Pistols fronted by Johnny Rotten, *anyone* could pick up a guitar, quickly learn three basic chords, and become a star. This kind of pop did not require any form of musical training whatsoever.

So what did audiences trussed up in torn T-shirts and safety-pins make of Annie from the Royal Academy with her freshly peroxided crop and Day-Glo outfits, Peet with his introspective lyrics and gentle voice, and the three odd-looking musicians lurking behind them? Initially at least, the infant band faced alternating nonchalance and heckling with occasional violence thrown in. One night, particularly poignantly for Annie, a Scottish punk group called The Rezillos covered The Tourists' dressing room in graffiti, and another time a friend of the band was attacked by an incensed bouncer at the Nashville in West London, a popular punk spot.

Annie's worst incident during this period occurred outside London, in what was supposed to be a 'friendly' venue. Spying an angry, drunken, bondage-clad crowd awaiting The Tourists from behind the scenes, Annie was reduced to tears. "Our roadie told us the last time he'd been there, the audience had gone wild and set fire to the PA system," she later recounted. "I was terrified and the stage had to be lined with bouncers at every side while we were playing." This was not the life she had imagined for herself on entering the pop world.

Not all memories of this era were negative, and Dave and Annie made great friends with members of Ian Dury's band, The Blockheads. Guitarist John Turnbull recalls, "I did get them some gigs with The Blockheads supporting us on our tour of Odeons, at Lewisham and Streatham or somewhere like that. They went down really well and had a bit of a name. I think because it was Odeons there was a smattering of everybody in the audience." The welcome change provided Annie and the boys with some much-needed encouragement, and they defiantly continued to develop their look.

"I went to see them somewhere in Camden one night," says Blockheads keyboard player Mickey Gallagher. "I thought they were very strange when I first saw them, because there was this girl in a pac-a-mac, playing a keyboard and jumping about the stage!" Annie's bounding enthusiasm was an interesting comparison with Peet's retiring reticence, and the two sharing lead vocals could either work very well, or sometimes not at all. As Geoff Hannington remembers, "They were a bit raw around the edges for their first live gigs, but that's to be expected." Interestingly, according to Annie, it seems The Tourists' aim was never to come across as particularly polished. "We never spend too much time on rehearsals," she said at the time. "We work out basically what's required and everyone puts their own ideas into it. And if we're pleased with what's come out – right, we'll try it on stage."

Peet was from the start an extremely prolific songwriter, and felt himself to be the natural voice of the band. Annie was, however, the visual focus, even though at first the majority of her vocals were restricted to backup. As a singer, Peet was certainly proficient, but in the early days his voice did not have enough strength to pass muster against his friends' backing, and his performance style was rather limited to the bowed head, shuffling, no eye-contact school of presentation. He was strikingly clever, quiet and thoughtful, but notwithstanding his immense songwriting input, it was Dave and Annie who were requested for promotional interviews from the very start.

In contrast to Peet, Annie was an arresting figure on stage; the only female in the group and attractive with it, stampeding up and down the stage, often pounding her fist on the ground. Having come from an intensely secluded background of writing very personal songs on the harmonium in her bedsit and performing only to a select few, her transformation was truly remarkable. What was even more stunning was how she took to singing lyrics that stemmed from an intimate and also masculine viewpoint, from a personality with whom she was often at odds.

"There's a lot of isolation and despair," she later said to *Record Mirror* of Peet's compositions. "To me and Peet, life is a duality that's composed of all types of extremes. And if you look into Peet's lyrics, he contains those polarities in his songs. There's a lot of contradiction in his songs. I find that's a valid thing to sing about, because life isn't black and white and there are crossovers. One day you feel full of despair and the next day for some unknown reason you're up." With this solidarity in mind, Annie continued to tackle Peet's distinctive lyrics with ebullience, whilst simultaneously holding down her role as part-time flautist, percussionist and keyboard player.[15]

Concurrently, Annie would do her best to portray a fun, bright image on stage. Her outfits became more and more extreme, and she would

---

[15] According to *Rolling Stone*, during her time in The Tourists, Annie played a Vox keyboard once owned by John Lennon.

typically appear wearing a brightly coloured mini-dress, gaudy plastic jewellery, pink headscarf and fringed leather waistcoat. "The trouble with the punk thing was that the music was great but so many of the people looked really drab," she explained. "I was just doing my bit to try and bring a little colour back into things." The boys took a little longer to find their own individual style, which was eventually to evolve into such memorable outfits as Sgt. Pepper jackets, ruff-necked shirts, waistcoats and scarves, but for the meantime remained nondescript, save their moddish skinny ties.

★   ★   ★

In March 1978 The Tourists, growing in confidence by the day, travelled again to Cologne, Germany, and spent the month immersed in Conny Plank's studio recording demos of their new material with the great producer. In April they returned to London and to Logo Records, armed with a clutch of tracks of which they had good reason to be proud. The Tourists had found their sound, and now they needed to release it to the public. While they waited for the go-ahead the band continued to perform in concert.

In preparation for the inevitable recording of their first album, the musicians honed their songs at these live gigs, which by now were being reviewed in the music press with some regularity. One critic was sufficiently impressed to write of Annie: "She throws herself into every number with boundless energy and a grin that you could read the small print by."

Logo boss Geoff Hannington remembers The Tourists' write-ups slightly differently, however. "Reviews of their live performances in some cases were not particularly good," he proffers. "I remember reading some reviews and I couldn't believe I'd been at the same gig! But I had implicit faith.

"When we went to see them live they were staggeringly good . . . They were wonderful – Annie was mind-blowing. Just the way she sang. Occasionally she'd bring out a drum and play it in front of the band, and she'd take her flute out once in a while. They certainly had their bad nights, but generally speaking I thought they were great."

As May turned into June, The Tourists received their first ever invitation to appear somewhere other than at a smoke-filled pub. Jim Toomey was a friend of Ritchie Gold (no relation to Rob), a producer working at Mickie Most's RAK studios. One day he was fortuitously standing next to the telephone when a call came through from someone asking if anyone had heard of a hot new band called The Tourists. Ritchie made the necessary introductions to the caller, who was in fact from Associated Television, commonly abbreviated to ATV. This led to a spot on the station's popular music programme, *Revolver*, where The Tourists performed a spirited rendition of 'Immune To Life'.

All this promising exposure was conversely set to a backdrop of growing distrust between the group and their would-be record label. Problems, which Rob Gold for one had anticipated some time ago, were now emerging within the very foundations of Logo Records.

"I was a bit disappointed when Logo got involved as their record company," he reflects today. "I think Olav had brought Geoff in to run Logo before there was even a job there. They had a rather large amount of money from Marshall Cavendish to finance the company. So there were two joint Managing Directors of Logo and of course they didn't really need two, but they took two or three years to find that out. Unfortunately the chairman of Marshall Cavendish seemed to side with Geoff more than Olav, so Olav was asked to leave and Geoff to stay on."

Ultimately Olav would indeed leave Logo, but he remembers being present during the onset of unhappiness between The Tourists and his company. "Dave and Annie were not the easiest people to deal with," he says. "I think they increasingly wanted to take total control of their own career."

When they look back on this period today, both Dave and Annie remain furious that 'artistic differences' between their band and Logo ultimately prevented them from recording and releasing a record. "It was incredible," fumes Annie. "We were playing every night to packed venues, yet the record company wouldn't release our songs." She went on to explain the crux of the matter in an early tour brochure. "We started to use Jim as a drummer and we were becoming aware of the sort of direction we wanted to go in, which was somewhat different from the way Logo had originally seen us, which was just with acoustic guitars. I didn't want to be lead female vocalist either and they didn't understand that, and because the contract was no good for a band set-up we kept away for nine months.

"When we joined them it was just the beginning of disco and if we'd gone like that they'd have been very happy. But since we didn't have any money to get electric guitars we didn't know what we'd sound like, and when we realised the difference between what we wanted and what they saw for us, we went home." Today Geoff strongly refutes that Logo had been remotely interested in promoting The Tourists in conjunction with disco fever. "I did read that," he allows. "There were a lot of alleged press comments made by Annie and Dave about our relationship with them and the things we wanted them to do, which I felt were wrong."

Either way, The Tourists were convinced that their new direction, aided by Conny Plank's production, should be captured on vinyl. So they stuck it out, even though it may have seemed for a time that they were burning their bridges. "We wouldn't even *speak* to Logo for about nine months," says Dave. "But we managed to stay together, we just kept on and on, even though things looked really bleak."

Staying true to their ideals, The Tourists spent the rest of the year playing to enthusiastic audiences, and defiantly planning their first album. Over this period Peet continued to write prolifically, soon accruing a surplus of material. Unable to record anything worthy of chart release, the bond between the five members of the band deepened as the winter set in, and as 1978 gave way to 1979 they reassured themselves that this year would be the one.

Understandably at this time of year, Annie sought the comfort of her family. "We used to meet round at Ann's Auntie Jean's house at hogmanay, and we used to have a big party where all the Lennoxes would appear at some point in the proceedings," recalls June Smith fondly of the annual festivities. "Everybody used to do their own bit, and Ann came up one time from London and that was the first time I'd heard her sing. Usually she played the piano or flute, but it was actually a super performance. It was a nice little Scottish folk song that her dad had taught her."

That December Annie decided to introduce Dave to her parents for the first time, surprising her nearest and dearest with not just a new boyfriend, but seemingly a new persona as well. "The next time I saw her, she came up with Dave Stewart as a couple, and some of The Tourists! I remember she wore a huge pair of fluffy slippers, very tight animal skin trousers, a fluffy pink jumper, and she had very short hair. The last time she had come up she'd been very conventional, and suddenly for this apparition to appear was quite different."

Returning to London after Annie's 24th birthday, the couple were more determined than ever to address their problems with Logo and finally record Peet's new material. Sadly for them, this pretty much coincided with the departure of Rob Gold whom they regarded as their one true ally. Rob was leaving for pastures new, and although he stayed in touch for a while, his exit was a little unnerving for Annie. Her recent visit to Aberdeen had re-opened old wounds, and she was just beginning to confide in her friend.

"I can remember having lunch with Annie at Jimmy's in Soho," he says. "It was one of the last times I saw her. She was talking about her father and how much she really wanted him to appreciate what she was doing. He was working-class and he probably didn't really understand what she was all about. It was a different world altogether."

8

PRECIOUS

"We rose to fame on a song that came out almost by accident. We did it so casually at the time, but the press absolutely slaughtered us and you can only take a beating for so long . . ."

– AL

It had been clear from the outset of The Tourists' disagreements with Logo Records that the band was in dire need of external management. After unsuccessfully sounding out a couple of agencies Dave, Peet and Annie came across a company called Arnakata, headed by another pair of businessmen, Mike Dolan and Lloyd Beiny. Their decision to ally themselves with Arnakata went contrary to the judgement of selected Tourists' friends, including Paul Jacobs and Rob Gold.

"Mike Dolan struck me as an 'old school' manager," says Keith Peacock. "I think he was the manager with The Strawbs at some point, and when I was a student I went out buying copies of their 1973 single 'Part Of The Union' – I think that says it all! They had big offices in W1 and Lloyd seemed like Mike's heir apparent – the understudy. His style was like a junior version of Mike's. I think they did a good job for the band – like all good managers, they were a pain in the arse for the record company . . ."

For better or for worse, Arnakata represented the band and reached an agreement with Logo whereby The Tourists would be immediately flown out to Cologne to record 12 of Peet's original tracks for their first album. Geoff Hannington maintains that the delay in negotiations was not so much a dispute between the band and his company over artistic direction, but a culmination of many things happening at once. He had been unhappy to allow The Tourists to start recording without any form of management, and over the last year had personally been more involved in the takeover of Transatlantic Records. With this deal completed, Logo was a new company altogether; Olav Wyper and Rob Gold had gone, and Geoff was consequently overseeing a full repertoire of Transatlantic's mainly folk artists and song catalogue. He was now in a more favourable position, with added sales, marketing and distribution power, to channel his energies into The Tourists. The band themselves were not about to budge on the next bit.

"They wanted to get into the studios and do an album initially," Geoff explains. "They had decided who they wanted to produce them – Conny Plank in Germany – which was unusual for a new group even to know about him at that point in time. He wasn't particularly recognised in the UK. How refreshing, but also how expensive!"

So, off to Germany The Tourists flew to spend three weeks in Conny's studio. Setting a precedent which would apply to the greater part of Dave and Annie's work over the next decade, the recording sessions were brief and the entire album, including the mix, was completed in just under a month. This was partly due to The Tourists wanting a convincing rough-edged feel.

"A lot of the album is live," said Dave at the time. "We put the backing tracks down live and then just put the vocals on top of that – that's the way Conny likes to do it. It gets that rawness. It's really gutsy and full, but there's only one or two tracks there with just a couple of overdubs, a guitar solo and some keyboards, no vocal or drum overdubs."

The plan was to launch The Tourists with their debut album and a double single within the next couple of months. Kick-starting their pro-motional campaign, a slot was secured supporting the recently reformed Roxy Music on a large-scale national tour, commencing in the UK in April 1979 before progressing to Europe, then America and Japan. The Tourists were present for the beginning of this undertaking, and Dave in particular was delighted as he was a self-confessed huge fan. "The best records are timeless really, like Roxy Music," he said later to *Zig Zag*. "I think you only get timeless music when the people making it have got an idea of what they want to do creatively, and they've got a certain feeling and a certain sound which they get almost instinctively."

The critical acclaim garnered from the Roxy Music tour was com-pounded when Logo employed the renowned Tony Brainsby as The Tour-ists' publicity agent. As Olav recalls, "At the time he was probably the leading independent publicist and would work for big companies and inde-pendents and adjust his fee accordingly." Press releases were soon winging their way to all the major music papers and radio stations, with excitable quotes from Annie about the upcoming release of The Tourists' first record:

"It'll just be saying 'THIS IS THE TOURISTS' and this is the music we play and if you like it, let's link on to something new again and get a good feeling happening – not a nihilistic feeling anymore."

Eventually in May 1979 the first Tourists' single was released; 'Blind Among The Flowers', a joint composition by Peet, Dave and Annie, featuring the two vocalists in a wholesome, power pop duet. Notably, it was also the record buying public's first ever taste of a Dave Stewart production. As promised, it was a double release, including a free single comprising two tracks, 'Golden Lamp' and 'Wrecked'. The nonchalance of the lead title was immediately noted by the critics, and capitalised upon by the band members in their enthusiastic first interviews with the press.

"I feel there is very much a Tourists sound, but within that there is plenty of variation," justified Dave. "We are not just a pop band. To me the lyrics for 'Blind Among The Flowers' are among the strongest statements that have been made for ageism, but it is not heavy intellectual pretension." Said Annie, no less boldly, "You could say that we are trying to use our music and our act to offer some kind of reassurance to people who're anxious but afraid to step outside conventional barriers." While 'Blind Among The Flowers' proved to be a mild success with the reviewers, The Tourists had a little way to go before they hit the mainstream, and the single peaked at number 52 in the UK charts, aided by an appearance on *The Old Grey Whistle Test*.

Not far behind it was the eponymously titled LP, *The Tourists*. Released on June 8, 1979, those in the know remarked that it failed to capture the band's raw, live appeal. *Sounds* magazine summed up what appeared to be the popular critical opinion by calling it a "confusion" of "misguided excursions", with "infectious hook lines and compelling arrangements . . . spoilt by inconclusive ideas."

As the album dipped into the lower end of the UK charts at number 72, the small circle of devoted concert-goers must presumably have contemplated what appeared to be an engagement ring on Annie's finger, on the staged photograph adorning the cover.

'Blind Among The Flowers' opens *The Tourists*, and following an up-front, punky introduction, the frenetic, fast-paced track evolves into a fairly straightforward and rather dated piece of power pop, with touches of new wave keyboards. Annie's double-tracked vocals are over-harmonised with Peet, which unfortunately presents her as a little insipid rather than dominant; her style at this stage clearly undeveloped and much softer than the demos recorded back in April 1977. A belligerent 'don't care' attitude is reflected in both the lyrics, "Nothing means nothing to me", and the messy guitar solos.

Peet then takes the lead for 'Save Me', a busy guitar-laden track, but the presence of Annie's backing vocals over the chorus adds a reflective touch. Although the third track, 'Fools Paradise', doesn't stand out particularly it is the first time on record where Annie's voice truly breaks through, singing regretfully of wasted chances, lost time and exploitation.

The first cheerful offering on *The Tourists* comes with the most welcome 'Can't Stop Laughing' – a catchy, riff driven song with sweet mellow verses and upbeat and danceable choruses. Peet and Annie emerge from their respective shells with a series of playful question-and-answer phrases, and the music ends with a shout of laughter against a backdrop of odd, flutey noises. 'Don't Get Left Behind' then provides Peet with the opportunity to display his best Buddy Holly impression in a positive, energetic burst, with Annie uprooted to backing vocals.

Peculiar yet touching, the brief musical poem of 'Another English Day' finds Peet backed, Fleetwood Mac style, with melancholy acoustic guitars. He sings softly of his home country in the autumn rain and of eternal waiting.

Folk influences aside, The Tourists are not afraid to experiment with elements of punk, and the introduction of 'Deadly Kiss' draws from Blondie's own eponymous album of the previous year. Annie again takes centre stage and her vocals are measured and sweet, yet with a fittingly bitter edge. The imagery of the lyrics; wind, thunder and pressure, is cleverly represented with a controlled, rushing feedback over the culmination of each chorus: "The wind is blowing a deadly kiss". Further echo effects at the end help to demonstrate that The Tourists are serious about not being labelled as 'just another pop band'; their occasional flashes of brilliance coming from the inspirational use of instruments and effects such as these.

'Ain't No Room' is something of an anomaly. Dub or reggae is hardly the style one would expect The Tourists to seize upon next, and Peet's incoherently slurred vocals sound ridiculously out of place for a singer hailing from sunny Sunderland. This is not his normal nasal commentary and the listener can't help but question his motives – what exactly is he trying to portray? Still, the melodic, catchy nature of the track is certainly refreshing, and the relaxed, lazy pace provides a very different backdrop to yet more life-questioning lyrics.

Annie is back as lead vocalist for 'The Loneliest Man In The World' and sounds uncharacteristically young on the verses, where her delicate high-pitched delivery comes across as a little too fluttery for the image she chooses to project with most of this album. She sings a pleasant and rather uninspiring tale of a friendless misfit, which at least deviates from the normal subject matter for a pop song.

The Tourists keep up the interest with the intriguing 'Useless Duration Of Time'. Its curious introduction features an Eastern-sounding saxophone and various distortion effects, while the following lyrical theme varies between teenage apathy and the existentialist undercurrent first heard in 'Blind Among The Flowers', as the twinned voices of Peet and Annie explore the matter of existence. Musically, there is an attractive quality of space interspersed with the military beat of the chorus. The close is just as bizarre as the beginning, with both the saxophone and guitar dabbling in half-tones – a promising musical inclusion in The Tourists' work so far.

'He Who Laughs Last' is frenzied and fast, with Peet again coming across as a whooping Buddy Holly-styled singer. Although the song is certainly spirited in performance, it is a bit contrived musically and soon becomes repetitive, with the F-word thrown in for no apparent artistic gain.

Finally, 'Just Like You' proves that *The Tourists* really belongs to Peet, as although Annie appears prominent during the album's opening song, he has by now forcibly established himself as the lead singer. This last number is full of twisted spite: "It's just like you to tell the truth", which Peet spits out with some venom. The long track closes with an exotic 'uplifting' choral effect and church organ – leading the either confused or delighted listener to contemplate whether The Tourists have found religion . . .

★　　★　　★

To promote the album, the group embarked on a tour throughout the month of June 1979, their first as headliners. The B-52's, the American new wave pop band whose two females wore extravagant bouffant wigs, took their turn as the support act. The concerts were relatively low-key, but undoubtedly respectable for a new band with just one single and album behind them; 13 dates at clubs and universities throughout England and Scotland, taking in Sheffield, Manchester, Leicester and Edinburgh. Troubles started towards the close of the tour as billing disputes emerged with The B-52's, and gigs at the Wolverhampton Lafayette on June 29 and London Lyceum on July 8 had to be cancelled.

Hot on the heels of this promotion, the follow-up single, 'The Loneliest Man In The World', was released on July 29, and aided by their growing live popularity, made a far better impression on the UK charts at number 32. The song was critically well received, with *Record Mirror*'s Mike Nicholls remarking on its similarity to The Beatles' 'Nowhere Man'. In response to this comparison, Peet Coombes was to hint in an interview later in October: "Well that song certainly did not consciously influence my own, but it could be about the same person."

The Tourists were not about to relax and bask in their initial success – Peet had written so many songs that the obvious progression for the rest of the summer was to return to the studio and record their second album. During this time structural changes within Logo would result in the departure of Keith Peacock. Although he retained a rather unpleasant aftertaste from his treatment by the record company, Keith had only praise for the sensitivity of The Tourists' female singer, who had by then attracted the first stirrings of media interest for her haunting lead vocals on 'The Loneliest Man In The World'.

"Logo was a company that was financed by a part-works magazine publisher investing in all sorts of businesses, on the back of massive success in their core business," Keith explains. "When things were not immediately successful the cutbacks were fast and furious. I was kicked out in about September 1979. I remember getting a really nice card from Annie – which I think says something about the sort of person she was then and probably is now."

The Tourists were currently coping with their own problems, as the honeymoon period with Logo had soured bitterly. Spurred on by suggestions from Arnakata, their notoriously cut-throat management company, negotiations were already under way to shift them to a major record label. By now the relationship with Geoff Hannington had broken down to a point where he and the musicians were no longer speaking.

As the band struggled to deal with this hostility *and* record new material, the beginning of the end was also apparent in Dave's outspoken dislike for the producer foisted upon them by Arnakata, to oversee their second album.

"Ours was a management company that I think is quite famous for getting a band that's already signed to a label, then moving them to another label for a massive advance by persuading this new label that they're just the biggest thing," said Dave of Arnakata's plans for the future. "They then take their cut and they're not interested in you anymore. I would go in there and say: 'What's the plan? There must be *some* sort of plan'; we didn't know anything about it.

"So the producer they gave us was a guy they managed called Tom Allom. The last album he produced was for Judas Priest and in The Tourists we were trying to sound like The Byrds, so this guy didn't understand us at all." The unhappy group booked themselves into Olympic Studios in Barnes in south west London, and did their best to recreate with Allom the success and friendship they had enjoyed with Conny Plank. It was clear that nerves all round were frayed, especially as Dave's respect for the new producer was in doubt. It was also exceptionally rare for a group to record and release a follow-up album within four months, and the demanding timetable threatened to reduce the quality of material.

Despite the strenuous conditions, the second Tourists LP, *Reality Effect*, was pleasingly successful – musically much the same as *The Tourists*, but with greater lyrical depth. It was released in October 1979, soon attaining the promising heights of number 23 and spending a total of four months in the UK album charts, which led them nicely into the beginning of the new decade. *Reality Effect* eventually went platinum in 1980.

A solid and honest review of the album was printed in *Sounds* magazine: "Some of this record positively flies. The Tourists are not brilliant. They're not inspired. They take themselves a little too seriously. They worry. But they've got just the right amount of suss to utilise their talents to generate some quite surprising quantities of agreeable sensations."

The most instantly notable aspect to the release was its striking cover sleeve. On the back was a photograph of a white, minimalist room, with a table laid for a meal. On the front was chaos; the same room contained The Tourists themselves, all clad in white sitting at the table, with Annie outstanding in a voluminous wedding dress. Set and occupants alike had been generously splattered with purple, red, yellow and green paint. It was a far cry from the static, posed portrait used on the cover of *The Tourists*, and already it seemed that certain members of the band were taking note of how image can be used as a key marketing tool.

The majority of the music was equally future-facing and is just as enjoyable today. Opening *Reality Effect* with the Coombes-penned 'It Doesn't Have To Be This Way', The Tourists continue their kooky approach to pop with a hotchpotch of Annie and Peet battling against each other vocally, and idiosyncratic inclusions such as the repeated breathy sigh panned from left to right. The track is a little too crowded and only really works when the arrangement is pared down in the chorus. Still, it stands well as an engaging opener.

Next came the Dusty Springfield cover, 'I Only Want To Be With You', a perfect crossover into the power pop genre, complete with chugging rock guitars and Annie's faithful Dusty impression, backed by Peet's tuneful harmonies. Everything is well-paced from start to finish, with an instrumental break punctuated by hand-claps just begging to be adopted by an eager teenage audience. The Tourists stick to an almost note-for-note version, taking no chances musically, and there is nothing here to incite wariness from their audience.

Peet's next track, 'In The Morning (When The Madness Has Faded)', betrays his New York punk leanings once again, with traces of Blondie's manic keyboardist, Jimmy Destri, appearing on Annie's organ. The song is in part disappointing – with a title like this, one would expect the vocalist (in this case Peet) to sound a little more 'insane' or even dangerous, instead he doesn't really do justice to the potentially exciting subject matter. However, the piano swirls towards the end of the track, blending with an Eastern-sounding string synthesiser, reflect the meaning more piquantly, the peculiar combination eventually fading much like the madness of the title.

The insanity continues with a wolf howl and another Coombes composition, 'All Life's Tragedies'. Reminiscent of The Police in instrumentation, the best part of this song is a stripped, stark chorus with Annie's devastatingly beautiful voice floating ethereally and anxiously over the top: "All life's tragedies/ Make me feel so ill at ease".

'Everywhere You Look' is a blatant rip-off of Buddy Holly's brand of cheesy pop – cheerful enough but incongruously twee in the edgy setting of *Reality Effect*. The lyrics hardly explore new, or even interesting territory: "Everywhere you look . . . there's always something to learn". Although some attractive guitar harmonics are used in the instrumental break, the rest is pure candy floss.

'Nothing To Do' is rather samey and straightforward, a bland rock'n' roll piece sounding much like the previous track; the only highlight is Annie's soft backing vocals. Soon enough she pushes Peet out of the spotlight as the pair harmonise together on the energetic 'So Good To Be Back Home Again' which is clearly drawn from the early Beatles. This is one of The Tourists' few love songs, especially unlikely with its cheerful tone. Critics rightly remarked that it bore a certain resemblance to 'I Only Want To Be With You', particularly with lines like "Only one thing I wanna do/ I wanna get back home to you".

'Circular Fever' revolves around a hard rock guitar riff backed by relentless drums. Both Annie and Peet camp it up considerably on the Police-like vocals. 'In My Mind (There's Sorrow)' recapitulates Peet's ceaseless pessimistic gloom, backed with chiming guitars. This track is really a lesser version of the earlier 'All Life's Tragedies' in terms of form and content, and leaves the listener feeling rather noncommittal.

The penultimate track, 'Something In The Air Tonight', begins with a blurred muddle of guitars and keyboards before Peet settles in to his trademark Buddy Holly impression. The music is slow and meaningless, making little impact. Fortunately, after the inferior quality of the last three tracks, 'Summer's Night' picks up in time for the close of this record. Intriguingly placed somewhere between Mexican and folk music, the song opens with a flurry of excited voices and then explodes into a fiery mixture of jangly guitars, enthusiastic percussion and even a mariachi trumpet part. Peet and Annie harmonise brightly with each other and *Reality Effect* culminates with foreign voices having a heated discussion over the fading music. Confusing yet brilliant, The Tourists' method of closing their second album effectively illustrates their sporadic bursts of genius which are all too often buried beneath the doleful personality of their retiring frontman.

With such strong material, it was only a matter of time before America bought into the act, and soon enough The Tourists caught the attention of Epic Records, a division of CBS. A selection of tracks from *The Tourists* and *Reality Effect* were combined on the group's debut US release, which a little misleadingly was also titled *Reality Effect*. This came out several months later in April 1980, and proved to be quite successful with the American critics, who immediately tagged on their own comparisons to native rock groups such as the early Seventies incarnation of Jefferson Airplane. Their reviews suggested that Annie Lennox and Peet Coombes were playing the parts of Grace Slick and Marty Balin. On the surface it was all good fun, but The Tourists' security blanket of artistic credibility was about to be seriously shaken.

★   ★   ★

'I Only Want To Be With You', The Tourists' remake of Dusty Springfield's 1963 hit was the first single to be released from *Reality Effect*. It was intended as a fun cover version that would further establish the group as a chart act. Without question the single achieved these goals, by strange coincidence rising to the very same chart position that Annie's childhood heroine Dusty herself had attained 16 years earlier. Even more bizarrely, the Scottish group Bay City Rollers also reached the magical number, with their 1976 take, 'I Only Wanna Be With You' – all round, a most impressive number four.

Such a huge accomplishment can be put fully into perspective only by considering that, at the close of the Seventies, Sixties covers were not just unfashionable, but complete anathema to critics in the hippest rock circles. Pop music was punk, disco, or even the fast fading tones of progressive rock, but it did *not* look to the previous decade for inspiration.

Twinned with a triumphant appearance on *Top Of The Pops*, where Annie camped up her biggest performance yet in a black PVC mini skirt and jacket, stilettos and enormous plastic earrings, The Tourists seemed to all those who had shared an interest in Peet's particular brand of introspective pop as if they had completely sold out. As close to 10 million viewers watched the gaudy spectacle on television, it was clear that The Tourists had arrived, but at what price?

"We rose to fame on a song that came out almost by accident," Annie was later quoted in *Sweet Dreams*. "We did it so casually at the time, but

93

the press absolutely slaughtered us and you can only take a beating for so long – no one came to ask me what I felt like. 'I Only Want To Be With You' was such a massive hit and it went across the board to grannies and to little kids of five. We were taken to the bloody cleaners for doing that bloody song and I swear to you we were not jumping on a bandwagon.

"It was just that we decided to do somebody else's song for a change and it sounded like a great single, so we stuck it out and it's as simple as that – and it was enormously successful. It drove me mad . . . it really wasn't wholly representative of the rest of the music."

Popular opinion within the media had suddenly swung from a growing respect for The Tourists as a decent live band, to condemnation of the group for cashing in. No band likes to be viewed as seeking easy money and equally quick fame, but to Dave, Annie and Peet, it was almost more than they could bear.

Dave outlined his personal regret in an interview for *Record Mirror*. "It was a bit out of proportion with 'I Only Want To Be With You' – the poppy side of it was really overplayed by everybody, and if you listen to the rest of our albums, apart from a couple of songs which are more sort of throwaway fun songs, it's not really like that. The throwaway fun songs became phenomenally successful, that's all – so what can you do?"

Geoff Hannington remembers being given the *Reality Effect* album on its completion, and offers that The Tourists themselves had chosen to release that single with their eyes wide open.

"If you put it out and it's a hit, then it's down to you. There was no pressure on them to have that recording out. However, it was pretty obvious that they'd made it for a reason. One assumes they had made it because Annie very much liked the song herself, but the second reason was, I think, that it was a very clever commercial choice to do a cover that would establish the band as a commercial band. And it certainly did."

Although Dave sounded resigned to the bad press, and was at least open to accepting that bands will always be synonymous with their more accessible songs, Annie was unable to let it pass. "The trouble in England is that commercial success and artistic success are seen as mutually exclusive," she moaned in June 1980. "If you're a hit you're a failure with the elitist rock press. We got a lot of favourable attention before we had the first hit and then they turned against us . . . We've had a lot of attention from the nationals and the Beeb and as a result the rock press regard us as having no credibility."

Her ranting continued less eloquently in another interview: "People think just because we did a Dusty Springfield song, that's an end in itself y'know – stick on a label, *categorise*. They seem to think we're just a bunch of stupid thickos who're only in it for the money! There's a great deal behind this group, and a great deal to be found out about this group. But nobody in the press ever gives us a *chance*! It's bloody unfair! Having bad press all the time limits our audience. Audiences really *are* affected by what they read."

It is unsurprising therefore, given Annie's retorts to any journalist willing to listen and her apparent ingratitude to the fans for making the song a hit at all, that almost overnight she gained a media reputation as being difficult, frosty and rather boorish. The 'steeliness' noticed by so many former friends and colleagues at the Royal Academy of Music and Logo Records had finally found its way into reviews, and all of a sudden she became the central figure of the group – and also the music papers' dartboard. With headlines appearing like *NME*'s infamous "The Tourists talk about suicide – Graham Lock wishes they did", Annie's new-found hatred of the press was quite understandable.

To pay Annie her dues, she made a point of standing up for herself and agreed to continue interviews in an attempt to smooth things over. Refusing to speak on behalf of The Tourists anymore would have been all too easy, but Annie felt a sense of duty to her group, fully realising that the delicate balance of their credibility could well rest on her young shoulders.

"Either I'm not very good at interviews, or nothing I say actually finds its way into print," she had shrugged to *Record Mirror* in October 1979. "It's shortened, taken out of context or whatever." Later in February the next year, she tried a little harder: "I don't want to be like Debbie Harry, or Gary Numan, because I think they have that slightly cold, unapproachable look. The papers will always talk about sex objects – especially the national press – they want to sell their papers. But I'm *not* cold and detached."

In August she appeared in the children's pop magazine, *Look-In*, in an effort to stress to her younger fans that The Tourists was not just about Annie Lennox and a nameless backing band. "It seems that no matter what you do to avoid being picked out and chosen as the focal point of the group it just doesn't matter. I've done loads of sessions where I've said that I don't want to be in the centre, that I'd stand at the side or at the back, but it just doesn't matter because they can pick you out anywhere if they want."

By October 1980, it was painfully apparent that no one was interested in the other musicians any more. Journalists would only ever approach them for interviews with Annie, and if Dave happened to be present (after all, he *was* her boyfriend), then all well and good. The crux of the insult was that the main creative force behind The Tourists, Peet Coombes, was completely overlooked.

"The music press don't even think we're valid enough to do an in-depth interview with Peet who's written three album's worth of songs, and to us, they're really strong statements," Dave sighed to David Sinclair. "This guy turns up in Edinburgh to do an interview for *Melody Maker*, and instead of Annie, we sent Peet to do it. The guy's sitting down with his photographer and Peet comes in. 'Hi, I'm Peet, I write the songs for the band.' The guy turns round to his photographer and says, 'Another wasted journey – if Annie's not coming, we're not doing it.'"

★ ★ ★

Now that the roles within The Tourists had unintentionally shifted, Annie decided that she might as well maintain the fun, visual image first established before the band had attracted any media attention, good or bad. She appeared again on *Top Of The Pops* dressed, uniquely, in a drape coat, tight shiny trousers and leather flying helmet from which trailed a fake long blonde plait.

Although The Tourists were beginning to see a little more remuneration as their singles hit the charts, Annie seemed determined to retain her Scottish frugality. Wearing an expensive-looking fringed suede jacket, she told Rosalind Russell, "We have about £60 a week each, and now I can afford to buy a jacket like this for £60 I still feel guilty about buying it. But the clothes I wear are an extension of my character. I would feel fragmented if I wore what other people thought I should. I still buy second-hand stuff." Annie had always been a regular at treasure troves like Camden and Petticoat Lane markets and, even though she was now famous, would continue to visit, perhaps picking out some eye-catching material to be made into trousers or a skirt. On the whole, she rejected any form of labelling by the press as being part of a 'fashion band', and strove to avoid personal typification.

This was in part due to an early perception of The Tourists as the 'British Blondie', on account of the style of their two albums, but even more to the very basic fact that the otherwise male band had a blonde female singer. Annie has never been one to take judgements lightly, and although she was flattered, she fought long and hard against these endless comparisons.

"I'm not a sexy lady," she protested to the *Daily Mirror*. "I dyed my hair [blonde] because my own is so mousy it's awful. But I would be daft to try to be a Debbie Harry. The trouble is people make comparisons about everything. The Tourists are different, and we don't identify with any of the current trends." The irony was that Annie had always been a fan of the diminutive New York sex symbol, and not necessarily for the obvious reasons. "She for me was so enigmatic as a performer. Not a great singer, but as a *popstress* she had this unique quality. She's never been given the recognition she deserves. It's too easy to dismiss Debbie Harry. Stylistically, she was unique."

Towards the end of 1979 The Tourists played some European dates to promote *Reality Effect*, culminating in a spot at the Nashville in Earls Court on December 22, 1979 as a Christmas "thank you" to their fans. As the holiday season passed, Annie turned 25 and faced an odd dichotomy; she had essentially achieved everything she had initially desired, yet the success was countered by an undercurrent of dissatisfaction caused by the ongoing criticism of her group. It was far removed from the anonymous restriction she had felt in Aberdeen.

In a surprisingly candid interview with Tony Jasper, Annie revealed her parents' stoical method of coping with their daughter's meteoric rise to fame. "My mum has been taken by storm, my parents are absolutely over the moon, because something is working out for me," she said. "But they don't tell people much about it. They're quite reserved people. Sometimes people tell them before they actually know because they read about it in the papers . . .

"I suppose if I rang up and said, 'Look, I'm not going to stick at this and I'm going to have a husband, kids and somewhere nice to live,' then they would be pleased. But only if it was what I wanted." With the full support of her family behind her and well aware of the constant need for self-promotion, Annie then tantalised the press by stating that she would marry Dave sometime during 1980, "If we can find the time."

The Tourists' publicity machine continued to grind on, and Annie's icy media persona was mercifully counterbalanced by an appearance on the popular children's television programme, *Tiswas*. Uncharacteristically, she seemed only too pleased to be pelted with custard pies and other such indignities, as the exposure provided her with a timely opportunity to show the viewers she was human and even possessed a sense of humour. "It's a good TV programme, I like it. Once I discovered that a bucket of water over the head is quite fun, I didn't mind. The first one is warm, but the other bucketfuls are freezing," she shivered in February.

Predictably, the next single released from the *Reality Effect* album was the similarly themed 'So Good To Be Back Home Again'. Comparable to, and therefore capitalising on, 'I Only Want To Be With You', it climbed to number eight in the UK charts. While the choice left The Tourists wide open for further criticism, no one was surprised by its success, not least Geoff Hannington at Logo. "The follow-up would certainly have been my choice as the first single from that album had we not had that cover," he says. "It was an obvious commercial song to go with."

The logical progression for The Tourists was to go on tour, in promotion for both the single and the album. The Last Laugh Tour (the triumphant title presumably aimed as a jibe at the music press under the guise of 'He Who Laughs Last' from their debut LP) commenced in February 1980 and took in some 14 British cities before concluding at the Hammersmith Odeon in London. Hiring tour manager Kevin Harrington, under the watchful eye of Lloyd Beiny from Arnakata, it was a success, with tickets priced reasonably between £2.00 and £3.50. More worrying than any press attacks for the party at this time were Dave's recurrent lung problems, and so as not to risk any complications, the band employed a doctor to accompany them across the country.

Annie relished the opportunity to command a stage, but still felt harassed by the disproportionate amount of media attention she attracted in comparison to the boys. "I do this sort of thing [interviews] because it gets the name of the band across," she told *Melody Maker*. "Unfortunately, the general media are so repressive, always exploiting a woman's sex, looking for an angle like, 'When are you and Dave going to get married?' I try and steer them onto another tack . . . but sometimes it gets depressing.

"However, I'm sure rock journalists yawn every time they hear a girl singer saying that she's looked on as one of the boys in the band. But the reason girls feel obliged to say that is because the mass media is so obsessed with keeping a woman 'in her place'." Annie's angst at being the victim of sexism, dating back to her unpleasant audition at the Royal College of Music, came across loud and clear. But her experiences of chauvinistic barbs within the music business took on a new and portentous aspect when critics of the Last Laugh Tour insisted on suggesting that she looked more male than female.

Sexist comments aside, Annie was delighted to return to Aberdeen in true style when The Tourists were invited to play at a fancy dress college ball. The following day Lord Provost William Fraser presented the band with a music industry Scotstar Award in recognition of their sales of LPs and cassettes.

In spite of the growing adulation and related merriment, Annie sensed an underlying edge to her surroundings and began to resent the relentless self-justification. No matter how many appearances she was willing to subject herself to on *Tiswas*, underneath the bravado was a deeply serious, intense young woman.

"If you were to ask me what life is all about, I'd say it's pretty tragic," she announced in June. "But the irony of it all is that we're not going on stage to make alienating noises to alienate the audience . . . there is such a thing as hope and some kind of positivity which we have in the way we present our music. So we're not alienating, we're pulling people in. We're saying this is our dilemma, let's admit it and face it." It was clear that this jaded musician was beginning to question the whole 'pop' aesthetic, and was wondering if perhaps The Tourists had a more profound role to play.

Needless to say, being in a band with her oddball boyfriend meant that he was always on hand to provide some much needed light relief. Arriving at a junction in their hectic schedule, the group as a whole decided that they would benefit enormously from a good old-fashioned summer holiday.

"We thought, let's go on a typically tourist holiday for a laugh, forgetting that Annie would be recognised by all the other tourists," said Dave. "We took the first holiday they had and it was to Yugoslavia. They couldn't tell us the hotel and when we got there they dropped everyone off apart from six of us. Then we got into a rowing boat which went off into the mist and finally arrived at an island.

"It turned out to be a nudist colony! Everyone recognised Annie and she spent half the time trying to avoid being photographed. I kept thinking I'd walked into a Salvador Dali painting . . ." In Dave's crazy world at least, it really did appear that truth could always be trusted to prove stranger than fiction.

9

FOOLS PARADISE

"Ironically I became a 'pop star' before I was musically ready for it. With The Tourists we just fell into this thing and, personality wise, the group was still at odds with themselves and how they wanted to be represented both visually and musically."

– AL

Midway through 1980, the atmosphere between The Tourists and Logo had deteriorated to such an extent that serious action needed to be taken. Says Geoff Hannington: "I suppose the relationship broke down really at some point fairly soon after the second album was released, it started to get sour. It was always a fairly sparky relationship, and that was good because it was fierce – Annie was fairly tough and Dave was Dave!" The band members were so disgruntled they began to make public statements indicating that they wanted to be released from their contract, claiming: "Logo have no understanding of our musical ideas and direction."

The group maintained that Logo had originally envisaged them as a disco band with Annie as a dollybird frontwoman, but this is disputed by those working for the label. In truth The Tourists' management agency, Arnakata, was behind the quarrel, stirring up trouble in order to pave the way for a better deal with a bigger label – as Dave had already surmised. Geoff recalls, "It became very obvious that the management of the band wanted to take them away and sign them to a major record company. We were a small independent label. The band had suddenly become attractive to major record companies, and more attractive for being suddenly all over the media. Here was a new hit band, with a lead singer; beautiful girl, sensational voice, great performer – it was all there."

It became clear that even if Logo did manage to hold The Tourists to their two-year-old contract, the group was likely to split or simply refuse to record because of the overwhelming tension. But Geoff believed that he had invested too much time and money into the band to let go without a fight. So Logo set about taking The Tourists to court, seeking an injunction to prevent them from signing with another label. For Annie, this proved to be the last straw. "I was *outraged* that people could exist simply to exploit others," she said. "It's despicable. I *hate* it."

While all three parties anxiously awaited the trial, Mike Dolan and Lloyd Beiny continued to negotiate with Logo in the hope of reaching some form of settlement. Arnakata's intention was to sign The Tourists with major label CBS, who were showing considerable interest after the impressive success of the last year.

"Meetings took place, the band made it very clear that they didn't want to go on with us," says Geoff. "It becomes acrimonious unfortunately once you get to court, and fairly soon after that I realised there was no way back – they didn't want to make records for us anymore. So the only way out was to let them go, on some financial basis." In fact Logo's hoped-for injunction was dismissed, with the judge ruling that The Tourists were allowed to move to another label. Logo would then have a strong case to sue for compensation for the time and money invested in the group. Unshaken, Geoff pursued the case, taking it to the appeal court, which overturned the first ruling. By this stage the court proceedings had dragged on for so long that CBS had lost interest and The Tourists faced an uncertain future.

The only way to break the stalemate was a trade-off of sorts. Unusually, Geoff maintains that it was he, and not Arnakata, who began to talk to other record companies. His version of events is supported by his ex-colleague, Olav Wyper, in that if he was successful in handing over the group, he would then be allowed to retain some of the publishing royalties.

"I went to Arista first and Arista turned them down," says Geoff. "I went to my old company, RCA Records, who had been distributing The Tourists' records, and I said to them, 'Would you like to sign this group?' They got together with the managers and worked a deal out, and that was it. Marshall Cavendish received what they wanted in terms of a cash payment and there were some override royalties, payable on future records."[16]

Annie, Dave and Peet were therefore not required to appear in court, and The Tourists gladly signed to RCA. The American-owned label, then part of the giant NBC Corporation, acquired all recording rights and Logo continued to benefit from a share of the publishing rights for the next five

---

[16] The agreement reached between RCA and Logo (via their recently purchased Transatlantic label) gave Transatlantic a 3% royalty on *Reality Effect* and *The Tourists* and 1% on future releases, which were to include *Luminous Basement*, *In The Garden*, *Sweet Dreams (Are Made Of This)* and *Touch*. Later Transatlantic were to sue Eurythmics for more than £250,000 in unpaid royalties.

years. To this day Geoff claims not to be bitter, just disappointed that events soured beyond his control. His overall memory is that he is glad to have been part of Annie Lennox's 'discovery', saying simply, "I was pleased that we launched such a great talent. It's not often that such talent walks through your doors like that."

★   ★   ★

In the interim, between signing to RCA and preparing for their first album with the new label, The Tourists set off on what became known as the 'Dolly Parton Tour'; a low-key 40-date trip around America. Their adventure coined its name because the five members of the band and their entourage travelled in the buxom country singer's tour bus, and as Dave quipped, "spent most of our time wondering how Dolly Parton fitted into any of the bunks, because the space between the bunks and the roof of the bus was so narrow."

This was the group's first trip to America, and its low budget and profile suggest that the group funded it themselves. Dave and Annie in particular recall their initial impression of the country as if it were yesterday. In Los Angeles, where they played at the Whisky on Sunset Boulevard, Annie remembers being refused a ride by a cab driver who expressed concern about her bright and uncommonly masculine appearance. When The Tourists arrived in New York, Dave was so terrified of the imposing city and its reputedly violent occupants that he and Annie stayed put in their hotel room with the curtains firmly closed, surviving on room service of questionable origin and rarely venturing out. By the tour's end, they were more than ready to get back to what they knew best, and ensconce themselves in a studio to record their third album.

RCA were immensely proud of their latest signing, and determined to invest sufficiently in them to make the negotiations worth their while. John Preston was later to become managing director, and today retains his first judgement of the group's female member. "Annie, although she would not wish this of herself, is naturally one of the stars with the greatest charisma I've ever met," he says with confidence. "She just has a natural aura of authority and charisma about her that makes her a star."

By now Annie and Dave were murmuring about their desire to do more within the group than just act as Tourists' spokespeople and perform the increasingly reticent Peet Coombes' material. They received a certain amount of encouragement from the staff at RCA, although it seemed initially at least, that the company were more interested in exploiting their unusual relationship for promotional purposes.

Chris Charlesworth was working as RCA's Head Press Officer from the autumn of 1979 to the autumn of 1981. Immediately under him was Richard Routledge, and below him Sheila Sedgwick, who had joined the department from RCA's international division. "During my tenure we signed The Tourists," Chris recalls. "I was informed that I had to arrange press representation for them."

Accompanied by Richard and Sheila, Chris travelled to a Tourists gig on the south coast. "I seem to remember the gig was sparsely attended and I'm not even sure The Tourists were topping the bill . . . I thought they were fairly competent but they'd be better off writing their own material than doing cover versions." After returning to London, Chris then delegated all The Tourists' PR responsibility to Sheila, mainly on the basis that the group had a girl singer to whom a female publicist could relate more effectively.

"RCA at this time was not a very successful label. It was very stagnant and seemed to suffer from ill-advised short-term strategies brought in by new management at the top, which was replaced every six months," says Chris of the company's coup in acquiring this major chart act. "The A&R department signed acts managed or published by their friends. Everyone was fiddling their expenses and not doing very much. I think a lot of money was wasted on ill-conceived ideas, though no expense was spared when it came to David Bowie. Whenever he arrived in London, he got the red carpet treatment. The artist liaison department seemed to have a bottomless pit when it came to funding his needs. Aside from Bowie the only successful acts were Al Stewart and Diana Ross, both oldies, not to mention Elvis Presley, whose records continued to sell."

From the RCA offices on the corner of Bedford Avenue and Tottenham Court Road, Sheila Sedgwick outlined her first publicity idea to Annie and Dave. She offered, on behalf of the company, that if Dave and Annie wanted to get married, they would hire a ship and fly out journalists for a huge reception. But the couple, who had previously toyed with the idea, turned this clever, life-changing request down flat. "We considered getting married and then starting divorce proceedings the next day, but it didn't seem worth it!" Annie said some time later.

★   ★   ★

Soon after the close of the Dolly Parton Tour, RCA flew The Tourists off to the tiny volcanic Caribbean island of Montserrat for the summer, to record their third album at ex-Beatles producer George Martin's Air Studios. They were tired from the rigours of touring, yet conversely fired up as a result, but the sessions were marred by bad-tempered spats breaking out between the two vocalists. Dave and Annie had discussed many exciting musical ideas they were hoping to explore, but the dominating presence of Peet as the main songwriter held them back and kindled jealousy on both sides.

The short fuses of all involved and the almost constant live work, which had honed the band into a cohesive unit, translated into a rough and ready feel on tape. Fundamentally, The Tourists were trying to capture on record what had attracted their now impressive following.

"Talking in musical terms, I feel our recordings are a very good representation of what we're doing live," said Annie shortly before their third album's release in October 1980. "We're getting the actual power of the band now and we're a lot heavier dynamically than before. That's a very difficult thing to get – sometimes you'll go to see a live band and they're fantastic because the visual aspect is right and the live performance is all there, but then you go and listen to that same group on record and maybe it's a big let-down."

But the biggest development by far on *Luminous Basement*, the title taken from within the album's arresting opening track, was the outstanding change in Peet's vocals. Now far more confident to take the lead without padding from his female counterpart, it seemed that Peet had truly found his voice at last and was free to drop any references to kooky icons like Buddy Holly.

Whether or not Peet was comfortable with his empowered result was negligible. *Luminous Basement* is packed full of clues that the main songwriter was feeling claustrophobic within his group, and something was about to snap. Titles like 'So You Want To Go Away Now (but no one's asking you to stay now)' and 'Don't Say I Told You So' positively dripped with venom, while the majority of the lyrics on the album described various cramped relationships, all on the verge of breaking up. The chorus of 'Walls And Foundations' runs along the lines of "I need to know/ I need the space/ I need to grow/ Out of this place" and at the close of the album in 'I'm Going To Change My Mind', Peet drops a telling reference: "It's time I realised, I opened up my eyes" after having walked around "blind" for so long. Notably, on the outer cover and poorly proofread inner lyric sleeve, the picture of the normally tidy songwriter is easily one of the most haggard and uncomfortable ever published by an official source.

Yet the troubles do not solely emanate from Peet, who lyrically loses mental control in the song 'Week Days'. With the inclusion of 'One Step Nearer The Edge', the track first recorded as a demo back in April 1977, so, evidently, does Annie. Even Dave's contribution, 'Let's Take A Walk', tells of the desperate need to patch up a severed relationship after a series of bitter arguments. If ever a group was on the brink of calling it a day, it was now.

With the switch from the UK to the US, The Tourists' third album featured two track listings, oddly shuffled into a completely different order. The UK release started with 'Walls And Foundations', a powerful opener showcasing Peet's strongest and truest vocal. Musically the track is based around a self-assured, thrashing rock riff, bursting with determined energy. Annie's contribution is reduced to backing vocals, cast aside to watch Peet portray a series of twisted and mainly negative images from his life. At the end of the track the protagonist gives up, lies down, and admits defeat.

With a quirky accordion sound punctuating the jumpy beat, 'Don't Say I Told You So' is ironic in that it stands as a fitting precursor to Annie and Dave's future outings, even though it is written by Peet Coombes. Annie's strange harmonies are excellent and there is an early hint of the aggression that is soon to break free from the inappropriate breathy punk girl style utilised on so much of her work with The Tourists.

'Week Days' tells of a nervous breakdown where the subject is, in some perverse fashion, actually enjoying the changes taking over his body and watching his dishevelled reflection in a mirror: "It feels so good/ Just like it should". Musically it is a paradoxically confident and hummable rock song, with Peet taking the lead and Annie contributing harmonies for the choruses.

'So You Want To Go Away Now' is a catchy piece of punky pop which lodges in the brain and indeed refuses to go away. It serves as probably the best matching of Annie and Peet's vocals, where their various inter-linking parts work *with* their differences, complimenting them rather than awkwardly underlining any competition.

The only solo track Annie contributed to The Tourists, 'One Step Nearer The Edge', stands head and shoulders above anything else on *Luminous Basement*, in both artistic merit and musical quality. This very personal composition has developed enormously since its initial conception back in the mid-Seventies, maturing into a far more polished and accessible piece than the simple, angry demo incarnation.

Introspective, ambient and softly psychotic, Annie's vocals are now well-crafted and intense, placed in the best setting the listener has yet heard on vinyl. Her talent as a singer has not until this point been fully exploited in The Tourists, and the straggling, bluesy tale of the world closing in is perfectly reflected in the slow and easy backing, which somehow seems to shrug off the lyrics' dark undertones.

'Angels And Demons' is a nondescript, incensed rock song which easily passes the listener by. In comparison to the raging surge of 'Walls And Foundations', Peet's indistinct tenor is not best suited to the hostility, and he is perhaps not the appropriate singer to take the lead. 'Talk To Me' is simply another take on 'The Loneliest Man In The World' – an organ-led, Blondie-ish track with Annie and Peet harmonising about a person living a secluded, hermit existence. Towards the end the song veers off into a poor attempt at progressive rock; a messy repetition of the same manic musical phrase over and over again, against a backdrop of extended electronic dissonance. Probably this track came across much better in a live setting than it did here. The next offering, 'Round Round Blues', is not actually an exercise in blues but more of a guitar-driven rock song. Annie gets only a very small part – once again it is an opportunity for Peet to explore his new-found vocal confidence.

Dave's track, 'Let's Take A Walk', is a fast, fun *Blues Brothers*-type number, complete with guitars, organ, harmonica and a four-on-the-floor beat under a strong Sixties influence. Annie and Peet even appear to enjoy their harmonies, striking a rapport which was considerable in concert. The ending turns into a yelling free-for-all with the two vocalists amiably attempting to outdo each other.

Immediately after the light-hearted diversion of 'Let's Take A Walk' enters the ominous beat of 'Time Drags So Slow'. Annie takes over main vocal duties, gently and thoughtfully delivering the attractive melody line which later develops into an intriguing cross between psychedelia and a soft rock ballad. The UK album then finishes on a typically Touristy track, 'I'm Going To Change My Mind', with Peet and Annie duetting in harmony against some most enthusiastic drumming and guitar riffs, and for some unknown reason, birdsong. The track, perhaps indicatively, has an unusually jubilant ending.

The British version of *Luminous Basement* came with a free single, appropriately pressed on luminous yellow vinyl, 'From The Middle Room'/'Into The Future' – the A-side one of the earliest tracks penned solely by Dave and Annie. This is a spacey electronic instrumental, borrowing not a little from Jean-Michel Jarre's keyboard work of the mid-to-late-Seventies. The track is based on a repeated theme which really ignites when Jim Toomey's drums kick in, heightened by unworldly guitar effects. After this ultimate Tourists chill-out song comes the B-side, 'Into The Future', which is a short but jolly piece with just a vague hint of a political theme in the lyrics. Peet takes the lead and Annie harmonises in the choruses.

★　★　★

"Personally, I was never 100 per cent happy with our first two albums," said Annie, unsatisfied with the lack of live punch on *The Tourists* and

Reality Effect, "but on our latest, *Luminous Basement*, it's definitely all there. Hopefully, we will continue improving on every album we make. As long as you want to keep working, and you're enjoying it, you forge ahead . . . I would like to think that we could go on from here. I certainly don't think we'll ever go back. Within the band we certainly feel that we've found our direction. What has happened with us is that it's taken us about three albums to get mature enough on record. Sometimes a band does that on their first record but I think we're happy enough about things now."

Her cheerful optimism seemed a little forced, to say the least. *Luminous Basement* was unhesitatingly massacred by bloodthirsty music critics, with the lead single, 'Don't Say I Told You So', halting at a poor number 40 and the album at a pitiful number 75 in the UK charts.

Luminous Basement's best quality was its very British sarcastic edge, but in the early Eighties this was hopelessly unfashionable. One of the kinder reviews came from *Sounds*: "This album shows greater breadth and sharpness from the two previous offerings, but it's still true that so many of The Tourists' best ideas were other people's 10 years ago." It seemed apparent the end was nigh.

The truth was that problems had been simmering under the surface since the very conception of the band. Dave and Annie were an extremely insular couple, and three, as they say, can prove to be a crowd. "It was a very uncomfortable situation because Peet was the main songwriter," recalls Olav Wyper of when Logo were first presented with the trio. "It had been suggested that he remained the songwriter and they became the front of the band. But he wasn't comfortable with it.

"Let's just say, Peet was less talented than the other two. He was very subservient to Dave. It was Dave who was 'all talk' and Peet would say, 'No I don't do that – I'm a musician.'" Unfortunately, that wasn't the crux of the matter. "There were obvious signs, although I wasn't getting them, that Peet Coombes had problems," continues Olav's erstwhile business partner, Geoff Hannington. "Peet started drinking too much, which was very sad, because Annie and Dave were very dedicated, professional people."

When the band had arrived in Montserrat the pressure had been well and truly on to prove themselves worthy of a switch from a minor to a major label, and as drummer Jim Toomey pointed out, they had been on the road since the previous autumn. "When you get five individuals cooped up, tempers are bound to fray."

Paul Jacobs was present filming the band on their travels and recalls the convoluted group dynamics, "Peet and Annie had come to hate each other, and Dave was caught in the middle. There were problems with Jim too; he was a great rock'n'roll drummer, but he couldn't make the transition to the type of innovative rhythms Dave and Annie wanted. So they almost had to tell him what to play, and Annie – being a trained musician – used to get very frustrated with him."

Annie herself reveals that when she looks back on the time she spent with The Tourists, her feelings are mainly negative. "I think if Peet had had a band on his own without me, it would have been better and he might have been happier. I never found him easy to get along with and I always felt a bit intimidated by him – and I'm sure he felt the same about me! He had a lot of creativity in him but he was always very self-destructive, which is often the case with gifted people. He was getting in a really bad state, he felt alienated."

Disheartened by the acrimonious events of the summer and the intensifying animosity within the band, The Tourists set out on what was to be their last series of concerts, the Luminous Tour. Travelling across the UK from September 2 to October 10, 1980, the group's star seemed to be on the wane. Ticket sales were sluggish and the turnout was poor. Dave put on a brave face for the media in *Record Mirror*. "Obviously because we've been away and we haven't had any publicity or any singles out, the beginning of the tour has been half full, but that's alright. We've been really enjoying ourselves and so have the people who've been there."

Supported by The Barracudas, the concerts commenced in Annie's home town of Aberdeen and, after the tour thankfully grew in impetus and extra dates were added, they eventually ended in Belfast at the Ulster Hall. The gigs were their most ambitious yet, encompassing a luminous slide show and dancers, with Annie placed centre stage in a body stocking. Plans were then made to continue to Australia, Europe and the US in late 1980 to early 1981.

Although on the surface things seemed to be picking up, behind the scenes the three key band members were affected in different ways. For Annie, the stress of the constant bickering and the pressure to succeed took a hold of her psyche, and before long she was a nervous wreck.

"It was a grey shadow with me every bloody day," she later confided of her rapidly diminishing mental state. "It first happened when I was on stage in Birmingham and I got through the song by pinching the side of my leg so that I'd concentrate on the pain and not panic. When it happened on tour in Australia, I was actually carried off stage." Travelling by plane from Australia to Tasmania, Annie suffered a terrifying claustrophobic episode.

She wasn't alone in feeling the effects of nervous exhaustion, as she explained in *Eurythmics* by Paul Roland. "We were going to Australia for a major tour and the plane got grounded in Bangkok 'cos Peet Coombes got absolutely wrecked.[17] His emotions exploded and the next morning he realised that was it . . . the end of the road for him.

"He came and told me and Dave, and we heaved a sigh of relief because we'd been feeling the same constraints for about a year . . . we wanted to go in another direction."

At that point The Tourists made the joint decision to split up after the end of the tour. But it didn't even last that long. Although Peet continued to play for a few Australian dates to keep up appearances, he was on the point of collapse and soon left, returning to the familiarity of England. The band struggled through a couple more gigs as a four-piece, before finally calling it a day. The Tourists were no more.

★   ★   ★

"Bangkok was the first time we'd been in an entirely different culture and as soon as we decided to split Annie and I started making loads of recordings on a tiny Sony recorder, things like Bangkok street noises and things off the TV," says Dave Stewart of the period immediately following the break-up of The Tourists. But although Dave was able to almost instantly throw off the skin he had adopted for that band and begin the transition to something else, both he and Annie felt a responsibility towards their fans. They decided to speak openly about the circumstances that had triggered the demise of the group, and welcomed the chance to put their version of events across rather than incite any further bitterness.

Said Annie, "Our musical attitudes were becoming polarised, as well as having to cope with our steadily deteriorating personal relationships. I am greatly relieved at the decision and glad it's all over, but it was fun while it lasted . . . Now Peet can be his own spokesperson. It was always part of Dave's and my dilemma that we were acting as spokespersons for someone else's work within a pop context, yet we weren't able to put across how removed he was from that whole scene."

Back on home turf it seemed Peet too was pulling himself together, launching, perhaps prematurely, into a fresh musical project. Together with bass player Eddie Chin he formed Acid Drops, an experiment that was sadly unexceptional and in time disappeared without trace. To complete the circle, Jim Toomey returned to the less pressurised world of session drumming, before eventually repairing to Australia on a permanent basis.

---

[17] This may be something of an exaggeration as all flights to Australia touch down en route for refuelling and a change of crew. The likeliest scenario is that Peet became increasingly intoxicated and was refused permission to reboard the aircraft until he was sober enough to continue.

While the individuals concerned were gathering the pieces for a new beginning, the ex-band were collectively informed of some bad news. In their wake The Tourists were left owing a total of £38,000 to Arnakata in un-repaid record company advances. Dave and Annie's share of this figure was some £15,000. After a year in the limelight, they were understandably furious.

"Look, The Tourists made a stack of money and a lot of people got rich – but not the band!" Annie cried to the press. "We were a bit naïve, I suppose. We'd gone headlong into The Tourists with piles of enthusiasm but little planning . . . The hairy situations that Dave and I have been in, people don't know. When we left The Tourists we were left holding the baby, owing a massive debt to RCA."

After the healing passage of time and all that was to follow, Annie came to terms with the distressing break-up of her band and made a surprising discovery.

"I don't have any nostalgia for The Tourists," she told DJ Paul Gambaccini in the early Nineties. "It's a terrible thing to say, but . . . I feel that perhaps my being in that group was probably wrong for the person who was writing the songs at the time. I think he could have probably realised his music better without me. Perhaps I might have been some kind of hindrance. Possibly my presence in The Tourists confused the image of that group; it would have been better as a male group, and not with me."

Famously, after a few years had passed she once admitted, "I don't own one Tourists' record you know, I never did; we just wrote these songs and played them. But the other night we were in this restaurant and an old Tourists' song came on. And when I heard this particular one, it struck me as quite advanced. I mean, it wasn't the realisation of *my* musical ideas – but it wasn't rubbish, it wasn't stupid, it was something I ought to have been able to be proud of. Yet I hadn't – it was something I'd been hurt by and confused about.

"And now, I just feel it was a damn disgrace . . . that someone who wrote as much as Peet just got nothing in the end. Not that he'd give a toss, it's just that . . . I find it very odd."

10

I LOVE YOU LIKE A BALL AND CHAIN

"The closer we got professionally, the more we needed our own space."

– DS

Swallowing infuriating financial losses on top of the band's messy demise left Dave and Annie reeling, but the dramatic turn of events made the couple more resolute than ever to fight back. Determined to use the benefit of hindsight to their advantage, the pair vowed to take more control of their career. "Right at the beginning Dave said to me, 'Annie we must have a manifesto,'" recalls the female half of the team. "So we wrote down all the things we liked to do on a big sheet of paper." Dave adds, "That way we'd be sure that if we got famous, it would be on our terms."

In this attestation of their aims Annie bared her soul, admitting to enjoying "dressing up, singing, writing lyrics and performing live," while Dave was equally true to his more light-hearted nature, writing "making funny noises and mixing backing tracks" as well as "working late in the studio."

Keeping their combined personal goals at the front of their minds, the duo instinctively knew they wanted to continue working together, this time without interference from others. Consequently they set about creating an isolated and stylised partnership in which they could pursue their quirky sound ideas. As their career paths entwined ever tighter, they found their personal lives suffocating as a result.

"Our relationship was too consuming, too frightening to continue," says Dave. "Sometimes we'd be together and one of us would have to leave the room. We'd each know what the other was thinking and found that the margins between us became blurred. We'd have to fight really hard to retain our individuality, it was terrifying."

After four long and testing years the unthinkable happened. The abject couple who had been through so much together, seen the rise and fall of a pop group, experienced the highs and lows of demanding tours and almost considered marriage for the sake of publicity, made the decision to part, citing an unbearable strain between them.

Dave, a naturally sociable person with few apparent cares, gained some of the personal freedom he perhaps felt he had lost, while Annie benefited from a developmental wake-up call. "I think I needed to find myself," she later acknowledged. "I had lived through a lot of other people, and through Dave, and I wanted to sort of break away from that. But I knew creatively I didn't want to work with anybody else except Dave. So there was this strange tension – the pain of the break-up and the excitement of working together on the music."

Incredibly, while their love affair reached its natural conclusion, Dave and Annie's unwavering musical respect for each other gave birth to a new, purely professional incarnation of their relationship.

"We've managed to retain, to harness the beneficial aspects of our knowledge of each other and to utilise them in our new situation," explained Dave. "But now we're careful to allow each other a lot of space, to socialise separately when we're not working. We're still closely protective of each other, but not in an exclusive or smothering way."

Naming this most unusual band was the next challenge. "We were both drawn towards making music with rhythm, where the voice is used in a special dynamic way," said Annie. To her, their ideology seemed strangely in tune with the dance patterns she had learnt as a child. Bringing Émile Jaques-Dalcroze's philosophy of combining intellect and intuition to express music to Dave's attention, they adopted 'Eurhythmics' as their joint alias. The first 'h' was dropped to aid spelling of the former Greek word, making 'Eurythmics'. Noticeably, to this day the incorrect prefix 'the' often appears in print.

Dave was quick to embrace the term from Annie's childhood, enthusing about its subtle inferences. "We also liked the name because of the 'Eu' for Europe, and we think that we're very European. It has 'rhythm' in the middle and we think that we are very rhythmical."

Their enthusiasm was not shared by the men in suits at RCA. The record company executives expressed concern about a foreign-sounding name, but Dave literally leapt to its defence, jumping onto the boardroom table to prove the point that 'Eurythmics' would look impressive on a billboard, as if it were a well-known brand name, like Coke or Adidas. As if to complicate matters further he added, "You can call everything Eurythmics. It's not really the name of a band. It's the name of a project."

Dave took initial control of Eurythmics' sound development, learning to play keyboards seemingly overnight. His theory was that guitars were heavily associated with the Seventies, and with past criticism of The

Tourists painfully fresh he wanted to stay one step ahead of the rest. John Turnbull remembers his friend's obsession with the new instrument: "Dave sort of locked himself in for a fortnight with this funny little synthesiser. The next thing you know he's in doing the demos for the first Eurythmics songs. He just mastered this thing but in a very unorthodox style, and he made this creative leap away from guitar." Dave also looked to pursue his love of unusual production techniques. "Annie can't stand anything to do with technology whereas I'm mad about things like that."

But it wasn't really his partner's wariness that mattered, more that RCA were sceptical about this reinvention of a defunct group, with a strange name and an objective light years ahead of its time.

"At the beginning of Eurythmics I did say to RCA that we wanted to be successful in a way that people wouldn't know what the next record was going to be," he said. "It's a bit like Bowie, nobody ever has a clue what he's going to do next." Bowie left RCA shortly after Eurythmics formed, largely due to clashes with the label over what he perceived as a lack of promotion, and possibly even respect, from the American side of the company.

Adamant not to be caught up in another volatile group, Annie and Dave decided to remain a twosome. "The first step towards Eurythmics was getting away from the usual format where you have five members in a group," rationalised Annie. "Dave and I never want to be in that situation again . . . We want to follow our own creative bent." Using two inexpensive WASP synthesisers they started writing and performing together in the electronic style which was becoming popular in the early Eighties. Other emerging synthesised 'odd couples' at the time were Soft Cell and a year or so later, Yazoo, with whom Eurythmics felt a kindred spirit.

While Dave was enjoying experimenting with Eurythmics, Annie felt herself slipping into a rather desperate state. Losing her lover and erstwhile band in just a few months had taken a drastic toll on her fragile nerves. She returned home over Christmas 1980. "I felt panic-stricken and exposed without Dave. I needed to think things out, so I went back to Aberdeen," she said. Yet even the open embrace of her family could not lift Annie's spirits and she began to flounder, struggling simply to get out of bed each day.

"I can never stop questioning things, I can never accept face values," she was quoted in *Sweet Dreams Are Made Of This* of her endlessly inquisitive mind. "I even question tangible things like the tarmac on the road and the fact that we're still alive. I wish I didn't think about things so much, it gets to be a burden. I can become very alienated by it . . . It was a delayed reaction to what happened to us in The Tourists, my own self-esteem hit rock bottom."

★   ★   ★

The one person who could encourage the fledgling band and help Annie regain her confidence was Conny Plank. Dave and Annie had kept in touch with him after The Tourist days and were invited to his annual New Year's Eve party at the end of 1980. Having already bumped into Gabi Delgado from Deutsche Amerikanische Freundschaft (DAF) at the airport, the musicians turned the party into a lively jamming session which included the multiple talents of drummer and brass player Jaki Liebezeit, bassist and brass player Hölger Czukay, and drummer Robert Görl, again from DAF. As well as surprising herself with an instant attraction to Robert, Annie has fond memories of the inspirational evening. "Eurythmics began there in the studio – just people listening to the music for a whole concept instead of *their* keyboard bit or whatever."

The impromptu session proved to be a turning point as Dave learned new techniques, co-producing with Conny and everyone present. Rob Gold remembers watching the sheer impact of the Germans from afar: "Hölger Czukay was somebody who influenced them a lot. He used to sample short-wave radio and use the different sounds and I remember Dave being totally enthusiastic about that." Dave was later to expound to *Musician* magazine: "Conny and his partner Hölger took me aside one day to show me what they were doing - all these weird, obscure experiments. They'd make rhythm tracks out of tape loops of pinball machine counters, and add a bass drum even though they couldn't play drums, and then they'd play some kind of scratchy violin part all the way through and I'd say, 'What the hell, that sounds terrible.' But they'd never use it like that. They'd kind of switch it in and out, and then run it through a space echo, and phase it . . . and it would sound really great.

"Compared to that, everything I'd ever done in a band seemed boring. I could see them running around, rubbing their hands with glee, and getting real excited – and these were 40-year-old men! They were like kids with paint pots and a blank canvas: they could do anything."

Annie confirms that Dave's fascination for studio equipment went into overdrive around this time. "Dave was able to assimilate many things about sound in relation to these machines so that you could do so much in a very small space. It was so exciting, because you felt that you had direct control. The ideas would come up and, with these instruments, were immediately on tape . . . Eurythmics has just always been its own strange little creature." Annie took to heart the valuable lessons learnt at the New

114

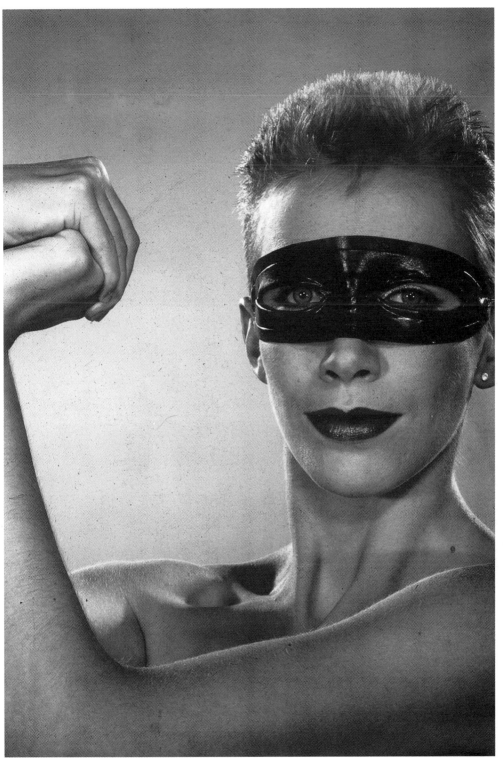

Peter Ashworth: "She's got strange eyes. She doesn't actually look straight at you; her eyes go slightly off. And somehow that can make the picture look compelling... A picture that you have to recheck is a powerful picture."
(Peter Ashworth/LFI)

Harlaw Academy 1971 class line-up prior to the 'Highers'. Ann Lennox is top right,
Colleen Sweeney is bottom row, second left. *(Colleen Gray-Taylor)*

Ann (front row, second right) participating in Military Band rehearsal, 1971.
(Aberdeen Journals)

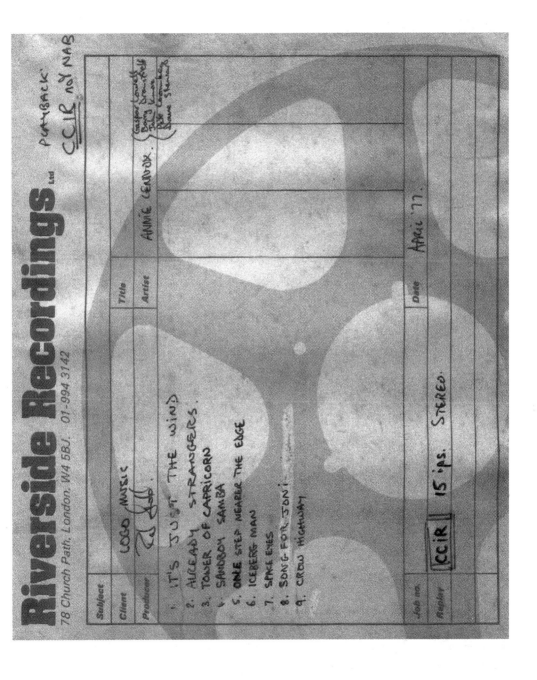

Riverside Recordings Ltd

78 Church Path, London, W4 5BJ.   01-994 3142

PLAYBACK:
CCiR noY NAB

Subject		Title	
Client	LOGO MUSIC	Artist	ANNIE LENNOX.
Producer	Rob Gold		Casper Conrad Bass Dan Ashlin Keys Rif Turner Drums Steve ???

1. IT'S JUST THE WIND
2. ALREADY STRANGERS
3. TOWER OF CAPRICORN
4. SANDBOY SAMBA
5. ONE STEP NEARER THE EDGE
6. ICEBERG MAN
7. SMAE EYES
8. SONG FOR JONI
9. CREW MIDNIGHT

Job no.		Date	APRIL '77.
Replay	CCiR 15 ips. STEREO.		

Original track listing for Annie's first ever demo recordings, April 1977.
(Rob Gold)

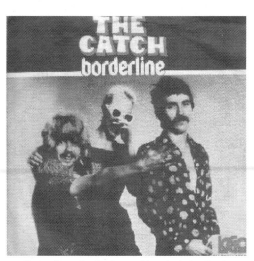

Cover sleeve for the first and last single by Catch,
'Borderline / Black Blood'.

The band of misfits. The Tourists, from top left,
clockwise: Eddie Chin, Annie Lennox, Dave Stewart,
Peet Coombes, Jim 'Do It' Toomey. *(Harry Goodwin)*

Annie: "Peet had a lot of creativity in him but he was
always very self-destructive, which is often the case
with gifted people."*(Barry Plummer)*

Last Laugh Tour, February 1980. "She throws herself
into every number with boundless energy and a grin that
you could read the small print by." *(Pictorial Press)*

Carol Semaine: "I don't think Annie realised at first how stunning-looking she was. That went hand in hand with her not wanting to flaunt her body. You'd *never* see her in a low-cut dress." *(Joe Bangay)*

An early Eurythmics incarnation: Dave, Annie, Sir Timothy Wheater, Adam Williams. *(Peter Ashworth)*

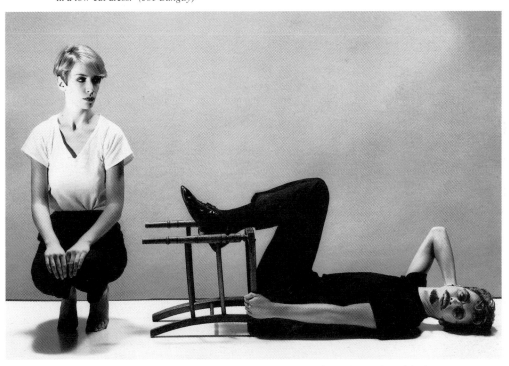

Annie: "We're not a conventional rock'n'roll band. We refuse to be put in a niche."
(Photograph by Gered Mankowitz © Bowstir Ltd.2000/ www.mankowitz.com)

Annie: "I knew creatively I didn't want to work with anybody else except Dave. So there was this strange tension – the pain of the break-up and the excitement of working together on the music."

(Photograph by Gered Mankowitz © Bowstir Ltd.2000/ www.mankowitz.com)

 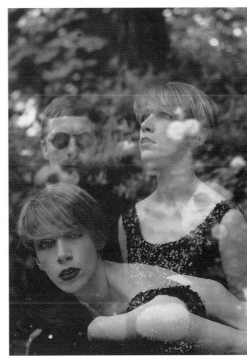

Peter Ashworth: "It was a typical little English garden, it wasn't full of roses, but it was meant to be like that. We were just playing around and they turned up with two masks…" Outtakes from the *In The Garden* photoshoot.
(Peter Ashworth)

"The person in the house is very sadistic, there's lots of leather around and strange things in the bathroom...
If we could, we would have had hypodermic syringes lying around in the video."
An outtake from the 'Love Is A Stranger' video shoot. *(Joe Bangay)*

Year's revelry, and savoured her mentor's lasting piece of advice. "Conny thought we ought to control everything and do everything in a smaller way. That's the basic philosophy behind Eurythmics."

★   ★   ★

Given a new lease of life, Eurythmics plugged away, ignoring RCA's disapproval. Deciding that they needed a new image to fit with their new ideas, they met up with freelance rock photographer Joe Bangay in his studio behind Harrods department store. Joe, then in his fifties, had accepted the assignment with reluctance as he had experienced a less than favourable run-in with Ms Lennox during her time with The Tourists. "It was the late Seventies. I was on a photoshoot as a news photographer for the *Daily Express* or something like that, and I met this very difficult woman, and a very funny fella in a group called The Tourists. Annie was very weird and didn't like newspapers. She exuded left-wing righteousness about a right-wing paper." Regardless of first impressions, Joe agreed to try again with Eurythmics.

"Dave and Annie came down and we found we liked each other," he recalls today. "We went across the road and had some lunch together. Dave came over as the weirdo he was and Annie came over as vulnerable and a bit clingy, but nice. And they decided I should do their first photographs, basically." As he got to know the ex-couple better he became very close to them. "I was mad about Annie, I loved her dearly. I thought she was a wonderful woman. She was very warm to her friends. She had beautiful eyes and a long angular body – a middle-aged man's conception of a stunning woman!"

Annie had grown to detest the bright mini-skirted look she had adopted for The Tourists and was seeking a bolder, more controversial image. It had been remarked on in the press that, due to her height (5′ 8″), strong features and short hair, she could easily pass for a man. Although Dave and Annie had parted ways romantically, their close relationship continued as if they were brother and sister and they capitalised on this affinity with a uniform visual image. They chose be-suited British artists Gilbert and George, well-known subversive social commentators, as their role models.

"Dave and I liked to think of ourselves as twins," Annie enthused. "Quite some time before this gender bender business we both went to a very ordinary gent's tailor and had identical suits made. It made us feel like a unit." Dave continued, "When Annie and I first formed Eurythmics . . . I had greased back hair and we both bought suits from Burtons, and a white shirt and a tie each – we actually copied Gilbert and George.

Because we'd lived together and we'd read a lot about them and thought, 'This is very similar to the way we go on.'"

Working closely with Dave and Annie, Joe observed the dynamics of their relationship at a time when Dave was particularly passionate about life and Annie was so low. "Dave was very innovative and he gave her most of her ideas," he claims. "Dave was also the boss, and Annie accepted that because she'd been brought up in a family where the father was the head of the family. My impression was that Dave was running the business of the show; a lot of the creativity came from him. He influenced her very much. He inspired her fantasies, started it all off."

Despite outward appearances, as 1981 began Annie found the situation between herself and Dave increasingly difficult to handle. When they split up they had been sharing a flat in Ridge Road, North London, but that was obviously unsuitable so Annie moved into the vacant room upstairs, not wishing to be too far away from the man who remained her soulmate, if not lover. But Annie found it hard to be 'just good friends' and occasionally turned to Joe Bangay for comfort. "She had a few weeps in my presence," he says softly. "She was pleased to have somebody to tell her troubles to. Troubles with Dave, that sort of thing. She hung in there, hoping he would come back to her. She loved him very, very much and she was reluctant to accept it was over."

The living arrangements only aggravated the tense situation. "She moved upstairs and then that didn't work because all we *didn't* do was sleep together," explains Dave of their predicament. "She'd be there for breakfast in the morning, knocking on the door. So then she moved down to the end of the street."

If rumours are to be believed, Dave celebrated his new-found freedom by embarking on a series of casual affairs. One particularly vicious story was that he noisily consummated a meaningless tryst within full earshot of his former partner. For Annie this horrible gossip was more than she could stomach, as if Dave's flaunting wasn't hard enough to handle.

In Joe's eyes the shifting relationship soon evolved into a power struggle of immense proportions. "Annie really loved Dave and she was clinging on to him. He was a bit wicked and he wanted to get rid of her," he divulges. "He used to go out with other women and make sure she knew about it – he used me a lot to photograph him with these other women." Over the next couple of years, as Eurythmics' fame grew, Dave would call on the photographer's services more and more. "He rang me up once and said, 'Joe, I've got this new bird, and we're landing at the airport, so will you wait and photograph us arriving together,' things like that. He was always encouraging me to build him up as a sex symbol."

In spite of Dave's apparent 'be cruel to be kind' theory, Joe denies there was any real animosity between the pair. "They never hated each other – they were close, they still are close, but in a different sort of way." He hints at one of the discrepancies in the couple's relationship that could have initiated ructions. "Dave never wanted children; he wanted a beautiful, colourful wife and no more. And Annie always wanted children. She was from a traditional family in Aberdeen. She loved her mum, she loved the family atmosphere. She always used to ring her mum and tell her what she'd been doing, but I think she was a bit scared of her father." According to Joe, Annie sought more of a father figure than a lover in a relationship, and this was a contributing factor to her split with Dave. As Joe himself was over 50 and the two became very close, it was unfortunately inevitable that whispers began to circulate about the true nature of their friendship.

Although fresh associations would blossom with time, Annie still found it hard to let go and Dave grew tired of her reactionary attitude towards their break-up. "Annie used to be madly jealous of me all the time. I never used to get jealous of her," he would later crow to *Rolling Stone*. "That was the funny thing. Annie used to be really mixed up as to why she thought we should split up. So she'd get dead upset about it. I would go out with different people, and Annie would be really moody for weeks, which was very confusing, being that she was the one who broke it up in the first place."

If they were able to overcome the loss of the physical side to their relationship, albeit with some difficulty, Dave and Annie could at least draw upon their past history to produce sexual chemistry and enhance their work together. Blurring the boundaries further, Annie protested nearly seven years later, "It *hasn't* ended. It isn't physical anymore, but it is romantic." Dave's shadow would always hang over her, she said, and he became a benchmark against whom all future boyfriends would be measured.

★   ★   ★

In February 1981 Eurythmics returned to Conny Plank's studio in Cologne, armed with banks of demo tapes and all set to work on some new tracks for what was to become their first album alone. Conny produced the sessions that were to last until June that year, and Hölger Czukay, Jaki Liebezeit, Robert Görl and Gabi Delgado were all only too pleased to lend their services to this exciting musical experiment. Close friend Roger Pomphrey played guitar on many of the sessions, and even collaborated on writing a couple of tracks. Annie was also delighted to welcome Sir Timothy Wheater, an esteemed flautist to whom she had grown close, to the proceedings. Blondie drummer Clem Burke happened to be in the studio at the same time, and soon formed a lasting bond with Eurythmics, who were flattered to be able to incorporate him into their sessions.

Annie and Dave were remarkably open to allowing so many musicians to contribute to their very personal project, and Annie commented after the record's release, "Dave and I are the nucleus but the LP songs were worked on and developed by the people who were there at the time. This is much more flexible than The Tourists. If anybody wants to put anything into it they can." The slight exception to the nucleus rule was brought in by Conny securing one third royalties as producer. The pair waived this as they were only too pleased to be finally working in friendly surroundings with people who understood and respected their musical ambitions completely.

From the outset Eurythmics had a very clear picture of the kind of music they were aiming to produce. "After all the hectic things that happened with The Tourists – it was like being tossed into the music industry and put through a big mincer, and then we were flying out the other end – we wanted to capture that calmer feeling, a melancholic calm after the storm," said Dave. With the aftereffects of their break-up no doubt swirling through their minds, the two seized on a slightly sinister but very attractive idea of an English garden, where the flowers and fruit had just begun to decompose. It was a highly evocative and divergent portrait – certainly a million miles away from Peet Coombes' particular brand of Tourist pop.

"We were intrigued by the idea of trying to create a sound that was melancholic," said Annie. "Having established this feeling, we wanted to take it a step further into something decaying – almost too sweet, like an over-ripe fruit. So the listener feels soothed but a little disconcerted at the same time." Soon enough, the album title *In The Garden* was as much a part of the project as the musical concept, and Annie and Dave lost themselves in its many different interpretations.

"I saw the garden as a place of growth and death – a cycle – and I see life as an ongoing thing of birth and re-birth, total circles," Annie continued. "I felt that *In The Garden* was a growth place for me and Dave as well, a nice place to be. There's a lot of beauty in the sound, Dave and I like beauty, but to make it with a touch of something – a slightly sickly smell – then that's really interesting to me. It's all a bit disturbing, a bit sinister."

The album as a whole is alternately beautiful and sour, with an overriding perception of Eurythmics as ethereally distant characters. The latter was helped in no small part by Annie's voice. Whereas in her work of The Tourists she had been on occasion aggressive, impassioned and fluffy as a cloud, here, with the help of Conny's mixing desk she explored a dreamlike, detached vocal style, somewhat difficult to focus on properly.

Coupled with the ambient production and abstract, impressionistic lyrics, *In The Garden* was so much of an artistic jump it was inevitable that

Annie and Dave were going to alienate a large section of their audience. They were unconcerned about what the much-detested music press thought, but the fan factor still had to be considered. Annie chose to tackle this by continually implying that she and Dave had moved on, and so perhaps should their fans. "I don't pretend that our new approach will go down well with many of our present fans; it's less instantly appealing but we don't want to make the commercial records you hear being played on the radio all the time," she said with an air of defiance. "That stuff is like musical baked beans."

The cast of characters featured in *In The Garden* is absorbing as it foreshadows the slightly more refined personalities yet to be created within Eurythmics' work. The protagonist, appearing throughout the album, is a solitary woman pictured in various rooms of her house and occasionally in her garden, who considers herself invisible and unimportant, and is unable to relate to the outside world. Belinda doesn't trust her man and none of the couples seem to be able to form a satisfactory connection. The strongest visions are of a whore-like seductress who could just turn out to be the victim, and a revenge seeker who plays with people like toys and spends her life plotting her next attack. All of these dysfunctional characters are placed in harsh contrast with the boring normality of the grey workers described in 'Sing-Sing', the monotony of these lives mapped out in their daily trek to and from nondescript jobs.

'English Summer' would have been a strange choice for an opener on any other album, but in the context of *In The Garden* it succeeds brilliantly. Dave described the overall impression as follows: "It's like on an afternoon when it goes a bit grey outside, it could be in London or Scunthorpe or wherever you are, and you look out of the window and the light changes – it's quite sunny and suddenly everything goes grey and seems a bit dead . . . we were trying to capture *that*."

Not immediately catchy, the track somehow induces an instant sense of nostalgia, with Annie's vocals floating ethereally over a slightly stilted guitar riff and plodding bass line. Her odd detachment, as well as setting a precedent for much of the music that follows, reflects the abstract snatches of memory in the lyrics.

A recurrent figure for *In The Garden* is now introduced, pictured in various different domestic poses yet disturbingly dislocated from everyday life. An undercurrent of unpleasantness runs throughout this character's reign and is present in 'English Summer' with understated yet suggestive lines like, "There's a mess in the kitchen". The contrast of sanity versus sporadic flashes of aberration also filters through to the music. In this track and during the rest of the album it frequently shifts keys from major to minor, often both at once, so Annie's wish of producing a 'sickly sweet' sound is effectively brought out instrumentally.

The second track 'Belinda' dates back stylistically to The Tourists with its straightforward, power pop tale of misunderstanding and a girl who doesn't trust her innocent man. Sonically, 'Belinda' builds up in layers with unusual drums and percussion while Annie angelically harmonises with herself, without getting too emotionally involved. The close incorporates a favourite Tourists' tool; Annie's Eastern wailing as heard on B-side 'Strange Sky'.

The excellent 'Take Me To Your Heart' epitomises the best of *In The Garden*; neurotic, nervous and intense. Distinctive keyboards are set against an equally hesitant and insistent beat, with Annie singing in punctuated whispers. A repeated picked bass run cleverly depicts the ticking of a clock and the passing of time, and the instrumentation and arrangement are reminiscent of the best work of The Cure, or even the darker side of Siouxsie & The Banshees.

'She's Invisible Now' brings back the vacant, dangerous personality introduced in 'English Summer'. This time there is a twist whereby the story is double-edged – is this an exhausted drug dealer (references to razor blades, dust and mirrors are hidden within the softly sung lyrics), or is the protagonist simply whiling away endless empty hours of solitude by counting? Either way, the human being as a calculator is an intriguing and unresolved image, heightened by Annie's computerised monotone countdown and the sound of a cash register *à la* Pink Floyd's 'Money'.

The blurry bubble of 'She's Invisible Now' is burst with the fast, chiming beat of 'Your Time Will Come', which despite its fresh contrast fails to impress and is too long to retain the listener's interest. Annie floats over the top as usual, continuing her tale of a bizarre, unconnected woman: "She is but a shadow of her former self".

'Caveman Head', like 'English Summer' written with guitarist Roger Pomphrey, is a psychotic babble of crazed guitars, percussive rumbles and tattoos and manic shouting. Over this impressive backdrop, not unlike a Talking Heads song with its skittering high-hat beat, Annie sings of the lure of a beautiful siren/victim, begging her counterpart, who could easily be a rapist, to touch her. The series of nightmarish images brought on by the music are heightened by the confusion in the lyrics – is she genuinely desiring sexual contact, or are there darker forces at play? "My hands are moving, my feet are tied/ My eyes are closing, my mouth is wide" . . .

On reflection, 'Never Gonna Cry Again' was the obvious single to herald *In The Garden*, as it is the closest thing to be found here to a pop song of the time; catchy, electronic and memorable with its quiet, smooth groove based on a simplistic, descending bass line. Annie's flute break comes over like a breath of fresh air, yet it is difficult not to question why Hölger's French horn is quite so badly played.

Even more laid-back than 'Never Gonna Cry Again' is the atmospheric ambience of 'All The Young (People Of Today)'. Annie's vocal is positively hypnotic and sexy in the verses, then hymnal in the chanting choruses. Once again discernible layers are apparent within the track, building up on the slightly sinister bass line as the song progresses. The lyrics describe the sexual conquests of the new generation, interestingly and maybe sarcastically in this case, showing the men to be more dominant.

'Sing-Sing' is based on a manic, unattractive and endlessly repeating electronic theme, with Annie singing, entirely in French, of the monotony of pedestrian life, commuting to pointless work, comparing the normality of everyday people to dumb animals. Unfortunately, it is simply too art-school experimental for Eurythmics to carry off, especially as it doesn't seem to go anywhere, not even building to an effective climax.

Touches of The Tourists materialise with the last track on this album, entitled simply 'Revenge'. This pop song with electronic beats is based on the bass line; the instrument taking the lead with Annie singing around it. The straight drumming makes a refreshing change from the programming on some of the other tracks. The song is about a sadistic woman who spends her whole life plotting revenge on people, playing with them like puppets, and is absolutely perfect as a taster for upcoming subject material. Unfortunately the lyrics are not yet refined enough to do the subject true Eurythmics justice.

*   *   *

With such a strong, distinctive album behind them, Eurythmics felt it would only be right to follow through with matching artwork for the album and singles. In March 1981 Dave and Annie were introduced to photographer Peter Ashworth by their mutual friend, art director and film set designer, Alexander McDowell.

Peter had grown up in Eastbourne, before moving to England's capital to study at the London College of Printing. An exceptionally talented photographer, the rise of his career was to be no less than phenomenal – his first shoot was the iconic Adam & The Ants album cover of the previous year, *Kings Of The Wild Frontier*, where the singer was dressed menacingly as a highwayman. Over the next few years Peter would become a top British music photographer, shooting covers for such Eighties heroes as Soft Cell, Frankie Goes To Hollywood, Tina Turner and Phil Collins. The partnership with Eurythmics forged at this first meeting would eventually secure Annie Lennox's fame as one of the world's most photographed women.

The photoshoot for *In The Garden* aptly took place in the garden of an ex-girlfriend of Peter's, in Swiss Cottage. "It was a typical little English garden, it wasn't full of roses, but it was meant to be like that," says Peter today. The rich greens of the setting were extremely important to the subjects who arrived dressed in funereal black, with respective altered images to fit the occasion. Annie, wanting a new look after parting ways romantically, had recently had an accident with a bottle of henna. Her normally cropped blonde hair was now distressed orange and she had allowed it to grow a little longer. Dave arrived with his hair cut shorter than ever before, sporting round John Lennon glasses and his trademark goatee beard.

"We did the shoot and it was very successful," Peter recalls. "We were just playing around basically, and they turned up with two masks, a frog mask and something else, and I couldn't really work out why they were doing that." Peter wondered whether Eurythmics were insecure about revealing their faces, having been so well known in The Tourists. "I'm not sure if they were trying to be anonymous at that point and produce really interesting music. Dave ended up wearing the frog mask for a portion of the shoot and Annie decided not to. I think she probably even did her own make-up, it was a very low-key thing.

"I was amazed when they picked the sleeve picture. It was an odd picture to pick, although they *were* trying to be a bit other-worldly and arty." The cover of *In The Garden* portrays neither Annie nor Dave in a particularly flattering light; blurred, lunatic expressions and abstract – but then that suited the music perfectly.

During the shoot, a subtle spark ignited between Peter and Annie that they tried initially to suppress, if for no other reason than Dave's immediate presence. To the singer's ex-boyfriend, however, it was all too clear what was going on.

"It was at that first meeting that Dave told me not to get involved," Peter remembers, "that she was very strong. Now I assume that that had come from him because he definitely still loved her. He was nuts about her. I think it was a relationship where he put her on a pedestal and she gave him a good shaking, every now and again. But she was also totally aware of where he could take her." The conflicting emotions between the three artists would normally have caused all sorts of problems at this point, but Annie was technically a free agent, and despite a parallel attraction for drummer Robert Görl, she was only too happy to explore her first flirtation for over four years in front of her ex-lover.

As far as Peter was concerned, their affinity was magnetic and instant. "I do remember being totally attracted to her on our first meeting. There was something about her. She had a power inside her. I wouldn't say she was one of those people who would walk in a room and everybody would stop, because she didn't have that sort of beauty. But if you actually spoke to her, took her on board in other words, you were aware that there was someone here who was very reserved, could hold herself within herself. She seemed to be very careful how she spoke, how she held herself; poise, posture . . . all that sort of thing was very controlled. Full of all sorts of angles on all sorts of things."

Aware of Annie's physical need for control, and no doubt put off a little by Dave's self-assured warning, Peter decided not to pursue the relationship. But he didn't have to wait long for Annie to react, although her method of rekindling the acquaintance was rather strange to say the least.

"First of all she called me up saying she wanted to buy the flat where we had done the photoshoot – this place where my ex-girlfriend's mother lived for 20 years and I think where my girlfriend had been born! It was just an extraordinary thing. It showed how powerful Annie could be. She'd see something she'd like – 'Right, I want it!' And this was then, this is very early. She already had that pop star thing."

It was clear that the garden wasn't the only thing Annie wanted, and while Peter firmly turned down her unusual request, the pair struck up an odd relationship. Annie was not open to sharing her personal space or even friendships, and insisted on conducting the affair strictly on her terms. Evidently she had been hurt deeply by the failure of her romance with Dave, and was not about to be burned twice. So, entranced by her aura and what he describes as her "power", Peter found himself agreeing to a series of secret meetings and night-time liaisons. She was far more comfortable with this than actually moving in together, and as Peter was also immersed in the development of his blossoming career, it seemed to suit them both.

★　　★　　★

As Eurythmics stood poised to release their debut single and album, they made many brave statements trying to define themselves to a music press that was both cynical and intrigued in equal measure. Annie went to great pains to stress that Eurythmics were not a conventional band, that they took risks and refused to be pigeon-holed musically, while Dave attempted to expand publicly on the new lyrical themes present within their work: "It's the subject of nearly everything we've ever written – the duality of *everything*: the tramp lying on the street while somebody walks by with a fur coat on; the feeling of love mixed up with terrible feelings of guilt and remorse. It's great, it's terrible – it's the way life is."

Against such a grand declaration, the pair continued to laud the importance of the synthesiser within their work, but also the visual awareness which was becoming a key element in their strategy. "We take advantage of the technology," said Annie. "Our songs are very visual, so we already have a scenario before we start. But we also use our imagination – it's not just a straight narrative . . . we get a lot of artistic control."

Well aware of the effect clothes and general appearance could have on an audience, Annie set about redefining her image once again so that Eurythmics would be easily recognisable. She had reached a dichotomy; her hair got shorter and she frequently dressed in the uniform suits that she and Dave had decided could be intrinsic to their charisma, yet she was still an extremely feminine woman. Her height and build had always set her apart from her female contemporaries, and she was now well used to the masculine taunts she had first attracted in The Tourists. On the other hand, her presence was unarguably traffic-stopping. Annie remained unsure of how best to project herself.

"Her clothing was 'jumble sale' at the time of *In The Garden*, and she liked to wear leery colours," says Peter Ashworth. "But she did it in a sort of odd, edgy style. It was an 'intellectual girlie' thing, rather than a 'sexy girlie' thing – almost a non-understanding of your own body thing as well.

"She was exploring and delving into black wigs with glasses and ginger hair in a crop, and playing around with clothes. It was interesting seeing how these ideas would start to evolve; how the myth was beginning. I know that she wanted to hide herself away from the public, whether it was that she didn't want to be recognised on the street or whether she wanted to just show that she was different from The Tourists I'm not really sure. When we went out she was sort of annoyed if no one recognised her and she was really annoyed if they *did* recognise her! It was very difficult to work out how to be protective to someone like that."

In May 1981, the first single from *In The Garden*, 'Never Gonna Cry Again' was released on RCA. Its catchy yet regretful beat received several good reviews, but it was slow to take off. Eurythmics' management, now chiefly Lloyd Beiny of Arnakata, promoted the single, and also the track 'Belinda' in Britain with a performance on BBC2's alternative music TV show, *The Old Grey Whistle Test*. A skull-capped Dave played a concoction of various computerised instruments, Clem Burke was drafted in on drums, Roger Pomphrey played guitar and The Slits' Penny Tobin guested on keyboards. They were joined by Timothy Wheater, who shared a crisp flute duet with Annie during the instrumental break.

The mis-matched group performed in front of an enormous poster of the disturbing single cover photograph featuring a close-up of Annie's fright-white face, with her pupils rolled back, which was almost as memorable as the set-up. "It was unusual," recalls Jack Steven, who at that time was working in the A&R department at RCA. "They had this computer which in those days was perceived as strange. It was really innovative, creatively, but it looked pretty strange. And then she started singing and she had one of the best voices ever."

A more obscure memory was to haunt the pair after this performance. "A big bomb went off in a club in Ireland, and on the front cover of the English papers there was a politician holding up the cover of our record, which had been playing on the turntable," Dave later told *Vox*. "They were using it as a funny symbol. But Annie and I woke up and didn't know about the bomb – we just wondered what our record was doing on all these covers."

Continuing the 'creepy' theme of the single's A-side, the ghoulish B-side, 'Le Sinistre', is about a séance, harking back to Annie's adventures at the Royal Academy of Music. Annie is the vehicle for Le Sinistre's warnings, and her stark, fear-laced vocals work dramatically well against the spooky low piano part, distorted trumpet and the incessant ticking of a clock.

Equally bizarre was the content of the promo video Eurythmics filmed to accompany the release. Videos had already made their mark as promotional tools in the UK, although it was still a few months before the launch of MTV, the American television channel dedicated almost entirely to their transmission. Fascinated as always by growing developments in technology, Dave and Annie had committed themselves wholeheartedly to this fashionable trend.

Annie, Dave and some extras including Hölger Czukay and Jaki Liebezeit had set out for England's south coast in the bitter month of February. The highlight of the moody video was the reverse photography used to film both Annie emerging, bone dry, from beneath the waves, and Dave rising from underneath the sand on the beach. Clever camera tricks entailed hours of patience, particularly on Dave's part: "I had to appear as though coming out of the sand, so I had to walk backwards into a grave dug into the sand and then everybody shovelled sand on to me until the ground was flat again," he explains. "They all forgot in fact that I was being buried alive and the sand was so heavy that I nearly suffocated before they could get me out." Annie's show-stopping entrance was filmed in a red, full-length evening dress, diamond tiara and earrings, and could only be done in one take. Soon after filming she was covered in towels and, teeth chattering, rushed off to a friend's house to get dry.

Aside from the otherworldly appearances from Eurythmics, the video features a king and courtesan figures, making odd faces and indulging in such dangerous pursuits as reading a newspaper that has been set on fire. They join Dave and Annie for a tea party, before Annie, in tears, heads back to the ocean.

Most unfortunately, this fascinating piece of work was never shown because Hölger and Jaki were not members of the British Musicians' Union, although they did belong to the German equivalent. Undoubtedly it would have assisted the chart success of 'Never Gonna Cry Again', which unaided by its stunning, experimental video, peaked at number 63 on July 4, 1981.

In August they tried again, with the follow-up release, 'Belinda'. This time there was no video budget from the frowning suits at RCA, who had watched the single sink without trace, just like Annie in her flowing red dress. 'Belinda' was joined by another B-side not on *In The Garden*, which itself was yet to be revealed to the public. 'Heartbeat Heartbeat', was a manic frenzy of a key-shifting, amorphous portrayal of this most necessary human function. Without promotion, Eurythmics were again ignored, and the single failed to chart. Afterwards, the downhearted Dave thought he understood its failings.

"The best test of what makes a good single is always what it sounds like when it comes on the air over little transistor radio speakers," he decided. "When I heard 'Belinda' on the radio I just knew it wasn't a good choice as a single. There was nothing wrong with the music or the song, but it was the way it was mixed and produced and presented. Nothing happened when it came on . . . We kept getting reports back saying that DJs found it weird, or what we thought of as weird they found commercial. We hadn't got the commercial thermometer well gauged . . ." Eurythmics had certainly arrived, but they had not yet been noticed.

The parent album, *In The Garden*, was finally released after much nervous anticipation in October. It too failed to make any impact on the UK charts, and wasn't even released in America, although import copies were sold there. However, although the great record buying public greeted it mostly with indifference, the music critics were pleasantly surprised, and said as much.

NME hailed the album as "A welcome step forward from the shrill and arthritic into mature music of subtle shades and true fluency . . . There's enough of quality to suggest that these two Tourists, at least, have finally come home." The *Guardian* commented: "A very agreeable, classy album though it's a pity that the material isn't as impressive as the performers." British entertainment magazine *Time Out* drew on its confusing Germanic origins, "An admirable experience but ultimately the album can't choose between nice pastoral art/pop or Kraut modernism. Frustrating." *Record Mirror* got straight to the point: "I'm still not sure whether it's a good album or a load of twaddle."

★　　★　　★

Although much of the criticism for *In The Garden* was encouraging, Annie sank deeper into depression, and her self-esteem was virtually non-existent. Towards the end of the year she attempted to play the up-and-coming pop star role by going dancing alone in an exclusive London nightclub. Hardly any time passed before she called her one trusted ally in floods of tears.

"Annie rang me up and she was crying and all over the place," Dave recalls. "She'd been to a club in town and it was full of Blitzy London people. She'd forced herself to go along to keep up with what was happening. She stood on her own for ages and then she started crying. Eventually someone came over."

Annie takes up the story. "It was Boy George. The George who'd come to Tourists concerts as a young lad – when he was only about 15." In 1977 George O'Dowd had tried to blag his way into visiting his idols backstage, but had been thrown out by a security guard. Undeterred he had climbed back in through a dressing room window and struck up a conversation with the surprised Tourist singer.

Annie continues about their chance second meeting: "He came over and I thought it was funny that the one who looks most extreme is actually the least of a poser. You know, people like us have gone through an awful lot of feeling exterior, of feeling very alienated. Actually we never could join in with the crowd." Boy George and his newly named band, Culture Club, were just recording demos for EMI who were subsequently to turn them down, propelling 20-year-old George into a similar state of flux. At their meeting in the club, the two relatively unknown singers formed a bond, supporting each other at a time when Annie needed it most.

Needless to say, Annie never quite overcame her fear of clubs after that unpleasant experience. "I'm not a nightclubber," she said a few years later. "The only reason I go is to check out the sound systems. I love to hear music loud. The atmosphere is usually too tense and pretentious for me to enjoy myself. I love to dance but I couldn't do it on a disco floor because it's far too peacock-like – that's not my idea of fun. I really like dancing alone in my own room."

In December 1981 Eurythmics set out on what was to be their first tour of the UK, having completed a couple of tentative dates in Europe with Timothy Wheater, and Dave's friend and ex-Selecter bassist, Adam

Williams. It was around this time that Peter Ashworth remembers doing a photoshoot of an early Eurythmics incarnation including all four musicians dressed in men's suits. This period was short-lived as Dave and Annie continued in the vein in which they started – just the two of them.

The winter tour, dubbed In The Garden Tour, took the novice duo around the snow-covered British Isles, taking in nightclubs and university venues across Coventry, Birmingham, Edinburgh, Glasgow, Stoke-on-Trent, Leicester and London. Learning from previous Tourist experiences, Dave and Annie chose to control both the sound and lighting from the stage, rather than relying on extra hands and equipment. "We've set up a way of playing live that's dead strange," Dave explained of their minimalist mobile unit. "Conny inspired this idea . . . We can play at a friend's party with an hour's notice or at the venue with the same equipment, just turning up the volume. We don't need any roadies either, we can do all the work ourselves."

Driving across country in a beat-up old Volvo towing their gear behind them in a second-hand horse box, Eurythmics endured one of the harshest winters for years. "We've had some terrible experiences on the road," recalls Dave. "The horse box was heavier than the car and so the whole thing jack-knifed – it was horrific. After that we humped the gear round in an old baker's van." Annie adds, "In our own car we hit this blizzard and had to drive about three miles an hour. What was so frightening about that was that we were going up the motorway at about 70 and this blinding snow storm engulfed us – it was just like a sheet of ice and snow."

The horrendous climate brought about a recurrence of Dave's ongoing health problems as one of his lungs collapsed yet again. In addition to the residual injuries from the car crashes six years before, Dave suffered other complications: "I had a condition in my other lung which kept collapsing, which is dangerous, because if they both did it at the same time you've got a few minutes to live." Clearly an intensive stay in hospital was imperative. As if the misfortunes befalling them weren't enough, RCA made the ruthless decision to drop Eurythmics after disappointing sales for their debut album and singles.

In the A&R department, junior member Jack Steven felt strongly that the duo deserved another chance. "I don't believe the record company knew what they had," he insists. "They treated *In The Garden* like a Tourists' album, not a Eurythmics' album which was a completely new band, with a completely new style, and new visual ideas, and that's one of the reasons why it failed.

"I joined RCA in 1981 and when I saw them on the roster I was in seventh heaven; I thought this was fantastic. I was like a young street kid and my brief was to get contemporary music rights of young acts for RCA. So I went through the roster and I said to the head of A&R, 'Look, the only act I think you should keep are Eurythmics, and get rid of the rest.' And he said, 'Oh, I just dropped them.'" Although Jack was seen as the new boy, he was respected within the music business and, as the Managing Director encouraged people with fire in their character, he was allowed a fair amount of leeway. But he admits, "I used to have huge rows in A&R meetings and particularly with the marketing department. We did a lot of things that they found offensive – I almost got fired three times!"

As far as Jack was concerned, Eurythmics were far too valuable a currency to let go without a backward glance and he made it his personal quest to fight their corner. Ridiculously he faced resistance from the group as much as the record company and had to take the time to persuade the dejected pair to persevere, while he negotiated with the higher echelons of RCA.

"I said to Dave and Annie, 'I know you've been badly treated and I can see that you're doing things differently. I think I can get involved and at least create a platform for your creativity'," says Jack today. They were understandably at their lowest ebb and to be shown signs of encouragement from someone within the record company was a much needed boost. Having been informed of their dismissal, Eurythmics were insecure and severely lacking in confidence. "It's very difficult when you get dropped from a major record label to be re-signed again by anyone. You are viewed suspiciously," comments Jack.

While Jack gave the band a new lease of life, its two members were battling against extreme health problems. Dave's latest chest problems warranted a lengthy stay in London's Royal Free Hospital in Hampstead for major reconstructive surgery. In a life-saving operation surgeons were forced to strip away the outer lining from one lung through an incision in his back to prevent further collapses. Similarly to his period of hospitalisation as a teenager, Dave's creative mind never ceased as John Turnbull recalls, "He used to ring me up from the hospital, mad as a hatter on painkillers, and discuss some bizarre projects."

Annie's psychological problems were not so easily cured. While her ex-lover was critically ill in hospital the Scotswoman was suffocating under the weight of the pressure. She had no choice but to return to her parents in Aberdeen, seeking the refuge of an existence less packed with emotional and vocational minefields. Over Christmas 1981 she grew to realise the possibility of a life for her away from Dave. The stress of still loving him in her fashion and having to deal with him on a daily basis had certainly taken its toll.

11

ONE STEP NEARER THE EDGE

"After Dave and I parted I tried to form new friendships but all I did was frighten people. People shy away from you when they think you've gone nuts. In the end you realise that you are devastatingly alone in this world. I lived on the verge of suicide."

– AL

After four years living with Dave Stewart, Annie Lennox felt helpless and alone, many times likening the agonising experience of their romantic break-up to the trauma of losing a limb. After all, he was the one who had picked her up and whirled her onto the runaway train of The Tourists at a time she was contemplating defeat. Annie in turn had revolutionised Dave's life, weaning him off his addiction to heavy drugs. They had lived together, occasionally joked about marriage together, formed lasting relationships with each other's friends and family, and shared everything from total poverty to moderate riches. Jointly they had formed such an impenetrable bond that they felt strong enough to survive the death of their affair yet still forge ahead with Eurythmics. But after the relative failure of their first 'solo' effort, *In The Garden*, RCA's refusal to pick up their contract for a second album and Dave's worrying period of hospitalisation, Annie had reached breaking point.

Surrounded by those closest to her in Aberdeen, as 1981 turned to 1982 Annie plunged into depression. With the support of her parents she was gradually able to work her way through it, but the effects were to linger for the best part of a year.

"I certainly went through a rough patch," she admitted years later. "My self-esteem dropped to an all-time low, and I was suffering from agoraphobia. I couldn't go outside the front door – whenever I went out, I started having panic attacks, I would get palpitations and come out in cold sweats. It was horrible."

Unable even to travel on public transport without hallucinating, it was clear that Annie needed more than her family could offer and so in desperation she turned to a psychotherapist for professional advice. "She didn't

130

help at all," Annie recalls. "She just sat there and looked at me while I got tongue-tied. I was more freaked out when I came out of her office than when I came in."

A close friend realised that therapy obviously did not suit Annie and convinced her to stop paying the exorbitant fees. The singer eventually agreed, and set about personally pulling her life back into some semblance of normality. This was to take many, many difficult months of supreme effort, and along the way she slipped back into despair several times.

"You go to such a rock-bottom feeling that you either decide you might as well cut your throat, or you start thinking about your own self-preservation. It was sheer hell at the time and I never want to go through anything like that again."

Annie's psychological troubles were rooted in her childhood. Since her early teens she had felt the overwhelming pressure of being an 'outsider', and as a means of coping had lost herself in music. But now, particularly with her trusted source of solace gone, she had to come to terms with the person she was herself; without success and without Dave.

"I spent a great deal of time crying," she said candidly to *The Face*. "It was unbearable. I felt so claustrophobic, experienced such terror that I hit rock bottom . . . It was like having a scar, you never believe you'll recover or function again properly." For a while Annie even considered suicide. "I don't mean that I'd ever do away with myself, but it's as if I'd toy with the idea for a long time . . . No matter how much you want to get out of that sort of thing, it's a very hard thing to crack. And in the end it has to come entirely from within yourself, you have to start thinking about your own self-preservation."

Annie has since described herself as a "manic depressive" over the difficult years that were to follow. She experienced periods where she was literally unable to rise from beneath her bedclothes, even at the zenith of Eurythmics' future success. She acknowledges that her chosen career in the spotlight serves only to heighten the extremes of her personality.

"It's just something I have to deal with," she said matter-of-factly to *Spin* magazine in 1985. "Obviously someone that performs and writes music like that and does the things that I do is not going to be exactly the most even-keel person in the world . . .

"I've suffered from a history of depression which I hope that as I get older, I'll come more and more to terms with. It's like an adolescent depression that you get when you're about 15, and it never quite leaves you. It's always there and it's also been the source of my creativity as well to a great degree, at least in the sense that I sense this awful sort of angst and greyness about existence. Part of the reason why I've ever written songs was to deal with that, to express what was inside, which was just something so awful."

It is true to say that Annie's best work has emanated from grappling with her feelings and on-going relationships with the key people in her life. Dave is a constant source of both positive and negative inspiration, her father has appeared several times in her lyrics, and later when she was again to find love and eventually have children, these characters would also provide touching stimuli for her work. Her transition into writing such confessional songs happened gradually, mainly developing after the worst was over, although at times her initial fevered output was a little too gauche to be recorded out of context. "Annie once came to me and said, 'I've written this song on my own and it's called 'Depression' and I'm going to play it!'" Dave revealed. "I told her that it wasn't that I didn't think it was any good; it was just that I didn't fancy going round singing it."

While her dejection at this time has been well-documented, it appears that aside from Dave, her parents and a couple of close friends, Annie mainly kept her feelings to herself. Her boyfriend during and after this period, Peter Ashworth, has no recollections of any spates of depression, claustrophobia or agoraphobia.

"I was with her all the time," he says today. "There were times when she was really down and we did stuff at home because she couldn't go out. But I didn't know anything about depression at all – I'd never had depression. I didn't know anything about therapy . . .

"But she was a moody girl, so what's new? Her highs and lows were beyond belief." He says that Annie would only ever take homeopathic medicine, never resorting to prescribed or illegal drugs, which are commonplace in the music industry and would have been all too easy to acquire.

The turning point for Annie, as she lay cooped up in her parents' house back in Aberdeen, came one day in early 1982 shortly after her 27th birthday. Dave had escaped from his hospital bed, seizing on a musical idea for the next album and running away with it without a backward glance. The foremost thing on his mind was to phone Annie and let her know.

"Dave was down in London and I was having a Christmas holiday up in Scotland," Annie remembers. "He called me up and played me something down the phone and said, 'This is the new thing.' He was really excited about the songs . . . I knew we'd found our new direction."

Annie agreed to return to London and give Eurythmics another try. Her parents were a pillar of support, and one morning Lawrence Wess witnessed her prompt 9.00 a.m. arrival at his knick-knack stall on Petticoat Lane. Accompanied by her mother and father, Annie was evidently furnishing her 'bachelorette' apartment, and gamely purchased a coal bucket for £12. When Lawrence recognised the former Tourist, she was reserved but seemed genuinely flattered by the attention. Thanks to Dave's boundless enthusiasm and Tom and Dorothy's ceaseless support, things were definitely looking up.

★   ★   ★

Back in London and armed with the bare nuclei of some promising and very different new material, Eurythmics' immediate hurdles were the lack of a record contract and, equally pressingly, a lack of funds. Dave's grand plan hatched in hospital was to develop their very own recording studio and explore his adventurous musical ideas in their own time and space. Eurythmics' combined debt from Tourist days was not going to stop Dave now he had a bee in his bonnet, and he hit upon the ingenious and rather cheeky idea of asking his local bank manager for a loan.

Dressing in one of his smarter suits and adding a businesslike touch with a tie and briefcase, Dave marched into the Crouch End branch of Barclays bank. There he confronted the manager Geoff Williams with a typically persuasive tirade. "I told him that Annie and I were going to do something absolutely amazing and that the bank should invest in us," he recalls. "I made the point that most bands spend £30,000 just recording one album, but that we could buy the equipment we needed for £7,000 and then make all the albums we wanted." Dave's plan had even more depth to it, as once the equipment was installed it didn't matter who worked there; Eurythmics would be able to rent out studio time to any band they fancied. Somehow the guitarist neglected to mention that the band had never controlled a studio in their lives and had only their time with Conny Plank and Tom Allom to draw from.

Geoff Williams had no musical training whatsoever, but couldn't fail to see the potential in the opportunity, as well as be amused at Dave's audacity. He agreed to the loan of £7,000 and Dave walked out of the bank on air. Annie could hardly believe their change of luck, and Geoff the bank manager was left with the firm conviction that Dave was "A determined young man with a good head for business."[18]

Dave and Annie had first met bassist Adam Williams when he appeared with his band, Selecter, at an outdoor festival in Finland alongside The Tourists. The friendship had been rekindled the previous year during Eurythmics' treacherous maiden tour of the UK. In 1982 Adam was

---

[18] Eurythmics were later to repay Geoff Williams' kindness by keeping him on the coveted guest list to all their big concerts and parties.

planning to move to London from Lancaster and was looking for somewhere to store his bulky musical equipment. In Lancaster he had enjoyed studio facilities, working with brass player Dick Cuthell who had been the in-house producer at Island before changing career to incorporate his love for playing the trumpet. Dave and Annie realised that Adam's relocation provided them with the perfect partner. On his side, Adam was only too pleased to agree to Dave's suggestion of pooling their resources and setting up a studio together in North London. Eurythmics agreed to use their £7,000 cash injection to buy the most sophisticated eight-track recording studio they could afford and the threesome set about looking for a suitable location.

They found the space they craved above a busy picture framers called Falconer Studios in Ferdinand Place,[19] Chalk Farm, not far from The Roundhouse, the old engine shed that was for many years a rock venue.

Above the workshop was a dingy, airless attic. It was not entirely conducive to recording purposes, with just one room with a window that wasn't sealed and no space for a drum or even vocal booth. Peter Ashworth recalls the less than idyllic setting, "They had a rehearsal studio right opposite the stables in Camden. Down a little alleyway. It was in the attic of this big old factory and they had a recording studio in this wood-beamed building. It was very rough, it looked like they had built it themselves, they had old mattresses and bits of wood." But to Dave, Annie and Adam, it was home. In this den they foresaw their future.

With the aid of Dave's bank loan, Eurythmics and their friend filled the room with a Teac eight-track studio, a cheap mixing board, two Beyer microphones and some very basic effects equipment. An unexpected sound effect came simply from what was going on underneath them: "If you hear sawing on one of the tracks, it's because I forgot to close the window," laughs Dave. Annie also remembers the problems of having to work around their neighbours' schedule: "Often we had to wait for the timber factory downstairs to turn off their machinery before we could record the vocals.

"We used so many different textures. It sounded so sophisticated," she continues of their dogged experimentation, which would often involve banging on wine glasses filled with different amounts of water and adapting normal instruments with ever stranger contraptions. Despite working well with Conny Plank, Dave was itching to produce his own material and moaned when other producers could not capture the right sound.

"When we worked with other people within the record company, someone was forever coming in and saying, 'This is the guy who's doing

[19] The site has since been taken over by funeral directors.

this for you.' And it never turned out right, because the ideas all came from us, but then they'd be taken out of our hands." With their own studio Dave was finally able to take charge.

Artistic control was all well and good, but not without a record contract. "We really had nothing going," said Dave. "Eurythmics weren't selling any records to speak of . . . Yet we were still going around with the same hopes which had always been in our minds.

"There was never a point at which we thought, 'There's no way. We'll never be able to be a group now.' Believe me, though, everyone thought we were *nuts*. People all said, 'Listen, this is unhinged, you're too far out there, you're not going to pull anything off.' Especially when we told them we were making our next album on an eight-track in a warehouse."

Their problems continued to escalate. They had shared close ties with their management company, Arnakata, for several years but had long since realised that the company's motives were more for financial gain than artistic integrity. From an opposite viewpoint, during the initial photoshoot for *In The Garden* Peter had witnessed the committed side to Lloyd Beiny. "I met Lloyd before I met Dave and Annie – he seemed like a pretty decent chap, a family man. He didn't really seem to have a mask – he appeared to be fairly straightforward. But I heard he was a bit of a wheeler-dealer. I remember Annie got very heated about Lloyd a few times. But he was the sort of guy that we wandered around looking at locations with, and I think a manager who does that is cool. He's preventing his band from wasting their time, he's checking on their behalf; he's doing what a good manager should do. At least he was prepared to go out on a summer's evening to look at gardens and drive all over London!"

Unfortunately Arnakata shared RCA's concerns for Eurythmics' future and their differences became too severe and remained unresolved. For a while Dave enlisted the help of his friend Alan Harrison, a Coventry art school teacher, but this didn't work out. So Dave determined to do the job himself. "I learned everything from maintaining a studio to how much equipment costs, to video budgets, to paying trucking companies," he boasts. "Just about everything you could imagine to do with running a group, I found out about it."

He was lucky to find an ally in the junior A&R rep at their former record label. "All the Eurythmics business was done out of my office at RCA," says Jack Steven. "They'd got rid of their managers because they weren't happy with them, so it was me, Dave and Annie working till nine or 10 o'clock at night. All the ideas for the record, artwork, tours and so on came out of my office." It was thanks to Jack's diligent devotion that the officials at RCA came round to Eurythmics' way of thinking and reluctantly agreed to re-sign the band.

"There was a lot of money that RCA needed to recoup because they'd lost a lot on *In The Garden*, so actually Eurythmics owed them quite a bit." Jack used his reputation as a 'street-wise' music fan to persuade the conservative company to gamble. "Basically it was my first demand of them, and obviously because it was a new job, they went with what I knew. But I never got a big budget or anything, it was never a priority. They thought, 'We've got this quirky A&R guy, so let him have a go at it.'"

Annie remembers that Jack's relentless badgering, aided by Sheila Sedgwick, finally began to penetrate the minds of those in power at the record label. "At the beginning there were a couple of people at RCA who were very enthusiastic. With their strength and their continual enthusiasm about us, it eventually percolated through to the rest of the company that we were really worth listening to." Eurythmics were invited into the company boardroom to outline their future plans. They took some very rough demos with them as a means of enticement.

"Let's face it," concedes Dave, "after signing The Tourists and then The Tourists splitting up, and then us coming up with Eurythmics and sounding pretty weird, RCA probably thought, 'Blimey! They're gonna go all sort of experimental on us and we're gonna lose a load of money.' And it took somebody with reasonable intelligence to realise that you can be a successful band and not follow the normal route of 24 tracks and big name producers."

Dave was well-versed in the art of persuasion after his display at the Crouch End branch of Barclays bank and felt that he had made some headway by the time he left the meeting, although his RCA bosses were not entirely convinced. Fortunately for Eurythmics, Dave's case coincided with some major changes within the structure and output of the label. "Slowly but surely RCA's fortunes turned, probably as a result of a wholesale clear-out of the creaking old A&R department. They signed some hotter acts [Bucks Fizz], and took on distribution of F-Beat [Elvis Costello]," recalls ex-Head Press Officer Chris Charlesworth.

★ ★ ★

At the same time as forging ongoing relationships with image-creating photographers such as Joe Bangay and Peter Ashworth, Annie and Dave decided the time was right to establish a corporate identity for themselves. They had become wary of record companies, managers and agents, and felt that only with their own company would they be able to command absolute control over their careers.

"RCA as a record label corporation was not really regarded seriously, it was Bucks Fizz's label, it wasn't like Island Records or Virgin, young trendy labels," says Jack. "So we decided to create an autonomous design for the group that encompassed all the creativity.

"I went to the London College Of Printing and met a lot of their young designers of that year. I came across this guy called Laurence Stevens. I literally pulled him out of the London College Of Printing into my office to work on all the Eurythmics stuff, because we all really liked the ideas he was trying." Laurence was young and enthusiastic, and because he was freshly out of college and relatively inexperienced, his services came cheap. Although he had a degree in graphic design, he had no previous training in conceiving record sleeves or other promotional artwork, such as posters, for a pop group.

During their discussions with Laurence, Eurythmics hit upon a simplistic, yet effective name for their company. Putting their initials together, they came up with 'D&A', and Laurence designed a logo using an elegant typeface called Palace Script. This was along the lines of the similar branding used to promote the New Romantic band Ultravox, who had been given a clever 'UV' stamp by Peter Saville. As Laurence explained, "It was an important cosmetic image, signalling music with irony. With Eurythmics I was going for something clean, with precision and lots of white space, giving it a strict, stylish sit-up-and-take-notice-of-me feel. This was in contrast to punk, which was all torn paper, splashed paint, pins and people making funny faces . . . There was new technology with drum machines and synthesisers, it was no longer four guys like The Clash – this was a proper production business, hence the business suits.

"Dave and Annie were two normal, almost common names and the idea of giving them an elegant symbol that wouldn't look out of place on an expensive box of chocolates or cigarettes or even on a solicitors' door appealed to us all." The three also shared the joke that the monogram sounded just like C&A, the clothing chain store, although its actual appearance resembled the arguably more up-market M&S sign for Marks & Spencer.

Over time, D&A was to evolve into a limited publishing company with the more witty name of DNA, and would be based at 147 Crouch Hill, Crouch End. Laurence Stevens himself would also later adopt the monogram idea for his own company name, Laurence Stevens Design. The initials LSD alone suggested this particular designer had fully embraced the leap into the world of rock music.

Back at RCA, the production loop was effectively joined with Sheila Sedgwick, who had proved a tower of strength during the bad press of

The Tourists' dying months. Following Chris Charlesworth's departure from the label in the autumn of 1981, Richard Routledge had become head press officer at RCA and Sheila was promoted accordingly. She continued her role as Eurythmics' own press officer and was so determined to override the negative criticism Dave and Annie had endured from 'I Only Want To Be With You' through to *In The Garden*, that she moved from Epsom to Maida Vale to devote more of her time to the group. Says Jack, "Sheila was really keen on turning the press around. She got through to *Melody Maker* and finally got a front cover and double page spread and then it spread from there. She turned the press around single-handedly."

Sheila herself admits that redressing what she describes as the press 'hate campaign' against Eurythmics was her toughest challenge whilst working at RCA. "It was a serious slog," she says. "Annie was very hard on herself, sometimes ridiculously hard. She has high standards for herself and other people, and can be quite aloof if she feels someone's not behaving right, which perhaps gave her the 'difficult' tag. She felt many people she came across were idiots with no understanding at all – that comes out of her own high ideals for herself in work and relationships." Sheila's devotion was later to earn her an industry award and promotion to Head of Press at RCA.

★   ★   ★

Now solidly in place, the dedicated Eurythmics team set about lining up some live appearances for the group to test out their new material. Annie was convinced that she should shed the skin of the performer she once was and adopt a different persona to reflect the change in their music. She was coming to the end of what Peter describes as her "intellectual girlie" stage, and with his encouragement and constant ideas from Dave, she began to delve deeper into the extremes of her psyche.

"It was a matter of finding things that really reflected their character, and the music which they felt comfortable with," says Jack. "At one point Annie was constantly wearing black, and then she started wearing clothes from sex-shops. It was just a learning process for her to find out what she felt comfortable with. One day she walked into my office and she'd cut all her hair off, and it looked fantastic and brought all her features out in her face. At that point it was a statement that she felt confident of who she was."

However, Annie wasn't quite confident enough to reveal her shorn locks to her audience just yet. On January 11, 1982, Eurythmics played a memorable date at the Barracuda Club in London. For this performance they appeared alone, merely with the aid of backing tapes. Dave wore a business suit and, alongside the synthesisers, played a double-necked guitar suspended from the ceiling. Annie, clad in black leather, hid her man's haircut under an asymmetrical black wig.

Eurythmics legend has long since been twisted regarding the events that followed. Some fans believe this momentous occasion occurred at the Barracuda Club, some at the notorious gay night spot, Heaven, and Peter Ashworth, present in the front row of the audience at all these concerts, claims it was at Regents College.

"She was going to be wearing this long wig, she wanted to hide herself," he recalls today. "Possibly because this was at a student college, and I don't think the media had been told about it. Basically it was an experimental gig in front of students . . . And she did have this long black wig. It wasn't pre-arranged, but somehow she either shook her head or bent down and someone grabbed her hair. She lost her wig during the performance and didn't bother putting it back on."

Her slicked-back, orange hair exposed, if she wanted to save face in front of the crowd Annie had little choice but to continue with the rest of the set. Suddenly she felt released, as if it was possible after all to carry the same physiognomy on the stage as it was off. No doubt the gasps of surprise emanating from the students now uncertain of the singer's gender heightened her resolve. Instantaneously Annie held attention, confusion and awe in the palm of her hand, and it was an intoxicating feeling.

"When she decided to go with it, it was such a definite decision," Peter continues. "It was, 'That's it, that's what I'm going to be now.' All of a sudden the stage persona was the same as offstage, unless she was going to start wearing wigs in the street, and she didn't. She never disguised herself on the street that I was aware of."

Pleased with the impact of Annie's androgynous image on audiences, and much encouraged by the small crew working diligently behind them, Eurythmics shut themselves in their attic studio for days at a time during 1982, recording an immense amount of work with the aim of paring down their best songs for one outstanding album.

It has to be said that, despite the sheer quantity of material produced by Dave and Annie during the next year-and-a-half, the extra and discarded tracks, many recycled for use on B-sides and promotional tapes, do not stand up to the quality of any of the tracks on their next album. That aside, many of the songs have been adopted as 'cult' classics with fervent Eurythmics fans, and are well worth a listen. Some also became firm favourites in earlier concerts, such as '4/4 In Leather', 'Satellite Of Love' and 'Tous Les Garçons'.

Looking back on this material, it is fascinating to follow the composers' progress as they try out idea after idea. Some fail dismally, but many of these concepts later ended up on Eurythmics' commercially released albums.

The best thing about this 'surplus' output is that Dave and Annie are not afraid to try anything. Often Annie's voice comes over as ugly and harsh, and frequently a musical snippet is spun out for too long and becomes irritating, but at least these ideas have been put through the Eurythmic mill, sparking off an interesting twist. Many songs, such as 'ABC Freeform' or 'Monkey Monkey', seem experimental, but tracks like 'Step On The Beast' and 'Invisible Hands' are worthy additions to any discerning fan's collection. They are all hummable pieces of pop in their own right, but would be completely out of place on a typically confident, hit-strewn Eurythmics record.

By March, both band and label were agreed that it was about time to release a single, and a track was chosen called 'This Is The House'. It had potential as a dance track and was therefore pressed up as a 12″ as well as a 7″ in the hope that the longer version would be played at nightclubs. Surprisingly, the song begins with the voice of Timothy Wheater's girlfriend, Maria El Vira Behro-Garcia, reciting excitable, flirtatious Spanish. As Dave explains, "Certain languages sound as though something is going to happen any moment now, the world's going to explode . . . That's why we used Spanish – it gets you on the edge of your seat." During Maria's recording session she was much amused with the whole process of wearing headphones and speaking into a microphone, so her bubbly laughter is completely natural.

The song is a Peter Gabriel-esque snapshot of family life, based around a powerful bass line, with John Turnbull's guitar taking the lead. "I just played a tiny little bit of funky rhythm guitar," the musician recalls. "I remember Annie going, 'No, I'm not sure.' But Dave liked it and so in the mix he flew a bit of it in on spin-off echo and it sounded really cool." Annie sounds clearer and more menacing than ever before and, poignantly, her lyrics reveal cracks in the family's happiness and an undercurrent of tension: "Nothing there but the dust and the rust . . ."

The 12″ version remained faithful to the original but was simply longer, featuring two B-sides hailing from Annie and Dave's indefatigable work. '4/4 In Leather', a popular live track at early Eurythmics gigs, features a futuristic Annie singing mainly in a sinister monotone about suggestive subject material which amply suits her threateningly androgynous image: "I want a leather dress/ I want a leather lover, nothing left to spare." The other B-side, 'Home Is Where The Heart Is' is a good example of Eurythmics' willingness to experiment. Annie's voice is soft and arrestingly close over a seemingly random electronic loop and a sampled whistle. There are two vocal tracks in which she melodically echoes herself, spinning a hypnotic web which peters out to the yearning whisper of "Can't be far away".

Despite the undeniable strength of the twin releases, 'This Is The House' failed to chart. The label, though guilty of lacklustre marketing, was unimpressed and was reluctant to contribute further towards Eurythmics promotion.

Annie was distraught, and the spectre of depression loomed once again. She flung herself into exploring her altered stage presence with a series of UK club dates including one in April at London's Heaven nightclub. As well as their increasing portfolio from the attic, the set would include the stronger tracks from *In The Garden*, 'Never Gonna Cry Again', 'Take Me To Your Heart' and the hopefully premonitory 'Your Time Will Come'.

On June 18, 1982 Eurythmics, goaded on by Jack Steven, decided to release another new song as a single. This was totally against RCA's wishes.

"I said to Dave and Annie, 'They're going to hate me for this at the record company, but why don't we just put out some feelers, some extended mixes on vinyl'," recalls Jack. "At that time there was a club called the Embassy – I used to go down there and insist they played their records. So people who were respected in the music business were hearing their songs and saying, 'Ah, that's Eurythmics' – it was planned."

'The Walk', described by Annie as a "crafted song done with a lot of love and care", features an atmospheric introduction bringing in a slower, shuffling groove accentuated by a glockenspiel heartbeat – completely alien to the baleful insistence of 'This Is The House'. A brilliantly inventive mix of authentic and synthesised instruments, it features real brass supporting Annie's prickly vocals, and a piano ringing out bright chords throughout the second verse. Dick Cuthell's muted trumpet solo at the close of the song helps maintain its musical integrity. The lyrics about seeking perfection within a potential relationship ring out in true Eurythmics style with some inspired touches: "And when you touch my skin/ I smell disaster".

'The Walk' was also released in various formats, with a host of B-sides enticing the collector to purchase them all. These tracks included 'Invisible Hands' (at that stage the planned title track of the coming album), 'Step On The Beast', 'Dr Trash' and 'The Walk Part II'.

'Invisible Hands' is totally electronic and bizarrely jolly, with Annie taking on the role of a monotonic dictator, delivering the intriguing lyrics with no emotion whatsoever. 'Step On The Beast' sets up an infectious beat akin to Soft Cell's best vinyl moment, 'Tainted Love', and continues with a most un-Annie-like vocal more typical of the likes of Alison Moyet or Carly Simon. Understated and bluesy, she grooves along to the underground Sixties vibe, worrying that she's "half-way down and can't get up". Perhaps The Beast represents Depression and Annie needs to climb up it like a ladder to find relief at the top.

'Dr Trash' aptly reflects its own title – musical trash, which is simply an assortment of voices and noises played at various speeds and backwards. There is little or no artistic value in the cacophony at the end, but maybe that in itself was what Dave and Annie were intending when they recorded it. Finally, 'The Walk Part II' is a piano-led, atmospheric instrumental, using the brass elements of the original. Annie's vocal presence is reduced to some heavily reverbed grunting and whooping.

Sadly, such an impressive variety of material failed to ignite the public's attention, and without backing from RCA, even in the form of a poster campaign, it sank without trace. It was all getting a little hard to bear in Eurythmics' attic studio.

★   ★   ★

Relishing the chance of escape from the disappiontments of London, Annie was enticed to another studio, playing keyboards alongside old friend Jaki Liebezeit and help Conny Plank produce Italian vocalist Gianna Nannini's 1982 album *Latin Lover*. Peter was present at the sessions held at Stone Castle studios in Italy and Conny's studios in Cologne during the month of August.

"They were still delving into Germanic things. They just wanted to break away from their past, they were really haunted by it. I think Annie was," he reflects. "Annie invited me out on a number of occasions. One was to Lake Como, where she was recording in this castle with Conny Plank and working with a girl called Gianna Nannini – she was massive, like the Rod Stewart of Italy!"

Although everything looked friendly enough on the outside, Annie was experiencing problems, whether it was with the current project, or the longer-term Eurythmics work back in England. Peter Ashworth arrived looking forward to the unusual sessions, but instead faced a startling development.

"It was really weird because I was met by Gianna's manager at the airport and taken to this castle. Annie was working, fair enough, but she came out at suppertime, somehow took one look at me, blanked, and walked away. And I'd been invited for a week, or two weeks to hang out. So there I was, isolated, in a place I didn't know . . ." Unexpectedly on his own, Peter had little choice but to socialise with the other members of the recording crew, particularly the inimitable Conny Plank. "One of the things I loved that he said to me was that he saw everything in film," Peter remembers. "Everything he saw, he saw as a movie film, not just a sound-track to a film, but an actual film. I think *In The Garden* was meant to be a series of filmic scenes."

Obviously there was trouble brewing between Annie and Peter at this stage, possibly exacerbated by the pressure on the singer to work in a studio without Dave. For Peter it seemed that despite the initially friendly invitation, he had arrived in the right place at the wrong time. "Maybe I wasn't what Annie remembered me to be, or I wouldn't give her the right thing, I wouldn't say the right thing about her, or I was a stranger. *Or* she was schizophrenic – it was one or the other, and I could never work out what she was," he muses.

Annie spent the best part of three humourless weeks recording a mixed bag of Europop-meets-Eurovision Song Contest material in the presence of the gravel-voiced Gianna Nannini and her deathly serious backing band. A month later she was glad to be back in Britain, performing a Eurythmics concert for BBC Radio 1 on September 25. Dropping the backing-tapes idea for the time being, she and Dave put together a band especially for the occasion, which consisted of Timothy Wheater on oriental flute and keyboards, Adam Williams on mixing desk and effects, Raynard Falconer on synthesiser and Dick Cuthell on trumpet. To make a bit of a change, Dave took over bass duties as well as guitar. Together they covered the usual tracks from *In The Garden*, plus the two latest singles and B-sides, a cover of Lou Reed's 'Satellite Of Love', and a new track in its very early stages, called 'Somebody Told Me.'

Hot on the heels of the concert came another single, 'Love Is A Stranger', released in September. Despite being burnt in the past with the criticism following The Tourists' take on 'I Only Want To Be With You', Eurythmics were painfully aware that they needed a commercial hit single to maintain RCA's financial support. Accordingly they worked on making this song more radio-friendly, incorporating an insistent dance beat and a catchy melody, but managed to retain their artistic individuality with spectacular results.

'Love Is A Stranger' was and remains a masterpiece of early Eighties pop music. Dave's synthesisers chug away like a rhythmic train, accentuated by odd grunting provided by a chef from a neighbouring restaurant. A willing participant in a typically bizarre recording session, his exertions were later processed through a reverb unit. The dance-oriented backdrop with its strange human beat works ridiculously well, showcasing Annie's heart-stopping voice and the tender torment of her lyrics. "What I did was put

143

opposites together, because love and hate are so close to each other," she explained of the theory behind her words. "Instead of saying, 'It's the most wonderful thing that's ever happened to me,' I put, 'It's the most *devastating* thing that's ever happened to me.'"

Annie's most impressive vocal performance yet captures her at a particularly poignant moment, her voice sweeping softly against the insistent background pulse but able to switch on impulse from sweet to threatening, highlighting odd words like 'subway' with unexpected aggression. Dave had become friendly with singer Kiki Dee, another Elton John protégée, and she agreed to record backing vocals for 'Love Is A Stranger'. Kiki contributes more than expected to this very female tale of obsessive love, blending surprisingly well with Annie as she takes on the higher harmonies of the lyrics.

Two B-sides accompanied this promising release. 'Monkey Monkey' is drawn out over a spacey dance rhythm with a similar musical thread to a forthcoming track, 'This City Never Sleeps'. Ambient, junglisitic and repetitive, it is difficult to decipher whether this is in fact a worthwhile Eurythmics experiment, or merely money for old rope. 'Let's Just Close Our Eyes', which was featured on the 12", borrows heavily from 'The Walk' and brings an element of science fiction to a powerful dance track. Annie's vocal has been treated so that it sounds distant and removed from the music, although punctuated with energetic "yeah"s above the backwards chanting at the end.

Eurythmics and their supportive team were so convinced of the power of this latest release that they decided to record their second promo video after the debacle of 'Never Gonna Cry Again'. Since the launch of MTV in August the previous year, many young British bands, notably Duran Duran and Depeche Mode, had made striking impressions on US TV screens, at the same time enjoying a boost in their overall sales. Whereas before it had been sufficient to make the odd television appearance and go on tour to promote a new single or album, now the world stood poised on the brink of the video age. If a band was unprepared to accompany their latest song with a short film, then they were playing severely against the odds.

Not that it was Eurythmics who were unprepared for the extra expense. RCA would have been totally unwilling to fund such an expensive exercise on such a low-profile and thus far disappointing group. So, unbelievably, Jack Steven decided not to tell them. "'Love Is A Stranger' got commissioned behind the marketing manager's back, because they didn't want to do a video. I really did stick my neck on the line for Eurythmics."

Filmed during September 1982, in a limousine and bathroom, on

Hammersmith Bridge and outside Dave's mother's Maida Vale flat, the video was produced by Jon Roseman. "All people were doing in videos in those days was having the band playing," Jack explains. "Jon Roseman was the guy who did Queen's 'Bohemian Rhapsody' with Bruce Gowers, so he was a pioneer of pop video. He was brilliant. He took a loss on the 'Love Is A Stranger' video because he thought this was fantastic and crazy." With his budget of £12,000, Roseman decided to shoot the scenes on 35mm, which gave a higher quality, more like a feature film.

Annie seized on the project with glee. Here at last was an opportunity to exercise her latent acting skills, and place on the song a visual interpretation which could alternately shock and impress. "The video is basically a little cameo story," she later described in *Eurythmics*. "I would say 'Love Is A Stranger' is a song about love objects. The concept of love in relationships is very often a person projecting what they want onto another person. We are all in love with the idea of love but what we want is not always good for us. We might get obsessed with something very dangerous. I wanted to put these ideas into a pop song."

Following her theme through to the video, Annie decided to act the part of a love object herself – an expensive-looking prostitute dressed in fur and wearing an obscene amount of make-up and a curly blonde wig. She reclines in the back of a limousine, the part of the chauffeur played by Dave. In his efforts to look cool, Dave was soon to find that his dark glasses were rather impractical, as the car mounted the kerb more than was strictly necessary!

Annie's pouting and Dave's grim-faced driving are interspersed by sinister shots of a dummy 'miming' the rhythmic grunting noise that punctuates the music. Drawing on her real-life experience, Annie fixes the camera with her piercing gaze, reaches back and rips off her wig to reveal her slicked back orange hair. Arriving at the Maida Vale pad, she gets out of the car and enters the house, where she becomes another menacing character, this time wearing a black wig and brandishing scissors. Again she pulls off her wig to reveal the woman underneath the costume, and then lies on the bathroom floor, twisting and choking in tangles of film. As Annie explains, "The person in the house is very sadistic, there's lots of leather around and strange things in the bathroom . . . The song is about somebody who is obsessed with something which is also a destructive thing. Like the love between an addict and heroin. If we could, we would have had hypodermic syringes lying around in the video." Unfortunately for Annie, this was not an image that either Jack Steven or Jon Roseman were likely to entertain, especially behind RCA's back.

Eventually Annie leaves the house and returns to the car. Her final incarnation is a masculine figure, pale and without make-up, an equally striking image. At the climax she turns into a dummy, the figure hinted at throughout, and performs a series of odd robotic movements symbolising that she is now being manipulated by Dave, the chauffeur. It was an ambitious project to say the least, but she tackled her quadruple transformation brilliantly, and the song was successfully metamorphosed onto another level.

It was all too much for America. On the video's first transmission on MTV, the screen went blank as the controllers watched in horror as Annie removed her first wig. To them it appeared that her gender had suddenly blurred, and the plug was pulled in the interest of America's innocent youth being exposed to what appeared to be a transvestite. The video was banned until further notice.

"When MTV saw this video they went bananas over it," guffaws Jack. "But the following day I got a fax from RCA: 'Could you please send Annie Lennox's birth certificate?' MTV weren't sure she was a girl and were worried that it was a bit sexually deviant." Popular Eurythmics legend dictates that Annie was then duly required to find said birth certificate to prove her femininity, but Jack smiles today, "I never did send it."

Other than being amazed at what she perceived as America's small-mindedness, Annie was quick to capitalise on the benefits of all the extra publicity. "I'm happier to be compared with a man than a woman," she stated defiantly. "I'm a very female person, but men seem to want to call my confidence, my positive awareness of myself, aggression. So many men still can't cope with the idea of the non-submissive female. I suppose it's part of some deep-seated castration complex!"

In *The Face* and other such magazines, over the following year she was to draw back from any bisexual tainting, stating rather insistently: "I think some men are threatened by certain songs. I have to admit it because I love men, I'm mad about them. I've always had this obsession about men. I'm not gay. I'm not really a kinky person or a practising pervert. A song like 'Love Is A Stranger' is emotionally sadomasochistic. It's not the love act, nothing so literal, but it is taken from my experience."

Tellingly she continued, revealing the extent of the personal nature that was increasingly penetrating her lyrics, "It's about falling for people who never want you and feeling ambivalent towards the people who do want you. I've hurt people and felt totally cold about them but when it's happened to me . . . I can't take it. My best songs come from suffering because I've indulged in my pain; a very typical masochism."

Somehow, amid all the controversy and daring remarks, the single did not do well as the video suffered from minimal exposure. A few weeks after its initial release it peaked at number 54 in the UK charts.

But all was not lost. Back in England, slowly but surely Eurythmics were beginning to reach a fresh audience. Their rule-breaking video for 'Love Is A Stranger' earned them the accolade of Video Of The Year from *Music And Video Week*. This was no mean feat, as Jack explains, " 'It was the first time RCA had won anything since David Bowie. But they wouldn't let me pick up the award because I had gone behind their back to make it."

12

THE POWER OF IMAGINATION

"I didn't know anything about production. It all seemed double Dutch to me, but I thought I'd give it a go."

– DS

In November 1982, amid the furore surrounding Eurythmics' first commercially released video, Annie quietly moved into a flat at 80 Stapleton Hall Road, Crouch End. Although money was tight, she was beginning to see a small amount of profit, as she said to the media, "I've just about made enough money to take on a one-bedroom flat. Before that I was in a bedsitter." Her new address was a ground floor flat in a semi-detached house with a share of a little back garden. There was a relatively large front room with distinctive shutters on the window, and down the corridor were a bathroom, kitchenette and bedroom. Annie was delighted with her new home and prided herself on being able to afford the step up into a respectable residential area. Dave and the studio were still just minutes away, but further than before, and Peter lived separately in nearby Islington. Annie set about decorating her new home in her own typically imaginative way, although in April the following year admitted to still living out of cardboard boxes. But by then she had the excuse of having no time on her hands at all.

The master tapes of Eurythmics' second album were delivered to RCA later in November, securing another royalty advance and thus making Annie's extra housing costs more affordable. It had taken some 11 months to record, and it arrived in a completely different form to their last effort. On the newly named *Sweet Dreams (Are Made Of This)* Annie and Dave had discovered their style.

Some 40 tracks had been written and recorded since the new year, and along the way plans for the album had shifted, blurred and shifted again. With so many extra songs at their disposal, RCA were later to master a five-track EP cassette from a selection which didn't make it to the album, comprising 'Intro Speech', 'Invisible Hands', 'Step On The Beast' and

'Angel Dub', a powerful yet non-eventful instrumental version of 'I've Got An Angel'. A version of Lou Reed's Bowie-esque 'Satellite Of Love', popular with both backing musicians and Eurythmics' audience, was also on the tape. During the early concerts there was a distinct lack of 'ballad' material, and this rendering would continue to fill the gap rather well over the next couple of years.

The album itself had originally been titled *Invisible Hands* after the track released on the B-side of the 'The Walk' single, but now the project had grown a different identity. Truly it had been a labour of love, set against the potent backdrop of Annie's gradual recovery from her depression and Dave's ever-devoted determination to flourish in the face of illness and disbelief. Jack Steven had proved a constant source of support through this testing time.

"For many months we just sat and talked about where Eurythmics were going to go," he recalls. "It took a long time. They were very suspicious of me at first, naturally thinking, 'He's a record company man – can we trust him?' And as an executive, you've always got a slight mistrust of an artist, so we spent time developing a relationship . . . It wasn't the normal record company/artist relationship. I was trying to encourage them to breathe." Jack was aware of the financial pressures coming from RCA, but was reassured by the fact that Dave and Annie had financed their very own studio completely off their own backs, and were cutting costs. "I was given a budget of £15,000 to do the whole album, most albums cost £60,000 to record. But I loved it, to me I was able to do real A&R. I was allowed to get on with it and didn't have the fascists of the corporation saying that the record has to go Top Five."

Jack was also privy to the inside changes occurring within the tight-knit band. "On the one hand Annie wasn't completely confident of herself, of where she was going. And on the other hand Dave wasn't completely confident about producing. There was one point where Dave was saying, 'Let's find a producer.' I said, 'No, the only person that can produce Annie is you, because you know her so well.' So all of that had to be brought out."

The overriding aftereffects of Eurythmics' work for their second album revolve not only around Annie's ever-improving vocal performances and Dave's growing ability as producer, but also around the couple's dedication to experimentation. It seemed there was nothing they were unprepared to try.

For example, the clinking counterpoint audible during the title track, 'Sweet Dreams (Are Made Of This)', is not an instrument of electronic or traditional origin – Dave and Annie resourcefully filled up milk bottles with different levels of water and tapped them in time to the chorus for that song. Also, all the piano on the album is there by chance and more than a little hard graft from the musicians. Coincidentally the owner of the picture framers downstairs was a pianist, who had installed a grand piano in his shop so that he could practise every morning before opening up. After much pleading, Annie and Dave were given his permission to use the piano after the picture framers had closed for the evening.

Of course, there was no way they were going to be able to lug the huge instrument up to the attic studio late every night and return it in time for the morning, so instead they hit upon the idea of suspending two microphones down through the ceiling on extremely long cables, and set up a talk-back system so that they could communicate from the different levels of the building. But their problems did not stop there, as the main power supply to the picture framers was shut down each night, and there was no electric light to play by. So not only would Annie be sent down a whole floor to play the piano beneath the dangerously swinging mics, she would also have to perform her part by torchlight, otherwise in total darkness. Electrical problems were to dog the musicians throughout the sessions, as Dave winces, "Sometimes we had the most outrageous connections. A real engineer would have been appalled."

On top of their lack of funds and the unorthodox techniques they were often forced to employ, Eurythmics also had to contend with 'knocking off' time at the picture framers to ensure the noisy machinery would not interfere with recording. "They had a machine that a guy would operate with his foot," Dave described in *Eurythmics*. "Only he would do it at unpredictable intervals, so we couldn't stop the sound getting on the tape with Annie's vocals. Eventually we had to wait till six to start every day, but that was OK, because this great empty warehouse was really spooky, and it had fantastic echo."

"I didn't know anything about production. It all seemed double Dutch to me, but I thought I'd give it a go," he later admitted. "I had no idea what we were doing as we were doing it. I just knew if I pushed that and this, it would sound like this." Yet Dave did such a good job that the resulting album sounds as if it was recorded in the sophistication of an expensive 24-track studio, rather than on a mere eight-track Teac. The majority of Annie's superb harmonies were achieved by 'bouncing' already recorded tracks together to make more space for more instruments. For the singer this meant standing right next to the studio and cueing herself in, most unprofessionally. But it's impossible to tell, as the mix sounds crystal clear.

"People think that album is so high tech. But we couldn't even afford a claptrap – the classic disco thing, you know, that goes ckkk-ckkk-ckkk!" Dave later confided. "It's just me and Annie, banging on the wall with a handful of picture frames! If we'd had the money, of course we would have used a claptrap. But not having it made us a lot more inventive."

One night a track was recorded for the album that sadly never quite made it onto an official release of any description. Ever striving to create interesting sounds, the song 'Armadillo'[20] involved Timothy Wheater playing a Chinese flute wrapped in onion skins, in an attempt to make the instrument sound like a snake charmer. Simultaneously, Annie, wearing a long black wig, got into the spirit of the session by wailing in Arabic tones and Dave played an array of guitars which were suspended from the ceiling. "Maybe it hurt him to wear his guitar because of his lung," muses John Turnbull of this latest contraption. "I remember he had this lightweight guitar, and then later on he had this harness, a bit like Lou Reed, you walk up and the guitar was on a bungy rope!"

The oddities did not end there. Timothy Wheater had been taught by the eminent flautist James Galway who, out of interest for his former pupil, decided to sit in on the session that night, accompanied by his manager and a friend. "Annie reckoned it was the most nerve-wracking experience of her life," Dave later divulged. "When you've got thousands of people watching it's one thing, but someone who's also a master of the instrument you love – well, that's something else. I mean, we were enthusiastic but we sort of related James Galway to *Stars On Sunday* – and then he really liked it!"

★   ★   ★

"If you look at the different style changes between *In The Garden* and *Sweet Dreams*, it's absolutely huge," says Jack Steven. "Technically as well we were doing things that nobody had ever done before, we were using drum machines, which nobody was doing in those days." At the time, Dave agreed, "We love the power of bass synthesisers, not the ones that do frilly bits of music. We used very powerful bass lines on the album. We left in the automation of a drum machine because it's so irresistible you can't stop it. It's incessant. That mixture with Annie's singing we felt would give the music an edge."

"All the tracks are strong," declared Annie. "I can put my hand on my heart and say, 'I really love every track on the album.' We rejected an awful lot of material and made sure there was no filler. All tuna, no celery. They're all quite different – and yet the Eurythmics' sound is there."

---

[20] Also known as 'Beautiful Armadillo'.

While Eurythmics waited the couple of months necessary for RCA to put the record together in a releasable format, they consulted with Laurence Stevens about the design for the cover sleeve.

Daringly, the threesome hit on an idea which featured a Lewis Ziolek photograph of Annie, naked and facing away from the camera. Her hair is shocking orange and cut shorter than ever before, her eyes are obscured by a black mask and in her gloved hand she clutches a lurid pink chocolate box, which is meant to contain the 'sweet dreams' of the title. Laurence's striking D&A typography completed the very different, businesslike image Eurythmics wished to project.

As with almost every stage up until this point, they were met with initial resistance from RCA. The record label favoured bold and basic images that caught the eye from shop shelves. The cover of *Sweet Dreams (Are Made Of This)* was simply too stylised and idiosyncratic for their mainly American tastes. They returned Laurence's distinctive artwork with suggested amendments to the chocolate box and Annie's nudity. This proved all too much for Jack Steven, who was swiftly tiring of the constant rebuffs.

"When I sent *Sweet Dreams* to America they rejected it," he recalls today incredulously. "But I thought America would fall in love with Annie. David Geffen had just started his record label. The head of A&R at Geffen then heard it and said, 'I love this, I want to put it out.' So I went back to RCA and said, 'Fuck RCA in America, I'll put it out with Geffen.' They all said, 'You can't do that.' So this fight started between me and America, but RCA grudgingly decided to put the record out.

"Anyway, they changed the cover on the album, because they didn't want to use the gold strips and they sent us this terrible design which was effectively a Polaroid of Annie holding a chocolate box. So I rang up the international department and found out that Alabama were the biggest act in the US at that time. I got this Alabama record sleeve and chopped it to shreds and re-glued it. I sent it back to America saying, 'I'm not too keen about your new design of the Eurythmics cover, but what do you think about my work on Alabama?' " Fortunately for all involved, RCA saw his point and backed down. *Sweet Dreams (Are Made Of This)* was set for release in January 1983 in the desired, show-stopping cover sleeve.

While Dave and Annie waited in nervous anticipation for the reaction to the album, they busied themselves with a series of club dates during November and December 1982, travelling from the Camden Palace in London to Bristol, Cardiff and Reading. Joined by aptly named drummer Robert Crash, who had assisted on producing the album with Adam Williams, they performed sets consisting of new songs plus Sixties covers of The Supremes' 'You Can't Hurry Love' and Nancy Sinatra's 'These

Boots Are Made For Walking'. But it seemed their hearts were not all in it, as Dave said in an interview at the time he would rather not be performing at all prior to the record's release. "Not because we don't like performing – but we would much rather mime to a song on TV. I mean, you've already played it once, so you don't need to prove it again – whereas on stage you have to concentrate on playing an instrument and you can't move around!"

Confusingly, around this time Dave was forced to change his professional name as it was revealed there was another Dave Stewart working in the music field. Acknowledging his middle name, Dave now became known as 'David A. Stewart' on all credits, discovering for himself how Ann must have felt when he enforced on her the new identity of Annie.

Finally, in the first week of January 1983, *Sweet Dreams (Are Made Of This)* hit the stores and the world was at last able to hear for themselves the fruits of Eurythmics' year of dedication.

The opening seconds of 'Love Is A Stranger' establish the no-nonsense mood developed from the occasionally faltering bones of *In The Garden*, with the immediate thumping dance beat, punctuated with grunts, suggesting a new, sexual bent to the couple's work. Without question, this is a fantastic opening track, arguably unsurpassed in Eurythmics' later work for its sheer impact at the start of an album.

The dance beat does not let up, but instead shifts into a bouncy jungle vibe, complete with simian screeches, for the second track, 'I've Got An Angel'. Synthetic pan pipes add to the all-enveloping, heavy electronic padding, providing once again a showcase for Annie's huge vocal range. This time though, she uses her voice more for rhythmic addition and the lyrics are more about the sounds of the words themselves than any real meaning. Projecting her visual image through her singing, Annie seems to switch from male to female, and back again. The music and the refrain "Time is time is time to kill" seem an apt precursor for the coming work on a future project, ending on a triumphant "Ha!"

'Wrap It Up' is a sexy, upfront cover of a song recorded by Sam and Dave in 1968 as the B-side of their hit, 'I Thank You', and is sung as a duet with Scritti Politti's Green Gartside. Annie and Green share the upbeat vocals line for line, battling against the near desperate pace of the extreme electronic backing.

Annie and Dave had long been fans of the Sixties soul duo's approach to music. "Sam and Dave were really underrated over here," said Dave. "They still are. Sam and Dave were *rough*, and it's their roughness that I love. We want to put that roughness back in – to have a soul feeling with that English power." Annie was especially proud of their interpretation, perhaps with The Tourists' treatment after their signature cover version at the back of her mind. She said, "Our philosophy about cover versions is that if you're going to do one, then do something original with it. I wouldn't want to do a lukewarm version of an original. We take a song and explode it rather than just doing a replica like a cabaret band would." Certainly on *Sweet Dreams (Are Made Of This)* Eurythmics gave 'Wrap It Up' a most distinctive imprint. Packed to the brim with energy and vitality, two thirds through the song, the emphasis shifts to funk for a quick but quirky instrumental break, with Eurythmics literally flinging more and more audible interest to their listeners.

Another track which chugs along like a train is 'I Could Give You (A Mirror)', predating the classic Queen sound of 'I Want To Break Free' by one year. Annie's soaring lyrics are accusatory and confrontational, "How could you be so cold with my arms to hold you?" and she threatens to give her unsatisfactory lover a mirror to look in, reflecting her disappointment in him. The track nods towards the dance floor and ends on a climactic muddle of voices and beats, culminating in a victorious shout.

After 'The Walk' brings the first break from the frenetic pace of the album so far, the title track emerges: 'Sweet Dreams (Are Made Of This)'. Opening with perhaps the most instantly recognisable and empowering synth lines in pop, Eurythmics' chugging rhythms are reinstated and Annie is straight in with her harshly sung tale of man's endless search for meaning or reason. Rarely does a straight pop song from this era present such a beautiful voice – here Annie balances soulfulness with strength, and she is snide rather than regretful. It is difficult to believe that this obvious lead track's composition really dates back as far as 1982 as it stands out as being particularly timeless. A work of genius and still their best-remembered song.

Another rare break from the combative strength predominant on *Sweet Dreams (Are Made Of This)* is the disturbing tone poem of 'Jennifer'. The sparse backing effectively contrasts the heights and depths of the music and twinkling synths well reflect the water, punctuated with a rather strange but somehow appropriate zipping sound, perhaps to pinpoint the termination of life. Dave's fuzzy guitar at the end sends the song spinning into orbit.

The disturbing lyrics and references to being underneath the water caused much confusion for fans curious to know the origins of the song. When Annie was first asked by journalist Max Bell who or what 'Jennifer' was attributed to, she replied, "I did want to write a very poignant love song, one that captured the distillation of feeling for another person. Once I had a boyfriend, and he died. After he was dead I tried to think of all the little things that summed him up. A piece of written paper on the wall, a photo or a shirt with a special smell. I made it simple and it ended up being about myself. It's called 'Jennifer' because the rhythm of that word is so lovely."[21]

Soon after Max Bell's report in October 1983, Annie made a swift about-turn and began to deny any links to 'Jennifer' and an actual death. "Someone asked if 'Jennifer' was written about a specific drowning incident," she said in another interview. "In fact it *was* written about a drowning, but not a real incident. I saw a black-and-white version of *Hamlet* when I was eight and there was Ophelia lying beneath the water and the weeds rippling over her and it was very powerful and that was another image in my mind." Either way, there is no denying that Eurythmics transformed Annie's simply phrased poem into something really special. "It's got the sound of the sea on it, and we wanted it to feel so intimate that it sounded like Annie was actually whispering in your ear when it was coming out of the stereo," said Dave.

'This Is The House' was the eighth track on the album, followed by the nervous lumber of 'Somebody Told Me', yet another dose of Lennox paranoia, with one more relationship stretched and faltering under the microscope. Here a lie has been uncovered and a love betrayed, and an unusual cynical edge of martyrdom makes an appearance, with the sardonic couplet: "I'm a silly little saint/ With a halo of smiles". This is all set against a slow, anthemic and ominous synth line and was later amply described by Dave as, "An angry, sad song with a very edgy sound."

The final track, 'This City Never Sleeps' is based around Annie's time spent in a miserable bedsit when she left the Royal Academy of Music. Peter Ashworth recollects Annie writing the evocative words quite some time before her move to Stapleton Hall Road. "That was in the little bedsit that we shared in Camden Villas. It was a tiny room, a bed in one corner and a sink in another corner. I remember her writing these lyrics while she was there. It was a very depressing place," he says today.

Elaborates Annie: "I'd regressed back to when you first come down to London and you have to rough it. That was happening in my private life – it was a telling strain on me, it was very hard to live with it. 'This City Never Sleeps' is simply to do with what was happening to me at the time. You know . . . the walls were so thin that I could hear the girl coughing next door! It was very depressing and I thought, 'Jesus!' There's millions of people all over the world who have this feeling where the city just hums all night and they don't know who the person is next door to them, and

---

[21] Intriguingly, extensive research for this biography failed to uncover any reference to an ex-boyfriend who had passed away prior to the song's composition in 1982. It is of course feasible that Annie's usage of the words "died" and "dead" could merely be symbolic.

they don't even wanna know because they treasure that tiny bit of privacy, that square box so much . . ."

When Annie presented Dave with her reflective, melancholic lyrics, he immediately seized on the imagery of the underground train rattling through the night and dashed off to nearby Camden Town tube station, where he recorded 15 minutes of train noises on Annie's small Sony walkman. Returning to the studio, Dave slowed down the tape until the recording was almost 'in tune' with the music, then literally held his electric guitar in front of the speakers so that it picked up on the squealing of the train wheels and began to noisily feed back into the system. In that way, the train sound effectively morphs into a screeching slide guitar, and the doctored sounds of the subway serve to heighten the lyrics. Annie is double tracked and low in this reflective, attractive semi-ballad, and the ambient synths and repeated bass line well reflect the boredom and frustration of being a stranger in the neighbourhood.

★   ★   ★

Within hours of its release, *Sweet Dreams (Are Made Of This)* was attracting rave reviews. *NME* announced it grandly as, "An immaculate post-disco view of urban romance with a few morbid edges," while *Sounds* described it as, "The absolute peak of heartbreak recollection". All the papers agreed that Annie's voice was the most astonishing yet to hail from the UK, and overall the album was lauded as, "A rich and captivating aural experience," from *Rolling Stone*, and "One of the most important albums of 1983," from *Melody Maker* – quite a compliment considering it was the very first week of the year.

Dave agreed with the critical acclaim. "I would say that *Sweet Dreams (Are Made Of This)* is one of the most important records of 1983," he said. "To us, the lyrics are so cutting and poignant, and it's been very carefully structured. We're not interested in creating anything unless it's really powerful." The stunning lead single, swiftly released in the album's wake, was undoubtedly one of those "really powerful" creations.

'Sweet Dreams (Are Made Of This)' had forced its way into the world at a particularly low period for Annie. It was conceived towards the end of the recording sessions for the album while RCA were expressing their concerns, and she was experiencing serious doubts about Eurythmics' future. "Out of that terrible depression, songs came very easily," Dave remembers. "It was like dragging teeth because we would end up in tears most of the time, and then we'd do a brilliant recording and be laughing and getting completely pissed together on a bucket of margherita. Then the tears got less and a sort of positive side came out."

"Dave and I almost split up the day we wrote 'Sweet Dreams'," Annie revealed a year later. "I'm very negative and he's very positive. But we were just having a terrible time and I couldn't take it anymore, and I said so. And he said, 'OK, fine, you don't mind if I go ahead and program the drum computer then, do you?'

"I was lying on the floor, curled up in a foetal position and he programmed in this rhythm. It sounded so good that in the end I couldn't resist it." Uncurling from her ball, Annie went over to the synthesiser and, as if out of nowhere, the main riff of the melody came pounding out of her fingers. Forgetting their argument in an instant, Dave and Annie excitedly started the tape machine. But that wasn't the end of the magic.

"Annie said, 'OK, let me sing,' and she went downstairs," smiles Dave. "Annie sang the entire song off the top of her head except for the part that goes 'Hold your head up', which we put in later. Some things you don't know how you did. Half an hour later it was just there."

The funny thing was, the sudden spate of genius that pulled Annie out of her foetal position had been inspired totally by accident. When Dave announced he was going to program the drum machine, the sound that came out was not what he had intended. "I pressed the button on the drum machine, and the track came out back-to-front," Dave finally admitted in 1999. "It was no great genius here – I switched the wrong switch! It had a mind of its own."

Annie's sudden lyrical flash of inspiration came through her experiences fighting depression. "The song 'Sweet Dreams' is a personal statement about people's motivations, in their lives, their own dreams," she explained. "I replaced the word 'motivations' with the word 'dreams'. I'm saying these are our motivations as human beings, and there's no way, whether I agree or disagree, that I want to change anything about that. And everywhere I look ('I travelled the world, and the seven seas'), all I see is that every person on the earth is looking for some kind of fulfilment. So you have the extremes from the people who want to use and be used, the whole spectrum."

Certain that their new song was capable of spearheading the Eurythmics campaign the world over, Annie and Dave first performed it live in concert while they were waiting for the release of the album. It immediately became a firm favourite, with the audiences' focus shifting from the verse's cynical overtones to the more positive chorus, which soon became an anthem: "Hold your head up!"

Although it seemed there was no way they could lose considering the pure strength of the planned single release, Eurythmics and RCA alike were taking no chances with the packaging. Once again designed by

Laurence Stevens, the sleeve photograph depicted Dave and Annie side by side with only the back of Dave's head showing and Annie with her wrists tied with rope. While many at the time construed this as a sly hint towards possible sexual innuendo within the lyrics ("Some of them want to abuse you/ Some of them want to be abused"), to Dave and Annie it simply symbolised that they would always be joined together, come what may. They had survived too much to let slip their esoteric relationship now.

'Sweet Dreams (Are Made Of This)' was backed by an earlier take of the album track, 'I Could Give You (A Mirror)', featuring a different melody with recognisable elements of the original, including Annie singing the normal verse. Intriguingly, the mix feels as if it has less impact than the album version yet is somehow more catchy.

One factor was missing. Eurythmics needed another promo for the video generation now hooked on MTV. Dave had a clear idea in his mind what was required, and fortunately he convinced RCA to indulge him. Dave's script was directed by Chris Ashbrook, and filmed on January 11 and 12 at Trillion Studio, Dean Street and on location in the Kent countryside.

The film opens with Dave's clenched fist banging on the RCA boardroom table. Across the table, Annie too pounds her fist down. She has bright orange hair, cropped as short as on the album sleeve, wears a business suit and wields a baton in her gloved hands. While she sings she gestures at film clips that include rockets and views of the moon, symbolising the infinite search of her lyrics. Meanwhile Dave, ever the scientist, works on an early computer. Suddenly they both assume yoga positions on the boardroom table and a red bhindi appears on Annie's forehead. The camera pans into the bhindi, taking us into a brief scene where they are both on a boat. This then changes to a field, where Dave and Annie simulate the main synthesiser line on cello and double bass. They are wearing masks and evening dress. Reminiscent of the 'Never Gonna Cry Again' video, Annie's ball gown is flowing and red in colour, on her head a long black wig.

In the field the viewer is suddenly aware that the musicians are surrounded by cows. When the scene returns to the boardroom, Annie and Dave lie head to toe on the table together, while a lone cow wanders in and out of shot, chewing the cud. This most memorable video ends with Annie falling asleep next to a book, with the title *Sweet Dreams* on the cover.

Evidently the cow was going to attract all the attention, as all concerned speculated on its significance in Dave's mind. "It's a bit off the wall, but animals, no matter what's happening, just go on eating the grass," he explained three months later to *Smash Hits*. "They don't have to go off flying to the moon or make a million dollar deal to know that they're OK . . . No matter what happens in civilisations, it all just drops down and then the grass grows again and time just goes on regardless.

"Everybody is scrabbling around the world looking for things; business-men looking for more money, gurus looking for more spiritual awareness and so on, so the video is just symbolising that, but it's up to people to look at it to interpret it how they want. Of course, to some people it might look like a pair of nutcases messing around in a boat and freaking out in a field with a bunch of cows . . ."

"I think that was a very subconscious thing," mused Annie of the cow's potential meaningfulness. "We put the elements together, then realised the symbolism. There was this animal completely out of place amongst all this technology and then when we put the technology in the animal's environment it was completely right." However highbrow the couple's definitions may have been, the cow and its bovine associates still managed to bring the crew down to earth on the day of shooting. "Obviously the cows caused all the fun," said Dave. "While we were outside they would-n't come near us, so we had to throw turnips around us and under the table." At least to the controllers at MTV, the animal contingent proved less offensive than the earlier sight of Annie ripping off her wig in the 'Love Is A Stranger' video, and the go-ahead was given for the promo to be shown.

To aid the single's promotion, Dave and Annie agreed to record what became known as the 'Breakthrough Sessions' for BBC Radio 1, the main UK station. Although they were both feeling under the weather and fight-ing off flu symptoms (possibly as a result of cavorting in a freezing field sur-rounded by cattle), it was clear that the 'breakthrough' had indeed been made. Jubilantly Eurythmics performed a special set for the programme including 'Sweet Dreams (Are Made Of This)', 'Love Is A Stranger', 'I Could Give You (A Mirror)', 'Never Gonna Cry Again', 'Somebody Told Me' and 'This City Never Sleeps'. Kiki Dee provided backing vocals, assisted by an enthusiastic girl singer called Eddi Reader. The show was fantastic. Despite the snuffles, there was to be no turning back.

13

SWEET DREAMS (ARE MADE OF THIS)

"There's no reason why I should be embarrassed about being rich, because in the past we were badly ripped off."

– AL

'Sweet Dreams (Are Made Of This)' was released on January 21, 1983. By the end of February the single had reached number two in the UK, halting just behind Bonnie Tyler's 'Total Eclipse Of The Heart'. While the album went on to achieve phenomenal success, being certified gold by the end of the year, the video gained equal critical acclaim, retaining its position within the 100 Greatest Music Videos some 15 years later. The song has remained a classic not only of the Eighties, but uniquely symbolising the peak of Eurythmics' music. Numerous artists have covered its harshly simplistic qualities, including notorious 'shock rock' act Marilyn Manson with his heavy metal version.

By February 1983, with their second album and its eponymous single achieving respectable chart positions, Eurythmics were thrown in at the deep end of fame. Unlike their last stab at success, this time the critics were behind them, hailing their quirky music and videos as the future of a new generation.

More importantly the duo were able to deal more maturely with the pressures linked to achievements and prosperity. Dave finally attained the dues for which he had striven so long, not only as a musician, but as a producer as well. For Annie to be taken seriously within a group and not just as a token female meant that she was able to drag herself up and out of her depression. The pair had grown up drastically since the split of The Tourists and it showed in the media hype surrounding their rapid ascension in the world of pop.

"Success this time round is very different, but much better," Annie gushed to journalist Karen Swayne in the thrilling summer of 1983. "I'm not so intimidated by it, and it's more directly under my control. We are both very clear in our own minds about what we want to do . . . You learn by experience, and I don't think I would've been able to cope at 18. Now I'm much more my own person."

Anyone connected to the instantly recognisable pair found themselves basking in the surrounding glow of the limelight. Annie's mum was traced and asked her opinion of her daughter's resurgent career. "Oh, I always thought she was musical, and I encouraged her, but sometimes it was difficult," Dorothy confided. "I never tell people I'm Annie's mother unless they find out. I'm really pleased, but I like to keep it to myself."

The Scots are traditionally renowned for being penny-pinching, and Aberdeen is the city most infamous for this trait. Annie, however, tried to remain true to her working-class roots rather than the popular image of a miser, but as even she discovered, ideologies change with the influx of royalty cheques.

"Wealth wouldn't come easy to me, I would be uncomfortable with it. I think being very rich is obscene," she had been quoted just before The Tourists fell apart in 1980, while only a few years later she was heard to justify the subsequent fortune she had made: "There's no reason why I should be embarrassed about being rich, because in the past we were badly ripped off. We've paid our dues financially more than anybody else I've ever met, actually. I'm not the kind of person who wants to have big status symbols, Rolls Royces, and flash around showing my Yves St Laurent watch."

Joe Bangay had stayed a good friend throughout and was able to see through to the core of the issue. "I think they both wanted to get away from their working-class backgrounds; they were very pleased to be rich. I don't think money was their driving ideal, but I think they were glad to be well off. Dave used to love his credit cards . . ."

While they tried not to let their sudden wealth go to their heads, the couple delighted in mocking the circles in which they now mixed. Dave's sense of humour combined with Annie's love of dressing up turned out to be a killer combination. At one music business party Annie turned up as the buxom country singer, Dolly Parton.

"She bought all the stuff, rehearsed 'Stand By Your Man', got a lime green fluorescent catsuit, a big blonde wig, padded her bra right out and got this friend to act as her manager," chuckles Dave mischievously. "They arrived at the party and acted out this part the whole time, for four hours, speaking in a southern drawl, then they just left afterwards. No one had any idea who she was but I was crying with laughter."

The fact that the most celebrated pop duo of the year were ex-lovers proved a popular media slant, and both Dave and Annie revelled in expounding on their remarkable ESP abilities.

"Dave and I have developed a fine sense of intuition about what we like, about what is valid. Things can be unspoken between us and still completely communicative," said Annie of their special bond, while Dave revealed they had separately bought the same record, This Mortal Coil's 'Song To The Siren', on the same day. "Our partnership . . . there's something about it," continued Annie. "You can't see it, it's an invisible thing, and I find it quite mystifying that there is this connection between us that is so powerful. People around us feel it as well. I'm always very touched by that."

While the popularity of *Sweet Dreams (Are Made Of This)* was like a runaway train, Jack Steven had to fight as hard as ever to secure backing for a promotional tour. "There was a shortfall of £70,000 for the first tour I got, and neither the A&R department nor the marketing department wanted to put that money into it," he fumes today. "So I stormed into the Managing Director's office ranting and raving, and swearing at him, 'You don't know what the fuck you're doing – you've got a genius act here and you're not even going to put them out on the road!' " The MD was outraged that a junior member of staff could accuse him in such a manner, so the resourceful A&R man offered a compromise.

"I said, 'You put the £70,000 in – if the tour works, give me a percentage of the record, if the tour doesn't work you can take my wages.' The MD just laughed and said, 'I've got to respect your audacity, you've got the money!' " But Jack's troubles did not end there. Having agreed the money with RCA, he found that Eurythmics' ex-management hadn't stopped recouping. "I received this huge bill and I thought this is far too much. I was going through it and I suddenly saw an additional 20% to the actual cost of the tour and I said to Lloyd Beiny, 'What's that for?' " Beiny was understandably trying to recoup the money he was owed through commission, while Jack was more interested in the future of Eurythmics, declaring, "We were starting from scratch, this wasn't about him earning money, it was about us working to get this going so that we all earn money."

Finally Jack managed to put together a promotional campaign for *Sweet Dreams (Are Made Of This)* consisting of performances on various television chart shows including *Top Of The Pops* and *The Tube*, and a 22-date tour of the UK, commencing on February 16, 1983 and ending at London's Lyceum one month later. It was clear that Dave alone was unable to organise the entire tour and luckily his friend John Turnbull stepped in.

"Brian Harrison lived upstairs from Kenny Smith and Sandra Turnbull. Sandra was my first wife and Kenny I knew as a friend. Brian said, 'Dave's looking for a tour manager.' So I said, 'Does he know about

Kenny?' I introduced Dave and Annie to my friends and they got on. Sandra became Annie's personal assistant, Kenny looked after Dave and the business."

Eurythmics were famous as a double act and had often performed on stage as such in the early days. However, accompanying musicians became necessary for the Sweet Dreams Tour as not only were they playing larger venues, but their audiences were also unaccustomed to seeing a duo on stage with just a portable eight-track. John suggested to Dave that fellow Blockhead, Mickey Gallagher, could augment the keyboard parts while the Eurythmic man experimented with his latest technology. Mickey was taken on board and worked closely with Dave, reconstructing the electronic aspect crucial to the Eurythmics sound.

"Dave was probably one of the first to actually use a computer live in this country," recalls Mickey fondly. "He used to have a computer on his side of the stage which would feed a pulse to my keyboard, and all I had to do was touch it and away it would go!"

Dave played guitar, keyboards and computer while Annie naturally assumed lead vocals and introduced her trusty flute. Eddi Reader, who had previously sung with Gang Of Four and later became the frontwoman of Fairground Attraction, was reinstated to shoulder the backing vocals while Clem Burke joined the touring party after the break-up of Blondie, accompanied by his girlfriend Diane. A few weeks of concentrated rehearsals at John Henry's managed to consolidate the unusual mix of musicians, and Kenny Smith was brought in as tour manager to organise the hastily cobbled together group.

Annie, not long out of her all-encompassing depression, spoke of her nervous anticipation of the tour. "I'm looking forward to it and I'm also frightened of it . . . I *have* had panic attacks on stage where I seem to leave my body, it's difficult to explain, but it's such an intensive thing and if your concentration for one moment goes . . . "

Cutting a bold image in a man's suit, in front of a backing band dressed in black, Annie had nothing to fear. Those close to her and lucky enough to witness the concerts express the aura that she exuded. "It was so powerful, the live set," says Mickey. "She was amazing with the suits and the haircut, the red hair. There was no doubt they were going to succeed."

Peter Ashworth was equally passionate about her vibes in concert. "She was already extraordinary, and just freaked people out. She just grabbed their minds and played with them and everyone would leave talking about Annie. She knew how to disorientate people on stage, to draw them to her. It was to do with the emotions she showed, which would suddenly and disconcertingly shift to a new frame of mind, and then just as likely shift back."

Alongside tracks from both albums, the set consisted of favourite covers 'You Can't Hurry Love', 'These Boots Are Made For Walking' and 'Satellite Of Love'. 'Stormy Weather' was often used as an introduction to segue into 'Sweet Dreams (Are Made Of This)'. Due to the popularity of the album's lead single, this track was usually played twice each night – once during the main set, and again as an encore. Eurythmics routinely closed with the Françoise Hardy song Dave listened to as a youth, 'Tous Les Garçons'. This was a curious number, which came across as an in-joke and did not always translate to the audience.[22]

The band put every effort into the concerts, riding high on their achievements and feeding off the tremendous audience reaction. "The show itself is very physical – I get very, very involved physically," said Annie at the time. "I only enjoy it when I can completely lose myself in it." Mickey Gallagher adds, "I think one night the computer went down and delayed the set for about 15 minutes – anything could go wrong, but Annie was such a good singer she could overcome any difficulty in terms of filling in."

Although Dave admitted, "We do feel a bit restricted at the moment in this band format, but it's the only way we could translate this album onto stage without it feeling cold," the anomalous group of musicians worked well together as a whole, despite their differing heights of fame. "While we were on the road, some magazine had 'Hunk of the Month', and it was Clem Burke," grins Mickey, "but there was no big ego with Clem at all, he was really good to work with."

Eddi Reader initially caused a little friction with Annie as it was the first time the latter had ever properly experienced another female presence with her on stage. "There was a slight bit of professional jealousy, but in the business that's healthy," Mickey continues of the two women. "It never raised its head or anything, and they sang so well together. We all parted very good friends."

The "powerful" yet "mystifying" connection within Eurythmics of which Annie had boasted was certainly sensed by others, sometimes to the point of causing problems. Mickey describes a curious moment during the UK leg of the Sweet Dreams Tour when Kenny Smith announced the logical accommodation arrangements of the two men, Dave and Mickey sharing, likewise the two women, Annie and Eddi. Meanwhile Clem and his girlfriend would have a double room and the tour manager could take a separate room.

---

[22] An original portastudio recording of 'Tous Les Garçons' was released on the 12″ version of 'It's Alright (Baby's Coming Back)' in 1985.

"There was a big silence, and Dave and Annie announced *they* were going to share a room! They weren't going out together anymore, but they wanted to. This left Kenny with a dilemma, because he couldn't put me in with Eddi. So, Dave and Annie shared, Eddi and I each had our own rooms, and it cost more."

With the bizarre sleeping arrangements finally sorted out, the touring party moved on to Scotland where Annie was able to show off her successful band to her suitably proud parents. Tom Lennox, who treated those present to some authentic bagpipe playing, simply commented to the press, "The music was wonderful and my wife and I had a really good time!"

On this part of the tour Mickey recalls a refreshing incident that illustrated how despite the press and audience hyperbole, Annie had retained her natural down-to-earth sensibility. "When we went up to Scotland, she was known up there, especially after being on *Top Of The Pops*. Of course everywhere we went people said, 'Oh Annie, give us a song!' It was very tedious. I remember walking into one hotel – she just walked up to the bar and before anyone could say anything, she had picked up an umbrella and did this version of 'April Showers', walking down the bar and standing on a chair. She just silenced the lot of them! We didn't get any hassle after that."

The tour was resoundingly triumphant and as they prepared for the closing gig at London's Lyceum Ballroom, over 3,000 people turned up, many with forged tickets as the venue held less than 2,000. A post-gig party at Barnes' Old Rangoon restaurant celebrated the end of the UK part of the first 'real' Eurythmics tour.

As the duo took stock of an exhausting month they were pleased to learn that 'Sweet Dreams (Are Made Of This)' had reached platinum sales in excess of 100,000. The single had dominated the radio for months, ultimately earning Eurythmics the cover of the prestigious rock magazine, *Rolling Stone*. There was no let-up as the tour progressed to France and Belgium. It was perhaps during their brief break in London that Dave and Annie first realised their new status, as the touring arrangements changed for the European section.

"The British tour was great – we travelled and worked just like a band usually does. It was a great feeling all round, although everyone knew it was Dave and Annie's thing," explains Mickey today. "But then when we got into the European thing about half-way through it all became a bit 'them and us'. As soon as they started getting success, then physically they were separated from the band. They travelled separately on the grounds of having to do interviews and having to get up earlier than us, that sort of thing."

Whatever the excuse, the pair's absence was noted by all the musicians left to travel the tediously long journeys between gigs by coach. "We did Hamburg on March 23, and then the next gigs were Bochum, Amsterdam and Paris," says Mickey wearily. "We were on our way to Bochum when we were told, 'The gig's off – divert to Amsterdam.' We travelled all through the night on this coach and then we got to Amsterdam and Kenny, who had been flying with Dave and Annie, joined us and said that the Amsterdam and Paris gigs were also cancelled.

"We'd been travelling all night and asked him when he'd known about it. He was very vague. We said we'd go and get a few 'Zzz's in the hotel, but he said, 'I've cancelled all the hotel rooms.' I was livid! There was just one room where we could have a wash. We asked when we were going back to England and he said that we'd have to travel back with the crew to Belgium to drop the equipment off, and then stay on the coach to England. It took us three days!" To add insult to injury the band were expected to take an exceptionally long route home.

Meanwhile, Dave, Annie and Kenny jetted off to attend to business in Los Angeles. Mickey concludes, "They cancelled the gigs and they flew off to America and left the band – it was very cold and ambitious. I remember going up to see Dave in his flat after they came back, and asking if there was any chance of a cancellation fee. But he just said, 'Oh, there is no money!'"

With Kenny Smith acting as buffer for Dave and Annie, Eurythmics had largely managed to escape the wrath of the unimpressed band members and avoid the depressing and tiring road travel. An experienced manager of some 20 years, Kenny had worked with artists ranging from musicians Ringo Starr and Kraftwerk to comedian Alexei Sayle. He found that he worked well with Dave and Annie, as did Sandra, and rather than leaving after the Sweet Dreams Tour, became the permanent Eurythmics tour manager, lending a significant helping hand to the running of DNA.

With the onset of fame, sycophantic acquaintances crawl out from under the woodwork while others try to exploit the circumstances. Dave and Annie had certainly felt they had suffered these fools before, but ironically, considering the lyrics in 'Sweet Dreams (Are Made Of This)' ("Some of them want to use you/ Some of them want to be used by you"), their instant success prompted their previously dubious record company to cash in without thinking of the consequences.

Ludicrously a nameless, and subsequently jobless, RCA staff member sold the best-selling 'Sweet Dreams (Are Made Of This)' to the London-based employment agency Kelly Girl for use in a TV advertising campaign. Not only was the deal done without the knowledge or consent of Eurythmics, but the sum earned was a measly £1,000. Infuriating the duo further they found that the song was also being used as the theme for a new American big budget soap opera, *Paper Dolls*, starring Morgan Fairchild and Lloyd Bridges.

With their artistic integrity at stake Annie did not disguise her disgust with the cash-hungry record label. "I almost went into RCA and killed somebody over that," she ranted. "I put the television on and there was this ad with our music . . . we would *never* have given 'Sweet Dreams' away, even if we'd been offered a fortune. As it was, someone no longer at RCA gave our song away for £1,000 without even asking us. *We weren't even told.*" With the help of some astute lawyers, Eurythmics were eventually able to prevent further bastardisations of their work.

Legitimate offers filtered through, and Annie in particular received countless invitations to endorse products, including a financially attractive package from Vidal Sassoon worth a cool £3 million. Once again she remained true to her principles, refusing the offer saying, "I didn't want to turn myself into some kind of consumer product. Never." Her resolve was strong as she reiterated to journalist Alan Jackson, "It can be all too easy to be swept along by the offers that come along. But you have to be really careful not to end up as some horrendous caricatured version of yourself, available to whoever offers the right money. If you allow whatever element it is that people react to in you to be taken out of context, boxed and sold, it's no longer a natural organic part of yourself: it becomes just a commodity."

Turning all commercial offers down, despite the astronomical figures involved, Eurythmics found it increasingly difficult to maintain a modicum of respect for their music as their record company appeared to undermine them at every turn. Jack Steven, seemingly the only employee of RCA working *for* rather than against Eurythmics, was horrified when he inadvertently discovered the company's latest insulting ploy. "I was driving in to the office and BBC Radio 1 announced the follow-up album to *Sweet Dreams*. I slammed my car to a halt, I couldn't work it out because we hadn't recorded another album, I thought the act had stitched me up.

"Some smart aleck in the record company decided that he was going to re-issue *In The Garden* on the back of *Sweet Dreams*. So I stormed into the office and I gave him hell, because that could have ruined their career." He quickly ordered a recall of the copies that had already made it onto the shop floors, citing the potentially damaging impact such a release could have had.

★   ★   ★

With a strong team around them to save Eurythmics from further exploitation, Annie and Dave were able to concentrate on their visual stance. Now that they were commanding sell-out tours and television interviews they had to seriously address their common image.

Dave latched on to the label he had adopted as a kind of mad professor and elevated it beyond all recognisable proportions. Gone were the days of his neat little goatee and relatively sedate hairstyle; instead he allowed his mousy beard to grow and developed an unruly yet stylised hairdo that was long on top with short back and sides. Still insecure about his looks, he continued to hide behind his hair, but by bleaching it blond, and taking care to leave dark roots, he was unwittingly attracting attention.

Denying any interest in visually representing the band, Dave explained, "The public image is Annie. It is like a duo but we've always made Annie the front of Eurythmics because she's a fantastic singer – great visually with herself and everything – and I have always been like this hovering-around kind of chap, a cross between a Scotch Terrier and something else, pushing buttons and twiddling knobs."

Such a statement put the onus on Annie to consider carefully the persona she projected, as she would reflect the band as a whole. It had been clear from very early on that even as a teenager she enjoyed making impressions with her clothes and experimenting with various looks. Although she would return to certain favourites, Annie Lennox could not be contained in one style.

"The only contrivance is that you have to stick to an image or you confuse the public," she complained. "I've never wanted to represent myself as one thing: more a bit of this and a bit of that. If I want to don a wig and wear a mini I don't see why not." Some critics perceived her anonymous looks as a downside, depriving Eurythmics of being coherently categorised; it was this very pigeon-holing that Annie was so keen to avoid.

"I spent two years after the demise of The Tourists coming to terms with this thing called image," she continued. "I went through the whole stage of saying, 'What am I?' The image of Annie Lennox of The Tourists was so strong and easy to pick out – I just wanted people to realise I'm not this nice, popsy, happy-go-lucky Annie, whom I *detest*. So I decided to kill her, dead!"

In stark contrast, Annie's traditionally male suits topped with a bold orange crop as seen in the video for 'Sweet Dreams (Are Made Of This)' led people to believe that she was either gay, staunchly feminist, or both. Suddenly Annie found her name synonymous with labels like 'gender bender' and 'androgynous'.

Whether this was the effect Annie had hoped for is debatable, but she ended up constantly justifying such a dramatic change of face. "When I started wearing mannish clothes on stage it was to detract from what people had come to expect from women singers, the height of which was Debbie Harry, who I loved," she said in a *Rolling Stone* interview. "But I felt I couldn't be a sex symbol. That's not me. So I tried to find a way to transcend that emphasis on sexuality. Ironically, a different kind of sexuality emerged from that. I wasn't particularly concerned with bending genders. I simply wanted to get away from wearing cutesy-pie miniskirts and tacky cutaway push-ups."

In numerous interviews over the years Annie has blurred the lines of what she tried to achieve, sometimes aiming for neutrality, at other times wanting to make a stand against an archaic masculine view that is intimidated by a strong woman. "In a funny way being neither male nor female widens your scope," she elaborated.

"Unfortunately a lot of people, men particularly, only see the 'tits and ass' aspect, and that is limiting," she continued to *Boston Rock*. "So I play down the female role on stage, but in a way I feel it allows my sexuality to come out even more. By not fulfilling those expectations, by not coming on in a sexy dress or whatever, I feel that I can actually make a stand. I am very feminine . . . Sometimes I appear totally as a man, sometimes I appear as the ultimate macho idea of a female object. There's always a touch of irony in everything we portray."

As the shockingly asexual outfit turned out to be a passing phase, Annie was disappointed to learn that the classification-crazy media struggled with a constantly metamorphosing band. Eurythmics had to reiterate their joint image policy; "When we started Eurythmics Dave and I wanted to represent ourselves in a visually intelligent way, not by some cliché that would limit us for years. We wanted to give ourselves longevity by making sure we were allowed to change."

The most effective medium for individual expression was in videos. Here Dave and Annie had clearly made a mark, causing quite a stir with each video thus far. The pair both dreamed up the unusual plot lines, while inspiration for character ideas was often found by simply rummaging through the stock of costume retailers; favourite stores included Contemporary Wardrobe, Robe Noir and Chimes of Big Ben, all in Covent Garden.

Aside from videos, many of the child-like dressing-up capers occurred in front of a traditional camera, and Annie relied heavily on the two photographers with whom she felt comfortable, Joe Bangay and Peter Ashworth. "I don't think she wanted to reveal herself half the time," ponders Joe. "That's why she wore those costumes. She's a very private person. But I think she'd go to the limit, take all her clothes off if it were appropriate. She's very professional about photography and once we got the idea she'd do it to her best ability, always."

With her boyfriend Peter, Annie was able to relax and express her emotions through her choice of outfits and poses. "We had Annie exploring different areas; she was wearing wigs, she was wearing rubber catsuits," says Peter today. One session went a little too far. "She was looking melancholy. I did make her look really darkly depressed on one picture, which freaked her out actually. We had a raging argument on that shoot, I think she vowed never to be photographed by me again! We did about five or six photoshoots, and all of them produced powerful pictures."

The fact that Peter was able to delve deep into Annie's psyche to accurately portray one of her truest emotions obviously scared her, as she has since argued a case in favour of less-than-flattering pictures: "Although I'm terribly vain, I'm not afraid of looking unattractive. I want to set new limits on what women in the music industry are allowed to do. I can look beautiful or dreadful, and like to play with those two extremes."

Annie recognised the power of her adaptable looks early on. With the brief of creating a lasting impression she let her imagination run wild. "I'm just amazed by the power of make-up and costume," she marvelled. "I see image as a wrapping. Why not? It's something to play with, people take it far too seriously." With such a striking haircut, wigs were one of the most effective ways of altering her look, although as much as Annie enjoyed the idea, they did cause overheating and headaches. With regard to her own hair, Annie commented, "I love it short. There's something very sensual about running your fingers through short hair."

According to future stylist Barry Maguire, Annie's orange crop was just as difficult to maintain as Dave's unbridled mop. "The thing with short hair is that it's harder to cut, because if you make a mistake it shows. A lot of photographs were close-up so it had to be right. She mastered the colour herself brilliantly. We'd bleach it and she'd bung on a colour, and then I'd cut it.

"Dave's hair was a nightmare. But we had a lot of fun with that. We did mad things, like punk stuff sticking out all over the place, big teddy boy quiffs, slicked back Elvis-style, depending on what mood he was in. One night he said let's do some Indian make-up with a star on his forehead."

★   ★   ★

In April 1983 RCA cashed in on the phenomenal success of Eurythmics both sides of the Atlantic by re-releasing 'Love Is A Stranger'. This time their gamble paid off and the single reached number six in the UK and a respectable 23 in the US, easily achieving gold sales.

This was the year when the duo could do no wrong. Interviewed that month, Annie may have been trying to keep her feet on the ground, but she risked sounding blasé: "I take chart success with a very big pinch of salt now. I think that the public now values the pop performer to the standard of his latest record. That's how it should be. It should be profound but disposable. It really excites me."

It was in the US in particular that Annie's face was at last being recognised. The American public could not fail to notice that one third of the American *Billboard* singles and album charts was occupied by British acts. *Newsweek* was among the first US magazines to identify this trend and devoted an issue to lauding the major British pop invasion, making a feature of Annie's androgynous appeal, alongside fellow import and gender bender, Boy George.

Such a prominent article stoked the fire on the already heated debate about whether Annie had undergone a sex change operation. Dave remembers the serious implications of wild speculation: "The American government demanded to see Annie's passport to prove she was a girl before she was allowed in the country."

"I think the papers wanted me to be the equivalent of Boy George," sighed Annie at the time. "That's wishful thinking, I don't fit that bill. If you have any intelligence you need to find a balance between acknowledging your sexuality and not conforming to a stereotype." Boy George was immensely popular with Culture Club's latest hit, 'Karma Chameleon', and recalled the bizarre events in his autobiography *Take It Like A Man*. "The day of the *Newsweek* photoshoot I heard Annie Lennox telling make-up artist Lynne Eastern not to make her look like Boy George. Annie was my female counterpart, the tomboy to my tomgirl. I enjoyed the irony of being photographed with her. I was the fan made good, even if she didn't want Boy George eyebrows."

Image boundaries had been continually tested by artists from David Bowie and Grace Jones to Alison Moyet and Marilyn. Consequently Annie received numerous comparisons and she was often quoted joking, "I think it's funny – they call me an albino Grace Jones; some say I look like David Bowie 'cos of the red hair . . . recently I've been compared to Brian Eno."

"My personal style is not ripping off Grace Jones at all, that would be far too simple, it's more complicated than that," Annie expounded. "She's an entertainer in her own right and she's incredible, but don't forget that she was a product of Jean-Paul Goude's imagination, whereas I've just taken the liberty of wearing more masculine clothes. It's more of a visual joke. Something taken to an absolute conclusion."

★　　★　　★

"Eurythmics is not a 'group' in the usual sense. Our partnership is the creative nucleus around which a variety of people will become involved depending mainly on compatibility and availability," said Annie of the unique relationship between herself, Dave and the other musicians involved in touring and recording. The pair were careful not to enlist any permanent players as they feared internal problems similar to those experienced within The Tourists. Unsurprisingly then, none of the band members on the Sweet Dreams Tour was present for a gig at London's Heaven nightclub in spring 1983, which was to be filmed by MTV.

Rapidly recruiting a new band, Dave and Annie replaced Mickey Gallagher with Vic Martin on keyboards, Clem Burke with Pete Phipps on drums and Eddi Reader with a trio of female backing singers, The Croquettes. They also took advantage of the change in line-up and added a bassist by the name of Dean Garcia. "I just went to an audition – they were after a drummer, not really a bass player," recalls Dean of his lucky break. "I think they were interested to hear bass, but they didn't really want it. I knew their manager, Kenny Smith, quite well through John Turnbull and he said, 'Just go in there and play.' So we did and it was great."

Unfortunately RCA had organised the concert and put Eurythmics under so much pressure that they ended up performing without any rehearsals. "It was the first time we'd ever played live with that line-up," says Dave. "We were almost forced into doing it. They said they wanted something for MTV. The band had been together for four days. Some of them had never been on stage before – and Annie had laryngitis."

Not the most auspicious circumstances in which to film a concert to impress America's largest pop medium, but despite the problems, Dean remembers the night fondly. "It was a bit of a mess, but a nice mess. It was quite exciting, we had a really good laugh as well. Annie holds it together anyway," he sums up, confirming Mickey Gallagher's observation that whatever happens, Annie exudes such cool confidence, taking any problems in her stride.

"I just made a beeline for Dave really," Dean continues. "I felt he understood because he was doing similar things, similar approaches to what I was doing, working on little eight-tracks and messing about. Annie was scary, because she was so brilliant. She doesn't mean to be intimidating. It was an odd sort of friendship, but really friendly, really warm."

The situation at Heaven was not repairable; the band were unrehearsed, Annie was hoarse and the filming and lighting weren't exactly going according to plan. "There was definitely a stress about it. With their success they could be a bit more choosy, so they wanted things to be done exactly the way they wanted them," expands Dean. "Certain things weren't done properly; the sound was a bit weird, the lights were a bit iffy, the way it was recorded. It was just technical stuff that they weren't happy with but they wanted to do it all themselves, so if things didn't look like Eurythmics, then that wasn't good enough."

Control of all aspects of Eurythmics' output was paramount to Dave and Annie, which not only manifested itself in their administration, but in running their own studios. With the success of *Sweet Dreams (Are Made Of This)* the pair had outgrown the tiny attic in Chalk Farm and were looking for something larger to house an office along with a well-equipped studio. Dave explains the problems they faced, "I was manager of the band, as well as writing the music and everything. My flat was knee-deep in files and papers, and every morning I'd wake up to phone calls and bike messengers banging on my door. I was going spare."

The answer came in the form of the right-hand side of a functioning sixteenth century church at 145H Crouch Hill, London N8, near the Haringey Arms pub. DNA was conveniently housed next door at 147. Dave maintains that The Church was one of two in England that had accommodated members of the Agapemonites, a cult popular in the 19th century advocating hippy-style free love. By the time Eurythmics saw the property in the early Eighties it was owned by two animators, Bob Bura and John Hardwick. The pair had converted much of the building's maze of rooms and corridors into studios for their film work, which had included the children's television programme *Camberwick Green*. They were finding it expensive to run and restore The Church, and so welcomed the chance to lease a portion of the building out to the two musicians.

"When they moved into The Church it was quite a shell," recalls Dean of the new venture, "just a big space. They developed it over time and put two really good studios in there." Having signed a 21-year lease on the property, Dave and Annie set about creating their ideal work space, taking full advantage of the natural acoustics on offer. They installed a 24-track studio, replete with new technology including a Lexicon delay and a harmonizer although they continued to use their two Beyer mics. Despite the upgrade in equipment Dave reassured keen music journalists that their haphazard artistic inventions had not been suppressed. "We're still banging metal bottles together," he joked. "I mean the very first thing we recorded in the place was a ukulele submixed with a Roland Juno 60. It's all in the brain, you know, not in the equipment."

The couple funded this brave step with an advance on royalties from the record company, and without a manager to subtract a fee they were able to live quite comfortably. Eurythmics remained based in The Church from 1983, continually expanding and modernising the rooms to the extent that they became one of London's premier recording studios with the latest technology. Tastefully furnished respecting the history of the building, the main studio was housed in the old chapel while the first room they acquired became a reception area. Many of the walls were lined with photographs and memorabilia reminding visitors of Eurythmics' past, including The Tourists, while Annie's harmonium occupied a coveted position alongside Dave's favoured guitars.

Although Dave boasted the financial benefits of self-management, Eurythmics had become too large a beast to handle alone. As the related branches of DNA extended, Kenny Smith teamed up with Steve Blackwell to form a company called Hyperkinetics, whose brief was to look after Eurythmics primarily, but also other acts. When DNA became the parent to sibling companies, Dave and Annie's stature within the operation grew, leaving some members of staff feeling mistreated. "It wasn't real," voiced one anonymous technician. "They had a feudal system, like something out of the Middle Ages – they were the King and Queen and you were the serfs." Of course to the fastidious duo they were merely taking pride in their work.

While Dave and Annie preferred to oversee everything, they increasingly had to rely on extra staff as Kenny as tour manager and Sandra Turnbull as Annie's PA were not sufficient. DNA recruited Karen Ciccone in July 1983, initially to run the fan club, but she took over the office administration when a previous employee, Mary-Ann Ellis, left suddenly.

The history of the fan club strengthened the incestuous relationships within the 'Eurythmic family' as it was originally organised by Dinah Marmery, the girlfriend of Dave's brother John, before being handed over to Karen when Dinah fell pregnant. The club offered the traditional activities of a regular newsletter, *Edition*, which included titbits from the stars as well as competitions, tour dates, and items for sale. Two years later, at the height of Eurythmics' popularity, Kim Hilton was seconded to help process the membership applications and merchandising sales. By late 1985 the club had expanded so drastically that the three divisions, International, British and American were brought together under one roof on Sunset Boulevard, Los Angeles, run by no less than Pam Wilkinson, Dave's first wife.

"Pam was always really behind Dave in the music and still thought that he was really talented," explains Barry Dransfield of the unusual set-up. "I think Dave kind of rewarded her with the job of running the fan club."

John Turnbull understood the continuing association. "She was very nice, easy-going, you know, like your sister or something. And she was around like a friend. I got on well with my ex-wife Sandra, and Dave got on well with Pam." Pam was approachable and friendly, enthusiastically running the club from this base for five years.

Annie and Dave used the independence gained by delegating the paperwork to branch out artistically with their new studios, inviting professional friends to use their facilities. They also took on an additional manager in America, Gary Kurfist, whose previous experience involved working with Talking Heads and The B-52's.

Realising the importance of keeping in touch with their fans, whatever age they may be, in June 1983 Eurythmics rather sweetly entertained the teenage magazine *Smash Hits* with tales of their daring decorative escapades. Recently both had moved into separate apartments near to The Church, so that they could be as close as possible to their work. With journalist Johnny Black they laughed and joked how Annie had just painted her room bright pink with little white clouds, while Dave had "rebelled" by painting his entire room black. "When life gets a bit too squiffy I go in the black room and chant Hare Krishna backwards," he announced solemnly, while Annie voiced the aside, "I was worried about him then. Thought it was a bit psychologically doubtful." Within the same interview, it was revealed to the delight of their young following that Eurythmics were so busy thinking about the follow-up to *Sweet Dreams (Are Made Of This)* that they had been forced to turn down the exciting offer of performing on the British dates of the upcoming David Bowie tour.

★   ★   ★

With no definite concerts plans, fans were pacified by the emergence of a new single. On July 8, 1983 Eurythmics released 'Who's That Girl?' It entered the UK charts the following day.

'Who's That Girl?' soon became acknowledged as another early Eurythmics masterpiece, and deservedly so. Almost entirely synthesiser-based, the introduction comprised a pseudo-symphonic-sounding but purely electronic string section twinned with a spiky synth, which plays the epic melody line introduction. Annie enters, smooth, seductive and in some twisted form of love.

As she later admitted to Q magazine, "With 'Who's That Girl?' I was rather desperately in love at the time, and a lot of my songs were about unrequited love. At the time the songs meant only one thing to me, but at different times came to mean different things. Songs are quite organic."

The tempo is slow, taking its time during the poetically phrased verses, but then the beats double as our broken-hearted heroine asserts herself with the fear that's been playing on her mind, "But there's just one thing . . ." The questioning chorus of "Who's that girl, running around with you" then adopts a military precision, with Annie yearning and plaintive against an enforced march. Even the ending is inspired with a fuzzy guitar effect pressed on and off over the fade-out. The beauty and brilliance in this track lies in its simplicity – nothing, but nothing is wasted.

This was clearly a most personal piece, and Eurythmics took full advantage of the potential role-playing behind the lyrics. "Everything had sparks coming out of it," Dave later reminisced to Chrissy Iley. "The lyrics were moving out of doom and gloom, and this was when we started to be very tongue-in-cheek about ourselves. We became a total parody of a couple. We played it to the hilt. I'd be the mad professor and Annie the manipulator."

The parody continued with the making of the accompanying promo video. Dave wrote the script, and Chris Ashbrook returned as director. The plot was simple: Annie plays a beautiful club artiste, singing of the torment of lost love. In walks her real-life ex-boyfriend, accompanied by a succession of beautiful new girlfriends, each and every one a celebrity. They are photographed leaving the club by a member of the paparazzi, played by one Joe Bangay. The continual taunting gradually becomes too much for Annie to bear, and she spots a lone man in the audience who is obviously attracted to her. Cutting short her performance in an angry tirade, she meets up with her admirer and kisses him full on the lips.

The twist was that Annie played not just the wronged singer, but also the man who embraces her. Once again she was blurring sexual boundaries, proving to the world that gender wasn't always instantly recognisable.

"I wanted to see if I could get rid of the woman completely, but for other reasons endorsed it as well," she intriguingly told the press. "I knew it would cause a few more raised eyebrows, there's something so subversive about it that I really enjoy. To think of someone kissing their ideal projection of what a man should be but to come back on themselves – to also *be* that man, it was great. Also the press are always saying how masculine I am so I thought I'd take it to its logical conclusion."

As Annie threw herself into her performance while shooting the video, those around her questioned just how seriously she was taking the whole issue. She later admitted, "Dressing up as a man wasn't enough – I had to *be* a man." Said Joe: "She really got into it. She became the man completely on set. She had all the vibes of a male attire and you felt very uneasy about it." Dressed in slightly dated men's clothing, adopting a certain stance and displaying a plausible five o'clock shadow with the aid of the make-up department, Annie certainly looked the part. She was only too pleased to confuse her audience further by sharing a supposed intimate moment, choreographed by Chris Ashbrook.

"I shot it by filming a locked-off shot in a camera, where the centre of the frame cuts down the centre of the picture. I got her to walk towards the camera, dressed as a guy. And then I got her to dress up as a girl and do the same thing, and never moved the camera . . . she leant in towards herself and pretended to kiss somebody, then she did the same the other way round." Chris proceeded to animate the gender-bending picture as if it was a cartoon, and video history was made. Annie's male character also appeared on the single sleeve; an Elvis Presley look-a-like with a Fifties haircut, thick eyebrows, sideburns and the stubble.

Annie dressed as a woman was almost, but not quite, an anti-climax in comparison. In her female incarnation, she wore a long blonde wig, delicate baby doll dress and enormous false eyelashes – herself semi-bordering on the drag queen 'look'. But as friend Barry Maguire later revealed, "She really hated that whole groupie thing. Those girls were so transparent. Her whole thing about dressing up was portraying these characters."

And what of Dave, flaunting his procession of ladies in front of his ex-girlfriend? By the time of shooting, Eurythmics were an immensely popular and integral part of the UK pop music scene, and it took very little persuasion to tempt a file of famous female vocalists to appear on his arm. The luscious line-up included Jay Aston and Cheryl Baker from Bucks Fizz, Keren Woodward, Sarah Dallin and Siobhan Fahey from Bananarama, Kate Garner from Haysi Fantayzee, Kiki Dee and Hazel O'Connor, as well as Debbie Harry and Meryl Streep look-a-likes. In an amusing nod to Annie's own gender confusion, Dave's girlfriends also included a small cameo by Marilyn, a notorious transvestite and friendly rival of Boy George.

The uncomfortable truth was that there *was* an element of reality behind Dave's screenplay of parading a string of famous ladies under Annie's nose. "He did tend to flaunt women in front of her," comments Joe. "In 'Who's That Girl?' he played himself – he just flooded it with women. Annie brought her boyfriend Peter Ashworth down, to get her own back . . . She'd got Ashworth on the set with her that day so Dave was popping off to drink with the girls and Annie was popping back to see the photographer in her dressing room . . . He was into quirky photography, he got her going in that direction. He was the flavour of the month for two or three years, as a contriving sort of photographer, into weird shots, and Annie liked it."

The strange thing about Dave is that somehow he managed to remain friendly with all the women in his life, even after they split from him romantically. He attributes his bohemian ways mainly to his mother, Sadie, who after leaving his father moved to London, became a writer and married a French Zen Buddhist, Julian Masseron. Despite the marital uprooting, in 1985 Dave described how she, her husband and her ex-husband would all go on holiday together, like one big happy family. To a certain extent, Dave continued this forgiving and forgetting theme by mixing and matching Annie Lennox with his own ex-wife, Pam, for fan club activities, and later Annie became firm friends with his future wife Siobhan Fahey, the Bananarama starlet he first encountered on the set of the 'Who's That Girl?' video. As already demonstrated with the inter-linking Kenny Smith/Sandra Turnbull/John Turnbull/Annie Lennox/Dave Stewart/Pam Wilkinson and Barry Dransfield relationships, the Eurythmic wheel did not just retain exceedingly close family ties, it was almost befitting a soap opera.

Dave's step-father Julian provided the main contribution to one of the B-sides for 'Who's That Girl?', 'ABC Freeform'. Described by Dave as "very calm and peaceful," he arrived at The Church one night to perform some Zen Buddhist readings, but after consuming quite a large amount of wine, ended up repeating the alphabet instead!

Needless to say, 'ABC Freeform' holds no great secrets. Julian recites the alphabet twice in French in various rhythms over a backdrop of wheezing harmonium arpeggios, a heavily reverbed flute and a pulse resembling a heartbeat. The applause at the end is from a tape Dave had made at the Royal Albert Hall. However, this wasn't the only weird and wonderful B-side attached to 'Who's That Girl?' The imaginatively titled 'You Take Some Lentils And You Take Some Rice' is a bizarre mixture of electronic squeals and dissonant tones placed together seemingly randomly against a very basic beat. Over the top floats a disembodied voice (origin unknown) reciting a rambling anecdote about plates made of leaves and an intriguing recipe of carbohydrates!

The single was an instant success, going straight to number three in the UK charts and rapidly achieving gold sales. To promote the release, Eurythmics launched themselves on a mini-tour of seaside towns, given the joke nickname of the 'Kiss Me Quick Tour' in reference to Annie's onscreen clinch with herself in the 'Who's That Girl?' video. The tour had the double objective of publicity alongside preparation for an upcoming trip across America, where Eurythmics hoped to storm into the charts in the same fashion as they had at home. The same line-up accompanied the two protagonists as for the Heaven concert filmed by MTV the previous spring; The Croquettes, Vic Martin on keyboards, Pete Phipps on drums and Dean Garcia on bass.

Although the tour was widely regarded as a lightweight rehearsal for greater things, as they travelled through the British coastal resorts of

Southend, Great Yarmouth, Scarborough, Southport, Margate and Poole, the latest adopted Eurythmics band began to appreciate the ex-lovers' professionalism. "Couples in groups can lead to fraught situations," said Vic Martin, "but Dave and Annie were unusual in that they could work so happily together, there were no weird dramas. They were more like brother and sister."

However, from the outset it was made clear to the band that there were certain boundaries not to be crossed with this particular 'family' team. "There seemed to be a divide," recalls Dean Garcia. "Dave and Annie were there, but they always travelled separately, and as well as possible. When you work with people who do that it causes an odd kind of tension between the people who aren't travelling with them and certain people get all cynical and twisted." A short while into the tour the extra members began to feel a slight resentment to being kept apart, and subtly treated as "lesser musicians". Whispered complaints began to increase in volume, and although there was little they could do, an air of quiet mutiny was introduced into the proceedings.

"It was all quite riddled with that really," Dean continues. "I didn't really like that much and I made it quite apparent. It didn't matter to me about how much we were being paid, where we were staying and how we were travelling. I was just really happy to do it, because I really liked what they were doing and I thought they were brilliant. The others were more seasoned, but I was into it for other reasons." Spurred on by their perceived feelings of inferiority, an element of the musicians and accompanying crew began to play up.

"It was the first tour I had done like that, so I became exposed to antics on the road," says Dean. "There was stuff that was going on that was really a bit stupid – dumb behaviour. I kind of shied away from it and wasn't really interested. You know, swinging on chandeliers in the hotel and smashing up things." While it seemed that Eurythmics kept themselves apart from this childish behaviour, it was certainly noticed in the upper echelons of power. "There is something about the rock'n'roll tribe that is quite ludicrous to me," Annie later commented. "The men are like pigs in muck when they get together. When they started doing the lads thing I had to go to my room. It drove me slightly mad."

Despite the turbulent undercurrent, Kiss Me Quick was a successful tour, with a brief set of around 50 minutes in length comprising material from both *In The Garden* and *Sweet Dreams (Are Made Of This)*. Already it was apparent that Dave and Annie's compositional techniques had progressed enormously since the concert at Heaven where the backing group had first convened.

179

"The harder stuff was the electronic stuff at the time, because you were dealing with the technology that was available to you," Dean remembers. "You'd work your way round it and do things differently. They would incorporate it. It wouldn't be playing to a sequencer, you would just have to make your own pulses by generating the sounds on stage, so sometimes I wouldn't be playing bass, I'd play bass synth, pulsey stuff like that so it felt right. And sometimes Dave would have a little drumbeat turning over. You try to keep true to the sounds. Their sound was quite precise, quite arty, it was the sounds they were combining that were really interesting. And so you have to retain those to sound like Eurythmics."

The Croquettes had by now evolved into quite a stylish set of backing vocalists. Hand-picked by Annie, the group consisted of Maggie Ryder, Suzy O'List and Gill Donovan. Annie had become firm friends with fashion designer Jeff Banks, who had taught her the Buddhist mantra *Nam-myoho-renge-kyo* in order to calm her nerves before a show. Since this unique introduction, Banks had provided Annie with her striking stage suits, and was now employed to find an effective antidote to her masculine image for The Croquettes. The girls wore a feminine combination of matching black 'china crop' wigs and Forties-inspired evening gowns, emitting a cool but classic vibe.

Nevertheless, Annie's trademark male clothing and extreme haircut stood out even more against the other females on the tour. Around this time she and Dave decided to take on their own full-time stylist to carefully maintain their image while they were away from home. Said stylist, Barry Maguire, was then just 17 and lived in a children's home.

"A friend of mine had a local band, Virgin Dance, who were 'in' then. I used to do a bit of hairdressing for them and they got the chance to support Eurythmics on a British tour, and they wanted me to go with them to do their wardrobe to make sure they looked great for Eurythmics." Barry struck up a close friendship with the more famous band, and soon he found himself working directly for Dave and Annie. It took him a while to completely relax in their presence, for obvious reasons: "On that first tour I'd be pottering around backstage and minutes before they were due on stage, you'd suddenly see this amazing woman appear with bright red hair, with this black and white checked man's suit on, red leather gloves and a flute in her hand – looking really intimidating. She'd always be psyching herself up to go on stage, and she'd have her head down, pacing and pacing. Not talking to anyone, just pacing around. Quite masculine really, quite frightening – just getting into character I guess."

Soon enough, the youngest recruit was accepted as one of the team and began to help out in any way he could with all aspects of hair, clothing and make-up for the band. "Annie's really great at that kind of thing," he says today. "You could knock at the door and she would turn up with the most bizarre outfit on. But I think it's just part of her slightly eccentric character. The image was a combination of both their ideas. The suits and the androgyny was a juxtaposition, the music had a certain sound that was new and fresh, it contradicted itself, and they made a conscious decision to do the same thing visually.

"The male look for her was clean-edged and cold, and her vocals were quite monotone, brilliant, but cold and hard. Jeff Banks at the time was a very creative person and Annie and Jeff would spend a lot of time sitting down together chatting about ideas.

"The sound was quite quirky and weird and you'd look at Dave with this weird professor thing going on. I would have ideas for looks for Dave; hair ideas, just putting clothes together differently for photo sessions and stuff. But to be honest they always seemed to be there, between the two of them everything would get done."

But the Banks/Eurythmics-inspired costumes were not to everyone's taste. "It was the dubious styling period!" laughs Dean Garcia, who was himself initially invited to take part in the band's dressing-up sessions. "They had set ideas and wanted funny braces and that kind of thing. It was one thing I did actually make a fuss about. It moved on to, 'Wear what you want.' But they always liked people in costumes."

Despite the negative aspect of having a detached couple in control of everyone else, the overall opinion of this short tour seems to be that it was an enjoyable run-up to what was to follow. As Annie summarised in *Eurythmics Melody Maker Starfile*, "It was fun – like taking a deep breath before America."

14

MONEY CAN'T BUY IT

"It's kind of fiery . . . because we lived together. It's like writing songs with your ex-wife."

– DS

In August 1983 the Eurythmic bandwagon travelled on to play a series of European festivals, culminating in an open-air gig entitled 'A Day At The Races' at Dublin's Phoenix Park, Ireland. They were there to support local heroes U2, along with Simple Minds, Peter Gabriel and Van Morrison on August 14. The night before, Annie expressed her apprehension about playing in front of a 20,000-strong crowd to a *Smash Hits* interviewer, then later chose to stay alone in her hotel room rather than go out and party with the rest of the rock stars.

Her nerves were well-founded. Appearing on stage dressed in a white suit and displaying a face painted with a *Blade Runner*-esque red stripe (remarkably similar to Peter Gabriel's current onstage garb), Annie was greeted with firecrackers, flying bottles and shouts of "British bastards! Fuck off!" Although the crowd's heckling was more to do with their nationalistic leanings rather than any dislike of Eurythmics' music or Annie herself (although one reviewer did note that she appeared "tigerish"), it was enough to reduce the singer to tears.

"Remember that we're all human beings," she pleaded to a backdrop of jeers. "I'm doing this because I believe in human spirit, in positive thinking . . . It's hot and people have hot temperaments. Be kind to each other. I can't play to faces full of hatred." As their set commenced the abuse continued from a small contingent towards the front of the crowd. Without hesitation, the distraught singer halted the music and, in her usually soft Scottish accent, proceeded to give as good as she got. There was a stunned silence before the audience erupted into scattered applause, then all-out cheering. Dave cried, "Let's play!" and the show went on.

"It was the best concert I ever went to in my life," says Joe Bangay, who was in the thick of the unpleasantness, acting as official photographer.

"She stayed on stage and gave them a mouthful; 'You fucking idiots!' I never heard her swear so much, before or after that concert. It was the U2 fans wanting their band to come on, basically." In a gesture of support for her bravado, Annie was later coaxed back on stage by U2's own frontman, Bono, and the two duetted on the song '40'.

Like the others, Dean Garcia, playing bass for this event, was blown over by her bravery. "There were these scuffles going on – Nazi paraphernalia, bad kind of shit – just a small group of people in the front. But she fronted them out because she wanted to express, 'Stop everything, you are wrong.' I think they were outed in a way and then she carried on. Annie's the sort of person that if she's not happy with something, she'll make it known."

Annie continued to make her feelings known about the upset in Ireland long after the event. She expressed in an interview that October, "What happened in Dublin I cannot allow. When you're trying to make music it's futile to be faced with blank hatred." More specifically, she launched an attack against a Dublin newspaper which had unkindly suggested the Scotswoman was simply "temperamental", responding with a scathing letter:

"I was so disappointed to read your report of our recent appearance at Phoenix Park. I did not stop the show because 'someone threw something at the stage.' I stopped it because a small minority of people at the front were agitating the audience by fighting, pushing and throwing bottles and cans onto the stage. A very dangerous situation was close to eruption with young people being trampled underfoot and tempers being lost in the sun. Thanks for nothing – you failed to spot the *real* reason why I put a stop to a potential riot. Maybe you were in the bar at the time."

Partly due to her unique appearance and powerfully feminist image, over the years Annie has often had to deal with other stage threats, thankfully less violent. "Quite often I've had something like a girl at the front staring me out, curling her lip and sneering," she said to *The Face* in 1983. "It's a way of taking attention away from the entire audience and turning it onto them, a perversion of the proceedings. If that happens I go and whisper in their ear and ask them to leave. I used to shout but that's a mistake. There's something about a quiet power which is stronger than losing your temper." Annie in fact possessed quite a temper that was to rear its ugly head in the near future, but for now was perfectly reasonable in the way she dealt with such objectionable situations.

A fortnight later Eurythmics arrived in America. *Sweet Dreams (Are Made Of This)* was becoming so well known worldwide that the band were required to promote their music personally. Their first concert took place at the Kibuki Theater in San Francisco on August 21, and from there they travelled to two different venues in Los Angeles; the Magic Mountain and The Palace.

Following their recent performing experiences, whether good or bad, the band had progressed to a powerfully sophisticated standard, with a more refined sound for the selection of songs from their first two albums. In particular, 'Never Gonna Cry Again' and 'Take Me To Your Heart' had been transformed into soulful masterpieces, far superior to their vinyl versions. Several recordings of the concerts were made and later certain tracks were released on record as B-sides and promos.

Although normally the ultimate professional, Annie's Irish encounter had instilled in her a desire for all stage operations to run smoothly, without a hitch. One member of the crew witnessed a fiery outburst from the hardened redhead. "We were on at The Palace in Los Angeles and Dave often had a little portastudio sometimes there with him. The tape recorder came in in a funny place and made Annie sound silly, like everything was on tape. It was only a cueing thing from the monitor manager, but she was very angry and went over to give him a piece of her mind."

Such an abnormal spurt of violence was repeated once again this month, this time with fantastic consequences. Late one night Annie and Dave were hanging out in their room at the Mayflower Hotel in New York, and dark clouds began to descend over Central Park. Perhaps sensing the tension in the air, as Annie stared out of the window watching enormous raindrops trailing patterns down the pane, the couple began to scrap.

"After the excitement of becoming massive all over the world, we had to readjust," Dave explains. "We were having this terrible row, and I was sulking and I just started playing this tune on a little Casio keyboard. It's funny, 'cos if we have a row and something's happening like that Annie immediately goes, 'Let me play that,' then she starts playing it, then I start fighting for the keyboard . . ."

Physically struggling over the miniature keyboard, the two fell onto the floor in an angry tangle of hair and fists. Winning the battle, Dave triumphantly began to tap out some notes while Annie skulked back over to the window. Without turning to face her ex-lover, she began to sing the line, "Here comes the rain again, falling on my head like a memory . . ."

"In the end this song came out of it," continues Dave of the resulting composition, 'Here Comes The Rain Again'. "It's one of my favourites, but it can be born out of such a stupid thing . . . you're arguing and suddenly it turns into something really beautiful." Later he and Annie were to take their ideas back to The Church and add the chorus, "Talk to me like lovers do" while experimenting with odd whistling noises and different rhythms. After a lot of work they came up with one of the most exemplary examples of early Eighties pop music.

For a while they toyed with the idea of offering the song to ex-Led Zeppelin lead singer Robert Plant, but fortunately recognised the track's importance; in Dave's words, it set a "turning point" in their career. Along with the brilliantly successful 'Who's That Girl?' it was to herald their third studio album.

The strange, compulsive relationship between the two songwriters added a certain piquancy to all their work, not just those tracks first ignited by the passion of a quarrel (of which there are many). Dave readily admits, "It's kind of fiery . . . because we lived together. It's like writing songs with your ex-wife. But underneath it all we're much stronger, so the argument will never last more than 10 minutes, whereas before it would last three hours. We don't actually get on each other's nerves as people, but we fall out over artistic things. We're both quite headstrong and sometimes we go in different directions." Said Annie at the time, "Being together 24 hours a day can be a bit of a strain, especially when you're both under a lot of pressure . . . Admittedly we spend a fair bit of time shouting and screaming at each other, but we are able to laugh about it about five minutes later. We just clear the air with a blazing row and get on with the music. We've built up a good understanding and our relationship with each other is a very personal thing."

In autumn 1983 there was simply no time for being anything but a united front. Dave and Annie were truly at the top of the mountain as, on the back of their US performances, the single 'Sweet Dreams (Are Made Of This)' smashed straight into the *Billboard* chart at number one on September 3. It stayed there for just one week, but continued to sell in droves, eventually chalking up sales of over a million.

★   ★   ★

Back in England in October, a party was held at The Church to celebrate the presentation of a silver disc for the success of 'Who's That Girl?' in the UK. As recording commenced that month on Eurythmics' next album, the effects of intensifying fame began to tell on the group's main man and woman.

Celebrity sat more comfortably with Dave than it did with Annie. "It opened major doors for both of them, especially for Dave, being the kind of character he is, to these people who he was fascinated and inspired by – artists, musicians, producers, everybody," says Dean Garcia. "Suddenly everybody wants to work with you. It probably did affect the way they worked together."

Harmonica player Judd Lander well remembers going out to dinner with the guitarist and being astonished at his down-to-earth approach. "We were in the restaurant and he told me about the day he got a royalty cheque in for about a million. He just looked at it and kept looking at it, and he said, 'I didn't put it in the bank for weeks, I just kept looking at it in disbelief.' I thought that was sweet, I thought, 'Here's a guy who realises his roots.'"

While it was easy for Dave to retain some semblance of genuineness, Annie found the ongoing scrutiny increasingly hard. "Success isn't always a wonderful gift. It can be a bind, honestly," she said in October to Max Bell. "On a stupid level; if I go to Habitat people wonder why I'm not in Harrods. Or if I go by bus, as happened the other day, I was surrounded by these four girls pulling my hair and ordering me: 'Go on, sing that song.' I wouldn't do that to anybody. You become public property . . . It's, 'What are *you* doing on a bus? Why aren't you in a limousine?' If I go in the pub round the corner they talk about me behind my back and if I don't, they think I'm stuck up."

In the same interview Annie divulged that she was unable to forget bad reviews of her work or performance. "I remember what was said about me in the past. I compare that with any praise we receive now and it balances me. Occasionally I go home where I have this chest full of newspaper clippings and I sit down and spread them out around me . . .

"I found this Joni Mitchell interview in *NME* where she was asked why she'd agreed to be interviewed after so many years of silence. She said: 'There are times when it's good for everyone to hate you, and times when it's good for everyone to like you. At the moment people like me.' I agree with that. I'd rather be liked at the moment. Everybody wants to be really liked, don't they?"

★   ★   ★

Although by now Eurythmics commanded great respect in all facets of the music business, Annie continued to be wary of reporters. Understandably, she was convinced that at any moment the papers could turn on her as they had during The Tourists, and with a couple of choice headlines, once again wipe out any success she and Dave had built up over years of effort. "Annie had been very spooked by the music press," recalls Peter Ashworth. "I think she had been very hurt by them because she had great abilities. Far more than most kids who just don't do anything and think they want to be in a band . . . she obviously felt superior to most.

"The trouble with coming from her academic background is that she wasn't streetwise, so to be actually savaged by London media, in other words southern English kids writing for a rag and giving her a good kicking every now and then, was something she didn't like."

For a while, Eurythmics had brandished the power to turn down interviews that were, on the face of it, intended only for their own good. One example of this occurred during the promotion for the 'Who's That Girl?' single. RCA had arranged an interview with the journalist, Jim Reid, for *Record Mirror*. When Reid arrived to do his job, Eurythmics took an instant dislike to him and sent him packing in the full knowledge that they would be portrayed badly in his paper. The reasons they cited were he was simply not "on their wavelength", and did not have anything positive to offer.

Annie's caution, although wise and sensible, led to the rather ironic aftereffect of published interviews frequently containing elements of her hatred of that very medium. "You have to learn to see that other people's motivation is sometimes very bitter and twisted," she raged in one such interview when queried on the personal effects of negative criticism. "So you have to expect it, 'cos most people *are* bitter and twisted. So now I realise, yes, people will sometimes hate me. It's paranoia that makes you try and explain everything so very carefully."

Unfortunately, Annie's self-admitted paranoia proved justified – in summer 1983, one of her closest friends seemingly 'betrayed' her trust.

"I had a call from *Life* magazine and I was asked if I'd like to write a piece about her," says Joe Bangay. Joe had come to photography late in life after an impressive career in the RAF, and was keen on developing his journalistic talents in tandem with his art. The offer was too good to resist and, he reasoned, it could only help raise Annie's public persona. "So I wrote this piece about Annie Lennox; beautiful, exciting, reluctant star. I thought it was a beautiful piece of writing. We got the cover as well."

To his horror, without any explanation, Annie immediately refused to have anything more to do with her former confidant and father figure, on the grounds that he had penned what she saw as an 'exposé'. "I had written that she was a reluctant star, that she would rather be down the supermarket, shopping. She took offence because I bared her soul," he says. It was to be two full years before they spoke again.

★   ★   ★

Annie's other major associations were also beginning to suffer under the spotlight as Eurythmics attained world domination. Peter Ashworth had been Annie's boyfriend since the photoshoot for their first album, and as they commenced work on their third, the relationship took on a new twist.

"I never really got to feel I knew her that well, in a funny sort of way," he says today. "I might have pulled back from Annie, which would have upset her. Maybe I was a bit nasty as well at times. I know I told her off . . . I don't think Annie was a bad person. I think she had chemicals running through her that put her down at times . . . You can talk yourself out of anything if you get too intellectual about it, and I think she was just too goddamn intellectual! She tried to control herself and others and life doesn't work like that. I think she wanted to be good. She wanted to be important in the world history of music. She wanted to be valid. I wanted to be valid."

During this period Annie seemed to distance herself publicly from Peter, until it got to the point that although they were spending most evenings at her flat, they would rarely be seen together as an 'item'. "I did find it strange that I couldn't even pick her up from the studio, it was more like 'meet me back at home later'," he says. "So it did become a relationship of the night, and maybe of the weekend." He was also uncertain of his new twilight role as 'unofficial chauffeur', explaining, "Annie didn't drive. She seemed to hate driving, found it a very destructive thing."

Nevertheless, Peter was Annie's only serious relationship outside of her family and the Eurythmics camp, and probably also the only intimate to whom she could confide her conflicting emotions as Eurythmics' fame grew.

"She threatened to leave Dave so many times . . . but there was nobody else she could work with." Privy more than anyone else to Annie's inner turmoil, Peter formed an opinion quite different to everyone else interviewed for this book. "I understood that *he* was clinging to *her* . . . Right at the beginning Annie said, 'Dave still has a crush on me'." In the Eurythmics circle of friends, the general consensus had been that Annie was the one clinging to Dave, not vice versa, and moreover Dave appeared to enjoy flaunting his latest sexual conquests in his ex-lover's face. Whichever way round the truth lay, Peter had no choice but to come to terms with the musicians' abnormal codependency.

Several years later Annie was quizzed on this very subject. When asked the direct question, "Isn't your history with Dave difficult on your lovers?" she replied honestly. "Definitely. It wasn't really Dave's fault, it was more my sense of loyalty to him. Invisibly he's always around. He was always my mentor. For years I probably would undermine relationships I've had because of Dave, I have to admit that."

Peter persevered at his romance with Annie, although by now his career had taken on a life of its own and he was widely regarded as *the* UK rock photographer. In spite of his escalating prominence, Annie presented an unusual request which he found quite hard to stomach. "At one point in our relationship she did say that she'd quite like it if I became her personal assistant, which I found a little bit strange, because my career was taking off." Peter declined Annie's odd appeal, realising that she was only asking because he was one of the few people she trusted with her affairs, but finding it difficult not to take offence at her somewhat patronising vision of his own life.

As for the physical side to their relationship, Peter maintains that their life together revolved more around the need for support and mutual understanding. "The sexual physicality wasn't an experimental thing to her. It was more about warmth; souls connecting. It wasn't, 'Let's try position 59!'" he laughs. Annie has always kept understandably quiet about her private life in this respect, rarely even drawing attention to it in her lyrics. Once, when queried on the matter in 1986 she proffered an intriguing tantaliser: "The really fascinating thing, I'm afraid I can't divulge. I'd run into a lot of trouble. I have lots of fascinating stories, but the terrible thing is, I'm just too cautious to divulge an awful lot of what I do."

As most couples tend to travel together in the normal course of their relationship, so Peter and Annie attempted to holiday together on various occasions. "I went on holiday with her to southern Ireland quite early on in our relationship," he recalls. "It was the most wonderful thing; she got Kenny and Sandra to book us a holiday, and boy did they book us a holiday! We flew to Dublin, drove from Dublin across to the North-West coast of southern Ireland. This hotel had salmon fishing, its own private lake, it was a massive place, really something special."

Unfortunately, as previously with Peter's trip to Italy during the Gianna Nannini recording sessions, this break ended with a sour tinge of dissatisfaction. Halfway through the trip Annie's mood shifted and for no obvious reason she returned to London one week early, leaving Peter in Dublin.

"That was the beginning of knowing that something strange was happening here. That either she didn't like being isolated with somebody, or people out of context aren't right. She was just contrary sometimes, she could be recording, want to get away and go on holiday, get there and think, 'I don't want to do this!' That's fine if you're by yourself, but if you're with someone else . . ."

In the course of his interviews for this book Peter described various incidents where Annie flew off the handle with only the slightest provocation. One such time was when he unwisely criticised a Eurythmics demo tape that she played to him back in her Camden bedsit. Another time he remembers being present during one of Neil Tennant's last interviews as assistant editor for *Smash Hits*. During their conversation, Tennant mentioned that he was quitting his job in favour of trying his hand as a pop star, in the duo Pet Shop Boys.

Peter recalls that Annie recoiled at the suggestion. Perhaps this was due partly to her hatred of music journalists, and partly because she believed 'not just anyone' could make it in the industry; her own success had only come through years of perseverance and hardship.

"What we like to do is make commercial music that is very special, so it can be commercial but also very *individual*," she stressed in no uncertain tones in the overlapping March–April 1985 edition of the magazine. "We're always looking for something really fresh. It's a bit like mining for gold but now with the idea of loot at the end of it. I'm talking in *artistic* terms."

"When you're famous," she warned Tennant, "it's a bit like having an extra leg. You can't forget about it because other people don't let you forget about it – there's always an extra thing around you." Wise words spoken in earnest, it seemed.

Gossip about the Eurythmics frontwoman speculated that, alongside Peter Ashworth, Annie was also continuing an alliance of sorts with Robert Görl, the German DAF drummer she had met at the beginning of the Eighties. Handsome, tall and blond, he seemed the perfect antidote to Dave's string of equally fair-haired conquests, and provided Annie with an ambitious yet humorous counterpoint for her troubles. When Peter confronted Annie with her rumoured affair she denied it, but their musical chemistry at least is in evidence on Görl's 1983 self-penned solo album, *Night Full Of Tension*. Recorded in darkest Surrey, the album is an amusingly intense example of mid-European pop-meets-Kraftwerk, and Görl does a passable impression of David Bowie against the overly electronic and largely stilted backing. Annie's vocals can be heard on the tracks 'Playtime', 'Charlie Cat' and 'Darling Don't Leave Me', which was released as a single and became a favourite among collectors.

15

HERE COMES THAT SINKING FEELING

"You want me to be a gender bender? Here I am."

– AL

On November 6, 1983 Eurythmics released their third album, entitled simply *Touch*. RCA proudly announced that it was the first pop LP to be simultaneously released on record and compact disc format in the US. Inconceivably Eurythmics had spent just three weeks at The Church writing, recording and mixing the music into its final form. As Dave said, "We started to write songs ridiculously quickly – like, people would go and get a sandwich and come back and we'd written a song."

Admittedly the group had already written two of the lead tracks on the album, 'Who's That Girl?' and 'Here Comes The Rain Again'. Even so, their relaxed approach to creating music so rapidly amazed all around. Dave: "Spending ages recording destroys any creative spirit. What we do is create space to be totally spontaneous – create the atmosphere, get the tape ready, and then capture it. We virtually put out great demos."

The demo idea wasn't as difficult as it sounded, as Annie and Dave surrounded themselves with the same personnel with whom they had spent the best part of the year performing, and also some respected musicians who were well-versed in working to a tight deadline. Michael Kamen, an orchestrator, conductor and composer in his own right, was the most notable addition to the team, which also consisted of Vic Martin, Dean Garcia, Pete Phipps and the eminent horn player, Dick Cuthell.

"We were working in The Church and it was exactly the same, they had a little tape recorder and were just throwing things at it, put this on and take that away," says Dean. "Their songs were very well crafted. They would write and craft them onto the tape recorder as they went. Under Captain Dave! But he'd be really loose and inspiring."

Dave's compositional method was to commence recording from the bottom up, first laying down the rhythm and a bass line, and then building in the rest of the instruments around it. Simultaneously, Annie would be working from the top end downwards, starting with lyrical snippets she had scribbled in an ever-present notebook, and using her musical training to notate chord changes for the other players.

Dave had already decided that after spending the majority of 1982 refining one album, the contents of its follow-up should be both fresh and improvisational. "The last thing we wanted to do was to make another record like *Sweet Dreams* – in fact we just forgot about that completely and went in to make a record as though we'd never made one before . . . often before, we'd found that an original demo is 100 times better than the final master, it's got that initial spontaneity."

"We did the album very quickly and even the softer tracks have got that edge," he said to Tony Jasper. "The recording of this album was a lot more like a sketchbook. We'd literally have one bass drum and Annie singing something and the whole song would build from that. We wouldn't actually write a whole song and then go and try to record it. The album's a real mixture. It's got everything from the British Philharmonic Orchestra to Annie playing a toy piano from Woolworths."

Above and beyond the recording process itself, Annie had grand ideas for the content. "What we were striving for is a cross between gut level feeling and intellect; pop music that is saying something, but is not so intellectual that you have to join a cult to understand it, something that's wonderfully functional and slithers between the extremes," she expressed eloquently.

With such an exciting collection of songs, clearly striking artwork was required for the outer packaging – a design to rival Laurence Stevens' sleeve from *Sweet Dreams (Are Made Of This)*. Peter Ashworth had recently taken a series of pictures to accompany an interview with Annie published in *The Face*, which had taken full advantage of her shocking hairstyle and willingness to experiment. The shoot, which had taken place in Bagley's warehouse, had included poses with Annie in a bright pink ballet dress contrasting sharply with her orange hair, and also in a gold glitter suit and platform boots. There had been a variety of different masks available which she had seized upon and incorporated into nearly every shot. "I recognised then she was a mask person and liked to play different roles, but in a theatrical manner," Peter recalls.

The outtake chosen for the cover of *Touch* was similar to that used for *Sweet Dreams (Are Made Of This)*, in that it featured Annie naked with a black mask shielding her eyes. It was a commanding visual statement that had originally been shot against a textural background, but was such a strong image that it became more effective when placed simply against white. The main focal points were Annie flexing her muscles, as if preparing for combat, and turning her eyes to the direction of the camera in a most unnatural fashion.

"The flexing of the wrist is a purely male thing," says Peter of Annie's method of adapting her androgynous personality. "She did it very elegantly. Putting the mask on was her idea. This weird thing of rolling her eyes back was her idea.

"She's got strange eyes. She doesn't actually look straight at you; her eyes go slightly off. And somehow in photographs, that can make the picture look compelling, because you have to keep checking it again. A picture that you have to recheck is a powerful picture . . . she did a bit of 'eye popping out sideways'. She's always wanted to be a bit otherworldly . . . a little bit like Kate Bush on acid!"

The cover was a brilliant finishing touch to a fantastic set of songs, and was to become recognised as one of the most memorable images of the Eighties. The most successful aspect was Eurythmics' own visual reference, as Annie herself explained, "I'd turned the previous album picture round the other way, so the heart had gone, and it was almost like a stance of defiance."

Following the success of their second album, Annie had mentioned to an interviewer requesting details on their upcoming creative intentions that, "One of the things I want to do on the next album is to make music that is so incredibly sweet, really touching." Her aim had been far excelled with the recording of *Touch*'s opening track, 'Here Comes The Rain Again'.

The most famous pizzicato strings in pop introduce Eurythmics' follow-up to *Sweet Dreams (Are Made Of This)*. From the start they are twinned unashamedly with synthesisers, forecasting the partnership of old and new which is one of *Touch*'s best features. After such a fresh and striking introduction, it is apparent from Annie's first breath that 'Here Comes The Rain Again' is one of those songs that simply transcends pop music and stands as a great composition in any artistic field. The backing memorably exploits pretty much every pop trick in the book before Michael Kamen's inspired line-up of eight or so violins is even taken into consideration. His sublime arrangement heightens the already powerful base with a series of swoops, swirls and plucks much unheard of in the charts at the time.

Meanwhile, Annie sings a compelling tale of her desperate need for love against a gorgeous mix of strident keyboards and attractive guitar harmonics. The rain she sings of symbolises the torrent of emotion she feels, with the music darkening to depict storm clouds and a flurry of weather. The chorus encompasses elements of Sixties pop, with a cute girl group "shoo-wop" behind her telling plea of "Talk to me . . . like lovers do". She gains power towards the end, recognising a surge of pain she has felt before, "Here it comes again, here it comes again – ha!"

The second track, 'Regrets' is a million miles away stylistically – a stark, electronic contrast of major and minor keys. Annie has taken on the persona of the dangerous android of the cover photograph, a sexy androgynous robot depicting peril. Against a purposefully relaxed backing she fills the track with allusions to her perturbing violent temperament: "I've got a delicate mind/ I've got a dangerous nature/ And my fist collides/ With your furniture". The sci-fi personality is exploited to the full with further imagery of the robot as a "hungry Mohican" who has 15 senses and a "razor blade smile" – not a character you would wish to meet in a dark alley!

Behind this menacing story, attacked with such obvious relish, is a fascinating musical backdrop of multi-layered parts, again both synthetic and authentic in fairly equal portions. Throughout the spacious soundscape with its leisurely beat appear muted trumpets which pip like birds cheeping, guitar and bass solos bubbling around in the background and many rhythmic and special effects. Towards the culmination of the track, Annie begins humming which, although seductively sinister, serves only to stress the laid-back vibe. Spiky slap bass takes the foreground against the synthetic bass line and Annie's "That's right, that's right" shows the robot caught in a triumphant loop. The ending belongs to Dick Cuthell's trumpet, stealing the show with a seemingly random scat, which suits the music perfectly.

After two such mind-blowing tracks comes the carnival horror of 'Right By Your Side', a calypso mish-mash of whistles and rolling tongues, Martin Dobson's baritone saxophone, and steel drums. Undeniably bubbly, the track stands out like a sore thumb on this otherwise serious-minded album, and doesn't really suit Annie's image or indeed Eurythmics of this era. At least when Blondie chose to cover 'The Tide Is High' in 1979 they somehow injected a cool, New York vibe into a style which wasn't necessarily befitting a rough-edged punk band, but 'Right By Your Side' comes across as fake and plastic – in a nutshell, they are literally just too British to carry this off.

Lyrically, the song is rather corny as a pure celebration of love and devotion which doesn't really ring true. Annie approaches the vocal with plenty of enthusiasm but this in itself becomes rather strained during the "yeah yeah yeah" refrain. This song was mistakenly given the wrong showcase on *Touch*, but paradoxically it isn't hard to fathom just why it became a huge hit – it is accessible and easy for a non-Eurythmics fan to appreciate.

Taste and continuity thankfully reappear on 'Cool Blue', opening with a clock-like rhythm matched with guitars that accelerate before the rigorous main beat makes its debut. Annie delivers a cold and emotionless vocal workout against the fast-paced drum machine, reinstating the 'water' theme of this album which began with the precipitation of 'Here Comes The Rain Again' and has now been frozen into the ice of a broken relationship. Although impressive in its sheer, compulsive energy, 'Cool Blue' becomes a little repetitive towards the end, indulging the guitar part a little too much.

After the well-known, slow and sedate measure of 'Who's That Girl?', Eurythmics travel back to fast and furious with the confidence and aggression of 'The First Cut'. This provides Annie with an energetic springboard for some more disturbing imagery, the idea of cutting referring, as always, to Annie's broken heart. She rapturously seizes on her pain and determination to fight like a chained tigress, ready to spring. She articulates perfectly, pronouncing every 'C' and 'T' with cold precision, and her vicious exclamation of "Ha!" is repeated almost the entire length of the song. Fortunately, the depiction isn't allowed to become overblown as her caustic sense of humour makes an appearance after some particularly soulful harmonies, with the ironic quip, "I'm a white girl, you can see my skin". Musically the track is just as biting, with lots of spangly guitars interspersed with a bouncy synth line. After two sets of verses and choruses, Eurythmics are free to explore the beat, which they do with an excitable sense of adventure.

In contrast, the ponderous, lumbering groove of 'Aqua' leaves the listener with an unnerving feeling, a masterful touch due to the electronics being slightly out of tune with the acoustic guitar. The bass line is set unusually low allowing Annie the freedom to explore a large amount of melodic space, which she does at her leisure. The water theme has reappeared in its most obvious guise and Annie's "Bubble up" samples are extremely effective, as are the various electronic water effects, many backwards or flittering upwards while heightened by tinkling bell-like sounds.

Lyrically, 'Aqua' is about a closed-off personality who cannot bear to be touched or spoken to and no longer feels anything. This leads nicely into the analogous numbness of 'No Fear, No Hate, No Pain (No Broken Hearts)', which features a long ambient introduction and a similarly plodding bass line. Then, without warning, the listener is suddenly assaulted by the sheer power of the re-emergence of Annie's violent robot, whose lyrics suggest disorder with frequent reference to guns or even drugs; "cold steel", "killing gun" and "shoot it up". Somehow, beneath all this intimidating delirium lie delicate oboe and string lines, thus demonstrating the inventive genius of the best of Eurythmics' work. The two tracks are a perfect illustration of Annie's overall objective: "The thing that motivates me is to put something down that will bring out a response, that I myself have a gut reaction to, that lives and breathes on its own."

The final track on *Touch*, the equally ominous 'Paint A Rumour' features another laid-back bass line; druggy and super-cool. Annie simmers away menacingly against an electronic high counterpoint. Trumpets appear as the 'real' instruments next to the rather static keyboard chords, and the highlight is Dean Garcia's funky slap bass solo in the midst of the ambient electronics and computerised, repeating vocals.

'Paint A Rumour' is quite long and is the track that lends itself the most to future remixing. The close of *Touch* becomes fittingly even more sinister and dark as Annie's cry of "Promise not to tell" takes on a panicked, desperate edge, the swirling synthesisers shift to an Eastern tonality and the beat develops into a more clubby, chilled-out vibe. Such is the perfect ending to this most enigmatic and intriguing album, which has surely fulfilled its joint ambitions of exploring Annie's forbidding, androgynous figure, and asserting Eurythmics as a startlingly experimental group.

★ ★ ★

On its release, *Touch* shot to the top of the charts in both the UK and the US, demonstrating that the British group had truly conquered the all-important territory across the Atlantic. Dave and Annie were beside themselves – from three weeks' work they had become invincible. "I can honestly say that *Touch* contains some of the best work we've ever done," said Dave excitedly. "My favourite track is 'Here Comes The Rain Again'. I'm more drawn to actual songs than weird sounds and that's why I like singles so much, because you've only got a certain time to do everything . . . and when you get that it's like the ultimate art form for 1983."

Very few critics expressed reservations about the release, and generally agreed wholeheartedly with Dave. They praised Annie's brilliant vocals, the album's extreme versatility, its well-constructed balance of spontaneity and careful planning, and welcomed the lyrical thaw towards more vulnerable, somehow *human* emotions. *Melody Maker* in particular voted *Touch* as their Best Album Of The Year.

Of course, not everyone yielded to Eurythmics' global domination. One unfavourable reviewer, Graham K. Smith, described the album as, "A disappointment . . . perhaps I was just expecting too much. The manner in which Dave and Annie have emerged from left field experimentalism into the chart mainstream has been a joy to witness – their sublimely credible synthesis of music and visuals being one of the year's finest singles . . . *Touch* promised the world. Promised but failed to deliver."

"I felt it was rushed, in terms of creativity," says Jack Steven, who from now on was to take a back seat, gradually extricating himself from the Eurythmics hit machine. "The only thing I thought the sounds had developed with was in terms of the expense. I thought it had lost a bit of the grittiness of *Sweet Dreams*, and the juxtapositions – on the one hand there's glamour, on the other hand Annie was living in a flat with rats. I felt that *Touch* didn't have that contradiction or twist."

Overall however, it seemed that Eurythmics could do no wrong in the eyes of the public, and they set off on the Touch Tour commencing just prior to the album's release on October 31, 1983.

The ambitious tour was to last almost an entire year. Beginning in the UK, the entourage next flew to Australia and New Zealand in January 1984, then on to Europe in February, USA from March until May, and Japan throughout the rest of that month. With such a demanding schedule the tour was dubbed after the popular British sitcom, *Only Fools And Horses*. Eurythmics stalwarts The Croquettes (with Sarah Fisher replacing Maggie Ryder), Pete Phipps, Vic Martin, Dick Cuthell and Dean Garcia continued the live accompaniment.

The set list for the tour ran through a comprehensive mixture of all three albums, and the band's sound was their fullest and most confident to date. But worryingly, on the eve of the tour Annie admitted to experiencing considerable problems with her throat.

Ill health aside, Eurythmics took advantage of all the publicity and released the second single off the album, the bright and up-tempo 'Right By Your Side'. The track represented a diverse change in mood during the recording sessions for *Touch*. "We were getting really fed up with ourselves being so down," said Dave. "It came out sounding like a calypso and at that time we really were right by each other's side."

" 'Right By Your Side' is probably one of the first genuinely happy tracks we've ever recorded," said Annie. "It's so simple that the words might almost be trite, but I *feel* that. I feel like just lifting up those lyrics. The real meaning of that song for me is even simpler – it's that happiness really does exist as a possibility. That it can feel every bit as real as the most frightening depths of depression." The single came out on 7″ and 12″ formats, with a limited edition 7″ featuring the free cassette containing the outtakes from the *Sweet Dreams (Are Made Of This)* sessions.

On the single sleeve photographed by Peter, a maniacally grinning Annie wore the gold glitter suit and red platform boots, resembling a garish cross somewhere between Elvis Presley and Gary Glitter. "That was my glitter revenge!" Annie declared to the press. "Well, sometimes I just like to do something tacky . . ." Soon enough the single hit the UK

197

charts at number 10, easily achieving equally golden sales.[23]

Eurythmics were too busy touring to film an ambitious video to accompany the single, and so instead one was produced using a combination of lip-synched performance mixed with live footage from the show in Manchester.

"The reason why we did 'Right By Your Side' with just our band playing was because we were getting a bit tired of seeing overblown Hollywood-type videos for songs that were just normal," Dave explained. "We had quite a funny one worked out, but instead we wanted to remind people that we're a live band too!" The irony, of course, is that Eurythmics shamelessly mime throughout the short, lacklustre film, which most memorably depicts Annie in a horrific concoction of a leopard skin wrap (with the legs hanging down), pillbox hat, gloves and large earrings. As she winks at the camera and holds the microphone lead in her teeth, it really seems like she's going through the motions.

The less than inspired performance hid a problematic day. It was on this occasion that Barry Maguire was fully accepted into the entourage. "One day they were shooting the video for 'Right By Your Side' and they said because of the lack of time they would shoot a live stage performance," he recalls. "But the make-up artist didn't turn up – it was some mistake with the booking.

"I was there early because I was interested in watching the video shoot. They said to me, 'Have you got your equipment with you? Could you please do some make-up for Dave?' Because it's such a physical contact, giving them a little shoulder rub and head rub to calm them down, there was this really bizarre connection." Barry was set to travel with Eurythmics for a long period after this event.

The single was given a little extra promotion with an appearance on UK pop programme *The Tube* in October. Here Eurythmics performed a more acoustic version than on record, and Annie wore yet another ghastly outfit. While they were filming at *The Tube*'s Newcastle studios, she eagerly took the opportunity to introduce herself to Tina Turner, who was also appearing on the show. During the meeting Annie informed the legendary American singer that she had been inspired by her track 'River Deep Mountain High' in her teens. The belated US release of 'Love Is A Stranger' hit number 23 in the *Billboard* charts just a fortnight later, so it was evident that Annie was surpassing the heights of her heroine's career.

★   ★   ★

---

[23] 'Right By Your Side' later made number 29 in the US charts on September 8, 1984.

On December 2, 1983 the British leg of the Touch Tour climaxed with an extra date at the Hammersmith Odeon in London, which was recorded by BBC Radio London and transmitted over the Christmas period. By this point *Touch* had exceeded all hopeful expectations, shifting over 300,000 copies and remaining in the British charts for six weeks. Riding on the back of its success, *Sweet Dreams (Are Made Of This)* made a further appearance at the lower end of the charts and continued to sell steadily, also reaching the 300,000 mark during the year. Around this time Eurythmics won the category for Best New Songwriters Of The Year at the 1983 Ivor Novello Awards.

In spite of the celebrations, Annie could no longer ignore the pain in her throat. "She was continually singing, interviewing and so on for three or four years up to that point, it was just completely manic, you know, the whole schedule," says Dean. "People around her had got nodes from singing wrongly, and forcing certain things and continual abuse and I think she became quite concerned that she would screw her voice up."

The situation worsened and Dave was obliged to announce her predicament in interviews, as by then Annie was not allowed to speak. "She seems to have nodules on her throat, which is fairly serious, so she has to rest her voice when she's not actually on stage," he told *No 1*. "Actually, it's quite serious and two specialists have told us that she must have an operation – but two other specialists have said, 'No, that's the worst thing she could do!' It's ludicrous." With Annie's operation set for Christmas time, the whole crew were horrified to learn that she would be taken out of action for three months of recuperation. For a while it seemed that overseas dates would have to be postponed indefinitely, but then a Swiss specialist with a miracle cure came to the group's attention.

"He places electric vibration pads on the throat for days on end, and eventually they get rid of the nodules without the need for any surgery," explained Dave. "I think Annie will be going over to Switzerland to talk with him about it when we finish our current tour."

On December 8 the singer flew out to Vienna to meet the throat specialist. He confirmed the presence of nodules and set Annie on a course of his electric vibration pads. As if by magic the treatment worked, Annie was given the all-clear (though still advised to rest her throat as much as possible) and surgery was avoided.

With the aid of her occasional voice coach, Tona de Brett, the star embraced a new way of living. Whenever she was appearing in concert and the pain flared up, Annie would cease talking completely, communicating only in sign language and hastily written notes on scraps of paper. Dave would take over the vast majority of the interviews required of the band, while Annie looked on in silence. For someone prone to bouts of depression, ill health was at first extremely difficult to cope with.

"One of the worst things about having a voice problem is that every-body asks you how your voice is – and you have to *speak* in order to explain!" she was to cry in frustration when her ailment subsided a little. "The problem is that I can be terribly over-talkative and tend to rattle on like a milk-truck when the mood takes me. Of course, this is precisely the wrong thing to do as you're *supposed* to keep absolutely silent all day long, which I find unbearable and almost impossible to do.

"Psychologically, of course, it's really awful to live with – night after night having to sing for a solid hour-and-a-half, knowing that you're almost completely hoarse. People get a shock when they hear me speak after a concert – I sound like something from another planet!" Annie had earned herself a well-deserved holiday, and over the Christmas and New Year period she flew to Nairobi, Kenya, travelling on later to Watumu.

In a sweet gesture she wrote a comical postcard to her fans to be pub-lished in the club magazine.

"Now the question you've all been asking! Did la Lennox get a chance to bask 'seal-like' in the African sun? Did she burn, peel and blister or did she turn from a milk bottle into a rich dark mahogany brown sultry sun goddess? Did the sand crabs attack? Did the mozzies bite? Did those fear-some savage tribes of Masai pillage, rampage, and plunder? – The answer – well . . . not exactly!!!" Poor Annie had arrived in the rainy season, and hadn't anticipated being under strict doctor's orders not to speak when she'd first booked the holiday. But all things considered, it was a much needed break before the Touch Tour progressed overseas.

Dave fared slightly better. He flew to Barbados on December 24, enjoy-ing a Christmas dinner of courgette and curried chicken on a white sandy beach the following day. While on holiday he met up with ex-Beatle Paul McCartney and his wife Linda, visited Guyanan reggae star Eddy Grant's studio and relaxed, "playing footy on the beach." It was obviously the place to be.

Cashing in on Eurythmics' incredible success, the first compilation from the days of The Tourists was released on CD in early 1984, rather wistfully entitled *Should Have Been Greatest Hits*. It contained all their singles plus a few of their better album songs, but still only totalled 10 tracks. In 1997 a more comprehensive 20-track collection would appear on the market, simply titled *Greatest Hits* and included an anomaly or two. 'Strange Sky', a 1980 Coombes composition, had not been heard on a Tourist album before, only previously released as the B-side to 'Don't Say I Told You So'. It is an atmospheric, quasi-funeral march which sounds like Annie is singing about life in a mental hospital. Quiet and reflective and set against a slow beat, the insistent and repetitive theme to all Tourists' work, "I'm losing my grip", shows the character of the lyrics singing to a lonely desert sky at night. The younger Annie lets go for the first time at the close of the song, where her semi-Eastern yell depicts the hopeless feeling of the track.

★   ★   ★

Annie had turned 29 shortly before the beginning of the new year, and as she approached her thirties it seemed, career-wise at least, she was in about as good a situation as she could be. 1984 was to see an amazing 35 per cent of American record sales stemming from British acts, notably including Eurythmics, and over this year the now mega-group was to play over 170 dates promoting their latest album. Quite a feat for a supposed 'studio band'.

Hardly acting the martyr to her throat, alongside touring this year Annie fitted in a quick recording session with fellow Scot Billy McKenzie, former singer with The Associates. Together they worked on a track called 'The Best Of You'. Annie was delighted to collaborate with a long-time hero of hers, stating, "When Billy McKenzie formed The Associates I thought, 'Here's somebody who's got something really special to offer.' . . . He's the most talented person I've met among creative people. He's a very inspired singer." Hinting at a possible concern, she later added, "He could do great things but he's got to be more disciplined."[24]

On January 27, 1984 Eurythmics played their first date in Sydney. For the next fortnight they were to continue around Australia and New Zealand, rapidly gaining impetus. It became a standing joke among the party that Annie would quietly sign into hotels under the pseudonym of 'Mrs Egg'. Quite where her inspiration for the name came from was a mystery to her friends.

"When you're on tour, life is such a surreal existence and you either can or can't deal with it," says Barry Maguire. "Annie's way of dealing with it was by trying to make it as normal and everyday as she could, by keeping herself to herself, going back to her hotel room and not going to the parties. Perhaps what she should have done really was to mix with people – don't be frightened, don't isolate yourself, because you don't do that in real life."

However the travelling was affecting her in private, Annie's onstage

---

[24] Distraught by the death of his mother, McKenzie was later to take a fatal overdose at his parents' home on January 22, 1997.

persona was certainly larger than life. Kitted out in a Jeff Banks tartan suit, the singer advised the rest of the band on what to wear and how to present themselves during the act. At one stage a choreographer was brought in to teach the musicians a few steps. The dancing idea was immediately rejected by the instrumentalists, although The Croquettes took to the movements quite well. "I was allowed to do what I wanted to do," says Dean the bass player, "just as long as I didn't stand in front of Annie too much, or Dave!"

The latest single release during this intense period of publicity was the inspired 'Here Comes The Rain Again', which shot to number eight in the UK charts on February 4, 1984 and US number four a little later on March 31. Platinum status was soon achieved.

Learning from the criticism of the video 'cop-out' for 'Right By Your Side', Eurythmics had filmed an accompanying clip for 'Here Comes The Rain Again' back in early December 1983, directed by Jonathan Gershfield. The group had planned to film on location in the Loch Lomond region, but looking for even more bleakness, they settled on the freezing Orkney Isles off the coast of northern Scotland. The area is so remote in winter that by midday most of the natural light has gone, so the crew were faced with an exceptionally early rise in bitterly cold conditions. Perhaps not so bad for the hardier of the party, but for Annie it was particularly difficult as she was to spend most of the video dressed only in a flimsy white nightie. The Scots lass did not so much as flinch, and retains only fond memories of the shoot.

"We were just in such an amazing location," she enthused later in a radio interview. "It was an incredible day and it stands out in my mind so strongly. Sometimes you can't capture on film successfully what you're seeing there. We had to get up very early that morning and drive to a ship-wreck. It was very, very cold in Orkney. It was about five o'clock in the morning, it was the first crack of the first light, and as we drove towards the shipwreck we passed the scuppered German fleet in Scapa Flow, and you could just see the tail end of the boats in silhouette in the water. It was so memorable that that image has never left me."

The resulting video is equally striking. With occasional visual references to the 1981 film, *The French Lieutenant's Woman*, Annie's onscreen performance for the first time presents her as an actress capable of displaying emotions other than dominance and control. She appears at the beginning in close-up, starkly beautiful and clearly very cold. Then she and Dave are shown walking along the windswept cliff tops together, filmed from the sky by a swooping helicopter. All around them the sky is animated to exaggerate the dark, stormy conditions, and the sea rises and falls with enormous, threatening waves.

Initially Annie is wrapped up in a blanket to cover her nightie and looks tired and drawn. Dave stalks her with a video camera, bringing to mind the unease of the 'Never Gonna Cry Again' promo where he followed her around with a pad and pen like a reporter. Annie goes into a house where she stands alone in her nightie, holding a candle. As she sings, expressions of semi-ecstasy cross her pale features. Dave is reflected watching and filming her from outside in the mirror, then later in the water. Annie then returns to face the elements on an unexplained quest, crossing freezing rivers (with the unseen aid of two sets of thermal underwear and rubber waders) and ending up by the shipwreck on a beach. She appears to be searching or waiting for something, perhaps an indication of the song lyrics about an ensuing torrent of emotion.

The whole video has a clandestine and sinister feel. Stalked and dressed in her nightie, Annie endows an erotic, virginal and even sacrificial image which is a far cry from any power suits or leather-bound whore figures. The freezing temperature is reflected in her face and breath, which brings a whole new edge to the song and the film – literally sending a shiver down the viewer's spine. It proved popular with fans and non-fans alike, and many began to speculate on the possibility of Annie expanding her talents into an acting career.

★   ★   ★

Just before the Touch Tour moved on to Europe in February 1984, Pete Phipps, Vic Martin and Dick Cuthell were informed their services would no longer be required. The line-up was changed to feature Swedish drummer Olle Romo and Patrick Seymour on keyboards, while Molly Duncan on saxophone and Dave Plews on trumpet were to perform *Touch*'s trademark bursts of brass.

"Half the band had changed," says Dean. "Luckily I got on quite well with Annie and Dave, and made it known that I really respected and liked them and wanted to work with them. But it was a case of a different band for the next thing, because of the general cynicism and dodgy behaviour from certain people." Not wishing to repeat the "chandelier swinging" episodes from the Kiss Me Quick Tour, Dave and Annie chose to continue their work ethic of Eurythmics as just the two of them, supported by a developing line-up of outside musicians.

Those who had been let go were extremely disappointed and confused at their treatment, in particular Dick Cuthell, who had performed on their second and third albums. He said at the time: "I was told they couldn't afford me. It really is a blow. I feel upset that they left it so long to tell us while secretly rehearsing new guys." But Dave and Annie were set. A spokesman for the band stated: "Eurythmics are essentially Annie Lennox and Dave Stewart, and it is their decision to keep the rest of the line-up flexible." Perhaps if any one musician either got too close, or became uncontrollable in any aspect of the business, it signified the end.

While some friendships were extinguished, others flourished. Barry Maguire had certainly never expected to enjoy a continued alliance with the band, but was about to be pleasantly surprised.

"After that first tour ended I went back to the children's home totally depressed. Then the phone rang one day and it was Eurythmics' PA at the time, Karen Ciccone, asking whether I was around, and whether it would be possible for me to join them on tour for a month in Europe as the assistant wardrobe guy."

Barry was still only 17 years old, and in order to employ him, some legal procedures had to be addressed. Amazingly this did not put Dave and Annie off in the slightest. "They became my legal guardians for a short period of time because I wasn't 18 yet, they were responsible for me. Then they asked me to join them full-time, so I ended up moving to London and it went on and on from there. At the time it was an 11-piece band, and I found I was doing everything myself, because I could do the hair and make-up as well. They explained that after the tour they were going to scale the whole thing down, make another album and the tour was going to be a lot smaller after that like a regular band, which I could handle on my own anyway."

Before long the relationship between Annie and Barry crossed the boundaries of professional acquaintance and the singer willingly became a mother figure to the young and openly gay assistant. "I was quite close to her because of the nature of my job, and it was always, 'Barry can you go and ask Annie this?' or, 'Can you go and find out that?', if they thought she wasn't too happy or if it was a sensitive thing, because my job was to be in and out of dressing rooms. So I tended to have more contact with her than most people.

"She was always incredible with me, always absolutely brilliant. At the beginning of the tour she sat down with me and she said, 'I don't know if you know about AIDS and HIV but this is the deal.' And she told me all about it. She said, 'America's a weird place, be really careful and please, we'd prefer it if you didn't wander off on your own to clubs. We don't know what you're into but there's always something happening with the band every night – just find out what's happening and keep in touch with each other and try not to stray on your own. If you do go off on your own, just make sure that somebody knows where you are, the address of where you've gone.' It was brilliant.

"She didn't have to do all that – she was paying me to do a job. They felt I was able to do the job and that's why they employed me; they didn't have to care the way they did. Ironically I think I only ever went to one gay bar in all those years of touring, not because she'd frightened me, but because I felt I was there to do this job, and I'd rather be around these cool people. But maybe if she hadn't have said that then I'd have been more curious. So, more than she probably realises, that was a massive help."

As a homosexual some 10 years younger than Annie, Barry posed no threat to the singer whatsoever and was allowed to become close to her in a way that only gay men and straight women experience. Such a relationship is usually clear cut, with no competitive jealousy or undertones of possible romance. Although Annie did not necessarily open up and confide her problems, even to her dearest friends, she saw her ties with Barry as an unspoken bond of trust, and treated him in a more gentle manner than any of the other crew members.

In the early spring of 1984 Annie was experiencing problems with her lover Peter Ashworth, and decided to end the relationship. Unfortunately the break was not a clean one and Peter certainly does not recall it being made clear to him that their affair was over. His version of events is that as two highly charged and emotional individuals, the couple broke up 'temporarily' many times, often as part of the separation enforced by Annie's touring schedule. But the singer was in a state of flux and continued the publicity for *Touch* under the impression that she was single once more.

"The problem was that Annie was in between relationships," says Barry. "She'd just finished with Peter Ashworth at the time and that was a bit weird I think. Annie was incredibly vulnerable then. I don't think she quite realised what powers she had and how she affected people. If she turned up for a gig and she had her head down, people just avoided her. If she was happy, she'd walk in, stop, sit down and chat to anyone. But because of her insecurity she was just very unhappy then. She didn't want to be on tour, she didn't want to be going from town to town amongst all this happiness, when she was painfully *un*happy at the time."

Everybody knew that there was only one person close enough to approach her at this difficult time. "Dave tried really hard to support her, to be a friend to her and to always be there for her," Barry continues. "She knew what he was doing and sometimes she'd take that in and sometimes she'd just put up an emotional block. In a way she was being nasty, the way you do to people you love. But Dave's a very different person to her, he sees the other side of things. She sees a wall and sees the height of it, whereas Dave would just get a chair and climb over it."

Unfortunately Dave's support, whether it was accepted or not, came at a time when the guitarist too was suffering, once again with ill health. His problems were not helped by a bout of unpleasantness in France, where French lorry drivers had rammed their tour coach off the road, badly damaging the vehicle and incurring huge repair costs.[25]

The European Touch Tour was interrupted when suddenly Dave gave in to the pressures of overworking. "In the end I just collapsed from exhaustion," he later explained. "I couldn't get out of bed in our hotel in Hamburg and they had to drag me to the phone and cancel the rest of the dates . . . My phone wouldn't stop ringing once we had success."

Dave was sent on an essential holiday following his breakdown, which gave him time to recuperate properly before the next leg of the tour. "I changed my number and went to Spain – the only place our records hadn't been released!"

Of course his cheery attitude belied the constant stream of health issues that had dogged him since childhood. "Dave always seemed very vulnerable to me, having a little lie down, and he was quite poorly a lot of the time," says Dean Garcia. "He'd have to be treated fairly gently, have a little snooze – you can't go mad all the time." The possibility of his symptoms not being 100 per cent kosher was often whispered behind the scenes, the rumours of hypochondria strengthened by his loud complaints to anyone who would listen.

"Dave was always ill," groans Mickey Gallagher, who had accompanied him on the previous tour. "'Oh my back, oh my neck, my leg' – you know! I never actually saw him knocking back painkillers or stuff like that, but he was a very good complainer!

"Everybody just basically ignored him. Sympathised, but got on with it. I think he had whiplash and he always complained about it. But he used to complain about so much all the time that it just became background noise. It rarely stopped him from working."

Dave had always been an extrovert, but his poor health and a growing realisation that Annie would always be the centre of attention forced him to slow down and take a back seat from the operation. "Right at the beginning, I was aware that any serious personality input from me would just capsize the Eurythmics 'thing'," he said. "In Eurythmics it's always Annie's psyche that's on display. I just play a counterpart – like in videos – to help diffuse it sometimes or to build it up. If you notice early press shots there's Annie right up front and a bit of the back of my head somewhere."

---

[25] Despite this and an equally concerning incident in Lyon where Eurythmics had been forced to drive across fields to escape violent protesters on strike, around this time Annie announced that she would be leaving Britain and moving into a flat in Paris, blaming unwanted attention from her English fans for her departure.

His observations were proved correct on February 21, 1984, as his more famous colleague was voted Best British Female Artist at the third annual BRIT Awards held at London's Grosvenor House Hotel.

Despite her near global recognition, Annie was frustrated that in some areas she continued to be viewed as a piece of fluff. Chauvinism had long since been rife in the music industry and in 1984 the number of female singer/songwriters with any clout was greatly eclipsed by the men. One afternoon she was invited to a Music Therapy luncheon held by the producers of BBC Radio 1. Determined to make a point about the emergence of women as respectable pop stars in their own right, Annie cynically dressed up in a large wig, false eyelashes and a mini-skirt. The irony was clearly visible to anyone remotely aware of her menacingly masculine image within Eurythmics.

Before the luncheon had even begun Annie was attracting exactly the kind of attention she had expected. "I looked like a groupie, because I was *being* a groupie," she said a year after the event. "All these men were patting me on the head saying, 'Oh, your hair is so beautiful.' Really! I looked the epitome of a prostitute and they were leering and winking."

Unfortunately the saga was to worsen, as Jack Steven elaborates: "The promotion department thought, 'Wouldn't it be a good idea to sit her next to a bigwig at Radio 1.' They started having dinner and the gentleman in question clearly said something that Annie felt was inappropriate. This went on and it was simply too much for Annie to bear. She just turned around and told him where to get off. She didn't mince her words!" Jack exclaims. "So the Head of Promotion took her out of this huge event, saying, 'You can't do that . . .'"

Annie was sick and tired of being told what she could and could not do at industry events. One week later on February 28, when Eurythmics were invited to attend the 1984 Grammy Awards for which they had been nominated as Best New Artists of 1983, it seemed the perfect opportunity to make another stand.

"The record company wanted us to make an appearance because they thought it would be prestigious, but we were very reticent about it," she later told the *Los Angeles Times*. "We felt our stance was not in the bosom of the conventional music scene. We wouldn't have been comfortable simply playing our latest hit. If we'd refused to be on it the company would have been really upset with us, so we had to think of a way of satisfying them but at the same time to do it on our own terms. There had been a lot of talk about sexual ambiguity that year, so we decided it would be perfect to kind of put it back in their faces . . . a way of saying: 'You want me to be a gender bender? Here I am.'"

Annie's chosen costume eclipsed even that of her friend Boy George, who congratulated America on "knowing a good drag queen when you see one" as his group Culture Club snuck the Best New Artist award from under Eurythmics' noses. In a back-handed snipe at the bow tie and dinner jacket brigade, Annie resurrected her male persona from the 'Who's That Girl?' video, naming him Earl the Rocker.

Following an introduction by John Denver, Annie strode on stage in a man's suit, black sideburns and a quiff, with no make-up and fake stubble on her face. She was met with a stunned and stony silence from the American audience, who completely missed any reference to the video let alone sly irony on her part, and worried amongst themselves as to the meaning of this outrage. Ignoring the blank faces in front of her, Annie gave the perform-ance of her life. But when the song was over, instead of clapping or cheering there was just loud discussion. Turning to each other in confusion, the sound technicians quickly substituted some pre-recorded applause. Furious with the response, Annie stormed off the stage and in a repetition of the pre-vious year's incident at The Palace in Los Angeles and indeed of the recent Music Therapy luncheon, confronted the monitor operator, verbally accosting him, crying, "We're fucking professionals, why aren't you?"

Eurythmics' American audience were of course unaware of the back-stage shenanigans and, as a result of the bewilderment prompted by the Earl disguise, faltered a little in their support of the British group. Annie was left to explain her behaviour to a number of US papers and magazines. "I didn't want to upset people," she attempted to clarify. "I wanted to have a little fun, that's all. Americans are famous for their sense of humour. I just wanted to give them something they didn't expect . . . It was a joke, but I think people often see me in a serious vein. Now I know I have to spell it out when I am trying to be light or funny." Having briefly enjoyed an easing-off in critical perception, Annie was back in the tabloid dog-house once again.

16

LOVE IS A STRANGER

"I believe you only experience love with strangers, so it doesn't last long. You're usually in love with the idea of somebody. Many of my own love affairs were projecting my ideas onto others."

– AL

In February 1984, during what had become dubbed the 'homewrecker tour', all members of the Eurythmics' entourage were experiencing an emotional rough patch. None more so than Annie, who was particularly vulnerable after her health scare and Dave's semi-disassociation as the effects of tireless touring took over.

It was at this exposed juncture that Radha Raman stepped into Annie's life, bringing with him undivided attention, spiritual mystique and tasty morsels of meat-free cuisine. He was simply a fan who had attended the Stuttgart concert late in the month, but felt so inspired by Annie's singing that he wanted to leave her a gift. Being a chef by trade, Radha prepared a lavish vegetarian dish and placed it outside her hotel room door. He went on to produce so many culinary offerings that Annie eventually agreed to meet him. The whirlwind scenario that followed has since become legend. They felt an instant mutual connection and the German Hare Krishna devotee invited himself along for the rest of the tour.

Surprisingly, Dean Garcia does not believe the dishes in question were *that* tempting. "His food wasn't very nice actually, it was horrible!" he grimaces today. "And I think Annie would say that now. But at the time she was playing with vegetarianism and trying to be healthy and spiritual and he was coming from there."

More than haute cuisine, Radha offered Annie an alternative lifestyle. She had been almost constantly by Dave's side for eight years, and now that he had quietened down temporarily it was Annie's turn to shine. "What Radha brought to her life, like Dave had before, was a gang," muses Barry Maguire. "Every night there would be another Krishna crowd from the temple, with all their cooking stuff, so Annie's dressing room would become a temple.

"You can't imagine this; from her being this really private woman, everyone terrified to knock on her door, suddenly every night there would be 20 Krishna devotees passing food with the most amazing smells around the band. So suddenly her posse kind of took over. That was really good for her, that was what she wanted. Radha brought a false comfort."

Most of the entourage who got to know Radha remained wary, and although many interviewees described him as being "really odd", few could pinpoint what it was that unsettled them. "A bit spooky, intense and weird," tries Dean. "Quite religious but not really – you could kind of see through that a little bit, which made it a bit odd; it all seemed a bit of a front. He was OK to us and we got on, but there was something missing."

One element elusive to their affair was a physical relationship, as Radha's religion dictated that an unmarried couple must remain chaste. "They were in Germany for a while, and he'd slept in her room, but on the floor. They weren't allowed to have sex until they got married," recalls Jon Roseman.

There was only one way around this obstacle and on March 14, 1984, 29-year-old Ann Lennox wed 30-year-old Robert Ludwig Rohnfeld at a registry office in Haringey, North London. Radha Raman was Robert's assumed Krishna alias, and his real name was just one of the many things Annie was soon to discover about the man she had married within weeks of their first encounter.

The secret civil ceremony was witnessed by Kenny Smith and Sandra Turnbull. Very few others even knew about the occasion. Painfully aware how easily the tabloid papers could distort such an expeditious affair between a headlining pop star and a Hare Krishna monk, Dave thoughtfully deflected any media scrutiny by announcing his engagement, albeit false, to rock celebrity Nona Hendryx.[26]

Although both Annie and Radha listed 80 Stapleton Hall Road as their address on their marriage certificate, the first thing the newlyweds did was set off on the American leg of Eurythmics' Touch Tour. As Radha assumed his position somewhat uncomfortably among the touring party, Dave made his excuses and steered clear of the honeymooning couple.

While maintaining their professional partnership, Dave and Annie were always simultaneously guarded and respectful of each other's lovers. "Annie adored Dave, and relied on him a lot," says Barry. "She was probably at the

---

[26] Former Labelle singer Nona Hendryx had suffered, as had Annie a few years previously, when her record company passed over her rule-breaking androgynous style.

Cover sleeve for the 'Sweet Dreams (Are Made Of This)' single.
(LFI)

The Church, Crouch End.
(Pictorial Press)

Joe Bangay: "It was the best concert I ever went to in my life. She stayed on stage and gave them a mouthful."
'A Day At The Races', Phoenix Park, Dublin. *(Joe Bangay)*

Posing as the expensive-looking love object and chauffeur during the 'Love Is A Stranger' video shoot. *(Steve Rapport/SIN)*

Still from the 'Sweet Dreams (Are Made Of This)' video. *(Steve Rapport/LFI)*

Outtakes from the photoshoot for *The Face* in Bagley's warehouse. The glitter suit later appeared on the cover sleeve for 'Right By Your Side'. *(Peter Ashworth/LFI)*

Who's that girl…
(Steve Rapport/LFI)

. … or is it a boy?
(Steve Rapport/LFI)

Still from the 'Here Comes The Rain Again' video.
(Steve Rapport/LFI)

Posing as angel and Sun King during 'There Must Be An Angel (Playing With My Heart)' video shoot.
(Steve Rapport/LFI)

'Missionary Man' was the first promo to be shown only after the watershed.
(Pictorial Press)

Aretha Franklin, Dave and Annie during the recording of 'Sisters Are Doin' It For Themselves' for *Be Yourself Tonight*. *(Corbis)*

Annie: "I have a deep respect and a great deal of admiration for Elvis." Annie and Elvis Costello recorded a duet called 'Adrian' for *Be Yourself Tonight*. *(LFI)*

Eurythmics at the height of their fame.
(Laurie Lewis/Retna)

Annie: "One of the proudest days of my life." Nelson Mandela's 70th birthday tribute concert at Wembley Stadium, London on June 11, 1988. *(Laurie Lewis/Retna)*

Barry Maguire: "When it happened it was a totally spontaneous action to an audience that weren't reacting. And it worked!" Annie's red bra as seen on the Revenge Tour. *(LFI)*

time pretty useless without him, from a creative point of view. Dave in the background of Eurythmics was just such an image thing, it just wasn't like that – he was definitely in the forefront.

"They were very professional in front of people. As soon as the amps went on it was pure Eurythmics, very professional. They were always very supportive of each other emotionally as well, because they'd spent so much time together." Regardless of Annie's recent marriage the show carried on and the US dates were a resounding success, with tickets at every venue sold out, often within a matter of hours. In Los Angeles Eurythmics were honoured when they were joined on stage for a duet by one of the original singers of 'Wrap It Up'.

"I was amazed when Sam from Sam & Dave got up on stage with us in LA during 'Wrap It Up'," marvels Annie. "We hadn't rehearsed but I knew he was going to come on and I was really worried about it. He was so powerful. Oh Lord he was so powerful. He said to me, 'Girl you've got it just like Aretha.' But I know I haven't."

A couple of weeks into their tour Annie's cover was blown, despite Dave's smokescreen. Although the press office and record company had to acknowledge the truth, they remained very protective of the couple. RCA simply and belatedly announced on April 3 that Annie had been married two weeks previously, but the identity of her husband remained unknown. The bride also played her cards close to her chest, letting slip only the following comment to *The Sunday Times*, "I'll say he's German, but that's all I'll say . . . I don't think it's anybody else's business but mine, so sorry, doors closed."

The shocking news of her secret union infiltrated the British tabloids the same week that *Melody Maker* awarded her Best Female Singer. Eventually giving in to relentless media badgering, Annie released a press statement saying of her husband: "He is a very special person who has provided me with a great deal of support and stability. We are both very happy together . . . We wanted our privacy to remain unspoiled." Slightly contradictorily, Annie then later commented on her marriage, "I hadn't thought of it as something to bring me security. There *is* something nice and stabilising about it, but it wasn't done to achieve stability. It was just something that came about – I didn't even know I was going to get married!"

Several months after the event, Annie opened up and finally explained why she had insisted on the cloak and dagger routine at the time. "I had to be very protective about my marriage to Radha because it was a very quick decision to get married," she said to *NME*, "and the person I was marrying has particular religious beliefs that I suppose to some people are

211

rather unusual. I knew that it would make brilliant copy for the gutter press. And I didn't want to have anyone, particularly me, exposed to that.

"So we got married completely in secret – I didn't even tell the group, actually – then it leaked out when we weren't in the country. And it was a funny thing, because when the story finally came out, it had already leaked out a little bit, so it was too late to make big headlines. Which I knew they would have done, like 'Pop Star Marries Hare Krishna Monk'. We were lucky we managed to avoid all that."

Having spared themselves the trauma of the mass media prying into their private life, Annie and Radha still had to face the family and friends who had not been invited to their wedding. "I did consult my parents but they didn't want me to go ahead," said Annie of what was supposed to be her parents' proudest day. "I'd rather not talk about it, it's too personal . . ."

"It was quite a shock to Tom and Dorothy," says June Smith. "Within themselves the Lennoxes are quite an open family, but that marriage was never even discussed. The first Tom knew of it was when the press phoned him up and asked him how he felt about his daughter marrying a Hare Krishna. And that's how he had found out. But she could be impulsive if she felt like it, and possibly it was an impulse thing!"

Having broached the subject, Annie had blatantly ignored her family's strong disapproval and married Radha regardless. Any student of psychology would have a field day with such a classic case of an only child rebelling against her father's strict control. Annie herself admits, "It was my statement to him that, 'You can't tell me what to do with my life anymore.' I had to say to him, 'I'm not your little girl. Let me make this mistake. Give me the respect to make this mistake. Give me the right,' and he wouldn't." Letting all her childhood angst boil up inside her, Annie had a blazing argument with Tom Lennox that was to signify the end of their relationship for a long time. "I was pretty severe with him. He wouldn't speak to me for a year. And I wouldn't speak to him."

Describing everyone as being "freaked out", Annie even included Dave who had been the willing mastermind behind her cover story. In fact, as much as surprising him, the change in Annie's marital status shifted their relationship onto another plateau. "My reaction was half shock and half that I was kind of pleased to think that she'd met somebody who would put everything on an even course," Dave summarised afterwards. The ex-couple were now able to admit openly that Annie had been jealous of Dave's numerous girlfriends previously, but that this was an opportunity for them to progress forward without any sexual tension.

"Dave was stunned by it. I think he had concerns, like everybody else, that Radha was an odd choice of person and where he'd come from," says

Dean of the bizarre month. "The rashness of it, the statement. I was quite surprised, and I think she was as well. I think it was a tour psychotic frenzy really. She wasn't of sound mind or something. It just seemed really rash, and the person was quite odd and the whole thing was completely extreme."

★   ★   ★

Coming to terms with the hurricane that had swept through Annie's personal life in the spring of 1984, destroying her close family ties while simultaneously providing the responsibility of a spouse, meant that she had to face the music publicly. At first she was very positive about the effects of married life, particularly in her unusual circumstances. "It's a very solid thing for me. I know it's a reverse role, I'm the breadwinner going out and doing my thing . . . He's very supportive of me and very nice," she said, adding a hint of justification for his financial dependency on her, "If we both had careers we would never see one another. Ours is a very modern role-reversal marriage."

Indeed, for many years to come, Annie did not want to be the housewife, cooped up indoors looking after the family and home, but her husband offered more than just a family life. "Radha wasn't particularly attractive," admitted Annie, baring her innermost thoughts, "but I thought I had found someone who was genuinely on a kind of spiritual path. I felt that with him I was going to give up everything that's ordinary in life to achieve something that is much higher."

That existence was the International Society for Krishna Consciousness (ISKCON). The members of this Hindu sect are known as Hare Krishnas after their distinctive chants, and commonly wear yellow or orange robes and have partly shaven heads. The cult became very popular within the music scene during the late Sixties when Beatle George Harrison demonstrated his support of the movement by producing a single, 'Hare Krishna Mantra', by the Radha Krishna Temple, which reached number 12 in the UK charts. Since that time the Krishnas have become a fixture in central London, operating from their base in Soho Street, also the location of their Govinda vegetarian restaurant. In the early Eighties lines of Krishnas were regularly to be seen and heard weaving and chanting their way around Soho Square and down the length of busy Oxford Street. Aside from Harrison, well-known converts include various Beach Boys, Donovan, Carlos Santana, guitarist John McLaughlin and punk singer Poly Styrene. Annie's friend Boy George had also recently dabbled.

It was inevitable that fans and the media would assume that Annie's marriage to a Krishna devotee meant that she too had succumbed to the devout lifestyle. The attraction of the faith lies in its ascetic living, which was a welcome breath of fresh air after the drug-addled Sixties and Seventies. Followers were expected to abstain from all forms of impurity in order to achieve enlightenment and remove themselves from the process of reincarnation. The ultimate sacrifice to attain a natural state of consciousness entailed the prohibition of gambling, intoxicants (alcohol, narcotics and caffeine), meat (including animal products such as eggs) and sexual intercourse (unless within a marriage, and then solely for procreation). In addition believers perform a hypnotic chant called a mantra, which is a vibration of sound that cleanses the mind, freeing it from anxiety and illusion.

Annie was weary of the materialism she had experienced since becoming famous and was enthused by the purity of her husband's religion. "At the beginning I didn't really know anything about the movement – most people don't, and it's just a strange, fascinating cult," she elaborated. "I didn't see them as religious nuts, because I've read enough about spirituality to know that there's more to it than that. But I didn't marry a Hare Krishna, I married a person." As she understood more about their beliefs and ideals, rather than become an initiated member, Annie tried to incorporate facets of the religion into her daily life.

"Initially I was very idealistic about the whole thing. I was full of it as one is, but then reality set in," Annie admitted realistically in an interview with *The Face* magazine. "Let's just say I'm struggling with it, not in a negative way but struggling to have time to sit down and say, 'OK what do I agree and disagree with.' I need to be able to talk to more knowledgeable people and say, 'Alright, tell me about transmigration of the soul, how does it occur?' Not everything can be decided by intellectual analysis of course, but most of all I need time to be with my husband, off the road, to try it out."

True to her word, Annie tried her hand at ISKCON. "I went to Bhaktivedanta Manor, the house where George Harrison has Krishna Consciousness meetings. The thing that really struck me, even though I was very much, 'I don't know about all this, it's very strange', [was that] I felt refreshed to be around people who weren't motivating their lives around purely material gain. I drove away from that place feeling just a little refreshed."

Radha too was aware that she was trying to understand his path to a cleaner lifestyle and appreciated her support. "It was quite an exotic thing," he later amplified in his only press interview. "Annie thought it was refreshing to be around people not focused so much on material life. I wasn't interested in her body or her fame or her credit card. [The relationship] didn't get physical for a long time. I lived celibate in the temple, and she knew we couldn't have a relationship like you usually do. But we were together 24 hours a day. Oh, it was very beautiful. To me, it was like a film; it wasn't real."

However poetically Radha spoke, there was still an underlying edge to his nature that unnerved those close to Annie. "To be honest, the guy was not to be trusted," says Barry Maguire, "although he came across as a nice guy, initially. He was a very gentle person in the way he communicated with you, but he looked strange – it was always weird that he appealed to her.

"But his oddness was a lot deeper than that. There was a lot more to him than his religion, he went into it to cover a much darker person than he allowed people to see. He had something weird happen in his background, it might have been drugs, and he went into the Krishna thing as a way out of that. I know for a fact that that never happened around Annie because she's so against that stuff, she was never into it."

Radha's background was certainly in question and it became apparent that he had embraced the wholesome religion as a means of escape from an unsavoury past, which many others have also linked with an addiction to hard drugs. The similarities between Radha's state of mind when he sought solace in Annie, and Dave's similar condition almost a decade before is startling. Likewise, when Annie met both partners she was at a crossroads in her own life, seeking direction and comfort.

"Maybe he needed a lot of help, a really strong person to lean on, because he'd had a funny background," speculates Barry. "They probably both needed the same kind of thing, they were both very vulnerable. But you need a strong person in a relationship and I don't think either of them felt that strong, or they felt strong in their own ways, but not in the ways that each other needed. Once they were married and he felt comfortable and convinced that this was the real thing, his barriers started to drop. So she'd be away doing things and he'd . . .

"Well, one night he phoned me up and said, 'Would you like to come round for some food?' I said, 'Is Annie going to be there?' He said, 'No, but that's OK, come round anyway.' So I went round there and he was there with a little pair of shorts on and his camera equipment was all out. He'd nailed this raffia mat on to her beautiful parquet flooring and covered all the furniture in weird drapings, and the shutters were all closed. He was drinking, which I didn't think he did. Just weird things – *not* very Krishna, let's put it that way."

★   ★   ★

215

Barry felt unable to say anything to Annie about Radha's more dubious side. Without family or friends to guide her the singer adapted her routine to accommodate her husband. Performing on stage is a physically demanding job for which Annie used to exercise each morning. During the Touch Tour she admitted to becoming lazy and instead of fitness, took more care of her overall health, inspired by Krishna cleanliness. Other than a few self-confessed adolescent cigarettes and experimental joints, Annie did not have a nicotine or narcotic habit, and her alcohol intake was not particularly high, so was easy to cut down. The hardest conversion then was to take up vegetarianism.

She became impassioned about the plight of animals bred for consumption, spurred on by the religious beliefs of 'action and reaction'. "We were horrified by the holocaust, but for some reason it hasn't dawned on the general public that the animals are suffering at our hands in an almost holocaustic way," explained Annie. However, these values effectively widened the rift between the singer and her loved ones as she winced in an interview with the *Vegetarian Times*: "Part of my family are farmers, so I grew up aware of animals. Granny would go into the yard and kill a chicken to eat for dinner. Grandfather was a gamekeeper. This seemed fair enough at the time and was the way of things. My uncle fattens beef cows for a living. It's all he knows, so discussing vegetarianism wouldn't make any sense to him."

All of a sudden, Annie became a crusader for the cause, using her public soap box to extol the virtues of her diet. "I feel rather than people saying to me, 'Are you a vegetarian?' my answer should be, 'You mean you're not?' Being vegetarian makes me feel more responsible. When I see people eating meat I'm aware of the slaughter that's gone on so instead of simply eating a meat pie when I'm hungry, I renounce it. From a karmic way of looking at it – and I know people are going to think I'm a complete nutcase now – one incurs a great deal of very bad karma through eating meat."

Despite this emphatic display of philosophising, Annie maintained that she was not a Krishna convert and that no one was forcing her to become a spokesperson for the movement. Radha was undoubtedly pleased that his famous wife was incorporating his ideals into her world, and even suggested that they did their own cooking while on tour to ensure that it was prepared without meat extracts. While this was a simple solution, it alienated Annie one step further from the rest of the group, who would eat sociably in the hotel restaurant.

"I think he probably wanted to keep her to himself to stop things ending before they did," theorises Barry. "I think if they'd have been more social together, people would have seen through the relationship a lot sooner. In a way I think he wanted to keep her to himself to maximise the power that he had, or thought he had." Annie was sympathetic to her husband's unusual situation and indicated early on that their marriage needed some attention. "It's not easy for my husband, 'cos he's suddenly forced into the limelight to a certain extent, from being just an ordinary guy. So we're both having to work at it, and I hope that it works out."

Part of the difficulty for the couple was that by the time Annie finished the tour a few months later, the two had not been able to get to know each other in private. As soon as the singer's schedule allowed, Annie and Radha moved into a house together, situated in a small village in the Swiss Alps near the Italian border. "You get to the airstrip and then there's a mountain and then you zig-zag for about 50 minutes up this mountain, thinking every minute that your life's in someone else's hands," describes Annie of the dramatic route to her latest acquisition. "There's this very tiny village, a sort of medieval village. It's not an opulent house, it's quite big, very old, and sort of farmyardish. It's very beautiful and it has a nice view."

The location was important to Radha as there was a Krishna farm community and temple in close proximity. Although retaining her London base, Annie was pleased to secure a peaceful haven. "Even now we've bought this house in Switzerland, I doubt if I'll have a lot of time to be there. But whatever time I get I'm gonna try and get myself down there," she explained. "It's a nice climate there. And it's near a Krishna farm community, where there's a temple, and it's good my husband can have a chance to have a connection with devotees, and for me as well to get away. I'm looking forward to it." As Radha fitted in easily, for Annie the house was obviously intended only as a holiday home that she would visit once or twice a year. She later divulged that she found herself bored after the first week, envisaging it as somewhere she would appreciate in the future with age and a family.

★　★　★

"Everything is calculated in the music industry and it's just calculated by us rather than from someone else," said Annie boldly of Eurythmics' artistic integrity. "Don't imagine for one minute that anything you see has not been thought about very seriously. But the difference between us and a lot of groups is that we've taken control of what goes out. There's nothing sinister in that, nothing devious. The ideas that come out are well thought-out, well prepared. We take a lot of trouble and we really watch the final outcome."

Notwithstanding this grand statement, Eurythmics were suffering somewhat as a result of their fame. Although they were awarded Song-writers Of The Year at the prestigious Ivor Novello Awards on April 29, 1984, they were losing some of their carefully created control over commercial matters.

Omnibus Press had published a book called *Eurythmics In Their Own Words*. Although it was just one in a series quoting many popular stars, Eurythmics took offence to the title as it appeared to be an official release. The fan club circulated a statement warning their members: "It is of very poor quality and we are advising fans not to buy it and therefore help to discourage the promotion of 'pirate' publications." Chris Charlesworth, who had progressed from his role at RCA to become editor-in-chief at Omnibus Press, recalls the ensuing tirade. "They were displeased with that. I remember there was a sharp exchange of letters. Clearly they were offended as they saw it as exploitation; that someone had done it without their permission." Despite their best efforts to thwart the perceived 'cash-in', the book sold well, indicating that fans were hungry for written material on their favourite artists.

Amusingly, several months later the tables were turned as Eurythmics submitted an 'official' book proposal to Omnibus Press. "Their manager Kenny Smith approached me when Eurythmics were still big," reflects Chris today. "He had hundreds of colour pictures taken of Eurythmics and wanted us to produce an official photo book. But he was asking for far too much money; a lot of money for the photographer, a lot of money for the designer, a lot of money for Eurythmics. And a 200-page coffee-table full-colour picture book, in hardback, was going to incur an expensive production bill. That means it would have had a high retail price.

"It doesn't matter how big you are, there's only a limited market for that sort of thing. So I turned him down. He seemed shocked that I turned down an opportunity to do a book on a band as big as Eurythmics. But it was simply a vanity publication."[27]

In May, Eurythmics next ran into trouble with the release of *Sweet Dreams (The Video Album)*. Dave and Annie were among the first to experiment with the use of film for an entire video album concept, tentatively nicknamed the V-LP. Bursting with ideas, Dave could hardly contain himself in interviews when talking about their current project,

[27] Johnny Waller and Steve Rapport's *Sweet Dreams – The Definitive Biography*, a considerably smaller and less expensive book than that proposed to Omnibus Press, was published by Virgin in 1985.

which was inspired by their landlords at The Church.

"Bob Bura and John Hardwick, two friends of ours, have developed a new filming technique that's going to revolutionise animation where you can make puppets do anything a human can do," he enthused. "People who've seen the film have had difficulty telling reality from illusion – and that's what we love, that trickery and deception . . .

"There is a lot of clever cutting where the puppet of Annie goes through a door and becomes the real Annie on the other side, or the puppet of me throws a baton into the air and when it comes down it is caught by the real me and I'm conducting a gospel choir in a beautiful Turkish Bath."[28]

However, that was where Eurythmics' enthusiasm was cut short. The video, released in May 1984 by RCA, included the footage shot by MTV at Heaven back in 1983, short promotional films for *Sweet Dreams (Are Made Of This)* and the sequences created by Bura & Hardwick Animation. Unfortunately the end product was neither piquant nor remarkable, which Eurythmics had intended. Moreover, the music was from the album of the previous year and contained nothing from the progression to *Touch* – Eurythmics saw such a move as equally short-sighted as RCA's attempt to re-release *In The Garden* on the back of *Sweet Dreams (Are Made Of This)*'s success. Furious at the blatant rip-off to which they felt exposed, Eurythmics issued another press statement:

"We were totally dissatisfied with this video. It falls so low beneath the standard of our work that we offered to buy it and simply remove it from the market so that it wouldn't embarrass us and disappoint our fans. Sadly our proposal was rejected, so it is now on sale with our name on it. All we can say is that we are distressed and disturbed by the whole business. We hate it when an artist loses artistic control over a product that boldly displays his or her name, and that's what happened. Unfortunately, large companies only think about the profit and loss statements to their shareholders and very little about the artist's future. We have a lot of regard for our fans and would have liked to put out something we are proud of rather than this. We would just like to say, 'Buy this at your own risk'."

Was the video really that bad? It starts with a man presenting an image of the future to a record company representative, the two characters played by Norman Bacon and Stephen Calcutt. The gawky man demonstrating the idea produces a model of The Church and two miniature puppets of Dave and Annie. The puppets magically come to life and open

---

[28] Batons had featured in previous Eurythmics videos, but this one in particular had apparently belonged to the North Nibley Choral Society in 1922.

the door to The Church, but walk into Heaven nightclub which segues into the live set.

The performance is almost overwhelming in its power, regardless of the immense difficulties and setbacks previously described by Dean Garcia. Annie is arresting with shorn red hair, wearing a white suit, a black T-shirt and red braces. She had adopted the famous red stripe of make-up across her eyes. "I plagiarised that from Malcolm McLaren," she later confessed.

While Annie constantly maintained her menacing stance by robotic dancing enhanced by controlled posturing, Dave looked every inch the 'mad professor' with his bird's nest hairdo. But even with Dean Garcia bouncing around on bass, Vic Martin swaying on keyboards and The Croquettes side-stepping in silhouette, Annie truly stole the limelight.

During their typical rendition of songs from the first two albums, Eurythmics gave 'Take Me To Your Heart' a soul treatment far removed from the original, and included 'Satellite Of Love' as the token ballad. The puppets were reintroduced to smooth the transition between Heaven and the promotional videos ('Love Is A Stranger', 'Who's That Girl?' and 'Sweet Dreams (Are Made Of This)'). Unfortunately the figurines were rather chunky and clumsily reminiscent of Tony Hart's British TV character Morph, which along with the rough editing lent the video an amateurish feel.

Clips of the video for 'Never Gonna Cry Again' were shown during the live version of 'Jennifer' to add interest to an otherwise sedate number. For variety also, 'This City Never Sleeps' was performed in The Church with Howard Hughes on grand piano and Dave on steel guitar, backing Annie's vocals against the magnificent rousing sound of a substantial gospel choir. The Church was dark and to make the most use of the light the musicians were filmed mainly from above. In stark contrast to the live set or pre-recorded videos it was very effective, but all too quickly became tedious and overpowered by the repetitive bass line on the piano.

'Tous Les Garçons' was clearly performed towards the end of the set at Heaven as Annie appeared exhausted, with her jacket off and her short sleeves rolled up. Her voice was beginning to feel the strain of a full concert and laryngitis.

As the order of songs on the live set has been altered for the video, Annie is seen alternately in this bedraggled state and fresh with her jacket on. This evident weariness, combined with actors of dubious credibility and dubbing, podgy puppets and previously released videos is a fair indication of why Eurythmics were not happy with the product. Then again, the majority of the live set was stunning, the promotional films were exceptional and fans were offered another medium on which they could enjoy their favourite band.[29]

Their professional misery was not to end there. The third unwelcome release this year was a remix album called *Touch Dance* containing just four songs from *Touch* reworked several times. Initially, as with *Sweet Dreams (The Video Album)*, Eurythmics felt the idea had merit and flew out to New York to put the finishing touches to the work done by François Kevorkian and John 'Jellybean' Benitez. They were also keen to appear fair, so while they tried to deny that the project was just a re-hash of old material, they ensured that a low price reflected the album's duplication. The result was intended to be of interest to die-hard collectors and DJs, although confusingly Dave pronounced that Eurythmics was not aimed at a dance audience. But then something went wrong.

Eurythmics announced they were unhappy with the final product, slating it as "predictable" and "inspiration free". Once again, they went to the trouble of advising their fans that the album was not endorsed by the band. Dave was particularly insulted as of course he had engineered the original versions. "When I say I can't stand it, I can't stand the principle of it," he explained. "It's songs that I've already recorded and mixed to the best of my ability. I don't think people juggling around with the sound of things makes them any better as songs . . . It was some bright spark's idea, it definitely wasn't our idea."

Indeed, Dave was right to query the point of remixing something which had already been mixed many times, including by Eurythmics themselves on the B-sides of several of their singles. *Touch Dance* cannot claim to add anything, no matter how small, to the original recordings, especially as the concept of remixing back in 1984 did not necessarily mean introducing any new instrumental parts, rhythms or beats to the material, rather just re-phrasing it, placing different parts in different places, or maybe just adjusting the tempo. That said, it was pleasant enough background music for any discerning Eurythmics fan who chose to ignore Dave and Annie's plea not to buy this cheap re-run.

There are only four tracks on *Touch Dance*; 'The First Cut', 'Cool Blue' and 'Paint A Rumour' each appear twice, once with vocals and once in an instrumental guise, and 'Regrets' appears solely on the A-side as a vocal version. There is nothing audibly different on 'First Cut' or 'Cool Blue' and only some very small rhythmic effects are added to the vocal version of 'Paint A Rumour'. 'Regrets' is slowed down to a rather laboured tempo

---

[29] *Sweet Dreams (The Video Album)* was repackaged, confusingly using a black and white photo from 'Missionary Man', and re-released in the UK in early 2000.

and doesn't especially work at a reduced speed. Annie's voice in particular suffers from this treatment.

The flip-side concentrates on purely instrumental remixes of the songs, which accomplish little without Annie's vocals. This is apparent in the verses of 'First Cut', where the guitar is not enough to carry the interest forward to the choruses, although there are some nice pairings of elements not matched on *Touch*. The last two tracks on *Touch Dance*, the instrumental mixes of 'Cool Blue' and 'Paint A Rumour', probably work better than anything else on the disc – the latter especially is already established as one of the longest and most experimental on *Touch* and this is just the same again in a slightly altered version.

Despite the derision handed down by Eurythmics, *Touch Dance* received major UK promotion with Woolworths and priced at a minimal £2.99 as promised, it reached number 31, amazingly surpassed by number 15 in America.

★   ★   ★

Eurythmics were beginning to establish quite a name for themselves as being somewhat precious, often as a result of their well-meaning fastidiousness. This unfortunate image was only exacerbated when Annie opened up and admitted her true nature in interviews.

"I'm not a very *happy* person. My happiness comes in fits and starts, up and down. This is a very *intensive* time . . . but then all times with me are intensive. I would say I'm *relatively* happy," she told Graham K Smith (his italics). To compound the situation Annie rejuvenated a long-forgotten diatribe about being the group's focal point. "Obviously I *must* be an attention seeker – but I want the attention to get the music across." Continuing elsewhere, "We struggled together to get where we are now. I'm proud of both of us. The magazines may stick me on the cover by myself. But I'm proud of both of us because I wouldn't be on those covers without Dave."

Finally the outspoken Scotswoman attacked Sting, lead singer of The Police, whose 'Every Breath You Take' was number one in the charts throughout June 1984. "I don't have a great deal of respect for The Police – I've met and I found them, Sting in particular, a very puffed-up sort of person. I sensed he was very arrogant – but nevertheless 'Every Breath You Take' really moved me. And I was surprised because it came from someone so arrogant."

The fans were undeterred and as Eurythmics continued their major world tour promoting *Touch* in the summer, visiting Japan in June and returning to America in July, the crowds were as strong and jubilant as ever. With 'Who's That Girl?' hitting number 21 on June 23, Eurythmics were welcomed into the US with open arms.

"When we arrived the reaction was so different from Britain," explains Dave. "Here they've been seeing you eight times a day on MTV, so you're a *star*!" Annie added her own considered reasoning. "America, you see, doesn't have much of a history or culture – I'm referring to contemporary culture as distinct from things like Red Indians. So I've come to realise that they look to Hollywood as their past, their glorification, their Golden Dream. So stars are, in effect, treated like royalty. That's why so many people are hunting for stardom without a care for good quality in their work."

At some of the dates, the crowd were so wild in their anticipation of Annie that they often mistook Sandra Turnbull's appearance on stage for the singer. When Eurythmics finally graced the stage they did not disappoint the multitude, sporting an array of outfits; Annie wore either a powder blue suit with red gloves or a red polka-dot dress topped with a black curly wig, while Dave unusually assumed a Scottish tartan. These new looks were complemented by a revised set list. Marvin Gaye's 'I Heard It Through The Grapevine' was added to the covers repertoire, while some audiences were treated to a glimpse of Eurythmics' latest project with a song, 'For The Love Of Big Brother', which they had just completed. Many of the concerts were given a spectacular close as Annie sang a traditional Scottish number, 'Farewell To Tarwathie', over the last strains of 'Jennifer', which was beautifully executed.

Although enjoying the thrill of the tour's reaction, Annie complained to the press that being on the road was harder for her than Dave. "Dave loves it, 'cos he's very gregarious and likes to talk to people. But I have this physical thing with my voice that makes me less sociable, because it puts a tremendous strain on my throat to talk as well. So I'm always the one who's back in the dressing room or off in a room somewhere."

Another addition to the set was the inclusion of pop vocalist Howard Jones as the opening act. As he was currently seeing success with his number one debut album *Human's Lib*, Annie was quite right to comment that she did not picture him as their support act, but more of a touring companion. "He's a lovely guy and he's going to be huge, he's the same age as me, he went to music school like me and he's a vegetarian, so we've got a lot in common," she enthused of her new friend.

As musicians joined, equally they left. Dean Garcia's departure came at the end of the strenuous Touch Tour. "I stopped working with them after the large American tour in late 1984. It was a band change and I wanted to carry on with a project that I was working with on my own and I had the choice. So I decided not to. People who do big tours with them go round and round and you jump off and somebody else jumps on. That's the way it works with them," he says philosophically.

Barry Maguire continued to work as stylist for Eurythmics and recounts some of the nastier incidents that occurred under the strain of the tours. "Annie was singing. This person was at the front of the stage, sitting still, with her feet up on the railing while most people around were stood up. Now, this person was either totally dumbstruck and couldn't move because she was watching her hero, or was totally unimpressed. Fairly early on in the concert Annie came off as usual, but at this one particular gig she said, 'There's someone at the front of the stage, I'm not sure what it is but I'm getting a really strange feeling, can we keep our eye on her?' So we let security know.

"As the concert progressed, it became apparent that this person was just sitting there, almost trying to stare her out. There were another two times when Annie came off the stage. The first time she came off and said to me, 'Can you get me a bucket of water?' So I get this water. The second time she comes off, grabs the bucket of water, runs back on stage, walks right to the very front, almost with her toes leaning off the edge, looks down, stares at this person and just pours the water over this girl! Then she stops, looks down, smiles, turns around and just walks off stage. And everyone just goes wild. She said to me, 'I feel much better now!' "

Venting her frustration in this way was a rather wet wake-up call for the unsuspecting fan, but amusing nonetheless. Not all tour incidents were unsavoury in nature. Annie was often careful to look out for the safety and enjoyment of those that she could see in the front row and was reported to have instructed the bouncers to let a young boy in a wheelchair through the line of security. While the public persona was often of a private woman, particularly after her clandestine wedding, Annie ensured that her fans were treated with the respect that they deserved.

"One of the most moving experiences I had was in Los Angeles," the singer recounted. "This 75-year-old woman had waited an hour-and-a-half to see me after I'd been on stage and she knocked on my car window. I wound it down and she said she'd driven 150 miles to see me 'cos her daughter liked me. She said, 'I wanted to tell you that you've given me something incredible and I think you're really great.' It wasn't like fan worship or anything, it was something very real, very emotional and I felt humbled by it."

Sometimes though, the rapport with the crowd got a little out of hand and whatever the truth behind the story, Annie needed protection on at least one occasion. "There was another situation when she was cautioned," recalls Barry. "One of the fans accused her of something or other. Now I don't know, I've never actually asked her, but she said it was an accident. As far as we could see there was nothing happening, but Annie's out there on stage and who knows what had gone on between them.

"The person had gone straight to the police and said, 'I want this woman arrested for what she has done, I've got proof.' He was brought backstage by the police and to sort it out Annie apologised and the matter was dropped.

"While this was all going on I was in Dave's room and there was this knock on the door. The chap said, 'Can I speak to Dave please?' I asked, 'Who is it?' He said, 'Bruce'. So I said, 'Hold on' and I closed the door – I didn't even know who Bruce Springsteen was! Apparently he had gone to Annie and asked her to come for dinner with him the next night, and she said no, because she was married to Radha of all people . . ."

Annie in particular was glad to finish the tour, leave the stress behind and concentrate on her marriage of just a few months. The singer was hot in demand as Eurythmics continued to chart on either side of the Atlantic, and she found herself being approached for numerous acting roles. Annie politely declined the various offers, although she was tempted by a small part in a Steven Spielberg movie which was sadly written out of the final edit. "I want some *serious* acting lessons first," she said. "But when I'm ready I'd love to work with Scottish director Bill Forsyth. I know he's interested."

While the female Eurythmic felt she needed more time before branching out into movies, her counterpart was embracing the film world with aplomb. His active mind could not rest for long and after the rigours of touring Dave saw films as his next creative outlet. "I think it's [fame] all so funny I've decided to make a film about it," he delighted in telling the press. "I've been offered millions to do it but that's not the point. I just want to make it really slapstick with a daft plot – like one in an early Beatles film where they try to catch Ringo and paint him red for a sacrifice."

Dave's suitably madcap film portrayed him as a Jerry Lewis-style bumbling buffoon falling into farcical, visual gags involving several notable musicians. "In one scene I deliver a message to Stevie Wonder and as I arrive I trip over all these wires and land on his drum computer. 'Cos he can't see, right, when all these amazin' rhythms start he goes, 'Great, we've got to do a song together!' It's all a bit like that." With his creative juices in full flow, Dave also imagined a mickey-taking sequel to Prince's *Purple Rain* called *Lime Green Drizzle* and featuring himself in a green plastic cape with a funny hat. Regrettably these ideas never saw the light of day.

At this, their height of fame, Eurythmics were undoubtedly on a winning streak and in September 1984 they were fittingly called upon to fly to Saratoga to present a cup to a victorious jockey and his racehorse named, of course, Eurythmics. Dave received approaches from other artists hoping to benefit from his string of hit singles. "I've also been asked to write songs for Tina Turner's next album with her," he said. "I do tend to get a lot of offers from girl singers because they tend to be unsure about asserting themselves with male musicians – it's the way rock'n'roll's been structured. And I'm fascinated by female singing voices anyway."

Eurythmics consented to try another collaboration after the doomed *Touch Dance* and in the early autumn of 1984 they teamed up with the electronics duo, Chris and Cosey. The resulting single 'Sweet Surprise' is indeed surprising as Annie's twin, unformed vocals harmonise with themselves over a lazy triplet beat and an ominous synthetic bass. A flute part matches the breathy focus of this deceptively simplistic and occasionally rough track, which at a push could be Annie scatting away in the privacy of her own shower. The second part is not dissimilar to an electronic version of Pink Floyd's 'The Great Gig In The Sky', only 11 years on.

To continue Eurythmics' run of success, on September 18 they won the Best New Artist Video category for 'Sweet Dreams (Are Made Of This)' at the annual MTV Awards.

17

CONDITIONED SOUL

"I wanted something permanent, binding, that would give a form and core to my life away from the pressures of the musical rat race. I thought Radha's faith might give me some spiritual comfort, but I married knowing it might be a terrible mistake. Naïvely, I thought I could make something binding overnight."

– AL

Unable to achieve a happy medium in both her personal and professional life, just eight months after Annie and Radha's wedding ceremony, the marriage was over. Barry Maguire, who had always been wary of Radha, watched the rather predictable events unfold. "The tour ended and I think Annie wanted to come back to reality. She realised that the marriage wasn't for her."

Although Annie had tried hard to embrace Radha's demanding religion, ultimately Krishna Consciousness did not support a feminist wife, and a pop star lifestyle could not accommodate strict abstinence. The couple's intimate relationship was also apparently a source of discord. Annie had never been an openly physical woman and according to close friends the marriage signified a green light for Radha who had an insatiable sexual appetite. Furthermore, while he stated clearly in an interview that he was not jealous or possessive of Annie when she was away on business, Barry's odd experience with Radha perhaps suggested it was Annie who should have been concerned about her partner's antics.

"Annie said that other things came out about Radha's past," acknowledges Barry of things more sinister which attributed to the split. Jon Roseman ratifies the transformation the relationship had on Annie, particularly after they married. "She changed completely when he was around – very quiet and non-communicative. I think she was scared of him, a real nasty piece of work."

Speculation about Annie's estranged husband further outside her immediate circle of friends was also rife. Boy George for one experienced a run-in with the German who was soon to be outcast, as he recounted in his autobiography. "One afternoon I received a worried call from the front desk. 'Mr O'Dowd, there's a Hare Krishna in reception. He insists on seeing you.' I was intrigued. 'Who is he?' 'He says he's married to Annie Lennox.' I knew Annie had married a Hare Krishna and I was desperate to see what he looked like. I told them to send him up.

"Radha Raman was handsome and a little pushy. He certainly didn't have the wounded innocence of other devotees I'd met. I ordered tea and he ranted about Annie. He told me they had separated, but wouldn't say why. He was so jittery, I couldn't wait for him to leave. I never found out why he came to see me."

Peter Ashworth who, to his understanding, had not even officially broken up with Annie at the time of her wedding, curiously maintains a sympathetic view of the man who wooed and stole his girlfriend.

"I met him at the end of their relationship and he was a shattered man," says Peter gently. "I don't know where we met, but it wasn't with Annie. He came to me. We had a chat, it was no big deal, and I think I commiserated with him! He only got positivity from me. I told him not to take it personally but I could see he was weak. He just appeared to be a bit of a shell.

"There was a viewpoint that Hare Krishna was searching out pop stars. They were doing it to boost their public image. I *might* have heard that he was an infiltrator on behalf of Hare Krishna, but I had a feeling that the guy was just getting screwed up."

Fifteen years later Annie was to speak candidly about this particular break-up. "I would undermine relationships I had because of Dave, he was the most important person in my life. I had a sense of loyalty towards him, and it seriously affected my marriage.

"I was tired of shallow relationships. I wanted something permanent, binding, that would give a form and core to my life away from the pressures of the musical rat race. I thought Radha's faith might give me some spiritual comfort, but I married knowing it might be a terrible mistake. Naïvely, I thought I could make something binding overnight."

★   ★   ★

After the failure of her short-lived marriage, the best thing for Annie would have been for her career to return to its former glory after a year of contentious releases. Unfortunately, Eurythmics' next offering was to be just as problematic. The project in question was the soundtrack for a film adaptation of George Orwell's last novel, *1984*.

While the duo had individually expressed an interest in films, they had already turned down lucrative deals to record soundtracks for *The*

Company Of Wolves and the sequel to *Flashdance*.[30] With this track record in mind, when Eurythmics were approached by Virgin Films to provide the background music for Michael Radford's film epic of Orwell's classic starring Richard Burton, John Hurt and Suzanna Hamilton, unsurprisingly they declined. Dave expressed the band's genuine concerns: "We turned it down – it's taken us *this long* to get our songwriting together – at the moment we just want to make great Eurythmics records. A lot of people tend to jump into all things when they get famous and spread themselves really thinly. I mean . . . we've *never* written a soundtrack."

Annie was wary too, not of the ethic of Eurythmics' sound, but of the nature of the task. "I was really worried about doing it, 'cos I actually thought I couldn't take it. After all, I'm not the cheeriest of chapesses. But the thing was, it was so interesting." Written in 1949, Orwell's novel describes an imaginary life in a totalitarian state where Hitler had won the Second World War. The world is divided into three nations; Oceania (UK, the American continent and a part of Africa), Eastasia (the rest of Europe and Russia), and Eurasia (Middle East, Asia and a part of Africa). While Oceania is at constant war with the other powers, two of that country's subjects try to find love and live a normal life under the restrictive and imposing dictatorship of Big Brother.

After persistent repeated requests, Eurythmics accepted that it would be an exciting challenge to cover such a moody piece after all, and despite their other commitments the pair positively relished the undertaking.

True to form, Eurythmics managed to record the pieces for the film in just seven days, and the entire album in under 20 days. "Consequently the music's still new to me," bubbled Annie at the time. "It lives, I love it. Without being egotistical I think it's some of the best work we've done." Such speed was no doubt aided by the idyllic setting of the Compass Point Studios in the Bahamian capital of Nassau. "It was weird. You'd come out of the studio and there would be blinding light, and turquoise sea. It didn't look real, it was so divorced from what we were doing," described Dave of the scenery in contrast to the sombre subject matter.

With the album written and produced in record time, it seemed as though nothing could go wrong. However, a basic lack of communication lit a fuse that blew up in the faces of all parties involved.

Virgin Films had invested heavily in the project and were under great pressure to ensure that the film not only emerged by the end of the year for chronological impact, but also that it was a box office smash to recoup

---

[30] 1983's *Flashdance* had proved very successful, securing a Best Song Oscar for Giorgio Moroder's 'What A Feeling', but the second instalment never materialised.

the finance. In this effort Virgin's boss, Richard Branson, was keen to procure a heavyweight artist to secure sales of the soundtrack in conjunction with the film. Virgin initially approached David Bowie, but while many believe his demand for a high fee was the problem, director Michael Radford explains the real concerns: "Bowie was the favourite, but when he announced that he wanted to do 'organic music' for the film (no one quite knew what he meant but suspected he meant a 'real' film score as opposed to a rock track) the Virgin executives got a bit anxious because they saw the possibility of a number one hit disappearing."

By August, and mindful of the tight deadline, Radford forged ahead and commissioned Dominic Muldowney, renowned composer and National Theatre resident, to complete the volatile soundtrack as he had already provided the majority of the 'Oceanic' score used for the live scenes. When Eurythmics were approached by Virgin Films' executives, Al Clark and Robert Devereaux, to write the movie's music they were not privy to this development. Radford was equally unaware of their progress, "I knew Branson was looking, but it was far too late. He never told me he had hired Eurythmics."

Although Dave and Annie were surprised that the director did not meet them in person, without any previous experience in this field they accepted the unusual circumstances. "We were working to a rough video," says Annie, "and I kept saying to Dave, 'Why isn't the director here?' We thought he must be too busy."

The director in question was horrified that they were working on the music before the movie was finalised. "Of course I'd have loved to be in the Bahamas with them," deadpans Radford today, "except I was finishing the movie in Twickenham."

The result of the director and backer failing to liaise left Radford with the very real problem of having two scores. Ultimately he felt strongly that it was his venture and he would choose the most appropriate style for his footage. "It was the first time they'd done a film soundtrack," recalls Radford who was nervous of Dave and Annie's lack of practice in this area. "They had even put sound effects into the music because they hadn't realised that we were doing the sound in London and thought that there was an absence of good effects."

Unimpressed with the pop-orientated product from Eurythmics, Radford favoured Muldowney's classical approach with anthems mimicking the rousing nationalistic fervour of the subject. After their stylised offering, when Eurythmics heard the rough cut of the rival score they were surprised. Dave was openly derogatory of Muldowney's music, likening it to the tackiness of a *Pathé News* signature.

Radford took control and finished mixing *1984* with Muldowney's soundtrack. His reasons were both practical and bitter. "When I got Eurythmics' music I had already finished the film and was into something else. I also felt a bit used, because I knew that Branson was trying to sign them to his label and I felt that he was using this as bait." Regardless, Radford failed to inform either Eurythmics or Virgin Films of this decision and the former were becoming increasingly disgruntled about the discourtesy of continually being kept in the dark.

"The first we heard was that our music wouldn't be used at the premiere of the film," said Annie at the time. "We still don't know what's happening. Last we heard, they'd edited less than one per cent of our score into the soundtrack." It was true Branson had eventually managed to persuade Radford there were financial merits in using Eurythmics' music, if only to spawn a charting album, but the director sustained his stubborn streak. "I asked Branson what legally was the minimum amount of music I could put on the movie to allow him to put out a record. He said 15 seconds, so I put 15 seconds of their music on the film."

Now it was Eurythmics' turn to get bolshie. After all, they had laboured over some powerful pieces. "When Branson came back to me and said that the Eurythmics management insisted that their music should be on the film, I was furious," claimed Radford. "I thought, 'If I had produced a record cover for them and they didn't like it, I wouldn't insist they used it. Where's the integrity of the artist here?'"

However, while the director rules the editing room, the financiers pull the strings when it comes to profitability. Just a few weeks after release, *1984* was retracted from the cinemas only to be remixed with Eurythmics' compositions covering 95 per cent of the music moments. The dividends resulting from the change were twofold: an increase in popularity at the box office brought about in part by the controversy, while the score's alteration helped secure a previously elusive distribution deal in America. Radford eventually conceded, "I've seen the film since, and I actually quite like the music now – it gives it a pace and intensity. At the time though it was the principle I was protesting – the director is the director of the movie."

Indeed, Radford remained vociferous in his attacks about the changes that he felt were "foisted" on his film. During an acceptance speech for Best Film Of The Year at the *Evening Standard* awards at the Inn On The Park, London, he made his views inappropriately clear.

"I'd planned the speech beforehand because I was so angry," he explained afterwards. "Actually during the meal that preceded I got rather mellow and thought I'd better not say anything, but I'd told so many people I was going to do it, I had to." His tirade included spelling out how indignant he felt that "a rock band should insist on its music being used when basically it was not good enough."

Annie had sensibly retreated to the sanctity of her Swiss hideaway throughout the crisis, and rose above the bickering to say, "We wash our hands of it. We did what we were asked to do, we made a soundtrack and an album that we both feel really proud of. But at this moment I'm so fed up with people saying one thing, and doing another, that I couldn't really care less."

Officially, Eurythmics were forced to issue their fourth exonerating press release of the year. "Our credibility as artists has been seriously jeopardised by Michael Radford's misleading comments – he knows that his real dispute is with Virgin Films. We would not even have considered a request to write a soundtrack for the film if we had known someone else had been asked to do so. We only discovered this by accident."

After the tedious altercation, Eurythmics did eventually release an album in November 1984 which was neither billed as the film's soundtrack, nor Eurythmics' fourth album. Instead it indicated on the jacket that it contained, "Music derived from Eurythmics' original score of the motion picture *1984*" and quoted a few lines from the film describing the love and loyalty for Big Brother.[31] While it garnered some open-minded reviews including *NME*'s "exceptionally good" and "one of studio-mad Stewart's most experimental works", it was often mistakenly viewed as a follow-up to *Touch* rather than as a stand-alone project, and much to Branson's frustration it suffered poor sales.

★   ★   ★

1984 For The Love Of Big Brother the film is a dark and uncomfortable piece, reflecting a Nazi-styled authoritarian society where the citizens are brainwashed by propaganda and trained to think, talk and write in a doctored language; Newspeak. Uncannily, it was shot during April–June 1984, exactly the same dates as the protagonist (Winston Smith, played by John Hurt) records his thoughts and experiences in his illegal diary. Radford, faced with the two completely different scores, chose ironically to use very little music at all in his finished edit. Muldowney's work features only in the Wagnerian songs and fanfares of Big Brother's announcements, and once or twice in fragments of wistful themes. Eurythmics' tracks on the other hand appear more frequently, but as basic instrumental versions of the finished music found on the album, and notably low in the mix.

[31] Notably Annie returns to her former incarnation of Ann Lennox on the credits – a hint that she wants to be taken more seriously or merely a careless copyist's typo?

In fact, music of any description is so scarce throughout the actual film that at times the footage runs the risk of being stilted and awkwardly silent. One can only assume that all three composers for this project must have been taken aback at the quietness of the movie after the vast quantity of work independently submitted.

The soundtrack to *1984* has actually stood the test of time better than some other Eurythmics work, and still sounds as fresh as it did on its release. The album is quite short, as are the tracks, and the instrumentation as a whole is spacious, uncluttered and never overproduced. This along with the only slightly more negative fact that some of Annie's vocals are not her most polished, reflects the short amount of time spent recording the music.

But that is not a bad thing – *1984* stands as an excellent example of Dave and Annie at their most raw and basic. The opener to the album, 'I Did It Just The Same', is one of the best and most durable tracks on *1984* as it leisurely builds up from a beat reminiscent of a falling drop of rain, to a delicious mix of a simplistic electronic groove augmented with bluesy piano and Annie's improvised, increasingly confident vocals, sounding alternately in pain and pleasure. With its infectious, toe-tapping beat, the whole song sounds like a catchy introduction to a full blown dance track. Unfortunately, despite this rather upbeat impression, 'I Did It Just The Same' is used in a more basic form in the movie against images of execution and the protagonist having sex with an ageing prostitute.

The most obvious example of dance music on this soundtrack album, however, is the fast and furious 'Sexcrime (nineteen eighty-four)' which took over the airwaves for the duration of the summer that year. The distinctive introduction of multiple sampled Annies confidently cry out a rash of the words "Sex" and "Crime" which are panned manically from left to right, creating total confusion. The song itself is then packed to the brim with funky, computerised energy, punctuated with scattered cries and samples.

Annie's performance is Bowie-esque in both musical tone and cynicism as she sings a difficult tale of the illicit act of intercourse in the sure knowledge that the lovers are being watched. Her pain is apparent: "And so I face the wall/ Turn my back against it all/ How I wish I'd been unborn/ Wish I was unliving here". Staying true to the Orwellian theme of 'Big Brother', later references describe her anger and desire to pull the wall down to spite the person watching from a hidden camera. In Newspeak the word 'Sexcrime' misleadingly refers to "love", which has been turned into a crime by the oppressive government of Oceania. The evil, insistent subject matter did not detract this otherwise excellent, straightforward dance track from being a major hit for Eurythmics, simultaneously helping the film to enter the public awareness via extensive radio play.

The mood of the album is then immediately softened with the entrance of the jangly bhangra-like theme introducing an ascending figure which is then repeated throughout 'For The Love Of Big Brother'. A piano bass line and sensitively chosen rhythmic effects serve to make this track one of the most atmospheric on the album, aided beautifully by Annie singing against the music in quiet half tones. This is one of the tracks where her vocals are a little on the rough side. Somehow this only makes the music more fresh and intimate, as if she is not afraid of wavering, or hitting her notes slightly flat. What is more striking is the similarity to the Nigerian/ English soul singer Sade in her voice and style of harmonies.

Lyrically 'For The Love Of Big Brother' keeps up the eternal fear of being watched, with chilling lines like "Even though there's no one/ Dark shadows move across the wall" and the subtle threat of "I still hear the echo of your footsteps on the stairs" against a hopelessly tumbling bell effect, portraying the helplessness of a nation's predicament. In the film a distorted version of this song is used while Winston and Julia, played by Suzanna Hamilton, make love.

'Winston's Diary' is an instrumental track that takes the form of a short hymn, combining an organ, gentle bass line and a harmonica sounding a melodic counterpoint against a soft chord progression. It is a fine example of how the two composers have taken their task of creating film music for the first time very seriously, and managed to cross over from their normal genre of upbeat pop music in a thoughtful, well crafted and delicately understated manner.

A shifted and altogether new mood is introduced with 'Greetings From A Dead Man', as busy tribal rhythms swimming with hi-hats and shakers form the image of a procession of some kind. Another example of choice film music, this is almost entirely instrumental except for Annie's rhythmic, mechanical "babababa".

'Julia' is the 'love interest' in the film; a young, rebellious member of the Junior Anti-Sex League. Eurythmics' theme is played at many conflicting times during the movie, notably when Winston and Julia are momentarily 'free' in beautiful countryside and then again when Winston is led to the torture chamber of Room 101. At the end of the film the viewers can hear the full version of 'Julia' as it appears on the album, if they are willing to sit staring at a blank screen once the credits have stopped rolling.

Eurythmics' 'Julia' is a moody, sometimes mournful ballad, which lyrically is a precursor to later work as it ponders human longevity through the changing seasons. Initially there is the strange *a cappella* juxtaposition of two different versions of Annie duetting with each other, one natural and untreated, and the other computerised. Soon after, bells and wind chimes twinkle in the background, introducing a light-as-air keyboard backing of an electronic harpsichord playing rippling arpeggios and a piano. Annie's repetition of the name 'Julia' sounds alternately nostalgic and insistent, and a synthetic trumpet sounds out a doleful anti-fanfare at the end alongside her hopeless question, "Will we? Will we still be there?" Unfortunately the ending, which includes a pensive acoustic guitar solo, drags on way too long; without accompanying pictures on the screen the music alone is unable to sustain much interest.

Newspeak for "very good indeed" in Orwell's book, 'Doubleplusgood' starts with a 'telescreen' announcement of a glorious victory in South India – foretelling of the supposed end of the war. This authoritative excitement is given the imaginative background of Burundi drumming, shakers and maracas of all descriptions, and miscellaneous shouting. Notably a high keyboard pedal point bleats out against the chorus, reminiscent of an alarm clock panned from side to side and piquantly increasing the sense of pressure brought on by the music.

But then something goes dramatically wrong and the news report seems to break down. The word "Attention!" is cut short and edited to a telling new meaning of 'tension'. The frenetic climax witnesses the announcer's voice counting down from 10 and stumbling quite a bit; intriguingly she never reaches '1'.

In Oceania, Winston and Julia's home, the Ministry Of Love represents one of four official government departments. The headquarters of the dreaded Thought Police, it is by far the most-feared office as it oversees 'law and order' (actually meaning the lawless acts of sex and love). Accordingly, Eurythmics' 'Ministry Of Love' is played every time Winston knowingly commits an illegal act, such as pulling down his diary from behind a loose brick in the wall and writing in it, and again when he opens a furtive note from Julia saying, "I love you" and arranging a rendezvous. Both deeds in themselves are punishable by death.

'Ministry Of Love' is best described as a dysfunctional instrumental ballad, based on a fluttering, descending scale of three notes, a techno bass line and inspired use of a rainshaker stick. Extra percussion is brought in gradually and Annie adds some tribalistic vocals, occasionally exclaiming, "Ha!" After a while, the title, 'Ministry Of Love' is spoken repetitively as if by a room full of people and the track fades out, accompanied by half-beats on the drums.

Beginning with a high pitched guitar harmonic, 'Room 101' leads into a grotesque psychedelic anthem swimming with squealing guitars. An electronic alarm beat and Annie's soulful "oohs" signal the abrupt entry of the depraved dance track. This mainly consists of an unpleasant repeated synth line and Annie making background noises that simulate the sounds of whipping and wailing. A sinister male computerised voice darkly intones the significance of 'Room 101'; "It's the worst thing in the world – I told you!" and the whole nightmare of a dead, futuristic prison culminates with an ear-shattering drumbeat.

While the album did not fare well in the charts, the first single, 'Sexcrime (nineteen eighty-four)' reached number four in the UK. As if to spite Branson for specifically seeking US commercialism, the single was banned by the majority of American radio stations for its so-called "objectionable content" and struggled to number 81.

Adding insult to injury Dave explained the gut-wrenching events surrounding the accompanying promotional video for 'Sexcrime (nineteen eighty-four)', poignantly soon after Radford's public harangue condemning those who tampered with his work: "They agreed to give us the film to put in our video and then I was really confused. I thought, 'Hello, the director doesn't want to put our music in *his* film but he wants to put his film in *our* video in order to sell the film.' And at that point we just stopped talking to them."

As Radford conceded, so too did Eurythmics and eventually included menacing clips of the feature film in their video, even going so far as to dress up in the shapeless boiler suits worn by the party members in *1984*. Returning to director Chris Ashbrook for the promo, the feisty footage of Dave and Annie was shot in a disused South London car park.

Commencing with a square pupil, TV images flicker in the eye bringing this video to life. Resembling a beautiful blond boy, Annie personifies Hitler's idea of the perfect Aryan specimen and, surrounded by bonfires and low-flying helicopters, the uneasy feeling of the film is effortlessly recreated. Dave too brings a nasty tone with a close-up of his long pinkie fingernail operating the mixing desk, before becoming violent and mindlessly smashing the equipment. Annie is captivating to watch as she is particularly animated, utilising jerky dance movements to the full.

"She's got energy, she's highly intelligent, and she's got an awareness of what she looks like," summarises Ashbrook. "The reason she gets crabby, which she does, is that because she works so hard at her performance, she gets the feeling that no one else is really working hard. I mean look at a video set, people just stand there with glazed eyes, and she's working to give a really decent performance. If she ever stops singing she could become an actress, she's stunning, she's such a beautiful performer."

With this more developed confidence came the ability to experiment with different images, and as 1984 drew to a close Annie's fans were initially astonished to see her change her style quite drastically. Gone were the orange crop and men's suits; in their place a softer, more elegant dress style and a feminine blonde hairstyle.

"Now I don't need to assert that kind of masculine sexuality as much, I'm allowing the feminine side of my sexuality to come through and I'm more comfortable with that," she explained. "Now I've established a certain persona, I can move into something a little softer." Annie's change of heart marked a turning point in her life as, on Christmas Day, 1984, she hit her thirties. "In my head I'm probably hitting 50," she shrugged to the press. "I said to Dave recently that I feel pretty good about being 30 because I felt I've achieved something I set out to do which until this point I didn't realise. It's not the motivation to be a star – that's a little tacky, but I certainly wanted to be a performer of note." No one could argue with that.

18

WALKING ON BROKEN GLASS

"It's so important for me to stress that I'm only doing what I'm doing today because of Dave. Without him I don't think I would have stood a hope in hell. I would have been like thousands, millions of other women singers who have great potential but get nowhere."

– AL

The year 1985 began with the unthinkable: a rumour that Eurythmics were to split. The group had endured a long year of problems with unauthorised and unwanted material, and had argued with their record company, publishers and film makers. As Dave buried himself under an ever-increasing workload as a producer in high demand, weary comments from Annie were easily misconstrued.

"We're finishing off years of work now – Dave and I haven't stopped working for six years and we've worked really, really hard every day. There has to come a time when you say No Eurythmics, No Annie Lennox, No Dave Stewart, No Nothing – just disappear – and that's going to come very soon."

The fire was fuelled by a seemingly incessant need for the two group members to prove how contrary they were in every aspect of their lives. "We're total opposites," said Dave to *Musician* magazine. "If I speak to Annie for more than five minutes she sometimes gets really confused and tells me to stop it . . . Annie is often very quiet. Before we go on stage, my dressing room's always full and there's always tons of people coming in and out, people cracking jokes, the trumpet player doing a dance in his kilt . . . In Annie's dressing room it's always quiet and sort of empty.

"That represents a similar thing to how it works, really. When we're on stage and in photos, Annie seems like the real extrovert. She's at the front and I'm the guy behind. But that's a very classic thing, isn't it? There aren't many people who are the same in the dressing room and on stage."

"He's always been like that," Annie would agree. "Very productive and irrepressible; he's an extraordinary character and he comes up with all these ideas. He's far more fruitful that I am and you never know what he's going to come up with next, but I like that chaotic creativity he has. We're both very keen that everything we do is sharp, like a knife."

Dave and Annie's personal history together was always going to be at the forefront of every journalist's mind, and in retrospect the two musicians appeared to play it to the hilt, leaving fans and critics alike to ponder how the pair could work together. "Our relationship ranges from really intense battles to very close friends," said Annie, then adding with some forethought, "where we know we'll never be able to work with anyone else.

"All the songs we've written have been in circumstances when we've been just about to split up, but something comes together again and each time it's stronger than before." As the music press delightedly digested each spicy morsel, even those unaffected by the hype wondered how a duo, whose best work came from violent arguments, could possibly continue for much longer. The charts this year were already beginning to reflect a declining interest in British synth-pop acts, and suddenly to the hippest music connoisseurs Eurythmics appeared somewhat dated. *1984* had pretty much proved to be a flop, the band seemed tired of both internal and external disputes – how could they carry on?

"The only way I could describe our musical direction is to say we never stop learning," said Dave diplomatically, "and each influence is apparent in our songwriting and recordings. It's difficult to stake a direction for yourself without being preconceived and a trap for yourself." Annie was never slow to rise to the defence of the couple's writing skills working as a team: "Dave is a very good barrier. We work together lyrically and he works like an editor. I usually say a song is rubbish, and he looks at what I've done.

"It's strange. I'm pessimistic about my own efforts – I think they're no good. It rather takes his encouragement, helping me to see what's good in a shared vision. That way I get inspired and have the guts to go away and do it quietly in a corner."

With a roller coaster year of emotional events behind her, Annie took the plunge and attempted once again to visit a psychotherapist. Now she was 30 her maturity made her more open to being helped than during the traumatic session years before, when she had perceived the therapist presented a brick wall. She signed up for a single meeting with a female practitioner in Los Angeles, and was later to say that it was the best $500 she had ever spent.

"It was significant, a great help," she confided in an interview with *Q* magazine. "I mean, some friends of mine see analysts once a week. It's a kind of fascination with their psyche. Me, I'm not so confident, not even so curious, so self-obsessed. But I did go to this woman at about the point when I was splitting up with the man I married, having difficulty with my father, everything was coming at me, I couldn't even face going outside my hotel room – I was just lost. I thought I deserved it all, I'm not worth anything, you know."

It was propitious that Annie's therapist was not remotely star-struck or overawed by her celebrity, and treated her patient as a normal individual. Most importantly she pointed out to Annie that the pop star's life was *ab*normal, and there were very few people out there who would be able to cope healthily with the incredibly intense experiences linked to it.

"Fortunately she was very good. She validated me. She said, 'Listen, you're not so crazy, you're not a bad person.' She made me realise that anyone who goes through these vast changes in their environment, in their circumstances, is going to come to a crisis point."

Annie was to view this sole appointment as a milestone in her life, on occasion specifying that her depression lasted from the ages of 14 to 30. This was not to say that the spectre was to magically vanish from her life without trace, just that now she felt more equipped to deal with her feelings. "I go through these three-month periods when I'm completely down," she said to Tony Jasper. "For years I've been a bad manic-depressive, but people don't see that in me so much because I can only do what I do when I'm feeling pretty up. If I'm down, I'm under the bedclothes, I can't see anybody – I just don't emerge . . . And now I feel I'm coming out of it. I'm sure there are millions of people like me who've been down so much. But although all these bad experiences can be horrific, with a bit of luck and a *lot* of grit, you can turn them into something creative. I do believe in self-improvement and I don't think one is always a victim, not at all."

With a clearer vision of her personality in front of her, Annie began to relax a little and unwind. She had been prohibited from consuming alcohol on strict instruction from Radha during their marriage, but now she would occasionally be seen with a drink in her hand. "I've never seen her really off her face, but she does like a drink," recalls Dean Garcia. "When she did drink she lightened up a little bit, she just couldn't do it too often for her voice."

"Actually, I drink to relax," Annie declared when questioned on her methods of recreation later in November. "I wouldn't endorse it for everybody, but I must admit I'm a better person when I've had a drink." Suggesting that the days of a Hare Krishna lifestyle were long behind her, she continued, "I'm afraid I don't meditate or do anything like that and I don't go to the health club that often. I wish I did.

"I have a strange dichotomy. You know those funny cuckoo clocks in Switzerland where on sunny days the woman comes out and on cold days the man does? I'm a bit like that. I can be very icy. It's either my defence mechanism, or because I really don't like that person and I want them to go away . . . [But] something happened to me on my 30th birthday that changed me. I feel more positive than I ever did before."

★   ★   ★

Far from being on the verge of splitting up, Dave and Annie were working hard on a secret album of covers including tracks like 'Last Night I Dreamt Somebody Loved Me' by The Smiths, The Temptations' 'My Girl' (with the suitable Lennox adaptation to 'My Guy'), David Bowie's 'Fame' and 'Come Together' by The Beatles. Tragically this release did not materialise.[32] 'Armadillo' and studio versions of '4/4 In Leather' and 'Tous Les Garçons' also adorned the cutting room floor, but were shelved within Eurythmics' vaults for future use.

On January 29, 1985 Dave purchased an apartment in Paris at number 5 Rue Jean-François Gerbillon. This stengthened his family connections with France through his stepfather, and also his brother John, who frequently visited the country on business with the British Film Institute. Dave continued to maintain a London base with his house in Maida Vale, but set his heart on doing up his new retreat, covering the walls with fabric and carpeting the floor for soundproofing, installing new theatre-style lighting in the bathroom and eventually adding reinforced doors as a result of an unsuccessful burglary attempt 18 months later.

In a mirror image of the period after the break-up of their romance, Annie too decided to follow suit, and acquired her own apartment virtually next door to Dave's. Neither star spent a great deal of time in these Parisian abodes, being more frequently required in London (where Annie also retained her flat, as well as the deserted place in Switzerland), but they fell in love with the charms of the French capital, and vowed to record their next album there.

Paris initially offered a welcome opportunity to escape from the die-hard fans who waited for their heroes outside their London homes, studios and media appointments. Annie and Dave were now well-versed in interviews and the necessary promotion required to keep interest in the band alive in between albums. The two videos for *1984* were shot within one week which also included a photo session and several interviews. This was during a period when they were beginning to write new songs.

---

[32] The covers were later pencilled-in for use in the 1986 *TVP* project.

"No one really gets used to media attention," said Annie. "It's a gauntlet you have to run through. If you are in the public eye, it is par for the course that you are scrutinised. You are fair game. I have to come to terms with being famous." Dave on the other hand had to be careful that Eurythmics' balance came across on paper. "It's difficult when there's two people – when Annie's talking I might disagree, but I can't stand interrupting because the interview wouldn't go very smoothly if we both did that. She's allowed to say what she wants to say and I'm allowed to say what I want to say. We don't walk around in unison doing double-tracked vocals, 'Hello!'"

Sadly for the guitarist who had always craved life in the spotlight, he was only ever going to be of secondary importance to the band's lead singer, whose every vital statistic could be found regularly splashed across the pages of *Smash Hits* or *Record Mirror*. Annie fans were delighted to read that her favourite films included *Fantasia*, Bob Hope and Bing Crosby classics, and she was also a documentary aficionado, especially those directed by Robert Altman. Her preferred food was "fresh clean fruit and veg" and her favoured tipple was a margherita or two from Ferdinands in Chalk Farm.

"I like simple, clean and uncluttered food," she said to the huge interest of her fans. "I like Japanese cooking because it's presented well and they put a lot of care into it . . . I tend not to eat a great deal of meat. I prefer steamed vegetables, nothing with heavy sauces and not too elaborate . . . I love drinking, particularly tequila. I wrestle with my conscience continually." The examination was completed by naming her latest clothing fad as "well-made classics in leather, silk, cotton or tweed".

It was nice to hear that the lady was human as well. "My nose should be a little smaller, my face shouldn't be as long," she whinged. "I'd like to lose the dark shadows under my eyes and the wrinkles now developing at the age of 30. I would like to have thicker hair, curlier, and thicker eyebrows though I like my eyes – I'm very happy with my eyes. I don't want to change them and I like my mouth and I like my teeth but I don't like fillings . . . Oh and I don't like my smile or my profile."

If Annie worried she fell a little short in the facial department it certainly wasn't apparent in Eurythmics' latest video. 'Julia' was the second and last single to be released from the *1984* album and failed to chart in the US, achieving only number 44 in the UK.

The intense accompanying promo clip was alternately regarded as Eurythmics' most uninteresting and their most timeless. It was simple, featuring only a head and shoulders shot of Annie performing the song, a range of emotions crossing her strong features. Few artistes would be able to hold the viewers' attention for the duration of such a slow ballad, but

Annie carried it off with ease, perhaps inspiring Sinéad O'Connor's striking video for 'Nothing Compares 2U'. Without all the brash excitement of a 'normal' Eurythmics promo the single sold poorly, despite ardent fans' examination of cryptic references such as a series of flute segments taken from the beginning of each verse and played backwards, audible at 4:36 to 4:18 on the CD.

★   ★   ★

Leaving behind the unpleasantness surrounding *1984*, Eurythmics resolved to return to the pop scene by recording a straightforward album of new songs. "I've already an idea what the next Eurythmics LP is going to be musically – lots more 'real' instruments," Dave hinted in the press. "An Eastern feel mixed with the heart of soul music. We're going to get a double-decker bus with a studio and drive off to France or Spain – it reminds me of *Summer Holiday!*"

Eurythmics had settled on Paris as the base to record their fifth official album, and rented a cheap rehearsal loft, kitting it out with some of the equipment used at The Church, including the original console on which *Sweet Dreams (Are Made Of This)* was recorded. They threw themselves into their new project, cleverly titled *Be Yourself Tonight* to reflect a musical development from the vastly differing *Touch* and *1984*, but Annie was not afforded a break from tabloid exposure.

Having formally separated from her estranged husband Radha in February, citing irreconcilable differences, divorce proceedings commenced in April 1985. Despite Annie's careful announcements to the contrary, the papers shamelessly printed reports on the ex-couple's supposedly bitter feud, suggesting that they were now only communicating through legal representatives.

"The split between Radha and myself is personal," pleaded Annie in a statement to the aptly titled *Celebrity* magazine. "The decision is amicable and mutual and something we feel is the best thing. There is absolutely no animosity between us and no truth in the suggestion that we're communicating only through our solicitors." Annie's last wish was to attract any public attention, especially as she was simultaneously trying to record a new album, but patiently she explained in interview after interview that she and her husband had grown apart, yet they were still very good friends and there was no need for all the fuss. Many celebrities at that point may well have refused interviews, but wisely Annie chose not to alienate herself further from her audience, realising that she had already reached the far side of sensationalism with the marriage and its religious connotations.

A fascinating read for followers of the headline stories came in the

October edition of *Rolling Stone*, which was ostensibly publicising Eurythmics' new album. Reporter Brant Mewborn secured an exceptionally rare interview with the elusive Radha, who claimed that the whole divorce issue had come as a complete shock.

"It's hard to get a real picture," the 32-year-old German outlined. "She's not an easy person. You always have to read between the lines, look behind the make-up. So I never really found out why . . . All I want is for her to be happy. I said to her, I don't want to talk about money and that sort of thing. All I want to do is straighten us out. I don't mind leaving the house, but I don't want to leave a mess.

"Sometimes I think she expected a miracle or something and probably I couldn't hold up with it . . . You all see Annie Lennox the pop star, but she's a small-town girl – very deep and very beautiful. But a small-town girl. She didn't drop down from heaven. She's like anybody else. Sometimes you go down and you need somebody to pep you up. It took a lot out of me to give so much strength to somebody else."

Having taken the opportunity to draw some sympathy from the readers of the eminent music magazine, Radha concluded by painting as curious a picture of his former wife as had many times been suggested of him. "For a while every article on Eurythmics began with the fact that Annie was married to this Hare Krishna person, and she got very tired of that. Around the time we were breaking up, she got very strange. It was like she wanted to show the world she's not so weird and crazy, that marrying a Hare Krishna was not such a good idea."

Fortunately Annie's "craziness" was twinned with a self-deprecating sense of humour, as she was quoted within the same article, "I'm so sick of reading about my divorce. Aaaaah! My broken heart! If I got obsessed with it, I could hate a lot of people. But I don't think that's healthy." To all intents and purposes it seemed that the messy affair was thankfully over, and Radha set off on a fresh career as a photographer in Los Angeles. The divorce would be finalised in 1986 and any time thereafter Annie openly referred to the whole business as a "mistake".

It was only natural therefore, that with her 'freedom' mercifully redeemed, Annie was to throw herself wholeheartedly into life as a single woman. She started by revisiting old ground.

Peter Ashworth was busy scaling the heights of his own career in photography when he received a telephone call from Annie during a shoot for the cover sleeve of the Phil Collins album, *No Jacket Required*. He was invited to visit her at the Portobello Hotel in London. Peter, intrigued by tales of her bizarre marriage, agreed to the meeting but was a little wary as to how she would react when he arrived.

"I had a shaved head at the time and I was rather worried that that would freak her out as Annie had never seen me with a shaved head before . . ." Not wanting to miss the opportunity to catch up on old times, Peter hastily disguised his new look and set off for the hotel. "I turned up and I had this sort of woolly hat on," he says. "I pulled it off and I saw the look in her eye that I got at Lake Como before, sort of 'God, you're not what I thought you were . . .'" Realising the flame that had once burned between them was long since extinguished, the two made their excuses and left, although their professional relationship was to be rekindled one last time shortly afterwards.

This left the path clear for Annie to begin a completely new romance with a dancer called Billy Poveda. The couple met in Los Angeles, when Billy was hired for the promo accompanying the first single from the upcoming album. As well as the physical attraction, Annie was also impressed with the former ballet dancer's commitment and credo, "Pain is pleasure; work is everything."

Billy's services were swiftly snapped up by Annie, who convinced him to leave behind his Californian lifestyle in favour of becoming her personal assistant. Billy was the third boyfriend the singer had approached with an offer of employment; Peter had refused the same at the beginning of their relationship, and Radha had for a time been Annie's unofficial chef during the Touch Tour.

After initially agreeing to an interview for this book, Billy decided not to speak as he is one of the few former partners of Annie Lennox who has remained friends save, of course, Dave Stewart. When those close to her were asked their opinion of this latest liaison, the general consensus was positive. Commented Dean Garcia: "Nice chap. Again a bit odd, unusual. Extremely artistic, creative. Obviously he was good for her. Kind of stimulating to talk to; he's quite visual, she likes that in people."

"Billy's great," said Barry Maguire without hesitation. "He's just full of life, lots of energy. They got on famously. He's a very encouraging, supportive person."

Billy's diligent work ethic and fun personality endeared him to the Eurythmics camp. Soon enough with his help an additional branch of business, of which Dave and Annie had dreamed for years, was to emerge. Eurythmics had always been a leading name in promo videos, and after one particular brainwave, Dave arranged a meeting between Billy and Dave's brother John, an established executive at the British Film Institute. Following a few months as Annie's PA, Billy's involvement in Eurythmics rapidly grew into the role of production manager. "Dave had the most prominent role in my integration into the company," says Billy today. "It was his idea to bring me into a professional relationship with Eurythmics. Dave put me together with John Stewart and that's how we formed Oil Factory."

In 1985, Billy and John started Oil Factory Films in North London. Before long they had recruited budding directors including Philippe Gautier and film student, Sophie Muller. Soon enough Oil Factory was living up to its name, producing an endless stream of videos for Eurythmics and other artists such as Sade, Sinéad O'Connor and Lenny Kravitz.[33]

While Annie was delighted with her current state of affairs, Dave had yet to settle into a long-term relationship. Having recently broken off a romance with actress Leslie Ash, a resident of Camden Square, North London, he had just started seeing Claire Evans. In a parallel reflection of Annie's relationship with Billy at the time, Claire was acting as Dave's own PA as well as being his girlfriend.

Annie and Dave had clearly come a long way since their break-up, but all was not quite right behind the scenes. After all, Annie had just followed her ex all the way to Paris.

Barry Maguire for one was aware of a certain continuing undercurrent. "I always thought there were a lot of unresolved issues there," he muses. "One time when Dave and I were in Spain together between a tour, we were in a restaurant in the early evening and we started talking about Annie. It was the only time we ever did this and I said, 'You still love her, don't you?' and he said, 'Yeah, I do love her.' I said, 'Call her,' but he never did. It was just the way he said it."

Patently, just because Eurythmics were willing to use their former relationship as an effective selling tool, it didn't mean they had completely smoothed things over. Their feelings for each other at this stage were never discussed in print, but five years later Dave was to offer a revealing insight into the inner workings of the odd couple.

"In the early days of Eurythmics I took almost complete control," he divulged in *Melody Maker*. "Then two-thirds of the way through I got less and less control, partly because so many things were happening and partly because Annie lost her confidence in me. She got worried that she was just doing what I was saying. And I got paranoid 'cos I know I can be like that

---

[33] Later in 1989, Billy was to return to his native Los Angeles and set up another branch of Oil Factory. Today, with more than 700 music videos on its CV, Oil Factory is among the cream of the industry's production companies and Billy Poveda is no less than the Executive Producer of Commercials and Feature Films.

so I just backed off. Around the time of *Be Yourself Tonight* I just said, 'Right that's it, I'm just part of the band.'"

★   ★   ★

The fifth Eurythmics album was recorded in Paris and mixed in Los Angeles. Faced with the challenge of appealing to the fans who had bought *Touch* some two years earlier, yet somehow having to reconcile their development into the world of soundtracks, Dave and Annie decided on a more rocky R&B sound. Favouring the Quincy Jones/Michael Jackson school of production, Eurythmics agreed that this fitted perfectly with Annie's transition from red-haired robot to blonde and beautiful sex symbol.

Since the last 'proper' Eurythmics record the singer had married, divorced, turned 30 and finally come to terms with her femininity. She no longer needed wigs, outrageous outfits, or props of any kind. With this new confidence she felt ready to tackle the world that had sniggered at her failings, religious, romantic or otherwise. Annie had grown up and was at last comfortable with herself. Depression was a dusty skeleton that no longer hid in her closet.

With the duo firmly established on the international rock circuit, Eurythmics were able to command guest appearances from Elvis Costello, Stevie Wonder, Aretha Franklin and Tom Petty's backing band, The Heartbreakers. Michael Kamen made a reappearance as their trusted orchestral arranger, and the musicians included a mixture of familiar names and new faces.

Be Yourself Tonight became a brave showcase for Annie's increasingly confessional lyrics, mainly revolving around matters of the heart. Un-ashamedly emotional, the result is a most moving album; alternately rousing, touching and sentimental. Considering what was simultaneously transpiring in her roller coaster love life, this was a courageous move as Annie later explained, "I'm not somebody who wished to draw attention to my romantic life or my emotions. It's been difficult, because at the same time that [the divorce] was announced, so was our album, so the papers wanted to write about me and my divorce instead."

As a first attempt at a less electronic, more energy-powered, all-out rock sound, Eurythmics achieve much, often with the old-style synthesisers peeping through the traditional band framework.

Be Yourself Tonight is a powerful album; not their best, but certainly memorable, made all the more poignant by the heartbreak of the subject material. The majority of Annie's lyrics appear to be about the death of one relationship and the birth, however indeterminate, of another. Annie was just starting out with Billy and bidding a turbulent farewell to her marriage. While open to interpretation, the apparent conclusions to be drawn from her lyrics are sometimes quite awkward in their candour of such love versus hate oppositions.

The hard rock opener, 'Would I Lie To You?', is about as far away from Eurythmics' earlier synthesiser work as they can get, and it seems that Dave and Annie are there to prove the point that they can indeed transcend this particular musical genre, with a little help from their friends. Particularly of note are Olle Romo for his enthusiastic, four-on-the-floor drumming, and Dave Plews and Martin Dobson, who produce a brass section to rival Phil Collins' trademark Phenix Horns of this era.

Annie harmonises with herself aggressively during the verse, which initiates the theme of leaving behind a failing relationship of lies and deceit: "You're the biggest fake, that much is true/ Had all I can take – now I'm leaving you". The sniping verse then leads into a stubborn, catchy chorus, full of energy and crashing guitars and cymbals. One of the most striking elements is the tremendous amount of confidence with which Annie sings. This in turn seems to rub off on all the musicians around her, who together put up an impenetrable front. The stunning opening track ends in a glorious cacophony of saxophone, vocals and guitars.

Stevie Wonder had long been one of Annie's idols, his music having been her initial inspiration to write. For his recording session Eurythmics uprooted from Paris to Los Angeles, but from the outset were a little sceptical that the session would ever actually take place. Recalls Annie: "We'd booked a studio in LA to record 'There Must Be An Angel (Playing With My Heart)' and rumour had it that Stevie Wonder didn't really know what time it is and we'd have to wait and see if he would turn up. It was getting very late and we were getting pessimistic whether he'd even turn up at all.

"Finally he showed up, and he was really an adorable person. He had these braids on his hair with beautiful gold beads, and when he plays he shakes his head so the beads make a loud noise. But the assistant who takes care of him took out this beanbag thing and gently tied Stevie's hair into it so it didn't make a sound down the mics. The man is a supreme musician, worth waiting for."

Reminiscent of the cloying, overwhelming happiness of 'Right By Your Side', 'There Must Be An Angel (Playing With My Heart)', is a camp, saccharine-sweet pop song which opens and closes with a death defying vocal stretching exercise from Annie. Soon the whole thing loses impetus in the chorus, which just repeats the same line over and over again against swirling harps and a warbling castrato.

By far the best bit is the gospel-tinged middle-eight, where Annie takes on a more soulful and interesting persona before Stevie Wonder's harmonica chimes out bright and breezily against a spiky clavichord. His effortlessly brilliant solo inspired the song's dedication to "Mr Stevie Wonder with love and thanks". As Annie herself declared: "To hear Stevie Wonder playing on a song that was dedicated to him anyway was heaven."

If there was ever a title to best describe Annie's ongoing relationship with Dave (and various significant others), 'I Love You Like A Ball And Chain' could not be far off the mark . . .

"That's where we got to the point of no escape," Dave later said seriously. "We had got such a history, we were prisoners of our own dreams. I remember recording it in Paris in just one take. Annie and I were trapped together. She was trapped in the persona she'd created and we'd started to wonder: 'How the hell do we get out of this?'"

On analysis, the lyrics for this song revolve around a relationship where Annie desperately longs for her lover, "Why do I feel so incomplete?/ When you're not here I'm just obsolete," yet is painfully aware that he is holding her back, "I'm a fool I know but I'm stuck on you . . . There's a river of blood/ There's a river of tears/ I've been wasting all these years".

Musically this song features a superior blending of authentic guitars and synthetic instruments. Annie teases with a gorgeous vocal melody in the verse, which leisurely makes its way to the chorus. The male backing vocalists, The Charles Williams Singers, are a most welcome antidote to Annie's feminine strength, and together they produce a male/female mix unheard since the days of The Tourists. The changing layers of vocals are dazzling, as are the sparing electric guitar fills, and when Annie goes up the octave for the second verse it all intensifies tremendously. Amusingly, the leisurely stroll of this well-paced funk/rock song is so laid-back as to be almost arrogant.

Later in the track we are treated to the novel rhythmic concept of "gravel and wood stomping", which apparently roped in Dave's mother Sadie. The extraordinary shaking, rattling effect is cleverly panned around the spectrum in circular movements against the building vocals.

Next Eurythmics travelled to Detroit to record the much-awaited duet between Annie and soul diva Aretha Franklin. From the very first beat of the introduction of 'Sisters Are Doin' It For Themselves' it is obvious that Annie and Aretha mean business. They begin by sharing a couple of lines each, but the partnership is not set in stone and by the time they reach the rip-roaring chorus of this up-tempo R&B stomp, the path has been laid for some sensational ad libbing. Everything sounds beautifully authentic, from Benmont Tench's Hammond organ to the gospel-flavoured backing vocals. Also impressive are the well-meaning witticisms such as "We're coming out of the kitchen/ Because there's something we forgot to say to you": a strong anthem for women everywhere.

After the cluttered stomp of 'Sisters Are Doin' It For Themselves', the breathtaking cleanliness of 'Conditioned Soul' is extremely effective. Chimes and pan pipes transport the song to a peaceful Tibetan hillside before it harks back to *Touch*, with crystalline synths matching an array of sitars, slide acoustic and electric guitars.

Annie is frustrated, pleading to her lover, or perhaps even herself, the title phrase, "Darling just be yourself tonight". She regretfully recalls past relationships and desperately wants to de-condition her partner's soul to get him to admit his true feelings. But, tellingly, by the end her lover has turned into a killer, demonstrating the agonising depth of her love/hate alliances.

'Adrian', a strange song about a besotted male Eurythmics fan, was recorded with left-of-centre singer/songwriter, Elvis Costello. "It was really special," recalls Dean Garcia, bassist for the session. "We worked in the studio, but then later on in the evening he came back up to the apartment where everybody was and there was food and stuff, and he sang a few songs on the piano. It was absolutely brilliant. Big voice, great big smile; really funny. It was lovely."

Annie also retains fond memories of this meeting of musical minds. "I have a deep respect for Elvis and a great deal of admiration because he's, mainly for me, an extraordinary lyricist," she said shortly after the recording. "One of the things he did when he came to the studio was to show us his book where he actually writes his lyrics. It's a huge hardback book and I just got such a buzz out of seeing his lyrics written down in this book that he obviously took a great deal of pride in. He's a very intensive person and I like people like that. I like people who put their beliefs on the line when they write a song."

With Annie evidently finding a soulmate in her co-vocalist, 'Adrian' develops into an up-front pop beat after an ambient, slow introduction with moody guitars and light cymbals. Annie and Elvis prove a pleasant match, but generally the song is a bit lightweight for Eurythmics and doesn't seem to evolve into anything spectacular. Annie's performance is indicative of the track as a whole as she is vocally noncommittal and after a while the well-meaning composition becomes too long and a bit repetitive.

Be Yourself Tonight is in need of something a little more persuasive after the nonchalance of 'Adrian', and with 'It's Alright (Baby's Coming Back)' Eurythmics succeed in recapturing the listener's attention. From the arresting start with its slow crescendo of soulful brass, this is another hit along the classic lines of 'Here Comes The Rain Again' with its striking brass counterpoint, sumptuous bass line and Eighties drum programming. Also worthy of mention is Dave's exquisitely understated guitar solo, making full use of delicate harmonics.

Annie manages to balance the yearning, desperate subject matter of the lyrics with ultimate confidence, and works especially well in harmony with herself in some nicely arranged, interlinking vocal parts. In this song she welcomes back her lover, and is literally so desperate to be with him that she doesn't care where he's been. As far as she is concerned, the two souls complete each other and there is nothing that can ever alter that. The end is a well-constructed vocal climax with Annie's soulful ad libs set against her own calming reassurance of "Make it easy on yourself tonight".

The last two tracks on *Be Yourself Tonight*, 'Here Comes That Sinking Feeling' and 'Better To Have Lost In Love (Than Never To Have Loved At All)' make good examples of the music Eurythmics were aiming to achieve with this album. Each stands alone as a somewhat standard rock work-out, yet the group retain some form of their earlier writing in vocal style, musical arrangement and unusual instrumental inclusions.

Neither song is particularly upbeat in subject matter, and thus the album ends on a low note. Although we have enjoyed glimpses of Annie in the ecstasies of true love, much of this album centres on the bitter failure of a long-term relationship. In 'Here Comes That Sinking Feeling' she is feeling the pain intensely: "Nobody hurts me like you do/ You cut into me like a poison dart/ Creep into my sleep at night/ Break into my dreams and tear them apart". Against a heavy rock guitar riff, her singing is backed by her speech as a dislocated announcer, which creates a detached, disjointed impression completely converse to the tortured meaning of her words. The most interesting effect though is when she pitches herself against the static rhythmic brass figures, very like the edgy Eurythmics of old.

'Better To Have Lost In Love (Than Never To Have Loved At All)' sees Annie grievously regretting the terrible things she has done to her lover. As Michael Kamen's manic string riff bursts with businesslike determination, she sings of fated lovers turning to enemies: "So I'll fill this bedroom full of mystery/ Hang our last conclusions on the wall/ And if this empty building starts to get to me/ Please remember that it just might be your fault". Admitting her own guilt is not a normal occurrence and here she seems to be sharing it out in equal portions with her disappointment of a lover. As the relationship and the album come to an unhappy close, there is no doubting her resolute strength. She affirms

"Hey, hey" to a dramatic, surging ending bearing an uncanny resemblance to the synthesised string introduction to 'Sweet Dreams (Are Made Of This)'.

★   ★   ★

Be Yourself Tonight was certainly an ambitious change for Eurythmics, and it paid off. Shooting to UK number three on May 18, 1985 and soon after achieving number nine in the US charts, it was eventually certified platinum by the RIAA. Eurythmics had made the necessary comeback after a couple of years out of the Top 40 on both sides of the Atlantic.

Openly revelling in all the excitement, Eurythmics held several press conferences and concerts in Paris to promote their new album. *The Old Grey Whistle Test* filmed them performing a raunchy live version of 'I Love You Like A Ball And Chain' in the studio. In the form of a music 'workshop' for the journalists and photographers present, Eurythmics ran through the song with just electric guitar and vocals, then gradually added drum machines and bass from the mixing desk. At the height of the song's emotional thrust those present were baffled to see the ex-lovers collapse together on a sofa; Dave lying on top of Annie and the two proceeding to 'get fresh' in front of an audience whose faces betrayed both confusion and delight.

The obvious first single to be released from *Be Yourself Tonight* was 'Would I Lie To You?' – printed on yellow, red and black vinyl in both 7″ and 12″ in an attempt to entice collectors to buy the single six times over. Ploy or not, the song bounded into the charts, and while it didn't quite achieve the placings they desired, it reached a respectable number 17 in the UK on May 11, and broke into the US Top Five later in July. Furthering the rekindled press speculation brought on by their touchy-feely performance in Paris, Dave said of the song's meaning, "We were trying to be honest with each other. It was the most played song in America and, again, it was a pastiche of our relationship, using the vernacular of Stax and R&B married together."

Such an up-front single required a powerful video behind it. Considering Dave's comments and that Annie had met Billy Poveda on the set of this very film a few weeks earlier, sparks certainly flew on screen. The promo was shot at the Roxy and gave Annie the perfect opportunity to flaunt her new image as a sex bomb. For the first time she appeared in a little black dress, and looked to Marilyn Monroe for inspiration on deportment: "She moved her hips in this incredible way, so I did that." This was all quite amusing as at the same time as the video emerged Annie was quoted in an interview saying, "I never felt that [cross-dressing] took away from my femininity. I love wearing trousers. Anyway, I've got the most awful legs in the world. If I were forced to wear a miniskirt, I'd have to see a psychiatrist."

The film begins with the 'band' hanging out in the back room of a club. Already behind the scenes there was friction as Martin Dobson and Dave Plews, the actual horn players on the recording, were not invited to attend and instead black stand-ins were employed to give a more 'authentic' feel.

Annie and Billy arrive on a motorbike and have a bleeped-out argument. Pulling herself together, Annie sits down next to a ponytailed Dave, who acts as mediator and advises her to "just be yourself tonight." They go out on stage to perform in a smoky club and Annie makes her slinky entrance in a sparkly, tasselled black minidress, the archetypal sexy 'rock chick' with her two-tone blonde hair. The audience is rowdy and the band enthusiastic. Some time into the performance an angry Billy revs his bike, which has been blended into the music on the album. He then gets up on stage and Annie sings the song to him. Presumably all is forgiven. The spirited performance was later nominated for a Grammy award with the rather convoluted title of Best Rock Performance By A Duo Or Group With Vocal.

Emotions were running high all round. As Annie was precariously juggling her feelings for Billy and Dave, one past relationship had to be put to bed. The end of Annie's association with Peter Ashworth occurred not through any personal meetings but a series of events linked to the artwork for *Be Yourself Tonight*.

In October Brant Mewborn's extensive Eurythmics piece in *Rolling Stone* opened with a dramatic description of an altercation between the group and the photographer. Mewborn summarised a scenario whereby, during the French recording sessions, Peter was brought in to take pictures for the album sleeve. Half-way through the shoot he supposedly convinced Annie and Dave to wear rather odd 'bird masks' over their faces, then encouraged Annie to stick her protruding beak into the gaping mouth of Dave's mask – openly indicative of sexual innuendo.

In Mewborn's report Annie storms out, feeling she's been made to look foolish. Peter then grumbles about losing his battle with the "damned masks", and Dave outlines RCA's reaction to the grotesque outtakes: "They were so S&M horror, a bit like a rapist's mask. The record company president almost had a heart attack." Eventually a blurred still from the 'Would I Lie To You?' video shoot would be used as the replacement artwork for the *Be Yourself Tonight* cover.

Peter himself has no recollection of this incident in Paris and remains unsure it actually happened. His memory of his final assignment as Eurythmics' photographer is somewhat different.

"The end was something else," he says today. "It was very peculiar. Dave and Annie were doing this album and they had been talking about using various different photographers. I got a call one day. They wanted to do it out in Los Angeles, so I thought about it as I got on really well with Kenny and Sandra. They took ages making a decision, and I ended up getting the job. I went out to a hotel called the Sunset Marquis, just off Sunset Boulevard. Laurence Stevens was there."

In Lucy O'Brien's biography Laurence recalls how the atmosphere gradually became rather awkward. "It was a bit hostile. I remember Peter saying, 'I don't know whether they brought me here to calm Annie down or to get us back together,' and Annie was saying, 'Don't bring Peter into the meeting because he's got quite a temper and he'll explode.'"

In fact, it seemed that Peter was lucky to be invited to a meeting at all. "I had been told to go out there by Kenny and Sandra, and spoke to them to keep them in touch with what was happening in Los Angeles," he continues. "Basically what started happening was I was getting isolated in this place and I would hear that Laurence had gone out for a meal with Dave and Annie and I hadn't. I began to feel a bit paranoid. I didn't even feel I had the right to go out and look for other work to occupy myself. I had nothing to do, I was really frustrated."

"He had a chip on his shoulder because he felt that Annie wasn't really treating him properly," Laurence accurately surmises. "He felt that because of their relationship she was treating him just as a photographer, rather than a photographer/friend." After a certain period of time, it became clear that Peter was being kept waiting on seemingly non-existent instructions, all the while unable to tout for work to maintain the expense of his studio back in London. Something had to give.

The showdown finally occurred during the video shoot for 'Would I Lie To You?' Many suspected tensions would be fraught anyway as Annie was taking a very obvious shine to her co-star Billy, and three of her lovers past and present would be in simultaneous attendance on the enclosed set. Nevertheless, Peter was duly invited to photograph the band as if he'd intruded on a live gig in an auditorium.

"This is the first time I've been able to get my camera out, and by then I'd been there about six weeks," he says. "It was ridiculous. Whatever fee I was getting had already been swallowed by the rent my studio was costing in London, that I wasn't using. But I wasn't going to walk away from the job.

"Anyway, I'm just getting into getting the picture that I know I need. It starts to work really well, and suddenly I hear, 'Stop! Right, photographer out!' "

Having been Eurythmics' photographer and friend since March 1981, let alone Annie's boyfriend, Peter was livid. In the heat of the moment he drew upon a rumour he had heard whilst out in Los Angeles. " 'I've waited six weeks for this shoot, you've let me come in here, I've been here an hour and you're telling me to stop *now*?' I went fucking nuts. My anger from all the years came out. I shouted to 150 people that ******** was shagging his secretary while his wife was pregnant.

"Now this was a very powerful music man in America. I wanted to tell him that it was between me, Dave and Annie. I felt so deeply humiliated then. What was even worse was that they immediately phoned up RCA and told them not to pay me. I'd done everything that was asked of me."

Fortunately Peter's friendship with Kenny and Sandra ensured that he was paid, but that was the last he ever heard from Annie Lennox, who along with Dave and Billy was left to deal with the ensuing turmoil on set. Peter concludes: "At the end of the relationship I did feel that there had been some torture involved. I did feel I'd been set up a number of times, I felt I'd been invited to things and then abused, and I didn't really know why."

19

THORN IN MY SIDE

"We're moving into leather, and getting away from vegetarianism."

– AL

In order to save Annie further problems with her throat, Eurythmics made the difficult decision not to tour *Be Yourself Tonight* and instead promoted the album with a series of videos. During six rainy days in June 1985 they shot promos in London for the two upcoming singles, 'There Must Be An Angel (Playing With My Heart)' and 'It's Alright (Baby's Coming Back)'.

"You can't run on a broken leg," Annie said bitterly of her painful vocal predicament. "But I don't want to talk about it. It's too negative. Talking about my voice being fucked up is the worst thing I can do. It's just made me depressed." Discovering yet more nodules, Annie was admitted to a Nashville hospital where she was placed under strict doctor's orders to rest. Even when she was allowed to return home she was unable to do normal, everyday things like speak on the telephone.

During this enforced silence, Dave busied himself with an immense amount of extra-curricular assignments: directing a video, producing two dozen tracks for Bob Dylan, an album for Feargal Sharkey, and writing 'Ruthless People' with Mick Jagger and Daryl Hall. Soon his name was well established as a respected force in its own right, away from the Eurythmic limelight.

Lying uselessly in bed and hearing of all his impressive achievements, Annie found it hard not to fret about her own future. "On one hand it was wonderful to see him developing in that way," she said in 1986. "But when I'm feeling insecure, I sometimes feel threatened by it . . . (still) it was good experience." Constantly she reassured herself that Eurythmics was his main interest.

One source of comfort came from the terrific reception to the singles released from their latest album. In June 'There Must Be An Angel (Playing With My Heart)' became Eurythmics' first ever number one in the UK, remaining in the charts for some 13 weeks. Across the Atlantic it attained number 22. Two versions were released; the LP track and a special dance mix by Jon Bavin and Dean Garcia, both with a previously unreleased track, the poppy, upbeat 'Grown Up Girls'. The A-side proved so popular that it was later famously sampled by alternative dance duo Utah Saints for their number 10 hit, 'What Can You Do For Me', and covered by Japanese band The Fantastic Plastic Machine on their album *Luxury*.

Once again, sales were aided by an unforgettable video in true Eurythmics style. Paying tribute to Ken Russell's 1970 film *The Devils*, Dave and Annie fully indulged their love of dressing up – Dave opulently made-up as a rococo Sun King and Annie, predictably, as an angel. This time Annie was responsible for writing the script, and joked that it was her attempt to humiliate Dave for a change.

The film was made at an Edwardian theatre in Wimbledon, and the court of the Sun King was filled with an extravagant cast of nymphs, cherubs, transvestites, a castrato and a gospel choir, costing RCA nigh on £100,000 and choreographed by Billy Poveda. During the piece Annie, pink-cheeked and wearing a long blonde wig, performs on stage for Dave. Children invade the set and a somewhat rotund cherub mimes to the operatic warblings. The king becomes bored with the display, yawns and dozes off.

He is awoken by the entrance of the gospel choir, arises from his throne and greets the performers who bow and scrape at his feet. Tossing money at his subjects, Dave then lets a dove fly out of a box, and the video ends on a close-up of his winking eye. Could Annie's irony possibly be that Dave is king of all he surveys and throws money around? "It's very tongue in cheek, but it's also very transcendental," she smiled. "It's about that feeling of being uplifted, which I rarely ever sing about. I do feel it, you know, on occasion."

Although Annie was not well enough to embark on a tour of any description, Eurythmics were glad this year to take part in The Montreux Golden Rose Rock Festival, a venture jointly organised by the BBC and the Swiss television channel TSR (Television Suisse Romande), with the help of the Montreux Tourist Office.

On stage Annie cut quite a figure in a sharp black leather jacket. In a reference to her bold rock chick image following her failed marriage, she made a little dig at the Krishna diet, announcing: "We're moving into leather, and getting away from vegetarianism." In actual fact the singer was to maintain her own vegetarianism for some time after this statement, although she did reintroduce fish into her menu.

Annie's all-round psyche seemed on a positive bent, as John Turnbull fondly recalls, "I had a great time there with Dave and Annie. I had lovely dances with Annie because she liked to warm up. We all used to wear these big black frock coats. Before we went on at Montreux Annie was spinning around and everything, we just started twirling round – it was so good to get your energy flowing. We were a bit of a whirling dervish!" Annie agrees that frequently she has to prepare physically for a perform-ance: "I have to psych myself up for a gig like an athlete in training for the big race. I talk myself into fever pitch and sometimes it gets so intense that I panic on stage, even hallucinate. It sounds dramatic, but I can't perform unless I feel totally involved and that's a rigorous process."

Understandably this is not the kind of mental state that the singer can be snapped out of easily, as she continues, "When I come off stage I'm in a kind of trance, I have to be left alone for a while to ease myself out of it gradually. I can't feel justified in what I'm doing unless I give 100 per cent and that means being exhausted afterwards."

One other incident was to arise from Eurythmics' appearance at the rock festival. Joe Bangay was present in the audience as one of the official photographers. After the concert he stood back as Annie came into view. Without hesitation, the superstar walked over to her old friend and gave him a big kiss in front of everyone present. It seemed that particular war was over.

★   ★   ★

The worrying nodules on Annie's throat caused her to miss out on more than just a promotional tour. One of the greatest events in pop history, Live Aid, took place on July 13, 1985.

The previous October a BBC documentary presented by Michael Buerk had brought home the true horror of the drought and subsequent famine in Ethiopia to the British public. Boomtown Rats singer Bob Geldof had been so moved by the incessant harrowing pictures of men, women and children who were little more than skin and bone, that he determined to raise money for their aid. Although Geldof's band were relatively low down the pop pecking order, the charismatic and unruly singer managed to coerce 36 artists to record the single 'Do They Know It's Christmas?' on November 25. Originally hoping to raise £72,000 from sales, Geldof and Midge Ure's song sold over three million copies in the UK and totalled over £8 million worldwide.

Much encouraged by this display of solidarity among the pop commu-nity for the Third World, Geldof co-ordinated two concerts to be held simultaneously; one at Wembley Stadium, London and the other at the JFK Stadium in Philadelphia. The shows were to cover 16 hours on July 13, 1985. Persuading more and more artists to join the event it became a veritable *Who's Who* of the music industry and included many with whom Eurythmics had been linked. They ranged from Eighties icons U2, Sting, Madonna and Phil Collins (the latter flying across the Atlantic to perform twice), rock stalwarts Elton John, Queen, David Bowie, Mick Jagger and Tina Turner, pop duo Thompson Twins to rappers Run-DMC and Dave and Annie's former support act, Howard Jones. Eurythmics were scheduled to join the throng of celebrities at Wembley, but ever concerned about her throat Annie felt she had to decline the momentous occasion.

According to Jon Roseman in *Sweet Dreams Are Made Of This*, Annie moped in front of the television on the day watching the phenomenon live, more than a little remorseful that she was not there. Jon described the impression he received from the hoarse singer, "The reason they hadn't done it I believe was because they thought, we're Eurythmics, we're too big for this. Then they saw what an event it was. Annie's always been confused as to what she is and isn't into." Annie herself revealed in a radio interview with Paul Gambaccini some years later that despite the good intentions, she sometimes feels uncomfortable watching healthy, young musicians jump around raising money for those who are dying.

Whatever the reasons behind their absence from the event, Dave and Annie retained a good relationship with the organiser, Bob Geldof, who was later nominated for a Nobel Prize and received a knighthood from the Queen. Dave helped out in the production room when Geldof launched his solo career in 1986 and provided a sanctuary for his friend when he needed peace and quiet to edit his best-selling autobiography *Is That It?* Dave and Annie were also called upon in August that year as best man and bridesmaid for Bob's marriage to TV presenter and journalist Paula Yates. For the occasion Annie wore a gold lamé catsuit and six-inch platform shoes at the Little Chapel Of The West in Las Vegas, and carried the couple's daughter, Fifi Trixiebelle, throughout the ceremony.[35]

Despite her absence from Live Aid, Annie's conscience was being aroused. Having previously become a vegetarian to embrace her ex-husband's beliefs, Annie had promoted the cause, speaking frankly and openly about cruelty to animals. "There are certain movements that I would like to become part of. I'm very much against animals being exploited and I'm planning to get involved with that. I find something intrinsically ugly about the mass consumerism of animals. There's a terrible brutal butchery which is governed by commercial greed. I always feel for

---

[35] Tragically Annie and Dave were to attend Paula's funeral 14 years later after her death from an overdose of drink and drugs.

the underdog and identify with those who are suffering."

While vegetarianism and animal rights continued to be current, hip causes, Annie felt that she had to bow slightly to Geldof's plea for help in Africa. "Live Aid made me question the solutions in the Third World. The issues are really immense: corruption in government, climate, agriculture and so on. Some of those issues crop up when we look at what's happening to the ecosystem . . . I haven't figured it all out, but it's the direction I'm heading in," she finished rather vaguely.

Annie's main problem was that she felt caught between a rock and a hard place. Acknowledging that the platform of pop music ensures an artist can reach an audience of literally millions, the singer was not sure she should abuse her power just because Eurythmics were enjoying the heights of fame.

"I think personally, that pop music puts colour into people's lives, and without it, if you took it away I think that people would feel very empty and very drab," she said of her career. "Our responsibility is to touch people in their hearts – to inspire the quality of their existence. And if it does affect people and make them more positive individuals then I think that politically and socially that's a wonderful thing to do. But in the future, because I feel strongly about things I've got no doubt that I'll get more actively involved."

In the first half of the Eighties some artists used their lyrics to provoke a reaction (Sting's 'Russians', Peter Gabriel's 'Biko', U2's 'Pride (In The Name Of Love)' and Dire Straits' 'Brothers In Arms'), but Annie explained at great length that as she writes from the heart about first-hand experiences, she felt unqualified to comment on social or political events and quite sensibly preferred not to try. Succinctly she summed up her philosophical muteness: "I just don't have anything interesting to say. I *do* have my opinions and values in life, but what difference does it make to anyone else? It makes *no* difference."

The profound change on her personal outlook since her 30th birthday, coupled with her contented relationship with Billy Poveda was apparently boosting Annie's confidence to the extent where she felt able to talk about her new-found poise. "I've never felt more in control. Well, not in control exactly, but I can see things more clearly now. Like all the chaotic things can actually be turned around to something so useful. And I'm not as afraid as I was; I was very anxiety-ridden."

Determined to become more vocal about topics in which she believed, on *Be Yourself Tonight* Annie made a remarkable departure from blurring the lines of sexuality to making a strong feminist stance. "It was a challenge, to write a pop song that could be played on the radio yet was a feminist anthem. I woke up one morning and wrote all the words. I had a vision of it, and said to Dave that this idea needs a fantastic woman to sing it with," she recalled excitably.

The single applauding female vitality, 'Sisters Are Doin' It For Themselves', was released in October 1985 and quickly powered through to number nine in the UK. The song not only surprised fans who were introduced to lyrical content with attitude, but it was also an unexpected experience for the singer. 'Sisters Are Doin' It For Themselves' had originally been intended as a duet with Tina Turner, but it seemed Annie's subject material had become a little too racy. "I really love Tina Turner's voice and Tina was really emerging at that period as a phoenix from the ashes out of that Ike and Tina thing. She was approached but she felt that the statement of the song didn't really suit her image and she declined the offer. I was very disappointed actually, because I really wanted to sing with her," said the snubbed Eurythmic.

Aretha Franklin had been brought in as a replacement, but the relationship between the two divas did not have an auspicious start, as Annie embarrassingly admitted that she only knew the song 'Respect' from Aretha's extensive repertoire. In addition, like Tina Turner, the older, more conservative soul singer had some issues with the song's solid stance. Annie, whose career was based on breaking rules, found it hard to understand the problems.

"I suppose that song's feminist in the sense that it's women singing about women, but it's really just a song for people in a situation like mine, people who now do things through their own assertion, through their own power, that they would never have been able to do before." The two strong-willed ladies reached a compromise as the line, "The inferior sex are still superior" was toned down a little to, "The inferior sex have got a new exterior".

Having settled the lyrical problem, the duet was ready to be recorded. Eurythmics flew to Aretha's home town of Detroit, as does any pop star who wants to work with her. "I got along alright with her but we didn't have an immediate rapport," remembers Annie.

"Aretha struck me as rather shy, a bit sad, a bit lonely. She had an entourage which I thought was a bit eccentric – I wasn't used to it." As the story goes, it was actually Aretha's snack etiquette that repelled Annie more than her surrounding posse. Feeling hungry during the session Aretha ordered some spare ribs for herself, and watching the buxom lady sink her teeth into the meat and tear it from the bone turned the stomach of the semi-lapsed vegetarian. Sensibly Annie refutes this tale, but Aretha is well-known for such carnivorous antics as both George Michael and

Lauryn Hill were exposed to similar events during their respective experiences with Aretha on 'I Knew You Were Waiting For Me' and 'A Rose Is Still A Rose'.

Overall the two singers maintained a harmonious relationship, if only for press coverage. Annie commented that Aretha was "eminently gracious and supremely queenful. She is the queen of soul. She can play incredible piano, too – she's not just a voice. She's an extraordinary woman." Aretha was equally complimentary about Annie, praising the innovative Eurythmics style, but admitting that she was more traditional at heart. When questioned about making a stand for feminist rights, she let the cat out of the bag, confessing that she did not whole-heartedly agree with the independent message. "I guess I'm old-fashioned, I like a guy who knows how to romance a girl. I like to be wined and dined, all that good stuff," she disclosed.

Annie had previously avoided 'message songs' and 'Sisters Are Doin' It For Themselves' confirmed all her reasons for doing so – with the single's release she found herself constantly quizzed about her perceived crusade for sexual equality and the effect it might have on the nation. Annie was undoubtedly in favour of balancing the roles of men and women in society, but was reluctant to be dubbed a modern day Emmeline Pankhurst.

" 'Sisters', you see, is simply a song about women. I think women are great, and I think men are great, and people are wonderful, potentially, when they're not killing each other," she babbled, desperately trying to express herself. "I don't have to say 'I bleed!' or 'I won't have anything to do with men.' Some of my best friends are men! . . . I don't want to be the head of a movement. I'm singing purely out of my satisfaction, my good feeling about women. And men as well, for allowing women to do that."

Annie's basic and genuine love of humanity became superseded as the single was released with four different covers portraying women in diverse careers and situations; an early female racing driver, a woman in the army, a secretary in the Forties, and a group of giggling girls. The quadruple sleeves proved an amusing gimmick to aid publicity in the absence of a tour, although cynics would suggest that it also encouraged extra sales to the avid collector.

The promotional video on the other hand was an odd combination of the two singers dancing in front of a cinema screen, which was used to show women at work and play. Aretha and Annie once again found themselves out of synch, ensuring that filming was as uncomfortable as the song's recording. "Annie had just had a photo session and the woman photographer was gay," said producer Jon Roseman. "Aretha has this thing about gays and assumed that Annie was a lesbian. She more or less ignored her throughout the entire session. After the video Annie didn't want to speak to Aretha. The atmosphere was strained between them."

The film certainly indicates this atmosphere as the two singers stand quite far apart and concentrate on their own show rather than working together as a team. The black and white footage behind them depicts women through the ages; punks, swimmers, martial arts experts, politicians, astronauts and nuns among others. This oestrogen-led shoot allows Dave his moment of glory in the instrumental break and he is shown on the screen leaping wildly around in numerous different costumes. Ironically it is therefore the man who steals the show as there is clearly no empathy between the women, even when they shift closer for the ending, awkwardly trying to dance together. This laboured effort is a precursor of Aretha's duet with George Michael just a couple of years later, as they too danced alongside each other in front of a large film screen. The similarity even extended to the vocals where George, like Annie, maintained the tune and allowed Aretha her soaring ad libs.

Following the success of 'Sisters Are Doin' It For Themselves' Eurythmics released 'It's Alright (Baby's Coming Back)' as the next single. Although this was the third song extricated from the album, its light, catchy insistence fared well in the UK charts reaching number 12, but stalled at number 78 in the US.[36]

As with 'Sisters Are Doin' It For Themselves' Eurythmics were concerned with the aesthetics of the single. It was originally produced in a stylishly plain white sleeve simply stating the group's name and song title in gold lettering, but this was soon withdrawn (making it a collector's item), and replaced by a cover showing a still from the accompanying video.

Furthermore the 12" version featured 'Tous Les Garçons', the old Françoise Hardy song Dave and Annie had recorded back in 1983 on their portastudio. 'Tous Les Garçons' was a favourite with early Eurythmics concert-goers, although its jollity always seemed to come across a little incongruously alongside Eurythmics' darker original material. Still, on the B-side to 'It's Alright (Baby's Coming Back)', it bounces along nicely enough, if a bit blandly. The song was released in its own right in France and Canada later in 1985.

The video for 'It's Alright (Baby's Coming Back)' transforms the simple forgiving song into an animated saga intended to highlight the duo's psychic connection beyond the grave. "We really don't understand a great

---

[36] 'It's Alright (Baby's Coming Back)' went on to win the Best Contemporary Song at the annual Ivor Novello Awards on April 15, 1987.

deal about life after death," Annie explained. "I feel this song embodies that unknown in a way. I was thinking about the good, gentle qualities that people have in their relationships, the things that pull us through, even though the physical body dies. It's those grander, nobler qualities in human nature that endure. It's like a collective soul."

Furthering this viewpoint, Annie is seen lying on an operating table in hospital, but before she dies she telepathically calls her lover back. Dave meanwhile is flying on a plane, and while he cannot physically attend to her needs, his spirit races across the globe to be with her. Or at least we are led to believe that was the design's concept.

The animation is rather dated and crude, where Dave's soul is shown as a shadow travelling in cartoon-like planes, trains and automobiles. Near-death apparently suits Annie, as she smoulders in icy blue, topped with a shaggy blonde mop. When she is finally set free by an embrace from Dave's spirit the picture ungainly explodes into a shower of drawn triangles.

"I do remember seeing the first cut of the video and throwing a diva-esque tantrum, floods of tears," says Annie. "We had to re-shoot it. If you do something, you have to live with it. That's why we're control freaks." One shudders to think what the first version was like. If the shoot for 'Sisters Are Doin' It For Themselves' was testing, so too was 'It's Alright (Baby's Coming Back)'. Dave brought along his girlfriend and PA Claire Evans, Annie was supported by Billy, and the respective partners watched as the ex-couple acted out their special ESP link.

★   ★   ★

Despite the everlasting bond with Dave, Annie's relationship with Billy proved to be therapeutic. Confident in herself and unable to tour for much of 1985, she channelled her talent into a new area: acting. Having turned down numerous roles just the year before, her career had allowed a momentary respite and she seized the opportunity to play a small part in *Revolution*, Hugh Hudson's drama set during America's War of Independence in 1776.

"So many people have said I've got a gift for acting that I've finally succumbed to the idea. I may fall flat on my face, but I'm excited about it anyhow," said a jubilant Annie. However, the fans might have been sorely disappointed with her first role on the big screen, which was little more than a crowd extra with half a dozen lines. As a bedraggled rabble rouser, Annie wears a plain period dress and a long, uncontrollable ginger wig. Branded with a skull and crossbones tattoo on her forehead and 'Liberty or Death' across her chest, the normally striking woman does not look her best in the torrential downpour. The film boasts first-rate Hollywood names such as Al Pacino, Donald Sutherland and Nastassja Kinski, and even though Annie receives seventh billing as 'Liberty Woman', her part totals less than her three-minute pop videos.

Annie's first appearance is easily distinguished by her strident Scottish accent and a spiteful spit at the British redcoats, whom she denounces as "filthy bastards". In her second and final appearance Annie leads a chant of "Liberty or Death" (perhaps the tattoo on her chest acted as a cue card), before she demands that Al Pacino and his son give up their boat for the greater cause.[37] Her final words are, "Give the patriot a cheer!" as Pacino is forced to surrender his vessel. The film was not a box-office smash, its failure attributed to its slow pace and dreary portrayal of a momentous period, and did little for the career of anyone involved.

Annie never spoke about Pacino with whom she shared a scene, but obviously took a shine to Sutherland, giggling like a schoolgirl at the mere mention of his name in interviews. Before filming she chattered excitedly to the media about the shoot and its settings. "I just saw some photographs of the wharf-side at King's Lynn [an East England coastal resort] which they've turned into an 18th century New York. The streets are thick with mud; it's quite extraordinary!" But ultimately, having caught 'flu from the freezing conditions experienced on set Annie concluded that she preferred her short promotional videos because, "I have direct access to the directors – and it's *our* project!"

Dave too continued exploring new projects while Eurythmics took a break from touring. Having created a name for himself as a master in the studio, he found himself bombarded with demo tapes from all manner of new bands and artists. Being the maverick that he is, he set up his own record label, AnXious Records, to produce and launch new acts. Dave was altruistic in intent, concerned that others might avoid pitfalls he had experienced, and resolved to nurture innate talent instead.

"I see this label as a long-term development thing. Too many labels these days are just desperate to have a hit single," he expanded. "When I work with other people, they always want to have something that I give to Eurythmics – that eccentric, English thing or whatever. But I'm always averse to doing that . . . I just try and get to the heart of what an artist is, and try to get them to enjoy themselves in expressing that."

Basing the label in his houseboat on Regent's Canal, Dave poured his own money into the company, which fell into £1.5 million of debt within its formative years. Impressed at her partner's stamina Annie summed up

[37] Discerning fans of the British soap opera *EastEnders* will spot a young Sid Owen playing Pacino's child.

his hyperactive mind: "He's a perfectionist and a total optimist. His health isn't always up to scratch but he has enormous energy. But if he's not careful, he could burn himself out. He has so many ideas . . . sometimes Dave really could learn to slow down."

Annie was adamant about the creative force shared between the two halves of Eurythmics, regardless of their individual ventures. "Dave and I still draw a lot of strength from each other, and when it really comes down to it, we are very, very close. We've ridden through the changes in our personal lives, and we value our relationship enormously." Together they were still an impenetrable force as Annie was named Best British Female Artist for the second time and Dave collected Best British Producer at the fifth annual BRIT Awards.

★   ★   ★

While Dave channelled his boundless energy into working with other artists, Annie's conscience had finally been activated by the power of Live Aid and now she was prepared to direct her energy into promoting worthy causes. Her first outing in this vein was at a benefit concert on February 9, 1986 for victims of the recent volcanic eruption at Nevado Del Ruiz in Columbia, where 25,000 people had died. Annie was invited to the star studded event by her close friend, the politically active singer Chrissie Hynde of The Pretenders. Together they joined respected acts such as David Gilmour, Mike Oldfield and The Communards on stage at the Royal Albert Hall in West London.

Annie performed a cover of Stevie Wonder's 'Blame It On The Sun', starkly accompanied by keyboardist Patrick Seymour, before reappearing at the finale to duet with Chrissie Hynde in front of a fantastic backing for KC & The Sunshine Band's 'Give It Up'. The concert, organised by native Colombian musician Chucho Merchan, raised £20,000 for the survivors of the disaster and was recorded for British television, Channel 4, as well as being released on video. A talented bassist with numerous jazz credits, Merchan became good friends with Annie through this event and went on to tour with Eurythmics for several years.

Just two months later, Annie was to suffer a personal tragedy far closer to home. On April 8, 1986 Tom Lennox died at the family home in Ellon, north of Aberdeen. In addition to cancer of the stomach, Tom had contracted bronchopneumonia and passed away one month shy of his 61st birthday.

After the bitter argument that preceded her marriage to Radha, Annie had not spoken to her father until she began divorce proceedings in the spring of 1985 and Tom celebrated his 60th birthday on May 12. The timing was fortunate as Tom's health plummeted shortly thereafter.

"He was made redundant. Men of 60 like that, they've only known their work, the work ethic, it's been their identity all their lives," she explained later. "It meant so much to him and suddenly he was dropped just like that. It actually broke the man. He became ill. For months they didn't know what it was. He was suffering terrible pain and they told him it was psychosomatic. Then I got a call from a relative who said she suspected it was something serious. It was cancer at a very advanced stage."

June Smith had remained a close family friend and witnessed the difficult and rapid demise of the head of the household. "It was quite tragic. I remember meeting Tom and Dorothy in a supermarket just before he died. He'd been in hospital trying to find out exactly what it was, but it was too late when they discovered it was stomach cancer. But he was a smoker and it was 99 per cent due to cigarettes."

Annie was horrified and sickened when she heard of her father's fatal condition but although she wanted to abandon everything to be with him, he insisted that she wait until he was ready to see her. In the meantime she had been able to ease her parents' pain, if only a little, by paying for what turned out to be their final holiday, to East Germany in the autumn of 1985. Tom did eventually call Annie to his bedside and fortunately she arrived in time to say her goodbyes. "It was about three days after I got home he died. We were with him, my mother and me. Well, whatever contact we could make between us, it *was* made.

"When someone is dying you long to do something. He suffered so much, *so much*. You're standing on the sidelines and there's this hopeless, helpless feeling. But then the communication between you becomes incredibly fine . . . he needs your gentleness, he needs your compassion. It's a very strange feeling seeing that fragility, that vulnerability, thinking, 'That's my father dying'."

The whole family found Tom's passing extremely difficult. "I think it was the first time that the Lennoxes had experienced a death," says June. "I know it affected Tom's sister Jean very much because she shared the nursing with Dorothy. I think his parents, Archie and Jean, also felt it particularly because Tom was their first born; even though he was older, to lose a child while you're still living is traumatic. They all felt the loss quite badly." Tom was cremated after a quiet ceremony which Annie attended along with her family and friends.

The necessarily cathartic course of action for the bereaved daughter was to pour her grief into the lyrics of her songs. 'Take Your Pain Away' and 'I Remember You' from the next album, *Revenge*, were the exorcists for her suffering.

"My father died recently of cancer and I had a very unique close experience with terminal cancer in my own life," she valiantly recounted of the lyrics to 'Take Your Pain Away'. "I'd never met anybody before that had ever had cancer and didn't know what it was about, and in my futile attempt to express how much I wanted to relieve him of his suffering at the time, the words to this song came through."

In another interview she continued, "There's another song, 'I Remember You' that was actually about my father. I wrote it down, looked at it, thought, 'Oh this is a love song', and then I realised that it really wasn't a love song it was actually about my father and that's how I interpret it when I hear it."

Dorothy returned to work as a school cook and life gradually resumed for the distraught family. Annie, who had always been closer to her mother, was suddenly shocked to realise Dorothy's own age and having lost her father, tried to help in any way she could. "During his illness I drew my parents' attention to diet. Even though this represented difficulties, mum has now virtually cut out all meat from her diet and has been surprised that the rheumatism in her hands has definitely improved. Her friends have also cut their meat consumption considerably. This is quite a shift for people brought up on a meat-based diet, but it shows that people are interested in their health."

★ ★ ★

Annie had already been recording *Revenge*, her sixth album with Dave, and as always in a time of catharsis, she immersed herself in work. Having taken a break from touring since 1984, she found that fame had momentarily taken a back seat. This was a relief, especially when she needed her privacy the most.

"I'm really a very quiet person," she said at the time. "I don't particularly go out to clubs and stuff because they're very smoky, full of people and sometimes photographers. When I'm just trying to have a nice time and somebody's flashing light bulbs in my face I don't really enjoy it very much, so I tend to keep myself in a low profile. I can actually walk about the streets at the moment fairly unrecognised. The thing is, I'm very clever at disguising myself because really my profile at the moment is low. But as soon as you start to get back into the machinery of live performances, television appearances, videos etc., etc., you see the difference in the street."

Despite her cunning deceptions, Annie was spotted stepping out with actor Steven Bauer during May 1986 and as promotion for *Revenge* took off, the singer found herself faced with constant media oppression again. The first single, 'When Tomorrow Comes' was released the same month, reaching a respectable UK number 30. The accompanying video was rather disappointing as the band, which included Clem Burke behind the drums once again, and a striking singer named Joniece Jamison backing Annie's vocals, were filmed rather statically performing the number in an empty warehouse.

They are all dressed in black and white, Annie with severely short platinum hair and a large black leather coat. Apart from occasional shots of Annie inexplicably rolling around on white sheets and Dave leaping about with his guitar, the footage is contrived and bland, without even providing a sense of unity. The criticism flowed freely as Eurythmics, who were typically seen to be an experimental 'video band', produced what appeared to be a filler. This unfortunately paved the way for future comments on live performances.

However, whatever the media felt about the album, which was released one month later in June, they could not deny its prosperity. *Revenge* immediately entered the British charts at number three and proceeded to hold a position in the Top 20 for an entire year, making it Eurythmics' most commercially successful album, achieving triple platinum sales in the UK and gold in America.

Staying true to their track record, Eurythmics wrote the songs in just one week and recorded them within a month. "It's frightening because it's so intense and argumentative," explained Dave of their peculiar schedule. "I even add to the pressure by saying that we have to make the album in three weeks or whatever. Annie will ask why and I'll make up some lame excuse, but really it's because I like that kind of pressure to make things work."

The creative process remained a combination of the two minds bouncing ideas off each other. "Dave is the facilitator," says Annie. "Very often he captures the idea as it comes from me and takes it several steps further. Then I take the idea a few steps further still, and we swap back and forth until the song is done. It's funny, we don't talk a lot during this process. I've developed a wonderful appreciation for it over time. I don't question it anymore, nor do I wonder how long it will work. I'm just grateful for every time it happens."

Recorded mainly in France at the Studio Grand Armée in Paris, but also paying a brief visit to Conny Plank's studio in Cologne, the duo set out once again to create something different. "We had guest artists on *Be Yourself Tonight* . . . but we haven't done the same thing on this album because we never like to retread what we've done before," explained Annie. "We wanted to show Eurythmics as being a live band, sounding like a live band, a real unit, and we've hand-picked a group of musicians who we're going to play with – not just because of their musicianship but because of their enthusiasm and their attitude towards work." Enlisting Clem Burke, Patrick Seymour and Joniece Jamison, the kernel of players also included Jimmy 'Z' Zavala, formerly with Tom Petty, while Michael Kamen conducted the orchestral arrangements and John McKenzie assumed most of the bass guitar parts.

Whatever the videos show along with the vision as described by Eurythmics, the cover artwork for *Revenge* pictures just Dave and Annie, but for the first time since *In The Garden*, they receive equal billing. The painting of the couple is from the shoulders up; Annie is naked with her eyes unnervingly drawn to resemble those of a snake while Dave is smartly dressed, wearing ornate earrings and a brooch saying 'Revenge'. This was Annie's third naked cover and it was hardly surprising therefore that she was questioned about it. "I like working with no clothes on," she started, quickly confirming her point, "I don't mean showing your breasts for the sake of it. It's just a really neat way of being who you are." The imagery inside the sleeve is of a rose, a smashed stopwatch and a snake – themes which were carried through to the *Eurythmics Live* video.

The music, like the video for 'When Tomorrow Comes', was not received especially well, the formerly cutting edge pair being judged as having sold out to stadium rock. *NME*'s attack said, "They're more showcase than song, designed to show off Lennox's larynx via constructs that dispense with perfunctory verses as quickly as possible to get the highflying fadeouts."

Other than Annie's two personal references to her father, Dave took much of the credit for the album's musical mission. "I was trying at that time to make classic pop songs," he described. "I was competing with myself in a way. It was like, 'Can we make a song that stands up next to this by so and so?' There's some classic pop songs on that, like 'Thorn In My Side', it's got 'Missionary Man' which is like a classic R&B American stormer and, 'Miracle Of Love' – can we make a slow ballad that's a bit heart-stringy but that isn't crass? It *was* a bit theoretical." However, proving that it takes two, the significance in Annie's lyrics picks up where *Be Yourself Tonight* left off, concentrating either on the wonderment of pure love, or the bitter end of a relationship.

Eurythmics' sixth album opens brilliantly with 'Missionary Man', a song with persuasive religious tones and an emphasis on monetary gain, suggesting that elements of Radha Raman's influence may still be lingering in Annie's psyche. Initially Jimmy Zavala's harmonica wavers against a growing moody haze of guitars and Patrick Seymour's sustained keyboard pads. After the pressure has been built up effectively, Annie bursts the bubble and enters, teeming with resolve and joined by an equally business-like Clem Burke on drums. The majority of Annie's singing is on one slightly twisted note, which lends itself nicely to the cynical persona of the storyteller. In this way glimpses of her former androgynous robot character can be heard, especially when it is down to Joniece Jamison to ad lib during the choruses.

From the outset of this catchy rock song with an up-tempo 4/4 beat, it is clear that the balance of power behind Eurythmics has shifted some-what. The players each seem to be there as dominant personalities and Dave and Annie could almost be described as being reduced to members of their own band.

The pace is then maintained beautifully with the stunning entrance of 'Thorn In My Side' with an affirmative whoop from Annie. This is a good, old-fashioned pop song with a slight Sixties influence on the vocals and arrangement, although unusually there are strings subtly placed behind the more up-front saxophone and guitars. Particularly for this album, Eurythmics appear to employ a fairly large orchestra in the very same way that they themselves once used multi-layered synthesisers. Perfect for the time, this song boasts a catchy chorus, cute sax solo and sing-a-long vocal breakdown with the aid of Clem's fabulous drumming.

Although on the face of it 'Thorn In My Side' sounds like cheery, good-time pop, lyrically its barbs have often been attributed to Radha and Annie wastes no time in building up a clear picture of the lover who has wronged her: "I should have known better, but I trusted you at first/ I should have known better, but I got what I deserved." It appears that she feels both used and abused with the explanatory "I was feeling complicated, I was feeling low/ Now every time I think of you I shiver to the bone . . ."

'When Tomorrow Comes' then comes straight in with a vaguely nostalgic pop/rock theme. It tells of the peacefulness of watching a loved one asleep and dreaming. Annie sounds soulfully reflective and there is a perfunctory guitar solo, but sadly this song lacks the biting edge for which Eurythmics are famous. It is far too straightforward – while 'Thorn In My Side' was rather fetching, this piece of anonymous pop could have been written and performed by anyone.

For 'The Last Time' the lyrical content swings back from high to low as this is about the end of an affair, due to an unfaithful lover. The music does not portray any feelings of regret or bitterness and is more assertive, based bizarrely as it is around a collection of juddering synths, chime bells and strummed guitars. Dave makes a vocal appearance in the chorus in unison with Annie, and amusingly sounds exactly the same singing as he does speaking.

'Miracle Of Love' proves to be the jewel in *Revenge*'s crown with one of Eurythmics' first true ballads. A spiky synth counterpoint, a lush, surging orchestra and soaring guitars provide Annie with the perfect setting for her most moving vocal performance yet, as she sings emotively about the promise of a new love for someone who hurts others as a means of defence. Her lyrics take on a bittersweet maturity, particularly with the rather beautiful line: "There must be a bitter breeze to make you sting so viciously/ They say the greatest coward can hurt the most ferociously" – this is by far the most profound example of Eurythmics' work thus far.

However, the overall tone of *Revenge* is not about introspection and soon enough 'Let's Go' bounds on to the scene, a playful song about lust. "I just wanted to write a song for everybody that encapsulated the feeling of meeting somebody and falling in love with them, just like that," said Annie. She sounds delighted at the turn of events and as a new development adds shades of raunchiness in her delivery, especially with the cheeky ending line: "He said 'Forget about the preacher man, let's do it on the ground!' "

This song was recorded at Conny's studio in Germany, continuing the ties to the first album, but Dave acknowledges that the couple wanted to move on: "We both wanted to meet somebody else – you know, 'Let's go, I want to fall in love.' That's how we both felt. We both wanted to meet someone solid. We wanted that for each other, we didn't want to be fucked up all the time." Although 'Let's Go' runs the risk of appearing trivial after the stunning 'Miracle Of Love', it manages to succeed mainly with the audible enthusiasm of the players, particularly Jimmy Zavala, who takes over the choruses with his jaunty saxophone and harmonica. The breakdown is especially fun to hear; Annie gamely tries out a variety of entertaining vocal effects, soon to be coined by the teen sensations, Bros!

'Take Your Pain Away' witnesses Annie soothing yet another troubled soul. This is one of her tributes to her father, although she sounds surprisingly detached and in opposition to the busy, fast beat, driven by a dominant bass line.

If memorable hit singles like 'Missionary Man', 'Thorn In My Side' and 'Miracle Of Love' were to supply the high points of *Revenge*, then 'A Little Of You' was surely its nadir. Truly a bad moment for Eurythmics, it is a perfect example of the kind of cheesy Eighties pop personified by the lesser outpourings of groups like Johnny Hates Jazz. Repetitive yet instantly forgettable, 'A Little Of You' is given some life by Michael Kamen's string section, but is generally too glossy to be taken seriously.

The underlying lyrical message though is quite telling of the Eurythmics' set-up. "If you look at all people's relationships they're fairly incestuous. I mean social groups of people that get together. It's quite incestuous, all our relationships are like that so it's a reflection on how people sort of invisibly hurt each other, really," said Annie, whose personal life consisted almost entirely of ex-lovers intermingling.

Making the final link back to *In The Garden* Dave describes the idea behind the connection. "When we made that album, everything was stacked against us – from Annie and me splitting up as a couple, to people saying we couldn't have a name like Eurythmics," he said of the concerns surrounding their first recording as a duo. "On that album there's a song, 'Revenge', with the line 'Revenge can be so sweet'. So for this album we went back to the same studio, and for one of the tracks – 'A Little Of You' – Annie sings the same line, 'Revenge can be so sweet'. You see, we'd been through all this stuff and come out of it OK."

The penultimate track, 'In This Town', was curiously recorded at a party thrown by Manu Guiot, one of the mixing engineers on the album, and a crowd can indeed be heard clapping and later cheering on Eurythmics. This is a rock'n'roll belter boasting a Def Leppard guitar riff, big drums and a particularly sultry Annie. Ironically for a song about terminable boredom, it seems to lose its momentum somewhere along the way – perhaps you just had to be there at the time.

Finally, 'I Remember You' closes the album with Annie's painful farewell to her father, including references to "The back yard boy" and "Standing by the railway line". Accordingly, the yearning refrain of "Oh – we were so young/ We didn't realise what we'd done" could well serve as an apology for her problematic relationship with Tom Lennox in both teenage years and their feud during her marriage to Radha.

Arranged as a military march tapped out on a snare drum, punctuating an interesting mixture of electronic oddities and a deep string line, it is interesting to note that *Revenge* both begins and ends with a march-like rhythm, as if the band are soldiers, putting on a performance. Annie is close and intimate, and effectively plaintive – here it is possible to hear traces of her former Joni Mitchell style, bringing the music back full circle.

One uniting factor through the album is the feeling of energy from the band, achieving Eurythmics' goal from the outset. "We wrote *Revenge* particularly bearing in mind that we were going to be touring live this year," demonstrated Annie. "So when we've been rehearsing the songs with our band I find that they transcribe very easily into live performance – and that excited me a lot."

★　★　★

273

Not having gigged since the fated Touch Tour, Eurythmics set off on the road afresh with their band of the last couple of months for a mammoth schedule taking them from America in July, through Europe that winter and on to Australia in spring of 1987.

Annie had worked diligently on her voice to ensure that it could withstand the strain of touring solidly for the best part of 10 months, and still create a "powerhouse" of sound at the gigs. This was a greater task than ever before, as for the first time Eurythmics chose to play large stadiums rather than smaller concert halls. They were backed by a winning combination of musicians; Clem Burke on drums, Chucho Merchan on bass guitar, Patrick Seymour on keyboards, Jimmy Zavala on harmonica and saxophone, and the robust Joniece Jamison amply backing Annie's vocals.

The band made quite an impression visually as well as acoustically. The stage was enclosed by black curtains held together by a giant metal zip which ripped open to reveal Eurythmics. With all members dressed in black and white, Annie and Dave remained the focal point as they proudly wore both black leather trousers and matching long coats with a plain white shirt beneath. Many shows were opened with the chant of "Sex, suh–suh–suh sex, sex" from 'Sexcrime (nineteen eighty-four)' before launching into a set consisting of new material and acoustic versions of their classics alike. While pandering to the old favourites such as 'Sweet Dreams (Are Made Of This)' and 'Who's That Girl?', Eurythmics had clearly moved on musically. At one press conference 'Tous Les Garçons' was requested and as Dave started to play it, Annie half-heartedly sang along, but at the end threw him a penetrating glare, muttering, "I'll *kill* you for that."

Starting in America, Eurythmics treated members of the fan club to an exclusive warm-up gig on June 19. Although performed at the Country Club in Los Angeles, this gig was recorded and rather misleadingly released as an EP under the title *Eurythmics Live – Rough And Tough At The Roxy*. The concert secured further promotion as it was featured on *Eurotube*, an off-shoot of the popular British television show *The Tube*. The programme was hosted by Paula Yates and showed performance clips interspersed with footage of Paula chatting individually with Dave and Annie, the latter shot extravagantly in the back of a convertible car driving round Los Angeles escorted by motorcycle police. Eurythmics hysteria was still strong despite their absence from the live circuit, and bodyguard protection was necessary in the form of Andy Michael, especially for Annie who received one surprise visitor backstage claiming to be her long lost mother.

While the tour was gathering unstoppable momentum in America, the singles continued to fare better in the UK. In August 1986, the second offering from *Revenge*, 'Thorn In My Side' was released, leaping to number five in Britain but sticking at 68 in the US. The 'thorn' stabbing Annie was an ex-lover, but in case anyone interpreting the song had missed the well-publicised break-up of her marriage, Dave was keen to point out that he was no longer the villain. "It had been so heavy for her, and this song was her release," he later informed the press. "This period was when we started to become affected by other people and bring them into our music. I can't say that we were no longer emotionally involved because being with Annie was, well, like having 7,000 emotions – there was never a straightforward day. You know, it doesn't have to be sexual."

That Dave and Annie were able to continue a very close relationship throughout divorce and family deaths was very important to her, particularly as it meant that she was able to express her anger in their music and videos. The promo aimed at exorcising the religious Radha from Annie's existence was a far more stylish affair than the repetitively dull 'When Tomorrow Comes'.

'Thorn In My Side' opens with an eye-catching shot of Annie holding a prickly red rose and releasing a piercing, infuriated scream. The band are playing on a stage together in front of an audience comprising tables of Hell's Angels and groupies, reminiscent of scenes from 'Who's That Girl?' Jealous glares bounce between Annie and a rival, focussing heavily on the women's eyes, a competition which Annie easily wins with a particularly maniacal stare. By the end of the song, the female followers individually approach the stage in a religious fervour to have coins placed on their foreheads before they collapse and leave.[38] As the song finishes Annie has overcome the pain of the thorny rose, reducing it to harmless petals which rest in her hands.

From one extreme to another, the next single to be released in the UK was 'Miracle Of Love', which achieved a respectable chart position of 23 in November 1986. As if inviting further speculation into the true nature of his exquisitely close relationship with Annie, Dave again commented that the ex-couple were only now able to go their separate ways: "We recorded the song and knew we really were ready to go out with other people." For two people who had split up six years previously, this seemed an intriguingly unnecessary statement.

Dave made his directorial debut on the video for 'Miracle Of Love', and was careful to avoid the obvious trap they were falling into of reinforcing

[38] This scene was later construed as symbolism for Radha's financial dependency.

275

the united band image. Overcompensating a little too much, the film is only just recognisable as Eurythmics. It opens with black and white footage of a liberation army marching through the streets of a previously war-torn city, but after images of an atomic bomb, a small baby and a woman gratefully kissing a soldier on the cheek, the lengthy guitar solo introduces a torrent of swirling sea and mist with Dave and Annie vaguely visible beneath. Where he excelled in abstract creativity, Dave's direction lacked the ability to retain interest, but he showed that after 'When Tomorrow Comes' he was not afraid to experiment.

In October 1986 the touring party had moved from America into Europe, starting in Scandinavia, working their way down to France by the end of November, before finally returning home for the run-up to Christmas. Mindful that their absence for two years may put them at a disadvantage, Eurythmics launched the European leg of the tour with a bang. An ingenious stunt was cooked up by the band, their management and record label, and not only secured media interest, but allowed Dave and Annie to mock their age-old foes.

Stuart Bailie reported the event in *NME*: "The location was a Covent Garden fitness centre, and a boxing ring was installed in the middle of the place. Dave Stewart had put up handsome cash prizes, and rival journalists were invited to climb onto the canvas and trade punches." With the winnings being donated to a charity of the victor's choice, the journalists fell over themselves to improve their public images. John Preston, Head of RCA, was wary about the ensuing mayhem, particularly as the headlining fight was between arch rivals Garry Bushell from the *Sun* and John Blake from the *Mirror*. Bushell bit the bullet, climbed into the ring and braced himself for the bell.

"The fanfare goes off and in comes Father Christmas, because it's in December, hood over his head," said Preston. "I look around, I'm pretty nervous about this anyway and I see John Blake beside the ring, and I thought, 'Hold on, this isn't John Blake – who's in the Father Christmas outfit?' So he gets in the ring, flips the hood off and it's Lloyd Honeyghan who is currently World Middleweight Champion!

"Bushell throws a punch, which is not one of the smartest things to do, because Honeyghan isn't very amused and clops Bushell, who goes down." The tabloid writers had a field day glorifying the scraps in the morning edition. Dave and Annie meanwhile delighted in watching those critics, who had many times severely bruised Eurythmics' ego, mindlessly clobber each other to raise money for a good cause.

★   ★   ★

Along with the raunchier leather-clad image, Annie had initiated a sensational trend on the Revenge Tour. Usually one to cover her flesh at all costs, the daring Scotswoman had taken to stripping off her jacket and shirt to perform in her leather trousers and a bra, which was alternately red and black. Many artists complain that onstage lighting can generate an immense amount of heat, and leather outfits are equally renowned for creating a sweaty body, but this was more of a shock tactic than an attempt to cool off.

The problem was that, coming from a woman so adamantly against using her sex appeal, the message seemed contradictory. Media interest was aroused to fever pitch when on December 2, 1986 at the Birmingham NEC, Annie, frustrated by the lack of audience reaction, finished a powerful version of 'Missionary Man' by defiantly divesting herself of even her red bra.

"When it happened it was a totally spontaneous action to an audience that weren't reacting," explains Barry Maguire of the bold gesture. "It was Annie's way of getting the audience to react. And it worked!"

Annie's liberation caused quite a stir in the press, but she insisted that it had ultimately proved her stance against sexism within the industry. "I'm relieved that our fans don't see me as a sex symbol. I don't want them to respond to me sexually. Too many bands have female singers just because they think it's a good media gimmick," she said, harking back to her bemoaning during The Tourists. Backtracking slightly, she then continued to other reporters curious at the time, "Now I'm able to let my feminine sexuality come through much more, but I still feel my mannish sexuality as a performer coming through on stage."

Astute critics married Annie's exposure with an apparently hypocritical attack on Madonna whose explicit video for 'Like A Virgin' showed her in a wedding dress rolling around exposing her thighs and a garter. Annie had said, "It was like she was fucking the music industry. It may have been a parody on her part, but I thought it was very low." Of course, the flash of Annie's breasts was far racier than Madonna's legs, but intended for a different purpose.

The allowable boundaries for female artists have often provoked heated debate, but Annie's apparent double-standards for herself and fellow colleagues was more than the reporters could bear. Criticism of Eurythmics' entire tour flooded the media, attacking the band for "selling-out" and producing middle-of-the-road synthesiser ballads for a standard stadium tour. Annie was flabbergasted that Eurythmics could ever be accused of losing their creative genius and rapidly retorted: "Run out of ideas!? Run out of ideas!! Christ, we've only just started! Run out of ideas!" She was apparently lost for words. "We could continue like this . . . FOREVER! We could do three albums a year if we wanted to. We made that album in a few weeks. It's not difficult." In her haste to jump to their defence, she had unwittingly suggested that Eurythmics churned out their material without musical integrity.

"We're not a conventional rock'n'roll band. We take risks musically," she was forced to back-pedal later. "You can't pinpoint the type of music we play because we refuse to be put in a niche. If anything we play compassionate music that doesn't lull people to sleep like most of America. We really don't concern ourselves with what the masses think, so we don't write our songs to fill their needs."

Writing from the heart, as Annie admittedly does, meant that each and every attack on their music hurt deeply. 1986 had not been a good year for Annie in this respect as she had been the victim of incessant public condemnation. The first assault was launched by cutting columnist Julie Burchill, who suggested in *Time Out* that Annie's morals were rather tedious. She wrote, "A genuinely interesting person doesn't mind being seen as a cartoon character; a frigging bore, on the other hand, will have 19 nervous breakdowns in order to prove to the world how uniquely intricate and complex they are." Annie took particular offence to Burchill's plea: "Let Eurythmics die painlessly in a plane crash."

Unfortunately Annie's retaliation did not endear her any further to those criticising her for being pretentious. "The aeroplane was our aspirations and ambitions, if you like, so we should have jumped out because we are not worth anything. It was hard not to fall because we were up there in the ether of stardom. What a place to be. I had so many crashes that I could not feel at all. I kept on crashing and crashing with myself." Lesley-Ann Jones of the *Daily Mirror* joined in the character assassination, simply stating, "I didn't like Annie Lennox. Frankly – I felt threatened by her."

Annie's media protests continued as she complained to *Rolling Stone* about its own reviewer who the previous month commented that she had no soul. "It was so painful to read. I felt like the writer had condemned me. I personally think I'm one of the few performers who has got a good deal of integrity and doesn't sell out. I think I'm the last person who should be given that kind of knife in the back." This self-important attitude did nothing to aid her case either.

Unable to open the media's eyes to her plight, Annie resorted to displaying a realistic appraisal of the situation. "It's painful, but then you have to learn to see that other people's motivation is sometimes very bitter and twisted. So now I realise, yes, people will sometimes hate me. It's a paranoia that makes you try and explain everything so very carefully. God, did

I go through that!" Seven years later Annie had matured enough to realise that it is not healthy to dwell on spiteful comments. "I'm not someone who sits and pores over their press clippings," she said, although she had admitted to doing just that in 1983. "You do something and it goes out into the ether and you have no control over how it will be received. You have to take it all with a huge pinch of salt. Everything you do and say goes into one great big mythological soup, so I have to be a bit blasé about it."

If Annie felt like the bull's-eye of a target it was not surprising. The negative exposure was not limited to strangers – Radha Raman's name cropped up again publicly, this time in the form of revenge by a spurned friend and colleague. Video producer Jon Roseman sold a tale to *News Of The World* who eagerly ran it under the racy headline: "Mad Monk Tried To Blackmail Naked Annie".

Jon had been close to both Dave and Annie throughout their working association, but believes their judgement was impaired by the trappings of fame. "I knew Dave and Annie when they were penniless. I worked with them in The Tourists and did the first three Eurythmics' clips for no mark-up, just to help them. There was every reason to have a good relationship, and we were close friends. Then they became rock'n'roll millionaires and it all changed," he explained bitterly to Lucy O'Brien.

Jon had turned to the duo during the mid-Eighties at a time of personal crisis; not only was his wife seriously ill, but his business was also suffering a rough patch. Jon says he sought company and comfort from his friends, but found himself swiftly cut out of their circle, his calls left unreturned apparently because he had been unable to accompany Annie and Billy on a previous vacation.

Appalled by their lack of compassion, Jon took the rejection personally and retaliated in a manner he knew would cause equal pain for the singer, if not her partner. He revealed to the scandal-hungry tabloid the more intimate nature of Annie's former marriage with the Hare Krishna devotee. Annie had confided some private details to a few people with whom she was close, on the strict understanding that it would go no further. One such piece told in confidence to Jon was that Radha had tried to extract money out of her to stop him publishing personal photos taken by the couple. While Annie would have been mortified had the pictures hit the media, she was not prepared to succumb to demands. It was rumoured that she eventually agreed to pay him £20,000 if he signed an agreement to return the photos and never produce them or speak of their marriage to the press.

20

AN IDEAL HUSBAND

"I'd like to have a home. I would. With another person. To really forge a relationship . . ."

– AL

Having struggled through 1986 amidst an endless stream of varied attacks, Annie hoped for a brighter future as she turned 32 years old. 1987 started with some unusual career twists for both halves of Eurythmics. A 12″ single containing a mix of songs, old and new, was released in Europe; 'Sweet Dreams (Are Made Of This)', 'There Must Be An Angel (Playing With My Heart)', 'When Tomorrow Comes', 'The Miracle Of Love,' 'I Could Give You (A Mirror)' and 'Baby's Gone Blue', the only previously unreleased track. The latter was a most curious exercise. The music is a juxtaposition of Annie crying "Ah – sweetheart!" while various male voices discuss a girl who has been found dead in her party dress. Piano driven, clumsy and harsh (the drumming pointedly leaving out any hi-hats), 'Baby's Gone Blue' was perhaps just a little under-prepared for commercial release.

Eurythmics appeared to be concentrating more on their own exercises than worrying about their joint output. Dave was in as much demand as ever from fellow musicians wanting to tap into his genius. Kiki Dee approached him to write and produce a song for her. The result, 'Another Day Comes', was recorded at The Church with a little assistance from former Eurythmics musician Dean Garcia, and appeared on Kiki's 1987 album *Angel Eyes*.

Meanwhile Annie was taking another tentative step into the world of acting, this time with a starring role in a screen version of Harold Pinter's play *The Room*. Directed by Robert Altman, Annie appeared alongside Donald Pleasance and Julian Sands in this short, dramatic story detailing a wife's thoughts and feelings regarding her bedsit accommodation. Annie is trapped in a marriage to an unpleasant and often near-comatose man, and the loveless couple have to deal with two mercenary strangers seeking shelter.

The combination of her slightly gothic appearance and strong Scottish accent certainly exudes an aura of intensity, but the performance on all accounts was criticised as being stilted. "It is hard to tell whether the acting from all involved is meant to be awkward and unconvincing or whether it simply is plain awful," slated reviewer Maria Arthur who suggested it was only of interest to the most ardent fans. The film was screened during Annie's promotion for the next album, but was swiftly transferred onto video as it did not prove successful. Released as *The Room* in Britain, it was teamed up with another Robert Altman short film, *The Dumbwaiter*, under the collective title of *Basements* for worldwide packaging.

Eurythmics' world Revenge Tour rattled ever onward, taking them to Australia and New Zealand as winter turned to spring 1987. Several of the Australian concerts were filmed for future use on the *Eurythmics Live* video. In February Eurythmics presented their fourth single from the album, 'Missionary Man'. England may have heard one too many Eurythmics singles in the last six months as it rested one place short of the Top 30, but its strident tones powered through to number 14 in America.

The inspiration for the song was famously provided by Dave's friend, the legendary Bob Dylan. Dave was in the kitchen of his house in Maida Vale with Dylan, listening to a selection of tracks they had just recorded at The Church. "Annie was there and we were all drunk on tequila," chuckles Dave. "Dylan was reciting the lyrics to these songs as the backing tracks were playing, but he was just making them up on the spot. And Annie was trying to scribble them all down as he went along. He did it for about nine songs just singing these brilliant lyrics, completely off the top of his head. It's then that you realise someone like that probably never sits at a typewriter for hours staring at a blank page." Thrilled with Dylan's improvisation Annie raced home and created a poem from his words, which eventually morphed into the lyrics for 'Missionary Man'. Starting off as a culmination of Dylan's ad libbing, Annie personalised the song by looking at fundamentalist religions, such as her dabblings with Hare Krishna.

To round it off, Eurythmics utilised Jimmy Zavala's expert harmonica playing, with only the aid of a stiff drink instead of a rehearsal. "I got him straight off the aeroplane in LA with jet lag," remembers Dave, "took him to the studio where we had a big drink waiting for him – tequila or something – and put him behind the mic with a harmonica and a song he'd never heard before. What you hear is the first thing he played."

The impact of the video for the single put paid to the recent criticism that Eurythmics had lost their creative spark. Achieving the claim of being the first promo to be shown only after the watershed Annie described 'Missionary Man' as a "cheeky look at the wages of sin." Dave opens the film as he acts out his usual mad professor routine, surrounded by test tubes and scientific equipment, creating a waxwork of Annie's head. Her face is slowly filled in and she starts singing as soon as the red lipsticked mouth is complete. When Annie is finished the camera pans out to reveal the Revenge band in the background.

The highlight is undoubtedly Annie, wearing a black leather catsuit with Madonna-style conical breast-plates, performing a robotic walk and dance. The real genius lay with the post production team as several frames were dropped from the final cut to produce the jerky motions. The effect is simply stunning, experimental and advanced for the time.

Continuing the threatening S&M stance, Annie's head is locked up in a machine which pounds computer-animated pistons into her cheeks, particularly reminiscent of Peter Gabriel's award-winning video for 'Sledgehammer' the previous year. Returning to the enticing black leather outfit, Annie unzips the front, peeling it back to reveal herself repeating the action until Dave penetrates the shot. Further aggressive imagery is included with furnaces and Dave typically smashing his guitar, but it is Annie's mechanical head and eye movements that are the most startling. "Some of the songs are very cold and sinister, about elements I've experienced and the way I portray them is sometimes a bit robotic," Annie said of this latest departure.

The month of February further solidified recognition of the group's creativity alongside the release of 'Missionary Man'. Dave was named Best British Producer for the second year running at the BRIT Awards and Eurythmics stole the Best Rock Performance By A Duo Or Group With Vocal category at the 29th Annual Grammy Awards.

★   ★   ★

Towards the end of the Revenge Tour, in March 1987, Annie's relationship with Billy Poveda skidded to a stop. The couple had lived together since 1985, but over time Annie began to distance herself from the former dancer.

"Something was never quite right there," said film producer Jon Roseman in *Sweet Dreams Are Made Of This*. "He got dumped. He was a choreographer, she fancied him, one thing led to another. Then he found himself in the terrible situation of looking after her life and living off her.

"I saw it begin to degenerate. There's a thin dividing line between using someone *per se*, and using them because you think there's a reason for using them . . . it was very sad."

Although Billy and Annie remained on good professional terms, the singer felt let down by both her partner and herself, and struggled to come to terms with the split. Following what was now a well established pattern, she channelled her energies into work, exploring her twisted emotions within her lyrics.

Her story would be openly recounted in the songs that became Eurythmics' next studio album, the aptly named *Savage*. "When I wrote songs for our new album *Savage*, I had just broken up with the man I had been living with for two years and it left me reeling," she clearly admits. "I wasn't prepared for it and I felt very betrayed. It was as if my world was caving in around me."

In the middle of this difficult time, the *Revenge* promotion took Eurythmics to Japan, where they performed in Tokyo on March 18. They had agreed for this part of the tour to be filmed for a feature length movie, directed by Israeli documentary-maker Amos Gitai and jointly produced by Agav Films and Oil Factory. The project was to be called *Brand New Day* after one of the new tracks on which Annie was working, and as she described, "It was an attempt to see the aspects of a country that we were touring, to break out of the bubble."

The film-makers tailed Eurythmics to such contrasting Japanese sights as Buddhist temples, bamboo forests and a Yamaha piano factory in an attempt to capture a slice of life on the road for their fans. The extreme sense of division between the Western pop stars and their audience is visually enhanced by following Eurythmics around outdoor settings where they are surrounded by an alien culture, and witnessing their performance in concert in front of a sea of Japanese faces. By situating the documentary in a foreign country Gitai employs the East/West stereotype as a metaphor for Dave and Annie's literal isolation.

Some electric performance footage was included, showing Dave and Annie at their peak on stage, and the film was set for preview at the forthcoming Edinburgh Film Festival. A striking poster publicised the event, depicting a bizarre shot of Annie; bald, naked and sprayed entirely white.

Sadly, that was as far as it got. Although there was nothing but praise for the concert coverage, the reviewers slammed the documentary side to the 83-minute film, slating Eurythmics as self-indulgent and dull. *NME*'s Bob Flynn presented a typical example of the critics' opinion: "The film fails in the task intended but succeeds accidentally in exposing the limbo-land vacuity of the oddest couple's rock-stardom tour-world, where fatigue and cosseted silliness prevail. It's as if Dave has said, 'Let's expose ourselves, warts'n'all, but you've got to do the talking and I'll just act daft.'"

Indeed, it was Dave's own personal behaviour on camera that came under the most unforgiving scrutiny at the press conference. Horrified, in leaping to his defence, Annie only exacerbated the situation, crying, "That's the way Dave is, there was no play acting. He *is* a guy who likes to show off constantly. He has an almost childlike quality which I find embarrassing . . . but others may have another reaction, possibly find it irritating. This film wasn't made for any specific target, like for fans or a certain cinema audience. It's not a strategy to project Eurythmics."

It seemed that even the star of the project was no longer certain of the film's actual intention, and as a direct result of the unexpected response at the conference, the plug was pulled altogether.[39] Annie backed down and admitted that she too shared the feelings of the majority. "Filming is too much of a false circumstance to be yourself on camera. I was shocked when I first saw it. Like everybody else I have a sense of vanity and when you see yourself in such harsh close-up you realise your age and how tired you were at that time. It's a tough experience being a performer." In an unnecessary show of independence, she passed the blame: "I was very reticent about making the film but Dave was very keen."[40]

Fortunately, one good thing was to emerge from the whole nasty business. A romance flourished between Annie and Uri Fruchtmann, assistant director on *Brand New Day*. Uri was an Israeli film-maker, born at Petah-Tikva and three months Annie's senior. According to biographer Lucy O'Brien, Uri, like Radha, had German origins. His father, author Bruno Fruchtmann, had left his hometown of Meuselwitz, Germany and settled in Israel just before the outbreak of World War II. Later, Uri worked in Germany with Bruno's brother, his uncle Karl, an independent film-maker in Germany. Karl and Uri joined forces on several films including the award-winning *Witnesses* in 1980, which centred on interviews with survivors of Nazi concentration camps.

As far as Annie was concerned, in the dark and handsome film-maker she had met her match, both artistically and emotionally. In summer 1987 she said, "I'd like to have a home. I would. With another person. To really forge a relationship – which I have, I've started another relationship with somebody and I'm very happy about it." Shortly after, she was even more vocal about her new-found happiness. "It's about time I had a relationship that works. It's marvellous that I've actually found somebody I love. I feel very happy, clear and clean." Uri was yet to make a proper name for himself within the film world, but his ideas were inspiring and the future looked bright. To top it all off, he proved a hit with the Eurythmics inner

[39] *Brand New Day* was in fact officially released in France, albeit in very limited numbers.
[40] In 1991 Annie's name was once again linked with Gitai's, as she contributed to his film *Golem*.

circle. "He's brilliant," says Barry Maguire without any hesitation. "He's quite an individual person. He's very gentle and kind, but he's also very motivated."

As the summer progressed, Eurythmics overcame their embarrassment of *Brand New Day* and, with the accolade of being named Songwriters Of The Year at the Ivor Novello Awards in April behind them, finished off the Revenge Tour with a semblance of pride. Notably, on June 4, 1987 while they were performing in Berlin, over 1,000 East Berlin fans gathered at the Berlin wall, chanting, "The wall must go!" The enthusiastic protesters were removed by the police – demolition of the offending barrier commenced on November 9, 1989.

★   ★   ★

Annie wasn't the only one with a blossoming love life. On August 1, 1987 a beaming David Allan Stewart married a heavily pregnant Siobhan Maire Fahey at Chateau Dangu in Normandy, France.

Ironically, Dublin-born Siobhan had been one of the throng of women adorning Dave's arm in the 'Who's That Girl?' video, at that time being one third of the successful British girl group, Bananarama. Having split from the band and formed Shakespear's Sister with Marcella Detroit, Siobhan was a pop name in her own right and had been seeing Dave for some time following his break-up from Claire Evans. His chat-up line had arrived over the phone: "I can't get you off my mind and that's the top and bottom of it. What are we going to do about it?"

After a whirlwind courtship, their summer wedding was a predictably glitzy, paparazzi-strewn affair and cost a cool half a million pounds. Hundreds of celebrity guests were flown in by chartered jet from Heathrow. Annie dutifully attended the ceremony with Uri, but kept a low profile and left early.

Although somewhat forced into each other's pockets, at least in the eyes of the media, Annie and Siobhan seemed to hit it off. Annie spoke generously to journalist Phil Sutcliffe about the latest addition to the Eurythmic family: "I think Siobhan is a great girl, a great girl. I don't know her *so* well but that's a relationship, between her and me, that will develop and become a nice friendship. It is already. When they first met I thought, 'At last he's got somebody who will provide him with the sincerity that was lacking before.'"

"In the past his affairs were all so frantic," she continued elsewhere, "as if he was looking for something he'd lost. There were different involvements with people and he was less settled, everything felt up in the air in a sense. Now there's a structure round him, something very positive that will deepen his experience as a human being. It will also be something apart from Eurythmics . . . Something wonderful, enriching."

Part of the attraction seemed to be that Siobhan really did come as a separate entity to the history that had bound Dave to Annie for what was now a decade. Drawing on his own past experience, Dave vowed to keep it so. "I have learned by my mistakes," he admitted. "I might give Siobhan's band advice, and we occasionally write songs together, but I'd never write songs for Shakespear's Sister. We'd turn into that same inseparable, claustrophobic mess as Annie and I were."

Something intangible changed after the pairing of Dave with Siobhan and Annie with Uri. Although both members of Eurythmics had been married once before, neither relationship had lasted, and children had certainly never been on the horizon. Annie had always been the one desiring parenthood, but now Dave was about to achieve it first, so the relationship shifted irreversibly.

Reflecting on the difficult period several years later, Dave realised that it was only through the stability of Uri and Siobhan that Eurythmics was able to continue. "We both thought: 'How are we going to get out of this?' It didn't happen the way we thought it would, because we both did meet the right people and felt totally alienated towards each other.

"We freaked out for a while, and that became the album *Savage*." Drifting apart, as work commenced on their next album after Dave's return from honeymoon, a definite crack was apparent in the very foundations of their partnership. Not only did they neglect to see each other socially, but they hardly seemed to meet up in the studio.

In autumn 1987 Annie and Dave worked, often independently, on the album that was to be called *Savage*. A taster appeared in October, the oddly titled 'Beethoven (I Love To Listen To)'. It reached number 25 in the UK charts.

"It was like an abstract painting," Annie attempted to explain. "The whole thing is very symbolic, using that line 'I love to listen to Beethoven', was just something I wrote down one day, and for me it's a symbol for when people feel really bad and they listen to classical music . . . They shut the windows, shut the door and listen to Wagner or something and it's symbolising feeling bad. The song itself is like going into a person's head and seeing all these fractured thoughts and emotions and everything being torn apart." Evidently her recent happiness with Uri had not yet eclipsed any feelings of bitterness towards former partners, and as Dave later confided, "Around the time of *Savage* she had a real confidence problem with me and would hardly join in on the LP until the very end. She was going through all these problems which in the end made the lyrics really good."

Savage was recorded at the same Normandy countryside chateau where Dave had married Siobhan. Returning to their early trademark sound from the days of *Sweet Dreams (Are Made Of This)* and *Touch*, Olle Romo was the only other musician on the album – the rest was just Dave, Annie and a computer.

Various stories tend to circulate around the recording of this album, but most agree that the majority of the work originated from Dave and Annie as individuals, rather than coming together as a team. Popularly *Savage* is *Annie's* masterpiece, exploring the extent of her heartbreak; her split with Billy, the death of her father and her struggle to come to terms with Dave's marriage and impending fatherhood. Before Uri brought some much needed calm into her world Annie had been stretched to her limit, sick of living in hotel rooms and with no loving home to return to. "I just didn't know what I was doing or who I was," she said. "It was as if I was all alone on a mountain top . . . an isolation that was quite dangerous."

"It was a very *faithless* album, you know," she said in *NME*. "In terms of the lyrical content, it was a betrayed soul. Things had reached such ironic proportions that there was nothing left to believe in any more. You can have despair, but you can have a little bit of hope at the end of the day. But *Savage* is just beyond that – when I say 'everything is fiction, all cynic to the bone' – that certainly was the way I felt at the time."

This was all in bleak contrast to Dave's content, but it appears he sat and helped her work through her emotions. "*Savage* was an annihilation record!" he later exclaimed. "A lot of Annie's words were about the despair and pain of being on the receiving end of men being so horrible. That was Annie's time out, it was almost a solo album except that I made the music with her." If Annie was behind the lyrics, his forte was the music. Initially Annie didn't like it, but then she wasn't often around.

"The thing was, I recorded the whole album without Annie being there," Dave later announced in *Vox*. "Annie came in twice in three months because she was so fucked up. She'd just split up with somebody. I made the whole album virtually on my own. Then I met Annie in Paris and we were great friends again, and she did the vocals in a week, just poured it all out."

Whoever is due the credit, the resulting album is little short of a miracle, as it successfully blends Dave's return to electronics with Annie's cold, dis-associated vocals and spiteful, hurting lyrics. As Annie said most eloquently, "There's a depth to it we haven't touched before. It's dark and I like the sharpness of its blade."

* * *

The pounding beat of 'Beethoven (I Love To Listen To)' tantalises for a good 30 seconds while a synthetic crescendo gradually builds, before finally bursting out into the title which is curiously transposed: "Listen To", "I Love To". Capturing both the listener's attention and imagination from the start, Annie's crystal clear tones cut icily through the music to tell the story of a woman sneering at a young girl's smutty lifestyle, alternately singing and speaking in a mock upper-class accent. The multiple layers of voice and sound persistently increase in complexity throughout the song, retaining the initial interest. Dave puts down his favoured guitar to experiment with a slightly demonic keyboard solo over the relentless beat. Towards the end, Annie's fake, breathy laugh is placed over dramatic synth power chords which are warped backwards to produce an uneasy, cold impression which grows before fading to end.

After the opening intensity, 'I've Got A Lover (Back In Japan)' is easier on the ear. Annie's voice gently weaves through the pleasant melody, producing a much softer, warmer sound. The occasional bursts of energy subside back to the meandering pace, sometimes leaving the impression that the song lacks a little direction. Annie utilises speech again, this time for reiteration as she says a line and then sings it back to herself. The lyrics detail the luxurious complications of keeping a lover in each port, but it is apparent that this is not the lifestyle Annie desires. She has wearied of the constant touring and in the last verse has met the man with whom she wants to settle down, clearly Uri Fruchtmann.

She repeats her state of mind to him: "I was bitter when I met you I was eloquent with rage/ Like honey from a poisoned cup I flowed from stage to stage", but reinforces that she wants to "Break away those ties". As a rather ominous indication of the immense succour required from Uri, Annie warns, "When the whole world descends on me/ I'll be waiting for you".

An intriguing percussive introduction draws the listener into the welcome sound of a real guitar, which expands to create a strong backbone for the third track, 'Do You Want To Break Up?' A persuasive synthesised bass permeates the melody and Annie's cute, recurring "Yeah" is regularly punctuated by stylish guitar twangs. 'Do You Want To Break Up?' demonstrates Dave's dextrous use of space and dimension to produce a fun and busy mix, but it is a remarkably bright and breezy song considering the nature of the lyrics.

Here Annie bares her soul, acknowledging that she is caught in a destructive relationship and must break away to find a happy future. Judging by the timing of the album it would appear that Annie is referring to her painful break-up from Billy Poveda, but the video for the song would later clearly portray her awakening from her obscure marriage to Radha Raman.

The deeply penetrating 'You Have Placed A Chill In My Heart' beautifully showcases not only Annie's fine vocals, but also her talent for expression. The drum programming and synths are slow yet insistent throughout, allowing Annie to expound on her personal disillusionment with the contradictions of love. "Love is hot and love is cold, I've been bought and I've been sold/ Love is rock and love is roll, I just want someone to hold". It is her despairing plea to find someone permanent, a partner with whom she can attain lasting, peaceful love.

Following the beseeching 'You Have Placed A Chill In My Heart', light bells lead into 'Shame', a somewhat dramatic cautionary tale. Annie explains that although the lifestyle of the rich and famous can appear enviable, the harsh reality is that stars are often artificially loved by their fans but lack the true undying love of a partner. Again it is her patronage for an enduring, meaningful relationship far removed from the glitz and glamour of the limelight. Annie's vocals are multi-tracked and used to emulate another instrument. It is a moving piece, but the strong emotional themes could be criticised as a little suffocating.

'Savage' marks a definite close to a monumental first side of the cassette and vinyl release. Instantly atmospheric, Annie takes this moody, dark song partly into the third person, with just two simple verses outlining her alternate repetitive theme; her emotional ostracism and the down-side of fame. Dave executes a superb extended guitar solo, before this unhurried song gradually builds to a dramatic close, but surprises with a disconcerting finish of a seething breath.

Blasting into the second side with a piercing scream of pent-up female frustration, Annie next becomes a lusty, domineering vamp. 'I Need A Man' presents the perfect dichotomy as this robust feminist rock number about needing a man solely for a raw, physical connection, was created by a woman who so desperately and blatantly craved a loving and nurturing relationship. It may be that Annie genuinely felt that she needed some outlet for her sexual desires without the complications of a serious partnership, but that would go against the grain of the rest of the album. Whatever the concept behind the song, it is an overwhelming success as Dave's searing guitar in the latter third helps propel Annie's powerful, Mick Jagger-like strut ever onwards.

Opening 'Put The Blame On Me' with a spiky guitar riff, the tension in the last number is immediately blown away to be complemented by a sensual bass beat and unusual keyboards. Although the title would suggest that Annie is to blame for an infidelity within the relationship, the lyrics are ambiguous as to who has been unfaithful. The story is filled with innuendo and deceit, with both physical and mental perfidy insinuated on both sides, and it would appear to a certain extent that Annie is trying to come to terms with her separation from Billy Poveda.

The first verse continues her need for straightforward sexual gratification as in 'I Need A Man' while the middle section hints at some serious communication failures within the relationship, and the closing verse sows seeds of jealousy and the distasteful realisation of an affair. Annie again speaks when asking, "Are you sleeping on your own?" but this time in an exotic, seductive voice to add weight to a fully loaded question. The use of steady repetition of "Get right up and go back home" interspersed with "Put the blame on me" to close, indicates that Annie was painfully aware of the problems in the relationship and desperately wanted to reconcile by accepting blame, but was ultimately unable to control the situation.

Whether Billy was the true target of these lyrics or not, 'Put The Blame On Me' stands as one of Annie's strongest yet most twisted songs. As Dave had previously commented, within her psyche lay the key to her genius.

"A lot of lyrics are to do with Annie and Annie's a very taut kind of person emotionally," the guitarist had said back in the early days. "She goes between complete ecstasy and complete tense depression and she stretches across the whole range in one song. Everybody feels these different emotions . . . it's just that Annie tends to fit them all into three minutes. She's a very razor-sharp kind of person."

Returning to the album, 'Heaven' is a refreshingly instrumental-based track, where the simple 14 words are just occasionally whispered or gently sung. The song paints a picture of a perfect heaven without specific narrative, leaving it open to be connected to any situation where peace and happiness is finally achieved. This relaxing, indulgent track consists mainly of swooping synths against Annie's ethereal vocals and is well-placed for such experimentation, halfway through the second side.

The synthetic, simple pop song of 'Wide Eyed Girl' has great potential sadly unrealised. Annie's vocals are harsh but the overall song is muffled, an unfortunate antithesis to 'Heaven'. It becomes apparent that the track has a live element as there is tremendous applause during the frenzied guitar solo and Annie's ranting at the end is rendered unintelligible. The track sits rather uncomfortably on a regular studio album although the concluding vitality is fairly infectious.

A false start and mutterings of "I can't hear you" stumble awkwardly into the most simplistic song, 'I Need You', with Dave accompanying Annie on acoustic guitar. Her lyrics have returned once again to the persistent imploring for a stalwart spouse as at the start of the album. Annie's voice is remarkably austere over the soft yearning lyrics, but alerts the listener to the reality of her distorted demands, "I need you to really feel the twist of my back breaking/ I need someone to listen to the ecstasy I'm faking". It is interesting to note that Annie seems to have outlined her emotional requirements for her partner, without a reciprocal offer. Slightly incongruous with the nature of the song are the voices murmuring and laughing in the background, as if at a cocktail party. When the music finishes and the crowd nonchalantly continue their conversations, one wonders if the song really *was* that uninteresting. Just maybe it's an apt reflection of Annie's feelings of alienation.

While 'I Need You' followed on from 'Wide Eyed Girl' in its live elements, 'Brand New Day' continues the minimalist theme. However that should not deter from the beauty of this uplifting, positive song. Annie opens this pseudo-spiritual number with a long *a cappella* introduction covering both verses, harmonising with herself and punctuating her points with breathy "boom"s and "huh"s. As she breaks out into "Hey it's a brand new day", delicate military percussion and samples are brought in. This is Annie's final showcase on an intensely personal album, describing how she has awoken from a bad dream and wanders the streets to clear her head for a brand new day; presumably an analogy for discarding her past and embarking on a new relationship with Uri.

★   ★   ★

Savage was released on to an unsuspecting public on November 18, 1987. After *Revenge* had initiated criticism of the band's commercial leanings against their actual artistic accomplishments, any weak-spirited Eurythmics fans were bound to jump ship. The latest album was so intensely personal and radio *un*friendly that without sufficient analysis it seemed to outsiders that the group had lost the plot. Certainly in America it bombed and all singles failed to reach chart placings of any significance. The UK remained a little more faithful, allowing it to reach number seven in the charts against *Billboard*'s disappointing number 41.

The album attracted mixed reviews all round. No one was quite prepared to accept that the hit machine of Eurythmics had gone AWOL and that Annie was so openly treating her music as a form of therapy. Although the bare bones of catharsis put many critics off, *Savage* was at least championed by *Sounds* writer Tony Mitchell, who wrote: "Blending delicate, textural layering, expected and unexpected gustiness, soft femininity, hard-line sexual politics and upfront sexiness, it is a more mature and complete collection of songspinning than we're accustomed to finding on any single album these days." Few were able to challenge his last comment.

In place of the customary world tour, Eurythmics chose to promote *Savage* via film. Cutting a little close to the bone, Billy Poveda produced the video album alongside John Stewart, and the two enrolled Sophie Muller to direct what was to become a themed epic. Working from Camden, London, Sophie struck up a good rapport with Annie, finding common ground both personally and professionally. The singer smiles, "When Sophie and I get together, our humour is really quite cruel. We both have a black sense of humour." The two had shared a similar upbringing, as although Sophie was born in London she grew up on the isolated Isle of Man, off the north west coast, later venturing back to London to pursue her further education. After graduating with a BA in Graphic Design from St. Martin's School of Art, Sophie went on to attain her master's degree in Film and Television at the Royal College of Art, gaining much vocational kudos in the process for her final year presentation.

Sophie continued to sharpen her skills as editor, producer and director for International Film and Video, before enthusiastically joining Billy and John at Oil Factory to expand her talents. Under Sophie's expert guidance, the videos for *Savage* combined her and Annie's similar temperament and outlook with the intensely intimate nature of the lyrics. "Annie liked the incredible feeling of voyeurism," Sophie explained in 1987. "Probably it was somewhat easier because she was female and we were dealing with female conceits."

When examined in depth the video explicitly portrays Annie's highs and lows in both her career and personal relationships. For a woman so intent on separating her private life from her public persona, it was startling that she should invite such speculation. "I think people will appreciate it and I'm very interested to see what they make of it . . . it's all to do with presenting ideas in an interesting and intelligent way." While there had been some conjecture over the balance of creative input for *Savage* as an audio album, the video left no room for doubt, not least due to Dave's limited appearance.

Laying bare the threads of Annie's life, the themes primarily explore the acknowledged polarities within her personality from the frumpy, brunette housewife to the slutty, blonde tramp, whilst tackling head-on specifically cloistered events such as her break-ups with Radha Raman and Billy Poveda. As a happy ending to her story is somewhat guaranteed, since she had found true love with Uri Fruchtmann before the project's creation, a cynic might venture that Ms Lennox is only comfortable with such close scrutiny having secured a seemingly perfect conclusion.

"I think *Savage* definitely represents the way I feel," she had announced of the music itself. "The darkness of *Savage* is very much on a parallel with the darkness within me but then I'm not always like that. I'm a very contradictory character. I know I am."

The actress dons a mousy wig to open the first video, in which she is dressed as a dowdy housewife, maniacally arranging flowers and talking to herself. Annie is visibly pale with dark circles under her eyes as we watch her sitting, rocking herself on the sofa. When she launches into 'Beethoven (I Love To Listen To)' Annie busies herself with everyday chores around the home, which is decorated in Seventies brown and patterned chintz. A young blonde girl representing her daughter appears in a pink meringue dress and ineptly tries on her mother's make-up. The child dances around the living room, methodically swiping ashtrays, ornaments and records off shelves, and messing the finely ordered room. The dutiful mother rushes around after her in a frenzy, simultaneously dusting and setting everything straight again.

In the background lurks a shadowy figure of a bald drag queen.[41] As Annie sings into the mirror on her vanity table, images of both faces are interchanged in quick succession. Annie typically reaches to her head and removes her brown wig, but instead of revealing her true self she replaces the look with a platinum blonde, curly wig, and liberally slaps on some make-up; the resulting look somewhere between her daughter and the drag queen. Unashamedly showing off her cleavage and black lingerie in a revealing dress, Annie marches around destroying the order she had so carefully created, before tottering out of the house. This detail-rich video snaps between images in synch with the pounding beat of the music, a technique that was to become a trademark for Sophie in her future work.

In 'Beethoven (I Love To Listen To)' Annie is apparently rebelling from the lifestyle of the docile housewife, but with her interpretation of 'I Need A Man' it would appear that she is not particularly proud of her initial moves after breaking this mould.

Continuing the tarty look in her tight pink dress and heavy make-up Annie stumbles into a nightclub and assumes the lead vocal to 'I Need A Man'. The camera pans wildly in and out focussing solely on the actress as she dances and sings. Any initial interest in Annie exposing herself as a slutty rock star is soon lost as the video becomes rather tedious and self-indulgent. The self-assurance of the lyrics is unfortunately swallowed up

---

[41] Popular Eurythmic rumour queried at the time whether this could actually be 'Adrian', the crazed fan of the *Be Yourself Tonight* album.

by the pitiful display of tacky sexuality. As the song closes she drunkenly staggers down the corridor.

The spiritual calmness of 'Heaven' allows Annie some time to reflect on her situation and although having hit the big time as a singer, it would appear that she still has aspirations of becoming a Hollywood starlet. Close-ups of the singer posing and pouting akin to Marilyn Monroe are juxtaposed with random shots of Hollywood and idiosyncratic Eurythmics images such as Dave acting as chauffeur for Annie.

The nightmarish trilogy outlining the changing visions of Annie's future from housewife, through pop star to film star comes to an abrupt end with 'Shame'. After a linking animation of saints on a stained glass window the shot turns to Annie and Dave in a naked embrace, viewed from the shoulders up. Clearly representing their time together both Dave and Annie sing in the video, while he provides emotional support for her melodramatic collapse.

Moving the story swiftly over the break-up with Dave, Annie and Sophie intelligently recall a typical, yet inevitably personalised, relationship between parent and child in 'Wide Eyed Girl'. The tale starts with a Sixties couple getting themselves ready to go out – they meet, kiss, and she falls pregnant. The pair marry regardless of the visible bump and shortly afterwards the baby is born.

A powerful montage is compiled to age the child through the years, interspersing Annie's face with that of a baby, a little girl (played by Dave's niece Laura), and a teenager. It is with the adolescent that the allegory is resumed. The daughter displays the usual pubescent fads in her choice of bedroom decorations, but it is the selection of boyfriends that causes the inevitable clash between mother and daughter. Parading numerous youths back to her room she settles on one who has a penchant for playing an electric guitar. Annie, as the exasperated parent, is clothed as a combination between the housewife and slut. She storms upstairs and shouts at the rocker boyfriend, who bears a strong resemblance to Dave. Having successfully 'saved' her daughter from one unsuitable boy, Annie is unable to protect her little girl as she travels abroad and meets a handsome foreigner. Upon the child's return with a strange man the mother screams at them both, resulting in a spite-infested pillow fight. Interestingly it is the girl's choice of boyfriend that leads her to pack her suitcase and leave home, closely mirroring the estrangement Annie experienced with her own parents when she married Radha Raman in 1984.

Of course Annie's marriage to Radha did not survive and it is fitting that the next video 'Do You Want To Break Up?' features numerous explicit references to the dubious German Hare Krishna, namely the couple's retreat in Switzerland. Annie is pictured in bed arousing from a deep sleep. While her awakening is calming and peaceful, shot in sepia, the marriage is illustrated as a farce. Once again she assumes the role of the deferential housewife, albeit plastered with make-up, while some yodellers in Leider-hosen sing and dance around her. Annie tries to carry on but has to keep ducking to avoid flying plates – these missiles could represent callous attacks by the press about the bizarre whirlwind romance. Fortunately this rather excruciating Julie Andrews rip-off closes as Annie is finally woken from her slumber.

Escaping the banality of the last video, 'I've Got A Lover (Back In Japan)' shows Annie back in her routine, touring and performing in Eurythmics, but it would appear that all is not well there either. Annie is being driven in the back of a car but for once there is no chauffeur. She dreamily traces a scenic picture of the Swiss Alps before tearing it up and throwing the pieces out of the car window to make a clean break. Annie and Dave are seen in concert footage, but it is painfully apparent that she is now uncomfortable with constant touring. Poignantly filmed looking out of a high-rise window over a vast city, Annie is permitted to observe everything yet is stiflingly trapped and unable to join in. Finally she imagines the slutty pop star lashing out at the constant media hounds surrounding her.

The visualisation for 'Put The Blame On Me' consists entirely of paint swirling over blurred film images of Annie. The feeling of confusion and lack of direction is accentuated by bright flashing lights and the pulsating heartbeat rhythm. These emotions appear to represent the two passionate years that Annie spent with Billy Poveda before the painful break-up of their relationship – the blame of which is left unresolved as in the lyrics.

After another setback in her personal life, and suffering as the victim of outspoken criticism of the Revenge Tour, it is not surprising that Annie utilised the video for 'Savage' to air her feelings about the media intrusion into her life. She portrays her vision of this daily invasion via her slutty character. The media persist in photographing and filming the starlet, oblivious to her blatantly depressive state. The helpless woman acknowl-edges that she is public property and prostitutes her soul for the price of fame, allowing herself to be captured with her wig slipping, looking positively sick with self-loathing. Although the video is remarkably monot-onous, it is highly indicative of Annie's state of mind after the last tour, and well explains the choice of video as promotion for the new album.

'You Have Placed A Chill In My Heart' is set in this seemingly bottom-less pit of depression to which she has sunk. A distraught Annie in a long black coat walks barefoot across a windswept desert, epitomising her hopelessness. The despair caught up in the lyrics is frequently spelt out, as the title is etched in the sand below a heart and the line "Show me the colour of your right hand" is illustrated with a neon dollar sign over a heart flashing intermittently. Annie has obviously been hurt in the past by partners more interested in materialistic items than love.

Dejected, with nowhere to turn, Annie considers returning to the notion of becoming a dutiful housewife, but as she shops for groceries she realises that she cannot simply buy love at the supermarket. Perhaps she should instead be content with the option of being a much-loved celebrity without a personal relationship. The ghostlike Annie then stands in between the housewife and starlet who are arguing the pros and cons of their lifestyles over the telephone. Wanting to be left alone she dismisses them and intriguingly walks into a 'Live Girls Show'.

Back in the wasteland of her emotion Annie looks healthier and happier as she is embraced by a faceless man, played by Uri. She has clearly found her one true love as she is simply ecstatic while the world spins around her. Notably this touching ending also borrows heavily from the 1986 video for Peter Gabriel's duet with Kate Bush on 'Don't Give Up', where they were filmed almost exclusively in an eternal embrace while the sky depicted the changing world in perpetual motion. It is only in the video that Annie's laughing "ha ha, ha ha" at the end can be interpreted as joy, instead of despair.

Having found her soulmate Annie uses 'I Need You' as a tool to amplify the simplicity of her plea to Uri. Shot in black and white, Annie and Dave are sitting on stools at a party. Even though they start playing, the conversation continues around them and they remain partly obscured by the guests' silhouettes.

Safe in the knowledge that Uri will provide unconditional love, the film launches into 'Brand New Day'. Although Annie admits that her life will still be viewed as if on the stage, she freely expresses her future desires, which clearly involve marriage and children. A group of young girls enters one by one, barefoot and dressed in dark tunics. They perform Eurhythmics, the Greek dancing that Annie learnt as a child. At the end of the *a cappella* section Annie herself bursts on to the scene in a flash of light. Dressed all in white surrounded by falling confetti and the dancing girls, this piece choreographed by Michael Clarke indicates a fresh start in life. As the curtains close wild applause spreads through the audience, and Annie and the girls step forward to lap up the overwhelming appreciation.

If nothing else, the culmination of the video would suggest that Annie has made her peace and is saying farewell to a substantial chapter of her life.

★   ★   ★

Further promotion for *Savage* included a one-off concert at the launch party for the video album. Accompanied solely and sporadically by Olle Romo on keyboards, Dave and Annie performed a short set including, 'I Need You', 'I Need A Man', 'You Have Placed A Chill In My Heart' and 'Savage'. During this time they also made a handful of live performances on television, but a tour was still not on the cards. 'Shame' was duly released as the second single, but failed even to crack the Top 40 in the UK, halting just one place short.

Frustrated by the cool reception towards her masterpiece, Annie threw herself into her relationship with Uri. In early 1988 the lovers moved quietly into a small apartment together above a baker's shop on Rue Delambre, in Montparnesse, Paris. This signified not just a fresh start in the singer's love life, but an ongoing need to stay removed from British soil for tax purposes and to avoid persistent fans. "I just love this city and I'm very happy to have any excuse to be here," Annie maintained, "but it's not a retreat because we're always working here. Paris for me is softer, it's a bit kinder, it's a bit more sociable and I enjoy that. I don't know many French people and I don't have much time to form relationships with people but it's just a marvellous place."

Colliding with the release of *Savage* the previous November was the birth of Dave and Siobhan's first child, whom they named Samuel Joseph Hurricane Stewart. Encouraged by the little family's obvious joy and the growing love of Uri, Annie began to think seriously about having a baby and the subject filtered quite naturally into her interview responses. "At 33, it's about time physically, and I know a baby will enrich my life," she said to one magazine. "Friends are getting pregnant all around me, but I don't want just to be part of the fashion. It is all a question of who you are with – you can't just buy a bag of kids in the shop!"

Although Dave now had fatherly duties to keep his whirling mind occupied at least some of the time, as a true workaholic he was unable to let the months following the last album pass without some diversion. Around this time he announced he had picked up an old project, started a couple of years previously, a feature film called *TVP*.

"It's for kids, though adults can understand it, but on a different level," Dave explained. "It's about teaching music to kids in a much more exciting way than they do at school. I mean, who wants to learn to play a recorder anyway?"

Gaining the interest and financial assistance of George Harrison's Hand-made Films, Dave also persuaded Annie to help him out. Seeing the possibility of using up some of Eurythmics' considerable surplus unreleased material, they earmarked some songs for the soundtrack and began to work on a screenplay. The story was typically Dave: a futuristic world orbited by a satellite operated by Annie, who would over the course of the film lose her mind. "It could be fantastic if it's done with as much integrity as I envisage," she said. Sadly this strange proposal has yet to see the light of day as George Harrison's business partner put a stop to its production and the matter has not been satisfactorily concluded.

In the meantime, RCA was extremely concerned with the poor sales of *Savage*, and decided to release a third single from the album, alongside a revised publicity campaign. 'I Need A Man' was released on five different formats, including a CD single in a metal tin. Eurythmics accordingly hyped it up on national television and in newspaper interviews.

" 'I Need A Man' speaks for itself," said Annie to *Record Mirror*. "It's a very angry song, a very ironic song and it's also very humorous in a violent way. I really enjoyed singing like that for a change. In an ideal world I'd be able to sing in all different kinds of voices because it's such a thrill to have that facility to interpret things. That's what I'm very interested in, interpreting ideas rather than just portraying a vocal style. When I sing, and I'm not the best singer in the world, I try to illustrate the song and I use all these different personae rather than just sing conventionally."

In fact, the Sophie Muller video accompanying the song attracted more attention than the music, or the message Annie was trying to portray. In her skin-tight dress and ridiculous blonde wig, Annie confused the audience totally. Some failed to read into it any irony and thus condemned it for her stance against femininity, while others stared at her flamboyant costume, wondering if she was trying to resemble more of a drag queen than a whore. Annie played their confusion to the hilt. "It's like a woman dressed as a man dressed as a woman, so there's a lot of sexual ambiguity in the whole thing," she stated, then threw in some extra spice. "It's almost a homosexual statement as well. It's a song that gay men could and will identify with very strongly. That's the beauty of it, that it can be really perverted in a sense."

With these efforts, the single struggled to number 26 in the UK and number 46 Stateside. A month or so later the fourth and final offering arrived, the forsaken 'You Have Placed A Chill In My Heart'. Dave and Annie once again did the rounds, appearing on *Top Of The Pops* et al. It came in marginally better on home turf at number 16, but sank without trace in America.

RCA panicked, and swiftly announced plans for a live video album hailing from the Revenge Tour. It would show Eurythmics with Chucho Merchan, Clem Burke, Joniece Jamison, Patrick Seymour and Jimmy Zavala in full-blown action in Melbourne, Australia and would be another Oil Factory production.

The curious fragmented opening sequence is a theme that recurs throughout the video in between the live footage and allows each band member to express themselves with an odd assortment of imagery. The symbols include elderly Aborigines, fob watches and Clem acting out a typical male fantasy as government secret agent, James Bond. Dave puts a broken mirror back together in the shape of a crucifix, which opens up as the camera swoops overhead to reveal a criss-cross of open plan rooms with each band member in a different room. This launches into live footage of 'Sexcrime (nineteen eighty-four)'.

Annie is dressed in a long leather coat with tails which she clearly enjoys swooshing around, leather jodhpurs, a white shirt and black leather gloves. Her hair is stark white and severely cropped. Each band member is involved in a different way, but this in turn detracts from Annie who is obviously struggling to hold the crowd's attention. She picks up a rose from one of her fans, but still seems unable to connect to the masses.

'Here Comes The Rain Again' starts with a promising guitar solo from Dave but swiftly dissipates into a boring, unEurythmical version of their classic song. The brilliantly cold original is destroyed with a schmaltzy stadium overtone, mid-Atlantic muzak more suited to Michael Bolton or Kenny G. Jimmy displays his talent with a bizarre saxophone solo while Dave adds a guitar part that is far removed from the song. It is all too easy when watching this kind of rock posturing to understand why Eurythmics were criticised for 'selling-out'.

The impact of 'It's Alright (Baby's Coming Back)' is lost without a horn section and strong harmonies, especially as Annie and Joniece's voices clash slightly. Perhaps the only redeeming factor is a close-up of Clem shooting the camera with his drumstick. Joniece opens the vocals for 'There Must Be An Angel (Playing With My Heart)' and Annie comes out on to the stage without her coat in a bid to pick up the pace a little.

Finally the accusatory 'Who's That Girl?' manages to forge a sense of atmosphere, and just as it seems that Eurythmics are managing to salvage the concert Annie leans forward and offers the unsuspecting audience to sing a line, shattering the tension. She then intriguingly brings on a searchlight to encourage audience participation in a lively reggae dub version of 'Right By Your Side'.

At last easing into the swing of the concert, 'Thorn In My Side' produces a modicum of audience reaction. The band join in the revelry as Joniece helps Clem out on the drums and Annie amusingly throws her microphone stand into the crowd below. This segues into an offstage shot of Patrick Seymour playing Annie's ancient harmonium. Over the sound of Pat pumping the foot pedal the menacing wheezy instrument bellows out the unmistakable chords of 'Sweet Dreams (Are Made Of This)'.

The anticipation is maintained as the introduction for 'Would I Lie To You' is punctuated by strobe lights before Annie triumphantly appears in her leather trousers and famous red bra, much to the crowd's delight. Aside from this raunchy get-up and Chucho and Joniece sharing a little dance through the song, Dave stole the show with a spectacular guitar solo, captivating his fans.

Annie covers up for 'Missionary Man', one of the most powerful songs of the set. Unfortunately its message is belittled as she sprawls about on the floor, out of view for the majority of the audience, before Dave smashes up his guitar.

Next Joniece and Annie take centre stage for their duet on 'Sisters Are Doin' It For Themselves'. Contrary to popular myth, when a fan breaks through security, creeps up behind Annie and touches her, rather than express abject horror, the singer hardly notices, shrugs and continues without breaking her stride. At the end the band come forward and Annie introduces each member to great audience delight; Joniece, Jimmy and Clem are clearly the crowd favourites.

Pleased with their performance, Annie and Dave walk backstage and give each other a hug and a kiss before re-emerging for the finale, 'Miracle Of Love', bathed in purple light. Of all the five minute-plus numbers, this is one of the few that deserved the extra attention and the slow and mean-ingful song is beautifully executed, capped with a semi-spiritual ending. Even Dave is reverent, performing his guitar solo sedately on a stool. As the audience express their approval of a good night out, Dave and Annie hold hands and take their bows at the front of the stage.

Quietly in the background, Annie didn't really care about the fate of this video release. She had just fallen pregnant.

★   ★   ★

Making up for their absence at Live Aid, Eurythmics were pleased to accept an invitation to perform at Nelson Mandela's 70th birthday tribute concert at Wembley Stadium, London on June 11, 1988. Having declined a tour for *Savage*, they felt a little out of practice and rehearsed for the upcoming event with a warm-up gig at the Town And Country Club, also in London. In the intimate setting Dave and Annie ran through an exhil-arating mixture of recent material and old favourites, thoroughly enjoying the preparation for the big day despite the onset of 'flu for both members, not to mention the fact that the singer was carrying a little extra weight . . .

The purpose of what was to become known as Mandela Day was to draw attention to the appalling reality that the African National Congress leader, Nelson Mandela, had been incarcerated for 26 years due to his devoted opposition to the South African Government's policy of apartheid. By staging a rock concert in celebration of his birthday to an audience of 72,000 in the stadium, and broadcast to some 63 countries via satellite, the organisers hoped to embarrass the South African authorities sufficiently to renounce his sentence.

A string of the biggest acts in the world supported and performed at this event, including Dire Straits, George Michael and Eurythmics from Britain, and American soul superstars Whitney Houston, Al Green and Stevie Wonder. They were pointedly joined by South African artists Miriam Makeba and jazz man Hugh Masekela. There is no underestimating the effect this most uplifting occasion had on Annie Lennox, who has many times since proclaimed it to be "one of the proudest days of my life."

Introduced by actor Richard Gere, Eurythmics were on stage for only half an hour, but they certainly made an impression. Launching straight into 'I Need A Man', Annie and Dave whirled furiously across the platform in black leather. They played a truly spectacular set from *Savage* and encored with a moving *a cappella* version of 'Brand New Day' and Stevie Wonder's 'Happy Birthday'.[42] At this point Annie chose to ignore the concert organisers' recommendation of not making strong political statements on stage, and set the huge crowd off chanting, "Hey Mandela! We want freedom in South Africa!"

Eighteen months later Nelson Mandela was finally released from captivity, undoubtedly aided by the immense TV exposure of this concert worldwide. As if in support of the musicians' efforts to change attitudes towards apartheid, every single act appearing that day would also watch his or her commercial products climb the upper reaches of the charts.

One month later, on July 15, 1988 Ann Lennox wed Uri Fruchtmann during a quiet ceremony in the fifth arrondissement of Paris, France. A pre-nuptial contract had been signed two days earlier in Palaiseau, negotiating that each party would keep 100 per cent of his or her property should the marriage fail, rather than dividing it 50/50 according to French law.

Although Annie was over four months pregnant at her wedding, her mother was delighted, and her grandparents were quite taken with her new husband. Assuming the name Annie Lennox Fruchtmann for all things bar her work, the singer enthused, "Uri is my refuge. My rock. It's about time I had a relationship that works.

[42] Dave's protégés Londonbeat on his newly formed AnXious record label joined them on stage for the finale.

"My life is all about relationships. They don't have to be sexual, but it's marvellous that I actually found somebody I love. I feel very happy. We are very happy together. He keeps me clued in. There is always a danger when you're famous that people around you will become afraid to say no to you and you lose the plot, but Uri would never let anything pass that he thought was rubbish." Many men would have balked at becoming linked to such a famous woman, but Uri seemed to take his role as *Mr* Annie Lennox completely in his stride, with his wife later hinting, "When couples have a particular cross to bear, it can actually make the relationship better."

21

YOU HURT ME (AND I HATE YOU)

"I don't know about working separately, I've never done anything on my own. I'm willing to have a bash to see where my weaknesses lie and where I can turn weaknesses into strength. I don't know what I'd do without Eurythmics though."

– AL

With just two months to go before the birth of her baby, Annie braved the critics and announced her first solo project. 'Put A Little Love In Your Heart', her duet with soul legend Al Green was included on the soundtrack to the seasonal movie *Scrooged*, starring Bill Murray, and released on October 24, 1988.

The two vocalists did not meet in person to record, instead working in separate countries to revive the song which was previously a hit for Jackie De Shannon in 1969. Despite Annie's best intentions, 'Put A Little Love In Your Heart' was a bit of an artistic sell-out. Fitting in perfectly with the current sugar-coated US soul popular this year, there was no doubt that this was an extremely commercial choice, both in terms of a film song and chart material. Al Green's voice is more angular than Annie's and not necessarily well suited, but the pair strive to create a perfectly *equal* performance, with each one singing a phrase that is then answered by the other, before falling into gospel-tinged repetition accompanied by claps and bells. It is difficult not to wonder how the track would have benefited from an actual meeting of its two performers, sparking ideas off each other artistically while physically standing together in the recording booth.

The B-side to the single was a song called 'Great Piece Of Love', with the producer's name given as 'Stewart' and the band credited to The Spheres Of Celestial Influence – the very name a certain young band had once dropped in favour of The Tourists. 'Put A Little Love In Your Heart' became a moderate success in the UK, rising to number 28 by Christmas, and was more suited to the US charts where Annie's profile was raised with a new year hit at number nine.

As the months counted down to December, Annie and Uri excitedly and nervously awaited the arrival of their firstborn. The expectant mother had enjoyed an uneventful pregnancy, taking care of her diet and attending gentle yoga classes. The big day was set for December 6, but two days prior to this Annie was admitted to a hospital in West London.

At first the Fruchtmanns had anticipated an early labour as Annie began to feel the onset of contractions. But during all the excitement the baby's movements lapsed, and then stopped altogether. Searching for a foetal heartbeat the doctors swiftly arranged for the traumatised mother to have a scan. Within one hour of expecting to go into full-blown labour, it was confirmed to Annie that the baby had died inside her.

It is impossible to describe the depth of grief felt by the singer and her husband as they were informed that, having lost the child she had carried for nine months, Annie would still have to go through the motions of giving birth. She was given an epidural, and after a heart-wrenching night of needless effort, watched the arrival of a small, stillborn boy.

Fortunately the hospital Annie and Uri had chosen to welcome their son into the world was in touch with the Stillbirth and Neo-natal Death Society (SANDS), and a representative guided the distraught couple through the long and empty hours that followed. Under SANDS' recommendation, Annie and Uri were encouraged to treat the birth as an experience in its own right, as opposed to trying to forget the tragedy. Ultimately Annie would later attribute this expert advice as the one thing that got her through what should by rights have been a period of joy.

Under the watchful eyes of hospital staff, the parents named their son Daniel and requested that he be washed and wrapped in a shawl, like any healthy baby. After taking some time in preparation, Annie and Uri held the lifeless little bundle in their arms and took photographs. This they were told would aid the grieving process, by creating real memories to attach to the experience. They then returned to Paris and spent the rest of the holiday season coming to terms with all that had happened.

The following day the sombre story left easy pickings for the tabloids, but the singer's friends and management made a superhuman effort to shield her from their reports. A statement was issued three days after the event by Steve Blackwell of Hyperkinetics, saying, "She will soon be on the road to recovery. She is coping admirably with what has happened. She is obviously sad, but is also a very resilient and realistic person."

In an action perhaps surprising to those who knew her, when she felt able Annie made the decision to speak openly in the press about the stillbirth. Given SANDS' eye-opening figures that one in a hundred babies are born lifeless, while countless others die in their first week, she reasoned that as a celebrity she was in a position to make the public more aware of this plight. She hoped that in so doing she would be able to help other couples come to terms with their loss. It was by far the bravest and most compassionate decision she had ever made.

"I didn't want to run away from it," she said a while later. "I wanted to face it and try and make something constructive out of Daniel's death. And I wanted to hold him and absorb what we could of him. For anyone to carry a child for nine months and then never see it must be awful. And however corny it seems, the experience taught me to view every day as a gift.

"After I lost Daniel I was determined to get pregnant again. I wouldn't give up on my dream . . . I want women who have experienced a stillbirth to know that there is hope of a happy ending." With time, when they felt ready, Annie and Uri determined to try for another baby. The Scots lass was not going to give up without a fight. Although it must have been diffi-cult, she did not avoid Dave, Siobhan and their year-old son, Samuel, and Annie later acknowledged the love and support she received from Dave's wife. "I couldn't have survived those dark days without her," she said.

★   ★   ★

Eurythmics started 1989 without a grand plan, although a fair amount of related product appeared on the market at various times. A previously unreleased track called 'Revenge Part II' surfaced on the soundtrack album for *Rooftops*, which also contained music from Londonbeat, Grace Jones and from the Revenge Tour line-up, Patrick Seymour and Joniece Jamison.

'Revenge Part II' revolves around a big, fat and distinctly Eighties synth line, with Annie rather agonisingly propelling herself through a series of whoops and yells proclaiming that revenge can be "dangerous", "refined" and "skilful" yet you must, predictably, "take your time". The general opinion of most of the fans was that they saw through the lightweight bravado, and pondered the disappearance of Eurythmics' ingenuity.

Another album that featured the combined talents of Annie and Dave was *Radio Silence* by Boris Grebenshikov. Grebenshikov was a gravelly-voiced, underground Russian folk/rock performer who sang partly in his mother tongue and partly in English, and was popularly described as "the Russian Bob Dylan". This earned him and his band Aquarium the dubious accolade of having their recordings banned and available only on the black market.

Dave and Annie were both fans of Grebenshikov's cross-over style in the face of Communism, and gladly contributed vocals, instrumental and production skills to *Radio Silence*. Other familiar credits on the album liner notes appeared, including 'Siobhan Stewart', Michael Kamen, and again Patrick Seymour.

The association did not end there, for during 1989 Grebenshikov also released a film entitled *The Long Way Home*. In this Michael Apted documentary he travels to Leningrad, London, New York and Los Angeles in search of musical collaboration with the western pop artists he has admired from afar. Dave is shown working meticulously with him in a Los Angeles studio, and Annie and her friend Chrissie Hynde of The Pretenders offer vocal assistance, willingly shouting out helpful suggestions. The end result is a powerful film which depicts the Russian's love of music triumphing against the odds of his country's predicament.

After working with Grebenshikov on *Radio Silence*, Dave and Annie began to think about Eurythmics' next project. Their initial conception of the infant album was set to a backdrop of change. Their American contract with RCA had expired and negotiations commenced with another, younger label, Arista, to sign them up for the US. With the latter company's enthusiasm, the group aimed to establish themselves fully in America with the next release, something which RCA had never satisfactorily achieved despite their breadth of experience. Confusingly, at this time the American Eurythmics fan club was shelved and returned to England, where it continued to operate from the original North London base.

Back in her home country, Annie was to discover that the tragic events over the Christmas period had endeared her to the music world, who were to demonstrate the extent of their appreciation by voting her Best British Female Artist for the third time at the 1989 BRIT Awards in February. Considering Eurythmics had not released an album during the qualifying year (1988), and had not enjoyed a huge amount of success with the singles released from *Savage*, Annie's courage had obviously been taken to heart.

However, it wasn't just the personal heartbreak that had heightened public opinion of the 34-year-old singer. Over the last couple of years Annie had become well established as a voice of the people, and following Eurythmics' association with Boris Grebenshikov, the Russian connection continued throughout the spring, when Annie began working with a high-profile set of rock musicians for the environmental pressure group, Greenpeace.

Donating the track 'When Tomorrow Comes' to *Rainbow Warriors*, a double album supporting the cause and including work from 26 American, British and Australian acts, Annie then travelled to Russia for its launch party, which corresponded with the opening of a Greenpeace office in Moscow.

Accompanied by Peter Gabriel, Chrissie Hynde and U2's The Edge,

Annie was appointed the official spokeswoman for the trip, and filmed a television report warning of the ongoing effects of pollution to millions of Soviet viewers. Posing for pictures in Red Square alongside the Soviet army, Annie, well-briefed and confident, spoke out for the cause:

"Somewhere in the back of my mind for years I had the feeling that things were not quite right. I never voted. I was completely cynical and disillusioned with all political parties, having a sincere mistrust of all politicians. Finally, after all these years it turns out that groups like Greenpeace have been quietly working away without much exposure, and now it's just clicked, everything's gone into place. Through a union of the media and people like myself, we're sounding a clarion call. The advent of the Greens is as significant as the advent of socialism at the turn of the century.

"Obviously it's useful for both Mikhail Gorbachev and Margaret Thatcher to be seen to be Green. But then Margaret Thatcher keeps promoting nuclear power, which in our country is one of the main ecological issues. One could be very cynical about the Russians inviting us here to put a human face on things, but what do you do, just pack up and go home?"

While Annie was out promoting Greenpeace, Dave worked quietly behind the scenes on a number of solo projects. Sessions for their next album had been pencilled in for the summer, and although the atmosphere had darkened since their respective weddings, both were confident that separate issues would not cloud their business.

"I think she was fine as long as it wasn't diluting any material they had worked on together, as long as he wasn't giving his best work away," says Dean Garcia astutely. "I think it does threaten any kind of duo situation if the other half is off doing something else. It's bound to be damaging."

★   ★   ★

The recording of the next Eurythmics album, *We Too Are One*, took place over five weeks in mid-1989. Arista had signed the group in the US, a huge promotion budget was agreed and a tour was planned to commence in August. On the surface at least the future seemed bright.

As always Eurythmics took the opportunity of recording a new album to alter the line-up a little. Retaining Patrick Seymour on keyboards, they re-enlisted Olle Romo on drums, and included guest performances from Nathan East on bass, another bassist (and husband of Joni Mitchell) Larry Klein, guitarist Mike Campbell and Dutch saxophonist Candy Dulfer. Dave thought it would be interesting to contrast Annie's vocals against a male singer for a change and so added backing vocalist Charlie Wilson, formerly of The Gap Band.

Dave felt it was time for him to enjoy the process a little and for the first time elected to co-produce the album, allowing someone else's imprint to infiltrate their sound slightly. He chose Jimmy Iovine, who had been a trusted friend for eight years, to complement his work. "On most of the albums I was in the group, but I was also trying to record my guitar, trying to tell the engineer to do this or that, producing Annie's vocal, finish writing songs," Dave elaborated to *New Hi-Fi Sound* magazine. "I was under a lot of pressure. This time I thought: 'Well, I want someone just to help, to be in the driver's seat for a bit so that I can lounge around and think about changing the chord structures on this and that,' and it was a very nice feeling."

Dave had been wise to take a step back from the pressures of omnipotence – with *We Too Are One* there were some frantic moments. The bulk of the album was recorded live to recreate *Revenge*'s band vibe rather than *Savage*'s contrived studio sound, with just a few details over-dubbed afterwards. This meant that a song was recorded in one take, but in the confusion of moving between different studios, some of the tapes went missing and several complete tracks were lost. Fortunately back-ups had been made and the originals were finally found, but nerves began to fray.

The declaration of solidarity conveyed in the album's title is unintentionally misleading on more than one level. A common misconception was that the 'Too' was spelt 'Two', a purposeful misdirection by Eurythmics, especially as the title track was written thus. The album was so named as a sly dig at the media, who had been speculating on a supposed rift between Dave and Annie. To complicate matters further, Dave had also assumed that the 'Two' indicated both halves of Eurythmics. He commented in an interview that they had really made an effort to revive their friendship after the natural demise following their separate family commitments. "It's like a statement, we've been through all this and we're still as strong as ever, with the same kind of vision," he confidently announced.

Annie had other ideas, which Dave only discovered during an uncomfortable interview on BBC television. Annie's reasoning behind the title in fact referred to the stable partnership with her new husband, Uri. This public shock only made it harder for Dave and Annie to be around each other without starting to argue, opting to work on the album separately where possible. The lyrics on the album are, as ever, excruciatingly revealing – it is difficult not to question how and why they pursued an album with phrases like 'You Hurt Me (And I Hate You)' and "I don't love you anymore, I don't think I ever did".

Ultimately it was the music that kept the Eurythmics machine rolling, and for their eighth album Dave was inspired to use similar guitar sounds to those produced by John Lennon and The Plastic Ono Band. "This guy came round who wanted to sell this Gretsch guitar that he had. I think he must have been pretty desperate for money," tells Dave of the story that provided the backbone for *We Too Are One*. "I picked it up and it was a really beautiful guitar. It was exactly the sort of instrument that would make this sound that I'd always admired. So I bought it from him, there and then, and that's the guitar on the whole record – really *ropey* but really great!"

'We Two Are One' opens the album rather deceptively with a jazzy riff punctuated by a piano, bass, drums and finally the Gretsch guitar. Retaining this original theme, the song opens out into a big, powerful sound, successfully merging synthesisers with real instruments and vocals. In keeping with the feel of the beginning Annie drawls her words for much of the song, and clumsily vocalises to compete with the guitar solo before learning to mimic and echo its pattern, which is more effective. The breakdown is more electronic as Annie's and Charlie Wilson's vocals zoom in and out with piercing "woohoos" to add interest. Sadly the song turns into a somewhat sickly declaration of "I love you".

A burst of drums jumps into 'The King And Queen Of America', a fairly cheesy parody of Sixties pop with an unchallenging melody. Annie's vocals remain rather low and boring throughout, with little tone or emotion. The brass however is persistent and jolly which, along with the sweet backing harmonies, helps keep the track alive. It does brighten up towards the end, particularly after the instrumental break, but the forth-coming promotional video proved to be the highlight.

As appears to be the norm on the album, '(My My) Baby's Gonna Cry' starts promisingly enough with a roaming electric guitar and fairly solid drumbeat. Annie's voice exudes more emotion but then, like a lead weight, Dave chimes in. In his latest vocal outing he sounds robotic and double-tracked, and ultimately appears to be holding Annie back. As he often repeats her words this track soon sinks into a slow, incessant quagmire.

This showcase unnaturally forces Dave and Annie as a couple down the listener's throat, and yet the lyrics are a perfect paradox, describing how the romantic flame in a relationship has faded. "It was a comedic thing between us – you know, 'here we go again'," pondered Dave of the potent meaning behind the song. "We were singing about the demise of it all: 'Now there's nothing comes from nothing/ That's what they always say/ Didn't mama tell ya/ That's the price you have to pay?'"

After nearly five minutes it ends and the bizarre combination of drums, a guitar and pizzicato strings open 'Don't Ask Me Why'. Immediately producing a sound more typical of Eurythmics, this brighter number stands at a better length of four minutes and 21 seconds. Easily maintained by the square beat and gentle guitar strumming, this quiet, unassuming number is complemented by Annie's tempered and growling vocals. A synthetic cello line creeps in to amplify the sound before real strings again lead the way to an inspired build-up of layers, backed by Annie's incessant and penetrating "Why, why, why, why". This is a fine example of a well-structured pop song which beautifully sets the scene for the next track.

Instantly mellow with delicate guitar work, bluesy piano and soft percussion, 'Angel' is a plaintive song about a 57-year-old woman who is dying but chooses instead to commit suicide. Annie spoke softly of the song's origins to radio interviewer Paul Gambaccini: "I once had written a poem about a woman who was my great-aunt, she had died – she was actually my first experience of death. I was about 11 years old. It occurred to me that there was a grave somewhere in Scotland where this body had been placed.

"It starts 'Underneath this canopy of snow' and I had thought of the seasons changing over this one spot where a person lay with all a person's fullness, their character, the memory of the person. The things that are left of that person that get dispersed after death; the items that they handled, their clothes, their jewellery, their letters. To me this is something very mysterious." Since the passing of her great-aunt, Annie had been forced to face two other deaths within her immediate family, those of her father and more recently her son. The lyrics took on a heightened meaning when she came to performing it, but the underlying message is of human mortality.

For once Dave was able to be truly involved in the emotion of the track. "This is one of the songs where it really helped to have Jimmy Iovine as co-producer," he explained, "because it meant that I could just stand there and play. The guitar I used is absolutely lovely to play. It's a funny acoustic guitar, actually, because you can get loads of sustain out of it."

Dave and Annie fully utilise an interesting combination of instruments, notably alternately understated and rousing strings but the track remains peacefully uncluttered. The sad and strangely uplifting tone is one of the most simple and elegant ways to finish an album's first side.

'Revival' is immediately catchy yet equally untypically unchallenging as it does not represent Eurythmics as we have come to know them over the last decade. The composers include Patrick Seymour and Chucho Merchan, which may go some way to explaining the lack of signature 'bite'.

"We were recording in one room, and Charlie Wilson and our keyboard player Patrick Seymour were messing around, just playing on their own,"

Dave recalls. "Charlie was singing something. It was actually just 'la-*LA*', but we thought it was, 'Re-vi-*Val*'. At least that's what it sounded like! So Annie said, 'oh yeah, *Revival*' and we all started messing around with it. Within 15 minutes it was a song! We were all clapping our hands with glee."

Animated with breathy grunts the snappy rhythm is pushed along by standard drums and guitar, while Annie's singing is quiet and restrained. When Annie and Co spell out 'Revival' the song goes against every Eurythmic grain but finally appears to spark, albeit at the close of the number.

Following the upbeat gaiety of 'Revival' comes the overtly spiteful 'You Hurt Me (And I Hate You)'. Annie's clear vocals are accompanied simply by a mood-setting piano and swooping fretless bass for the introduction, before the drums break out and the rhythm gets going. Annie then changes her voice to incorporate her contempt in the lyrics while the flute, keyboards and brass are wonderfully incongruous as a bright and breezy build up to "You hurt me and I hate you".

The song is simultaneously busy whilst retaining an interesting mix of instruments from the haunting flute and persistent brass to fidgeting guitar and threatening keyboards. It is a little strange to see Chucho Merchan credited in a composition that appears so clearly to come from Annie's heart. "There are millions of love songs – it's time to put an extreme one about hate in there. It seems to run parallel to love in so many respects – so many love affairs have fallen foul, ended up in horrendous circumstances, I'm sure everyone knows through personal experience what I'm talking about," she quietly summed up.

The next song on *We Too Are One* continues Annie's fascination with lone females; 'Belinda' could not find lasting love, 'Jennifer' tragically drowned and 'Julia' was restricted from love in *1984*. There follows 'Sylvia', inspired by a harrowing picture of a drug addict in Amsterdam, although references to poet Sylvia Plath can also be detected.

There is little more ominous than a bowed cello and short strikes on strings, even if they are electronic, except when accompanied by Annie's serenely haunting voice. In this uneasy song, borrowing from The Beatles' 1966 'Eleanor Rigby', Annie tells the harrowing tale of a young girl who has run away from home to eke out a living as an unhappy prostitute in London, ultimately preferring death to her miserable existence. When the song shifts to a happier tone it could appear out of place, but the lyrics reflect that Sylvia's death by overdose provides a restful, forgiving peace.

Snapping out of the mesmeric 'Sylvia', the band idly mutter to themselves before 'How Long' starts. The song quickly grows into a cluttered, full sound with the various elements merging into one another. Annie's rather laid-back vocals are uncharacteristic, but refreshing in their difference. As with most of the tracks on *We Too Are One* this song picks up after the instrumental break and perhaps should have started after the second verse. Strings and flute are again present alongside the Gretsch guitar and Charlie Wilson contributes high-powered backing vocals to the chorus.

The final number, 'When The Day Goes Down' was recorded live in one take, as Dave had hoped for the majority of the album, with a six-piece gospel choir overdubbed at a later stage. Easing the listener gently in, Annie's soft vocals float quietly over the mellow fretless bass, soft tinkling bells and watery percussion. The tune lifts a little when Annie proclaims, "That's when the rain comes down". After an exquisite instrumental Annie reappears and emotes with great feeling her lyrics about the plight of the homeless. The drums then pave the way for Dave's effectively simple guitar solo. The ending is particularly poignant, consisting of moving vocal harmonies over an extended drum roll to fade.

★   ★   ★

Pleased with the final result, if a little harassed with each other, Eurythmics presented their latest offering to the media at a press conference in Paris. Treating a gaggle of journalists to snippets of *We Too Are One*'s finest songs and describing their promotional plans, Dave and Annie were stunned by the deathly quiet that followed, before a smattering of half-hearted applause and a few murmurs. Sick of the awkward silences, Annie's patience snapped.

"This is very limiting for everyone. You probably feel as self-conscious as we do and we'll probably never do a press conference again. It seems more like a *funeral* to me."

The atmosphere in the small room where Dave and Annie faced the sea of critics was more strained than a wake. One reporter ventured a question to Dave regarding any future plans he might have, or rumoured work with The Traveling Wilburys. This was one insult too many for Annie and she erupted. Trying to retrieve a modicum of calm Dave pleaded for some sensible questions, "You've just listened to our album which we've taken a lot of time and care to make. Eurythmics music for us is like our *life*, and nobody's asked us *one thing* about the songs!"

As the audience begrudgingly allowed the pair to talk about their album and ensuing live gigs, Annie ventured that she would take a break after the forthcoming world tour to spend some time with her husband and try for a family again. When one reporter asked, "But won't that be frustrating for the fans?" Annie flippantly replied, "There's not a lot I can do about that."

Realising that the talks were proving fruitless the duo exchanged weary glances and left the room fuming.

The writer for *Melody Maker* took pity on the couple, but questioned the merit of the exercise as a whole: "Why artists of their calibre should be doing this, putting their all into bits of their songs while a selection of hacks from all over the world chortle and gape . . . is a mystery beyond all fathoming."

The press conference did not bode well for how the album would be received. But alongside comments of "overslick, uninspired career retrospective that borrowed too heavily from every period and style in their history together" lay more positive reviews: "The sound was varied and the lyrics were unusually well crafted. There is, however, an air of romantic resignation throughout *We Too Are One* appropriate to its valedictory nature."

Perhaps sensing the finality of the album, fans on either side of the Atlantic reacted in opposing ways. The album topped the British charts in September 1989 ensuring that Eurythmics were remembered fondly in their home country, while in America they were on their last legs and *We Too Are One* struggled to reach 34. The first single, 'Revival' managed a respectable number 26 in the UK accompanied by a jolly yet uninspiring video.

With this mixed success behind them, Eurythmics embarked on the 65-date world Revival Tour. Starting in France they travelled backwards and forwards between Europe, America, Australia and the Far East until the year's end. Despite the poor reception of the album at the press conference, the group continued to woo the British media, inviting some 50 journalists to a preview concert at Juan-les-Pins, near Cannes followed by a celebrity party.

Providing the extra live sound for the tour were Patrick Seymour on keyboards, Olle Romo on drums and Chucho Merchan on bass, while Joniece Jamison and Charlie Wilson competed on the backing vocals. Their image had changed drastically as the band appeared in Cinderella-style rags, Annie in a shabby evening dress and DMs, and Dave's hair and beard had been recently dyed black.

Musically the concerts were predictable, mixing songs from the new album with old favourites. To allow Annie short breaks in the demanding set, the band played a brief interlude of 'Sisters Are Doin' It For Themselves' featuring Joniece's incendiary vocal operatics and 'Never Gonna Cry Again' as a forceful duet between Joniece and Charlie.

For a change, criticism of the concerts was not directed at Annie and Dave, but instead at the overbearing performances from the two backing singers, and even Patrick Seymour for obtrusive keyboards. Joniece, who had been a much-loved member of the band for several years, had often received both praise and reproach for her stylistic ad libbing, sometimes even suggesting that she outshone the star of the show.[43] But the showmanship of Charlie Wilson was considered more of a threat to Annie, as on numerous occasions he threatened to steal the limelight a little too much for comfort. As had been the case with previous musicians who had become too big for their boots, after a while Wilson mysteriously left. Eurythmics, albeit flawed and flagging, was still a two man (person) band.

To relieve the monotony of touring, Dave and Annie experimented with acoustic versions of some of their favourites, and at one point there was a rumour that the next full-length release would be presented purely in this fashion. Although an album never substantiated this speculation, several acoustic tracks recorded on this tour found their way on to the market as B-sides to singles from *We Too Are One*.

Having returned to England during September, Eurythmics released the second single from the album, 'Don't Ask Me Why'. This was the last song Dave and Annie wrote together, finally admitting that they had grown apart irrevocably. It fared reasonably, reaching number 25 in the UK and number 40 in America. The video for the song, filmed by Mondino, was inspired by the movie *Blue Velvet*, paying respect to both lighting and Annie's pale colouring. Annie appears in a sparkling silver, off-the-shoulder, fish-shaped dress. She looks elegant and sophisticated during her performance, but her slight facial expressions fully exude the underlying bitterness of the lyrics as she directs numerous poignant glares at Dave. For his part, Dave has smartened up his image with a dark, neat hairstyle and beard. Much of the song relies on footage of the band playing, but towards the end there is a sequence of close-ups on Annie from different angles, interspersed in sharp succession with Dave's face.

As the tour progressed to America and Canada in November 1989, MTV released a documentary studying the life and times of Eurythmics. The group was also found to be contributing to a project designed to raise money for the Special Olympics. The album, *A Very Special Christmas*, was an assortment of festive covers by various artists to differing degrees of success. Eurythmics' version of 'Winter Wonderland' was the second track on the collection and was generally well-received with Annie's soulful inflection. Other notable performances were Chrissie Hynde's rendition of 'Have Yourself A Merry Little Christmas', Alison Moyet's stately

---

[43] After working with Eurythmics, Joniece Jamison was to enjoy a substantial pop career in France in the early Nineties, achieving chart success with 'Joue Pas'.

version of 'The Coventry Carol' and Sting's brief version of 'Gabriel's Message'. Madonna, who had at the start of her career encountered comparison to Annie, was commonly viewed as embarrassing with her overly camp interpretation of 'Santa Baby'.

Having assumed most of the organisation of the tour, Annie was keen to see its culmination. After spending the early part of December in Australia, the group moved on to Tokyo just before Christmas for the last gig that year. Returning home to the comforts of a loving husband, Annie quietly celebrated her 35th birthday and toasted the dawn of a new decade.

Regardless of the cool reception to *We Too Are One* and the strains of promotion, the Eurythmic office appeared to be functioning as normal as the third single from the album was released to moderate success in January 1990. Representing a healthy dig at American society, 'The King And Queen Of America' reached number 29 in the UK, but was belatedly rejected Stateside.

"American radio loved the song 'The King And Queen Of America' for the first 10 days, and then they had all these phone calls from irate fascist Americans saying, 'What the fuck are you playing that for? They're taking the piss out of our society.' And they took it off the air . . . They're so conservative over there it's unbelievable," chastised Dave, omitting to mention that both the song and video did indeed openly poke fun at the American dream, intimating that the natives were a shallow race who created stars out of anyone at the drop of a hat.

It is interesting to note that Eurythmics often used symbolism alluding to American ideals. Although the couple are British they frequently used the dollar sign to indicate money rather than the pound sign. It would appear that their blatant jibe at American society in the video for 'The King And Queen Of America' was a continuation of previous work, including lines like, "If I had a dollar bill for all the things I'd done" in 'Missionary Man' and images such as the neon sign flashing between a heart and a dollar sign in Annie's right hand in 'You Have Placed A Chill In My Heart'.

Pulling themselves together for one final gig on the Revival world tour, the band congregated at the Festival grounds in Rio de Janeiro, Brazil on January 29. The excitable audience of over 100,000 Eurythmics fans were unaware of the monumental significance of the occasion. At the close Annie simply said, "That's it, see you."

★　　★　　★

Standing on the podium having received her fourth BRIT Award for Best British Female on February 18, 1990, Annie Lennox announced that she would be giving up her career to concentrate on having a family and working for the charity Shelter. Extolling the virtues of the organisation set up to help homeless people, and acknowledging the pride she felt on stage at the Nelson Mandela tribute concert, Annie seemed more than content to finally turn her attentions to her home life. Although she didn't say as much, with her brave declaration of retirement, Annie had also signalled the end of Eurythmics.

The relief for Dave and Annie was immense. Throughout their 14 year relationship they had experienced a wealth of emotions as lovers, friends, business partners and creative springboards, but finally they had become weary of living the same repetitive existence in each other's pockets.

Annie admitted that although the gig in Rio a few weeks earlier now appeared to be their final outing, it had not been intentional. "We sort of left it saying maybe, maybe not." Dave elaborates, "I remember we were on top of a hill in Rio de Janeiro, the two of us sitting on a bench and somebody was filming us – you get so used to people filming you, so we just carried on talking. We said, 'I don't know, after this gig we might want to do something else.' We both knew at that moment that we were kind of saying let's just stop for a while."

Their record company was understandably shocked at the turn of events, as John Preston recalls, "I had just renegotiated the contract and I thought *We Too Are One* was the first album of a new ongoing relationship. Despite the fact that I was close to them as well, professionally close, I really had no real inkling that it wasn't going to carry on at that time."

Before Annie was able to retire to the quiet life she had dreamed of for so long, she was obliged to participate in explanatory interviews, answering repetitive questions as to why it appeared Eurythmics had split after a decade. Many of the answers pointed to her personal quest to relieve herself of stress, and to try again for another baby after the tragedy of Daniel's death.

However, both Dave and Annie were quite open about the difficult and incestuous nature of their own relationship and its contribution to Eurythmics' demise.

"We've been through such a lot and never had a break, like a divorced couple that want to be apart," she said to Q magazine at the time, hinting heavily that it might only be temporary. "Wanting to make music was what kept us together. But now we need space if we're not to destroy the goodwill that exists between us. It's a very strange relationship. But then, it always has been."

Although Annie talked of goodwill, it was widely acknowledged that both halves of Eurythmics were more than a little sick and tired of each other's company, particularly having finished an acrimonious album and world tour.

"It got to the point where if one of us walked into a room and the other was in there, you'd want to walk out," said Dave bluntly. "We came to the sad realisation that we had to get away or we would destroy each other. At that point, it was very funny – we'd be laughing, then we'd be not talking for two days. We would just go home to our different spouses and be reassured there. We'd come back to the relationship feeling alright about ourselves but not about each other."

Ultimately Dave and Annie had found that their personal lives suffered, partly because of their heavy schedules, but also because their current spouses struggled to deal with the intense Stewart/Lennox connection. "We made eight albums in nine years, which is probably about double of most bands, and we toured constantly. We didn't, for 10 years, have any sort of life or world other than that," said Dave openly. "We had to have other lives. I mean we were married to different people, and we needed space. It wasn't really fair on our partners."

The conclusion to this period in Annie's life may have been unavoidable, but as Dave and Eurythmics had been her life for so many years, even with the love and support of Uri, she found it difficult to cope. "When I left Dave it was like cutting off my legs," dramatised Annie to convey the helpless feeling of the necessary action. "Our relationship was really incestuous, really sick. I had to separate myself from that way of life."

Barry Maguire was able to appreciate her yearning to leave Eurythmics behind for a 'normal existence'. "She just wasn't happy anymore, she wanted a life," he sighs. "It was different for Dave because to him being on tour was part of his life. Annie isn't like that, she likes to go for walks on Hampstead Heath, and cook and clean the house. She was just longing to put down her roots, instead it was just another record, another tour.

"The tension was pretty weird. She was learning a lot about herself and how to deal with people. I just think she didn't know how to deal with people very well then, because she didn't trust them. Why were they talking to her, why were they saying, 'You're so fabulous'? Yet people meant it, and genuinely felt they had a connection with her, and wanted to be her friend. There was a lot of everyday life that she was missing out on – she knew that and she just longed to be in an environment where she could give that a chance."

Finally free from the pressures of the band, Annie knew what her goals were but, typically of the insecure Scotswoman, she found the real world overwhelmingly alien. "After the tour I went home and sat in the house and I thought, 'I don't know how to do this anymore.' I didn't know how to do the shopping, I didn't know how to do anything. I was used to the five star monastic existence of hotels. I didn't know who I was, what I was."

★   ★   ★

Annie desperately wanted another baby and so channelled her energies into looking after her own health to provide the best conditions for pregnancy. One reassurance for the hopeful couple was to be near a trusted doctor in case any unforeseen complications should arise. To this end Annie and Uri decided to settle at 26 Warwick Avenue, Maida Vale, rather than the apartment the Lennox Fruchtmanns had bought in Paris. The large white mansion block in West London is hidden behind dense foliage but remains surprisingly exposed to the public, situated on a busy road, near a tube station. The domestic preparations paid off and within just two months of publicly admitting that she wanted children, Annie was deliriously happy to find she was indeed pregnant.

Dave too branched out into areas far removed from Eurythmics. "I felt the need to experiment wildly, and in many different directions," he expanded of his first steps after the split. "Simultaneously, I got involved in about 100 different projects – as a songwriter, a producer, a photographer, record label boss, whatever. Then, finally, I felt able to settle down again, and to just pick and choose."

Annie would occasionally intimate that she had held Dave back, describing their new-found freedom, professionally and personally, as liberating. Remaining respectful of each other, while Dave and Annie admitted that the relationship had broken down, neither was publicly heard bad-mouthing the other, only ever wishing him or her well. Physically they kept their distance and suddenly their lives leapt in opposite directions.

While Annie settled into her second pregnancy, Dave's first project was a successful instrumental, 'Lily Was Here', with former Eurythmics saxophonist Candy Dulfer. In spring 1990 the single reached number six in the British charts and the parent soundtrack album for the film of the same name, held a respectable 35; both releases on Dave's AnXious label. As one half of Eurythmics Dave had often been overlooked in interviews, but it was now his time to shine and soak up the limelight on his own.

"I think Eurythmics was becoming a very frustrating experience for him, and that on many occasions he felt overshadowed by the Annie Lennox 'monster'," heralded the expectant diva. "Ultimately that got to Dave – he was always finding himself being lampooned as the 'wacky' figure behind me. Not surprisingly, it was totally appropriate that he should want to do something on his own." Dave too came to realise how he was often portrayed, "When you work as a duo with somebody like Annie, who everybody looks at as some kind of goddess–ice-queen character, you're written about as the werewolf in the background."

Keen to amend this image and having tested the waters on his own, Dave's boundless enthusiasm and ideas enabled him to launch a new band. The Spiritual Cowboys, as they were collectively known, consisted of John Turnbull and Izzy Mae Doorite on guitars, Wild Mondo on keyboards, bassist Christopher D James, drummer Zac Bartel and Martin O'Dale on drum warp. John recalls the loose idea behind the group, "Dave wanted two or three guitarists, keyboards, drummers, and everybody to sing. A big band of weird vibes," to which Dave agrees, "It was a raggle-taggle band, we were just pleased to try something that wasn't so organised."

As prolific a writer as ever, he released two albums with The Spiritual Cowboys, and although neither managed to produce a Top 40 single, it was refreshing to hear more of his solo work. "Dave had this saying, I don't know where he got it from, maybe John Lennon," muses John of Dave's overriding career philosophy. " 'Songs are like little postcards that you write and send to someone, or send to everyone, and the next day you write a totally different one.' They're just little things, they're not big and meaningful with deep pockets. They're just little vignettes of something, life or whatever."

If Dave's compositions were not intended to be meaningful, no one could ever say the same was true of Annie's lyrics. In April 1990, despite the official split Eurythmics released the fourth and final single from *We Too Are One*, the powerfully moving 'Angel'. Released with an equally exquisite acoustic version of 'Missionary Man' as the B-side, the single disappointingly stalled outside the Top 20 at number 23 in the UK.

In true Eurythmics style, alongside the album sat a full-length video. *We Two Are One Too* arrived in April as a posthumous salute to the band that no longer existed. It adopted a different format to the usual collection of short promotional films, by interspersing five tracks with live footage from the Revival Tour and candid backstage shots. As the album received mixed reviews, unfortunately the video was almost universally slated.

"If the film of the album of the tour is a harmless idea, the reality is excruciatingly and inexcusably lame," wrote Max Bell of *NME* scathingly. "This is still a bad home movie by any standards. Who in their right mind would want to watch a bunch of rock stars' children singing 'Rudolph The Red Nosed Reindeer'? Who could possibly give two hoots for a jokey song entitled 'Ballad Of Eurythmics Road Crew'? . . . *We Two Are One Too* has no redeeming features saving its brevity and even then the box blurb has the gall to claim a total running time of 'Approximately 60 minutes'. Approximately is right. Try 48."

Directed by Sophie Muller, the montage appears to have been intended as a rough video diary, unwittingly cataloguing the final days of Eurythmics. The first clip, 'We 4 Are 3', is a long ambient introduction comprising images of being on the road mixed with Dave and Annie messing around. During the footage of 'We Two Are One' the video cuts between the live version and a brief, acoustic informal version.

'I Love You Like A Ball And Chain' also offers a long, lazy start, exhibiting the travelling life. Annie rips off a curly blonde wig, but there the track is abruptly cut, segueing straight into the promotional film for 'Don't Ask Me Why'. Recovering from the rancorous feeling left by the latter, the grainy-pictured 'How Long?' shows Dave teaching an impatient Annie how to play guitar, rock'n'roll-style. Exposing their deep-rooted connection the duo reverse the roles and Dave sings along while Annie strums the guitar. Although this piece of film cuts in with off-duty clips of the pair frolicking on a beach, Annie manages to come across as petulant as they both overplay the rock-star role. 'You Hurt Me (And I Hate You)' exposes the singer's move away from vegetarianism as the 30 second shot consists entirely of her lounging on a fur backdrop.

'(My My) Baby's Gonna Cry' is performed live and is an over-indulgent display of Annie and Dave lying on the floor, flirtatiously rolling over each other and rather childishly play-fighting. While the video's viewers may find this extroverted display of the duo's strong bond a little uncomfortable, a thought should be spared for members of the audience beyond the front three rows, unable to see what was happening, not to mention the pair's respective spouses.

The live version of 'We Two Are One' commences after Dave's questionable monologue chronicling his five bouts of 'flu during the tour. The acoustic version of 'I Need You' is very similar to the official promo included on *Savage*. Presumably in an attempt to enthuse the band for Christmas 1989 as the tour plodded on, the next clip is of Dave playing 'Rudolph The Red Nosed Reindeer' on guitar, accompanying the three children singing and playing trumpets and a tuba.

There follows the promo for 'The King And Queen Of America'. If it's possible to overlook the lyrical attacks on American society, it's unlikely anyone missed the point in the video. Dave and Annie dress up depicting numerous American clichés; celebrities at a glitzy show-business party, the President and the First Lady, a game show host and his assistant, a cowboy and girl, a typically staid couple in a supermarket, Elvis Presley and Marilyn Monroe, a Playboy tycoon and bunny girl, Minnie and Mickey

Mouse, a preacher and his wife, and astronauts. Two of Annie's characters are particularly startling: uncannily she resembles her youthful self in a blonde wig for the cheerleader, and once again refutes her belief in animal rights as she watches leopards in a cage wearing a leopard skin jacket.

Looking out over a balcony Annie proclaims, in an extremely scripted manner, "Oh my god – what an incredible view!" before a tantalisingly brief clip of 'Love Is A Stranger' cut at the potent line, "I want you so it's an obsession", introduces mega-fan, Danny Chi. He proudly boasts to his favourite group that he has amassed some 490 Eurythmics records and 50 Tourists records.

Initially Chi comes across as a smiling, dedicated collector who has been following the duo for eight years, but as he continues his devoted monologue, Annie and Dave become increasingly unnerved. He assures Eurythmics, "It's not an obsession, it's love. I've been following you for eight years . . . I don't just love you as a video band, I love you both as human beings. I love your ideas, your philosophy, a lot of what you're about . . . I understand you."

Chi swiftly becomes heated, punctuating each demonstration of his fixation with a pointed, "Do you understand?" The excruciating crunch comes when he criticises Annie for briefly forgetting the lyrics to one of the songs during the previous night's performance. At this instant her face freezes with a forced smile.

Although Annie has previously been quoted as saying, "I think it's important to talk to the fans – people whom I would never meet otherwise – I find it very touching to get a real response from somebody," she backs it up with, "I don't look for adoration, I don't *want* adoration, I only want to touch somebody and for them to realise they're being touched."

Moving on from this awkwardness, the footage continues to Annie performing painful vocal exercises whilst Dave messes around in his dressing room – this is simply rock star excess at its worst.

The official promo release of 'Revival' is rather bland in comparison to most of Eurythmics' output. It shows Dave, Annie and a number of nameless dancers cavorting in what appears to be a factory or warehouse, until right at the very end the characters are shown to be part of a picture that's still being painted. Annie oddly comes across as 'one of the lads', standing with Dave and eyeing up the bunny girl dancers that parade across the stage, carrying letters spelling out R-E-V-I-V-A-L.

The introduction to 'Farewell To Tarwathie' reveals Annie the star, reclining in bed wearing dark glasses, watching the news. The broadcaster reports that "Scottish rock band", Eurythmics, have been forced to cancel a Perth gig just 45 minutes into the set, returning $200,000 worth of $40 tickets as a result of Annie's continuing throat ailments. The spectator laughs helplessly, and confirms that it was the worst night of her life as a performer.

'Angel' is the next official promo with Annie playing the medium in a séance as the camera looks down on the group of people sitting around a table with their hands spread out flat and fingertips touching. A spirit enters Annie and she appears to re-enact the moment of death. This is symbolised in numerous fashions including the onset of dusk, a light bulb extinguishing, flowers dying and petals falling. There are many scenes replayed with altering twists, where she is trapped in a room behind a table and chair which burst into flames, blocking her exit. Dave constantly runs to try to save her, akin to 'It's Alright (Baby's Coming Back)', and each time he fails, the scene is reset and they try again. Eventually he reaches her and the room spontaneously combusts just as she is saved. This controversial video was reportedly censored by MTV for its alleged occult and drug references. It is interesting to note the recurring theme in many of Eurythmics' videos that Dave plays saviour to Annie's victim.

Abruptly the serenity is dispersed as Dave performs the 'Ballad Of Eurythmics Road Crew'; a humorous ditty about the entire crew's exploits with references to Annie's impromptu drumming and his own numerous colds. The final track, 'When The Day Goes Down', features countless images of life on the road, centring on Annie and Dave sneaking some deserved time alone on a park bench, soaking up the sun.[44] Nostalgia is the main focus of these miscellaneous clips, but the sequence notably shows the negative side of touring, allowing some very tired and irritable-looking moments.

The close of the video aptly sums up Eurythmics' feelings by the end of the tour, and indeed all of their last year as a functioning band, as Annie walks off stage emotionless.

---

[44] It is possible that this moment captures the very conversation described by Dave which signified the split of Eurythmics.

22

THE MIRACLE OF LOVE

"I was very curious to find out what my own worth was, separate from Dave. I'd always been so connected to him musically and, to be honest, I didn't have a great deal of confidence in myself."

– AL

With Eurythmics firmly behind them, Annie and Dave pursued their separate ventures with considerable aplomb. Dave appeared on the *One World, One Voice* TV spectacular in May 1990 along with nearly 300 other musicians, before embarking on a tour with his group. Later in September, *Dave Stewart & The Spiritual Cowboys* peaked at number 38 in Britain while the single, 'Jack Talking', stalled at number 69. Their second LP, *Honest*, fared no better.[45]

Annie, on the other hand, was jubilant. In June she had enough confidence in her health to announce that she was pregnant again, expecting the child in early December. She was still unsure of her own solo ability and that summer she hesitantly agreed to contribute a track, 'Ev'ry Time We Say Goodbye', to the charity album, *Red Hot + Blue*.

"I was very curious to find out what my own worth was, separate from Dave. I'd always been so connected to him musically and, to be honest, I didn't have a great deal of confidence in myself. I didn't actually think I could do anything of value away from him," she divulged. The LP was an anthology of Cole Porter cover versions produced to support the Red Hot Organisation, a charity dedicated to raising money and awareness for AIDS.

World AIDS Day in October 1990 was symbolised by a global TV event. The 90-minute video was organised by Chrysalis Records, Initial Film & TV and BMG and the original intention was for it to be directed

---

[45] Dave quickly abandoned The Spiritual Cowboys and adopted a different approach, teaming up with vocalist Terry Hall of The Specials fame, to release an eponymous album, *Vegas*. After that he turned his attention to soundtrack work.

by Derek Jarman. Unfortunately he was unable to work as he suffered an AIDS-related relapse just before filming was due to commence. Ed Lachman at Palace Pictures instead completed the project, paying an emotional tribute to Jarman in the process.

Annie was delighted to be involved with such a worthy cause, proclaiming: "We should all be aware that the problem of AIDS is international and direct action by governments is certainly insufficient up to this point. Let's hope we highlight this fact."

Having enlisted Annie's performance of 'Ev'ry Time We Say Goodbye' for *Red Hot + Blue,* Derek Jarman then wanted to use it in his forthcoming film *Edward II.* The movie, released in 1992 just two years before Jarman's death, was an extremely ambitious variation on Christopher Marlowe's 16th century play about the monarch. Jarman's presentation of King Edward's open homosexuality, which ultimately led to his murder and succession, avoids the traditional pomp and glamour, instead opting for stark settings and smart suits to attire the cast. He was also able to incorporate seamlessly a cameo for Annie Lennox, who performed her beautiful rendition of 'Ev'ry Time We Say Goodbye'.

Her second foray into the realm of solo work proved to be the impetus Annie required. Even before she had carried her child to full term she was beginning to get broody in a musical sense. Gently setting the wheels in motion, she amused herself improvising a few tunes on her keyboard in her home studio. She taped some rough demos of her ideas, simple wordless sketches, but needed somewhere to take them.

Tentatively toying with an idea of working without Dave, Annie sought encouragement in the form of an independent manager. She happened upon Simon Fuller.

Formerly a publishing scout for Chrysalis Records, Simon established his own management company, the title of which came from his protégé Paul Hardcastle's number one anti-Vietnam hit, '19'. He based 19 Management just off Battersea Bridge in Parkgate Road, South-West London. While he was relatively new to the game when he met Annie, Simon later launched, and publicly lost, the Spice Girls. He brimmed with enthusiasm, which was vital for Annie's momentum. Simon realised Annie's potential as an artist in her own right and suggested that she should meet up with producer Steve Lipson, with whom she could discuss her ideas.

"I thought Steve was the strangest man I'd ever met," recalls Annie, "and got really depressed because I'd played him some demo tapes that I wasn't that confident with. I actually thought he hated them – my confidence went to an all time low and he left the house, and I was thinking there wasn't much point in even doing this, maybe I won't bother.

"And then he called up and said we have to talk to each other again. I was quite surprised and I said to him, 'Well to be frank with you I didn't think that you really liked anything that I was doing.' He said, 'Oh no, on the contrary, I'm just in the middle of working with Simple Minds and it's really difficult for me to think about anything else!'"

The misunderstanding prompted a friendship that was to prove enduring with great potential for artistic expression, but Annie's bump was the immediate priority and so creativity was put on hold.

★   ★   ★

Despite Dave and Annie's individual output, the fans were still desperate for Eurythmics releases and relished both the box set which went on sale in November 1990, and the inclusion of a Eurythmics track on *Rock The World*, a benefit album raising money for the London-based rehabilitation centre, The Phoenix House.

On November 16 Dave Stewart sold his Parisian apartment as there was no lift and the eight-month pregnant Siobhan was unable to climb the five floors. On December 5, their second son was born, whom they imaginatively named Django James Lawless Stewart.

Five days later on December 10, Annie gave birth to her own bundle of joy at the Great Portland Street Hospital in Westminster. Her healthy regime had paid off as the pregnancy was smooth and the labour thankfully uneventful, producing a hearty seven pound baby girl. She was called Lola Lennox Fruchtmann, the choice of Lola being something of a mystery. It has been suggested that Annie, being a Marlene Dietrich fan, coined the name from the actress' role as temptress, Lola Frohlich, in the erotic drama *Blue Angel*. However, Annie once hinted her point of inspiration was the 1970 Kinks number two hit, 'Lola', in which case she amusingly named her child after a legendary, albeit fictitious, gender-bending drag queen.

Annie and Uri were thrilled and relieved to be parents at last. While Annie gushed to reporters about the momentous experience of childbirth, she was mindful to draw on her previous trauma and instil faith in women facing similar difficulties.

"Giving birth to Lola was the most wonderful moment of my life," she beamed. "She is everything I ever hoped for. After I lost Daniel, I was determined to get pregnant again. I wouldn't give up on my dream. I want women who have lost a child to know that there is always hope of a happy ending." Annie and Uri ensconced themselves back in their Maida Vale flat in time for the first Lennox Fruchtmann family Christmas and Annie's 36th birthday.

Outwardly appearing to settle easily into the role of motherhood, behind closed doors the natural hormonal struggle began to catch up with Annie during the winter months of 1991. Initially she felt tremendous compassion for the families pictured on television being torn apart by the Gulf War. "After having a child, you identify with other children as if they were your own," she said sympathetically of the endless images of destruction. "You feel for them, because you see your own child within them. So, when you see kids caught up in warfare, you're all the more aware of what a terrible thing war is."

Eternally grateful for the safe arrival of her daughter, Annie began to sense tremendous pressure of the responsibility bestowed on her in raising a child. In an attempt to come to terms with her conflicting emotions, she turned to her GP. The doctor diagnosed post-natal depression and prescribed painkillers and barbiturates. Annie had rarely taken strong medication, favouring natural remedies for common complaints, and found herself unduly susceptible to the drugs, comforting her when she needed it, but leaving her low afterwards.

Admitting to herself that she was in danger of becoming addicted was not easy, but she reasoned with her strict morals. "They made me feel so good and really dreamy that I found it hard to stop taking them," she said later. "I managed to force myself to stop, I thought, this is no way to live – but it wasn't easy. I wanted to stay in that dream world."

★   ★   ★

Life continued around Annie regardless as she battled with the 'baby blues'. It had been a year since she announced her retirement in favour of a family, and RCA truly put Eurythmics to rest by releasing their *Greatest Hits* compilation. Available on March 30, 1991 the eagerly awaited album entered the British charts at number one, spectacularly marking the end of an era.

"As it is, I think it ended in a pretty perfect way," Annie pleasantly summed up, "amazingly so, considering that we each had many opportunities to be cruel or behave very badly towards each other. I feel very good about the fact that we didn't do that, and consequently the *Greatest Hits* represented something very important for both of us. OK, I know it's only pop music and all that, but we had a great sense of achievement about it. We could listen to all those songs collected together and feel proud to be associated with them."

As Eurythmics' popularity in America had waned towards the end of the Eighties, distributors included only 14 tracks on their CD, unlike the 18 enjoyed by the rest of the world, and consequently their chart placing was an embarrassing 72. Stretching British enthusiasm a little, 'Love Is A

Stranger' and 'Sweet Dreams (Are Made Of This)' were re-issued, but both failed to enter the Top 40. That summer, for a phenomenal 16 weeks, the number one song in the UK was Bryan Adams' '(Everything I Do) I Do It For You' from the hit film, *Robin Hood: Prince Of Thieves*. The producers had originally approached Annie to provide the vocal, but she refused, citing other plans on the horizon.

With the love and support of her husband Annie had stopped taking the drugs to combat her depression, finally managing to overcome the extremes of new motherhood naturally. Encouraged by Simon Fuller and Steve Lipson on the work front, she slowly gained confidence in her own abilities. As little Lola began to allow her mum to sleep through the night, a revived Annie began in earnest to write the foundations for her first solo album.

The self-confessed technophobe of Eurythmics, Annie surprisingly used a laptop computer to compose the threads of prose that evolved into songs. "Some people like to write in longhand, but I like the visuality of print – it looks more official than my own scrabbly handwriting which I can't take seriously," she explained. "And with a laptop I can edit and change things around. I write in snatched moments, in the same way you may get a sudden urge to write a letter to a friend."

Unexpectedly, the subject matter proved a stumbling block. Always writing from true emotions or real life experiences, Annie found that as the mist of post-natal depression lifted she had little to comment on. "Sometimes it made me feel I'm just not miserable enough these days," she sighed. "Usually when you write, you're in a blue funk, bitter and angry, there's such a lot you want to say, it's all welling up. I don't know why, but joy doesn't have the same magnetic hold and being so much happier with my life, I was at odds with myself."

Instead Annie turned to her favourite artists for inspiration. Yet, in spite of her natural flow of emotions and lyrics, and the desire to create an individual name for herself, she found the writing long and drawn out.

By April 1991 Annie had moved her studio to the top floor of her house at Warwick Avenue, inviting Steve Lipson and his engineer Heff Moraes there daily from 10 o'clock in the morning to midnight. Her house was not designed for making music and Annie recalls the chaos that ensued, "Steve and Heff took all their equipment with them and set up in the top room, and we recorded there in the house, until my husband was almost driven to distraction! The neighbours almost had us thrown out . . ." Despite the lack of sound-proofing Annie insisted on working from home so that she could be on call for her baby.

Work continued slowly and although Steve and Heff proved invaluable, only Annie could actually write the songs and it didn't get any easier. "A lot of the lyric writing was drudgery," she confided in Phil Sutcliffe. "Me alone in my room, Steve and Heffy working on some sounds upstairs, a big chunk of a song still missing and I couldn't see the wood for the trees. I'd go up to Steve and say, 'That's it, I'm through! I don't know what I'm fucking doing anymore, it's useless.' And he'd say, 'You're the writer, that's your gig, I'm not going to help you, go downstairs and *do* it.'

"I'd go off like a bear with a sore head, but I always need to be cajoled and kicked a bit." Steve turned out to be the driving link Annie had been missing since her split from Dave Stewart.

Occasionally her thoughts would wander to her former partner, and her attitude remained confused. "I'd realised that I have my own strengths. It was essential that Dave *wasn't* involved, though sometimes I found myself feeling guilty about it as if I was betraying him."

With more tracks laid down, Annie, Steve and Heff needed to move to a proper recording studio, to mix the music without outside sound and interruption. Keyboard-whiz Marius de Vries was brought in at this stage, again introduced by Simon Fuller.

★   ★   ★

The future looked brighter for Annie as the summer of 1991 rolled around. For a break she travelled 400 miles north, with her husband and daughter, to visit her own mother. Dorothy provided the warmth and comfort of a traditional matriarch, as described by Laurence Stevens: "She's what a mother should be – plump and grey-haired and always cooking, cleaning and worrying about Annie."

The singer has fond memories of the trip. "We drove around and went back to certain haunts that were part of my childhood," she reminisced. "I was surprised to see how little it had changed. I was very happy about that. I feel akin to the part of Scotland that hasn't changed; that is synonymous with hills and wildness and a kind of certain bleakness in the landscape, sometimes it's very beautiful, very wooded." Allowing the tranquillity of her childhood surroundings to soak in, Annie rejuvenated her strength, finally allowing herself to bask in the pleasures of parenthood, enjoying the transformation that Lola had brought to her life.

This change was reflected in the EMI release of *The Mermaid* the following year; a fairytale narrated by Annie and Peter Gabriel in both English and German, where it became *Die Nixe*. The mother also contributed two very brief children's songs, 'The Lovely Seashell' and 'Octopi Song'.

In the autumn the Lennox Fruchtmann trio were spotted enjoying family life in London's parks and high streets. Gone were Annie's striking looks and designer image replete with cropped, dyed hair. Instead she wore loose or even ripped trousers, a baggy T-shirt, a duffel coat and a hat disguising her distinguishing features.

As celebrations for Lola's first birthday commenced, Annie was making plans for her first public appearance since the BRITs in February. The tabloids had picked up on her shock announcement about helping the charity Shelter, thus making it a commitment. Annie had not intended to become a celebrity ambassador for the charity appearing at photo-opportunity soup runs; she felt she could be of more use providing contacts and pressure behind the scenes. The temporarily unemployed singer had astutely realised her worth.

"I understand that I am a kind of currency – I can be of value," she carefully told the press. "What I decided to do was help Shelter very quietly. I write letters on their behalf, I contact people, I try to get money for them, I try to obtain things for them, I try to really open doors for them. But I'm doing it in a way which doesn't put me up as being a sort of pop star patronising benefactor of homeless people, which I think is really disgusting; it's too serious an issue for that."

After the BRITs Annie was somewhat distressingly portrayed by the media as a saintly figure pledging to save the homeless, and so she tried to be tactful to avoid further damage to either Shelter's reputation or her own future career. "That remark was taken out of context," she backtracked. "Helping Shelter was just one of the things I wanted to do. It just came out as a shock horror story, 'Pop star turns herself into Mother Teresa'."

Resolutely remaining behind closed doors, Annie worked quietly to help with preparations for Shelter's 25th birthday campaign on December 2, 1991. She contributed her famous leather coat and jodhpurs from the Revenge Tour to the wealth of pop memorabilia that was auctioned off at Sotheby's, including Madonna's gold basque from the Blonde Ambition Tour, a suit from Phil Collins and George Harrison's jacket embellished with Hare Krishna motifs.

She spoke a couple of times to the media about the plight of vagrants, hoping that her child wouldn't have to experience such sad sights when she grew up. "I remember the first time I saw a tramp on the streets of Aberdeen, and I burst into tears," she said. "Now I'm a 'hardened adult', I don't burst into tears every time I see a tramp, but every time I see somebody in the street that is in a depressing situation like that – like a victim – I always notice it."

Shelter was flooded with requests for a representative to comment on the work Annie was doing for the organisation, and a standard reply was issued: "Annie is a very dedicated woman and a very hard worker. She just wants to take a back seat and will be working from her home in London. We're absolutely thrilled to have her on board."

Aside from donating a few stage clothes and putting pressure on friends to give money or time to the cause, it is difficult to determine whether Annie did much else except run Shelter through the press mill, for better or worse. It is possible that further work was extremely well hidden, but it appears she was wary of making another flippant comment which could be preyed upon by hungry journalists.

In one line of defence, Annie was heard to chastise the relationship between pop stars and worthy causes. With hindsight it becomes a rather telling statement for her actions later in the decade. "Let's face it, if I was towards the end of my career, I could go and blow it all on an issue like this or Amnesty or Greenpeace or AIDS," she generalised to journalist Phil Sutcliffe in 1992. "They could use me up, they could spend my currency; it wouldn't matter if I was lambasted in the press. But I'm not ready for that yet. I'm not ready to be mistreated in that way. And people in my position can do a lot of harm too, going into areas they really don't know enough about. All I'm saying is that with charity stuff you really have to do it carefully."

23

DIVA

"My life is divided into the public me and the private me. In the public me, I am seen as a woman on a pedestal, an artifice, who glides from place to place, a grandiose creature with no other life. That's the one I'm projecting. It's not me, of course."

— AL

In March 1992 Annie launched her solo career with the breathtaking single, 'Why', taken from the forthcoming album, *Diva*. Positively described by one critic as, "Confidently feminine, with greater lyric sophistication and hence greater artistic risk," the song steadily climbed to the heights of number five in the UK. "'Why' is a dialogue and a diatribe and a statement about feeling misunderstood," Annie explains. "For me words are very powerful and one person can misinterpret what the other person's saying so easily."

'Why' couldn't be further removed from the raw rock feel of *We Too Are One* and instantly introduces a more mature and mellow artist. The music is very mellifluous yet deliberate with piano, percussion and acoustic guitar painting a calming picture with a purpose. Annie describes the painful realisation at the culmination of a relationship when the problems become too prominent to be solved. The piece itself is realistically moving and resigned, and before it threatens to become turgid, echoing strings are brought in to add interest followed by a shift towards 'watery' music, a recurring sound throughout the album to come.

The stylish accompanying video was directed by Eurythmics stalwart Sophie Muller, and received kudos in the form of MTV's Best Female Video award.

It equally established Annie's image as being far removed from that of Eurythmics. With short brown hair she is pictured without make-up, a combination which exaggerates her masculine look. Sitting in front of her dressing room mirror she curls her eyelashes and brushes bold stripes of orange and pink across her eyes before pencilling in heavy eyebrows. The transformation into an ageing diva is completed with a pale white face, garish lipstick, heavy jewellery and a kaleidoscopic headdress sprouting orange feather boas. The ridiculous outfit leaves Annie resembling a glamorous, albeit fake, drag queen as she sits proud as a peacock on a *chaise longue*, posing for the camera.

With a return to the limelight came the onslaught of media requests and photoshoots, which Annie had been relieved to drop after Eurythmics. "The physical side is that it's daunting for me to be exposed in public again, using my face in photographs, this Faustian deal you do. I want to go carefully, slowly-slowly," she cautioned in an early interview.

On March 12, 1992 Annie performed solo for the first time on *Top Of The Pops*. She executed 'Why' with incredible dramatic intensity; dressed in a sequinned gown. Contemplating the self-doubting lyrics with an anguished expression, Annie appeared glorious in her role.

Two days later on March 14, she continued the usual promotional patter, appearing on Michael Aspel's chat show, *Aspel & Co* on ITV. This time Annie not only sang 'Why', but participated in the lightweight celebrity conversation with the other guests, Will Carling and Ruby Wax. Dispensing with the trademark Eurythmics short hair, Annie displayed dark brown locks, slicked back in an elegant, yet manly style. Obviously nervous and a little out of practice, she seemed coy, skirting around the questions. Unfortunately, despite her efforts to appear human, she came across as a little silly and unprepared.

Happily moving on, in April 1992 Annie sold her interest in The Church to Dave.[46] Otherwise their relationship was virtually non-existent. "We're not close friends, but we wish each other well," she attempted to categorise. "I certainly only want the best for Dave. Even though we've been through an awful lot together – both good and bad times – I have no negative feelings towards him at all. It's just that we've both travelled so far, that we've become different people to those we started out as."

★   ★   ★

Annie's forthcoming album sleeve was carefully chosen. She looked for fresh talent to help create her new image. "The cover is a photograph by a young Japanese artist who lives and works in Paris, he's called Satoshi," she said. "He's absolutely wonderful." In the photoshoot, Annie dressed to look like a Forties style diva who has seen better days. "We did this in very early December of last year and I didn't have a title for the album. In January the prints of the session came to me in Los Angeles and when I

---

[46] At the time of going to press, Dave had put The Church up for sale, signifying the end of Eurythmics' former base.

looked at these prints and I knew mentally the list of the titles that I had conjectured for the album, I knew exactly then what the title had to be. It just seemed to fit with the picture." Thus *Diva* was born.

Musing about the title Annie admitted, "It's meant to be partly ironic. My life is divided into the public me and the private me. In the public me, I am seen as a woman on a pedestal, an artifice, who glides from place to place, a grandiose creature with no other life. That's the one I'm projecting. It's not me, of course. It's myth-making, the lifestyle of the persona I am creating."

On April 18, Annie appeared on NBC's *Saturday Night Live*, the same date that *Diva* entered the British charts at number one. The album received three Grammy nominations, including Album Of The Year, was certified platinum by the RIAA and eventually sold 5.5 million copies worldwide.

Critical acclaim rained down on the diva herself in publications ranging from *Rolling Stone*, to *People*, *Time* and *Billboard*.

"The fashion and the passion, the tears behind the smiles, the fame yet the heartbreak: by her own account, this is what Annie Lennox's debut solo work *Diva* (a tragic, confessional *prima donna*, lest one forget) is all about," pronounced one such journalist.

Released via a worldwide deal solely with Arista Records, neither the head of the label, Clive Davis, nor the singer were entirely convinced by a launch in America, each for separate reasons. Annie was dubious as a result of recent apathy towards Eurythmics and the current market trends, as she outspokenly detailed to *Rolling Stone*, "I just felt rejected. I thought, 'Look at all that crap on the charts. I can do better than that. It's rubbish.' And then I got very blasé about it. I thought, 'Oh well, they're all fucked up anyway. Their culture's a mess,' and I really didn't care. In fact, I said I'd rather not put it out in America. But I couldn't do that, because I'm contracted. I had to put it out there."

Clive Davis was conscious of the way the pop scene had shifted since Eurythmics' heyday and informed Annie he thought she was brave for releasing a collection of unlikely hit songs. But Davis' wariness in turn made the singer re-think her outburst to the American magazine. Rekindling US interest with vigour, *Diva* went on to achieve double platinum sales in that country.

Calling a press conference in Venice, Annie appeared calm and serene. She acknowledged the media praise with grace, but resolutely maintained, "If it sinks without trace, well, I'd be crushed. I'd have to rethink my strategy, but I won't give up music."

Alongside Annie, Steve, Heff and Marius, notable musicians included keyboardist Peter-John Vettese and trumpeter Dave Defries. Surrounded by this insular team, Annie was able to shine as a calmer, more mature vocalist easily crossing over from a teenage fan base to the contemporary adult audience. The framework afforded Annie the opportunity to come across as a chanteuse rather than a popstress, along the relatively recent lines of the sympathetic orchestra of 'Angel'.

Diva was popularly perceived as the turning point for Annie, wherein she expressed her content with family life. But a brief insight into the lyrics reveals as much pain as ever.

"Personally I'm happier than ever I was, but I'm not naturally a happy person," she admitted pessimistically. "I'm very dark, and have a tendency to see things in a rather negative way. Much as I enjoy beautiful things, I don't want to be surrounded by them the whole time, because they cut me off from a different sort of reality. They lull you into thinking everything is safe and ordered and established, whereas in fact we're all hurtling towards whatever oblivion."

What seems to be a definitive opening for Annie's debut solo album is actually a question – 'Why'. After its mesmerising tones are brought to a close, *Diva* is brought to life with a plinking piano and emphatic synthesised strings in 'Walking On Broken Glass'.

Combining adult soft rock with breezy elements, Annie produces a catchy, interesting piece. Successfully balancing the deep instruments, namely a large string section, with sparkling piano and light, unusual vocals, the overall effect is of a full, robust sound. The lyrics revolve around the aftereffects of a relationship break-up, following on the theme from 'Why'. The lack of communication between a couple is a subject one would expect from Annie at the end of Eurythmics, but is quite unexpected on an album supposedly written in marital bliss.

Annie's soulful ad lib to start 'Precious' could not be more misleading as the song is actually an ode to the joys of motherhood, celebrating the arrival of Lola. Realising that pain is in the past and the 'precious little angel' has made Annie complete as a person, 'Precious' breaks out into an infectious funky rhythm with steady drums, simple throbbing bass and spiky guitar. Dave Defries' muted trumpet imaginatively fills in the instrumental break before the song takes on a life of its own, building to a vigorous climax. Here, at last, Annie seems to have broken the mould and taken on a personality in her own right.

'Legend In My Living Room', co-written with Peter-John Vettese, starts with dark synths hypnotically flickering from left to right, before electronic strings pierce and snap the listener back to reality. The cold, persistent ticking percussion acts as a clock counting down the time while the lyrics tell the tale of an eager teenager aspiring for fame and fortune.

334

Written as an exploration of what could have happened to Annie, who also moved to the city aged 17, the character in this story fails to hit the big time. Lines like, "Bright lights and trains and bedsit stains" hark back to 'This City Never Sleeps' a decade earlier. The synths swoop around the mix, using the space to full nauseating effect, highlighting the insignificance of the unsuccessful singer. Although jointly penned, clearly the material covers Annie's time at the Royal Academy of Music before she met Dave, again suggesting that this period of her life was still as important as ever.

'Legend In My Living Room' bands straight into 'Cold', unnaturally dropping the pace dramatically. In contrast this blues piece is slow and sparse with beautifully contained, breathy vocals, piano and percussion over an underlying string bass. This is another song which does not appear to be borne of her contented lifestyle as she sings of an unrequited love which is so right, yet unattainable. A little awkward in its placing, 'Cold' coolly shows off Annie's exceptional voice control.

Diving straight back into the watery feeling of earlier, 'Money Can't Buy It' combines hollow dripping sounds with waves lapping on the shore. The lyrics express Annie's eternal search for true happiness, but she is wise enough to realise that this can only be achieved through love and friendship, not wealth. The song could also be interpreted as a subtle dig at Dave Stewart, who has admitted to trying sex, drugs and wealth to attain satisfaction. Annie reiterated in an interview, "Money is not a currency for trust, and love, and genuine friendship; they just cannot be bought."

'Little Bird' opens with Annie's powerful and nostalgically robotic vocals of "aah, ahh" and "yeah", keeping the listener spellbound until the insistent keyboards and thumping bass permeate to provide a solid background for her yearning. She sings in a crystal clear voice of the trapped aching she feels in her heart for the freedom of a bird, a metaphor for her state of mind prior to the Eurythmics break-up. A few critics notably construed it as a particularly scathing attack on Dave, with lyrics including "They always said that you knew best/ But this little bird's fallen out of that nest". But as Annie explained in an interview, inspiration actually came from an endearing little bird who sat and sang on her windowsill during the recording of the album.

The track grows with the line, "But my my, I feel so low", and suddenly there is no stopping the runaway train. Her vocals have generally remained high over the deep music, so continue to signify her feelings of entrapment, but she suitably drops to *contralto* for "weighted to the ground" and "lay the burden down". Like some of the other notably successful songs on the album, Annie brings this track to a climax once more before softening it and ending it with a few choice warped tones.

Returning to the sploshing, hollow watery sounds once more, this time infused with an Eastern tinge, 'Primitive' is again calmer and more relaxing. The synthetic strings are Beatles-esque and the spiritual atmosphere completes the mystique. Annie sings of fate and mortality, and while her vocals are exquisitely calming, her audience is yet to hear the raunchy enthusiasm of Eurythmics.

The Middle Eastern intonation for 'Primitive' apparently came from her time living in France. "The human voice can be produced in many different ways," she explained. "I've heard these Arabic women and they stand in line and produce this wobble that comes from somewhere and it's terrifying but thrilling at the same time.

"There's a lot of Arabic and North African music in Paris. I'm fascinated by this. And then on top of this fantastic swelling orchestra usually will enter this woman's voice which is totally extraordinary, singing in pentatonic scales which will just blow your mind."

Many of the songs on *Diva* do not start as they mean to go on, and 'Stay By Me' is no exception. A classical piano arpeggio smoulders into a sparse percussion-led riff before culminating into a simplistic march with a childish recorder and glockenspiel leading the way. The bass is overpowering in the mix as Annie struggles to be heard over the numerous other instruments in this cluttered song. Finally she sings of her love for Uri, asking that he never leaves her, whatever may happen. Unfortunately she chose the most unadventurous song in which to do it, as it fails to ignite or even go anywhere. Several new sounds are introduced, none of which necessarily suit the song, but nothing can disguise the cringe-making sound of the squeaky recorder. After six minutes this song is a little too much.

The ominous distant heartbeat motif at the start of 'The Gift' is soothed by Annie's reassuring wordless vocalising, beautifully setting the scene for a moving penultimate track. A piano gently eases in, along with the ever-present electronic sound. Cutting through the album like a breath of fresh air, this poignant piece appears to be about Annie's previous suffocating unhappiness, and her gratitude at finally finding a partner, whose 'gift' is their daughter. Annie's controlled vocals are as haunting as ever, heightened by the piano. This remarkable piece about the enriching virtues of love was co-written with The Blue Nile from Glasgow.

Rounding off the album with a humorous summation of the title, *Diva*, Annie takes on the self-mocking warning of 'Keep Young And Beautiful'. Produced to mimic an old scratched record, Annie bounces through this fun number with a plum in her mouth and her tongue in her cheek. A lovely ending to a curiously mixed album.

★   ★   ★

Disinclined to take on the pressure of a promotional tour, particularly with a young child not to mention plans for increasing the family, Annie chose instead to produce a video to accompany *Diva*. With such a romantic location as St. Mark's Square, Venice and direction by Sophie Muller, it is hardly surprising that *Diva* the video won a Grammy for Best Long Form Video.[47] The release was a little premature as not all the promos had been shot, and so in the UK, at least, a second film was produced entitled *Total Diva* which included the missing footage for 'Walking On Broken Glass' and 'Precious'. A clip for 'Little Bird' still did not appear as the single was not to be available until later in the year.

While writing the lyrics had proved tough, Annie undoubtedly let her hair down for the film. "I always enjoy the visual bit, making the video. It's easier than writing the music. That is soul searching. This is fun. I don't want to sound too pretentious . . .

"OK, let me sound pretentious. I love bringing visual images out of a song. I don't use stylists. I create what I think will be suitable . . . The diva look is new for me, but it seemed to suit the mood of the album," she told *You* magazine. The overall theme of the characterisation in the film is of a faded Forties star, as per the album cover. "Some people have thought that I was a transvestite, because I'm tall and I used to wear bright, brassy stuff," smirked Annie. "I don't choose to be that way myself, but I like the way transvestites look, I like the tackiness of it."

Staying true to the sleazier side of show-business then, the word 'Diva' flickers into life on a blue neon sign to open her debut video offering as a solo artist. Not intended as a video album with a specific narrative but instead as a collection of promotional pieces for the songs, Annie experiments with different styles and ideas. Nevertheless there are several recurring themes, namely the expression of face and hands and an oriental influence. Ultimately the video was surrounded by great anticipation, from the fans to see what Annie would be like without Dave, and from the star awaiting validation.

As with the album, the first song is 'Why' before another flickering sign, this time of a star, leads into 'Legend In My Living Room'. Borrowing heavily from such diverse images as Madonna's 1990 video for 'Vogue' and Judy Garland's 1950 film *Get Happy*, Annie sports a black top hat and tails, a man's white shirt, white gloves and a cane. She is seen sitting manfully astride a chair, leaning on the back, and smouldering at the camera from under the hat before gracefully dancing around the set in the style of

---

[47] Sophie had previously picked up numerous awards for her work with Eurythmics and a Music Week Award for Shakespear's Sister's 'Stay'.

Fred Astaire. Aside from the striking image she portrays, the video is a little monotonous, but fun nonetheless.

The clip for 'Precious' comprises shots of Annie singing in close-up, dressed as an angel and wandering the streets of an imposing city. Possibly under Sophie's direction, Annie chose particularly heavy, panda-style eye make-up similar to that favoured by Shakespear's Sister on their 1992 video 'Stay'. Another major influence appears to be the Far East, as Annie introduces delicately expressive hand twirls to her dancing and an oriental green and gold dress.

Annie has often utilised angels as a theme for her songs and videos, a concept she tried to define, "We have no angels in our time. I have never met an angel, but there's this idea of a fictitious being that is somehow connected to a higher creative source, and that might be a protection for us."

Apart from the video for 'Precious' which is made up of several different interspersed images and the final piece on the album, 'Walking On Broken Glass', it is interesting to note that while pushing the visual boundaries as far as costumes and characters are concerned, the videos on *Diva* are simplistically straightforward in their storyline. 'Money Can't Buy It' is a prime example of an enticing concept for a short film which sadly becomes boring due to its lack of progress.

Annie is dressed in a glamorous red ball gown contrasted with a white towel wrapped in a turban on her head. Sitting in front of an oversized mirror in a magnificent stately hallway, she alternately sings directly to the camera and through the reflection. After suitably freaking the audience out Annie turns to face herself, and becomes wholly obsessed in her own image. In an attempt to induce life into what has now become a repetitive film, she turns her cheek to the mirror again and mists it with her breath, drawing dollar signs in the condensation.

Proving her diversity for characters once more, Annie wears full Forties mourning attire including a big black feather hat for 'Cold'. She stands at the edge of St. Mark's Square, taking cover from the relentless rain in a courtyard with imposing pillars. Her make-up is pale and harrowing, particularly as the camera frenziedly zooms in and out at the end, concentrating on her hands and face.

During extra music not on the album, she walks into a beam of light streaming down into a deserted warehouse. Clothed in a black bodice and a floor-length white skirt, Annie picks up brightly coloured saris, feather boas, scarves and capes which she twirls around her like a child delighting in a dressing-up box.

For the video of 'Primitive' Annie returns to the distraught woman

Posing for pictures in Red Square, Moscow alongside the Soviet army, Annie, well-briefed and confident, spoke out for Greenpeace in 1989. *(Adrian Boot/Retna)*

Billy Poveda was Annie's personal assistant and lover for two years. *(Richard Young/Rex)*

Uri Fruchtmann was Annie's husband for 12 years. *(Richard Young/Rex)*

Dave, Siobhan Fahey, Uri Fruchtmann and Annie.
(Tim Jarvis/Retna)

Annie and close friend Chrissie Hynde.
(Rex)

Annie finally meets her heroine Joni Mitchell at the
Grammy Awards on February 28, 1996. *(LFI)*

Annie performs 'Under Pressure' with David Bowie at the Freddie Mercury tribute concert
at Wembley Stadium in April 1992. *(LFI)*

The diva herself.
(LFI)

Annie performs with the 'draggy' male dancers from *Medusa*.
(LFI)

Annie in her pseudo-Minnie Mouse dominatrix outfit at the Grammy Awards on March 1, 1995.
(LFI)

Tom, Annie and Dorothy Lennox.
(Joe Bangay)

Annie: "Something had to give, and it couldn't be my daughters. That's why I made the conscious decision to go inside and close the door." Annie, Lola and Tali.
(Pappix UK)

Anne Dudley: "She's extremely down-to-earth and very normal. She's really got her priorities right, because she's very family-orientated." *(Rex)*

Stevie Wonder presented Eurythmics with the Outstanding Contribution To Music award at the 1999 BRITs; their first major public appearance in a decade. *(Popperfoto)*

Annie performs solo at Arista's 25th anniversary celebrations on April 10, 2000.
(Popperfoto)

The 1999 reunion album *Peace* was promoted by a world tour and a series of public appearances by the pair in army combats. *(Roy Tee/SIN & LFI)*

A newly-peroxided Annie smiles through the troubles at the launch of the rock museum, Experience Music Project, in Seattle on June 25, 2000. *(LFI)*

wrapped up in a black duffel coat last seen in 'You Have Placed A Chill In My Heart'. Similar imagery is used, but instead of wandering through the desert of her emotions, she is pictured floating on the waters of Venice in a gondola. Rather than the desperation seen in 'You Have Placed A Chill In My Heart', the passage of water in 'Primitive' implies that whatever happens, fate will take its course, wounds will heal and we will be led to safety by the powers-that-be. Annie lies on a bed with her face shrouded by a veil decorated with small stars, again indicating that the world is bigger than the mere mortals inhabiting it.

Returning to the faded diva outfit with a blue mask, Annie parades around the Italian square almost as a circus act for 'The Gift'. Looking faintly ridiculous with her extravagant headdress sprouting two pink feather boas, she poses for endless photographs with tourists bemused by the spectacle.

To mark the change between the last clip and 'Walking On Broken Glass' there is a brief scene where Annie, dressed in a man's pinstripe business suit with a short crop, sits at a counter in a café drinking coffee and eating a bun. She acts out an amiable response to people who can be heard talking and laughing off screen, pretending to join in with them. As abruptly as this bizarre sketch started, it ends.

'Walking On Broken Glass' has a more coherent storyline. English comedy actor Hugh Laurie makes a guest appearance as Annie's long suffering partner when the couple attend an extravagant Regency wedding. Through scenes mirroring classical paintings, it becomes apparent that the groom, played by John Malkovich, is one of Annie's ex-lovers, and she inwardly fumes at not being the bride.

As the party continues Annie becomes increasingly intoxicated and openly displays her contempt for Laurie's peace-making advances. Sick of watching the happy couple, she has a flashback to the time when she was with Malkovich and in a nostalgic haze she stumbles towards the bride and groom, forcibly shoves the bride out of the way and ushers the groom onto the balcony for some privacy. He shuns her advances and she returns to the party in a terrible state, drunkenly staggering with an evil white face and exaggerated make-up. Following a tug of love between the trio Annie totters down the grandiose stairs into Malkovich's arms to be swept off her feet.

For the final clip, 'Keep Young And Beautiful', Annie returns once more to the bare warehouse. This tongue-in-cheek song offered great potential for visual interpretation, but Annie chose simply to wear a Twenties style dress with angel wings on her back, while she gently danced round in circles. She changes back to the distraught mourner standing in the courtyard as the credits roll, clutching a hot water bottle for comfort which is amusingly refilled by a crew member.

Unfortunately the video as a whole leaves a feeling of bemusement, and a doubt over its overall conception. The various powerful images and original ideas seem sadly stunted before reaching maturity.

To accompany the release Annie appeared in a documentary, entitled *Diva*, which was aired on April 28, 1992, by BBC2. It featured Annie sitting in a chair, answering unheard questions. During the fake dialogue the lady rambles a little and doth protest too much about coping without Dave. Straying off the musical point, she also reveals that she would like more than one baby. In this way, Lola won't grow up thinking the world revolves around her, as Annie herself admits to doing as an only child.

★   ★   ★

Having decided not to tour in promotion of *Diva*, Annie dusted off her stage clothes for a one-off concert in memory of Freddie Mercury in April 1992. Marking the loss of one of rock's greatest personalities to the rapidly escalating AIDS epidemic, the three remaining members of Mercury's band Queen organised a spectacular concert for their late vocalist. All revenue from the star-studded event at Wembley Stadium, and the ensuing EP, went to the specially formed Mercury Phoenix Trust to be distributed to various AIDS charities worldwide.

Annie appeared in a fantastic costume and make-up with a Pierrot-style black mask painted across her eyes complete with the obligatory shiny tear. She finished the look with a full-length ballerina tutu and a sparkling gold top. With Brian May, John Deacon and Roger Taylor providing the backing, Annie duetted with David Bowie on 'Under Pressure', the song that Bowie had originally recorded with Queen. But the performance is best remembered for Bowie's extraordinary behaviour at the song's close; somewhat inadvisably he knelt down and offered what appeared to be a spontaneous prayer for Mercury's salvation.

After the concert Annie continued to promote her album. On May 8 she appeared on NBC's *Tonight Show* while 'Precious' reached number 23 in the UK. Gradually she was showing more confidence as a solo artist, playing at Subterania in London on June 21 as a 'trial gig'.

Performing in this rather ad hoc fashion appeared to suit the singer more than the rigmarole and planning required for a major tour, and the next concert appearance was at the Montreux Jazz Festival, Switzerland on July 3. Cashing in on Annie's surprise showing, MTV suggested that they film her set, airing it as part of their acclaimed *Unplugged* series. Still finding her feet, Annie was nervous of such an undertaking, but with a little help from her friends she was pleased to agree to both proposals.

"I thought, 'Well, I can't turn this down – this is ridiculous, people would die to do this!' " she exclaimed. "Steve Lipson actually said, 'To be honest about it, you can't *not* do this. This is wonderful, I will get the musicians together for you, I will organise it for you.' So he's been an absolute angel for me, as I couldn't do that myself."

The band itself was impressive, consisting of Steve on guitar, John Giblin playing bass, Peter-John Vettese and Joe Basharan sharing keyboard duties, Neil Conti on drums, and Mae McKenna and Sonia Morgan-Jones adding backing vocals and percussion. Annie ambitiously chose to incorporate unusual sounds from her past including a harpsichord and a harmonium.

The set's songs ranged from *Diva*, a selection of Eurythmics classics and even a rousing cover of Tina Turner's 1966 hit 'River Deep Mountain High'. As well as being shown by MTV on August 26, the recorded tracks later found their way onto a couple of collector's items, namely the bootleg *Rendezvous With A Lady* and the triple CD single collection *Cold, Colder, Coldest*. The main showcase, 'Cold', fared respectably at number 26 in the UK.

Reluctantly agreeing to occasional interviews, Annie carefully reconstructed the fortress around her private life. When accused of being "intensely private" by journalist Sylvia Patterson, Annie coolly retorted, "I'm human. I feel what anyone else feels. There is a big difference between what I do on stage and in my private life. I don't put my living room on magazine pages. I'm not 'intensely private' – I talk a great deal about my life and my work – I just don't play the game to excess."

But there was no need for Annie to pander to the press, as the singles and videos spoke for themselves. In August 1992, 'Walking On Broken Glass' maintained the pace, hitting number eight in the UK and number 14 in America. On September 9, the film for 'Why' won the Best Female Video category at the MTV Video Music Awards. By the time Annie appeared on Whoopi Goldberg's chat show in October that year, she was not only riding high on the success of *Diva*, but she had a few surprises up her sleeve.

Once again Annie was positively blooming in pregnancy. Partly reassured by the safe arrival of Lola and also eager to pursue her flourishing solo career, Annie did not take many breaks from work while carrying her third child. Capitalising on her physical situation, the mother-to-be appeared in videos with a visible bump.

By November and six months pregnant, Annie changed her priorities and took a rest from promotional work, concentrating instead on her health in time for the baby's birth. She also began to look towards activities other than music for inspiration. "Perhaps I'll go to art college, do a foundation year, the one I never did when I was 17. Oh I'd like to learn to drive,"[48] she dreamed, adding elsewhere, "I want to take photographs – that's something I want to develop just for myself. I'd also like to learn Spanish."

As 1993 commenced Annie was content to settle down wholeheartedly with her family and prepare for the big day. She agreed to one final interview, a special which was to be broadcast in two parts at the beginning of February on Britain's morning show, *GMTV*. She wore an understated black designer suit to cover her bump and talked candidly about life aged 38. "With Eurythmics, I really devoted my life to the band. It came before everything else," she confided. "Now I am not in that position. What I do musically – although it's terribly important to me – is not the most important thing in my life.

"Professionally and personally, I have grown up. Now I have a family and that is great because it has enriched my life. I am a better person for it. My life is in perspective." This declaration of needing a family to feel complete seemed a little unusual coming from the lips of such an outwardly independent woman, but was a great insight into her mature feelings.

One of the last recordings Annie made before her well-deserved break was for Greenpeace. She contributed a fresh version of 'Cold' for the charity's benefit album, *Alternative NRG*. The collection's gimmick was to boast that all the songs were recorded on solar-powered equipment. This turned out to be the only selling point as the assortment of live tracks was resoundingly uninspiring, even with contributions from artists such as R.E.M., U2 and UB40.

In February 'Little Bird', *Diva*'s fifth single, was released as a double A-side with 'Love Song For A Vampire'. The latter, a delicate, static ballad was written for Francis Ford Coppola's film, *Bram Stoker's Dracula*. Again working with Steve Lipson in the Townhouse Studios, Annie wrote what appeared to be a moving tribute to her lost son.

The promotional video is stark and cold. Annie is dressed in a white gown, looking pale and evil with raven black hair and what appear to be claws covering her fingertips. The film is interspersed with footage from the movie, but for her part Annie is clearly pregnant. In this happy state

---

[48] Annie's desire to drive unfortunately took a turn for the worse two years later, when she revealed to *Details* magazine that she had been stopped for jumping a red light and unceremoniously marched down to the local police station.

she also performed a magical rendition of the song on *Top Of The Pops*.

The double release leapt to number three as its profile was aided by the video, which was previewed at 30 Odeon cinemas before their screening of *Bram Stoker's Dracula*. The clip for 'Little Bird' was directed by Sophie Muller, the inspiration coming from Bob Fosse's film *Cabaret*. The promo featured eight Annie Lennox lookalikes past and present, and the real singer who was ready to pop.

Diva itself secured two more awards for Annie, notably Best British Female Artist and Best Album at the BRITs that February. Due to go into labour the week surrounding the ceremony, she gracefully accepted her award by video.

On February 9, 1993 Annie gave birth to her second daughter, once again at the Great Portland Street Hospital. Both mother and baby were reported to be in fine health and no less than 10 days later Annie was proudly showing off her youngest during a shopping trip, accompanied by Lola and a nanny. The latest addition to the family was called Tali, possibly after the Arabic, Talia, meaning 'lamb'.

With the birth of her child safely behind her, Annie looked to pastures new and the Lennox Fruchtmann family sold their home in Maida Vale for the sunnier outlook of the Spanish island of Majorca. Rumour had it that the move was prompted by extortionate British taxes, making her yet another pop star on the long list of tax exiles. Whatever her motives, Annie bought and converted a property in the island's pine woods, to create a reclusive family home and a professional recording studio. Enjoying her anonymity on foreign shores Annie lived a 'normal', peaceful life, partaking in a local petition opposing a new road scheme and shopping in the capital, Palma. The girls were of utmost importance to the proud parents and despite being abroad, Lola, now three years old, went to a private school nearby while baby Tali was looked after by a nanny.

"Suddenly you are there and you have this unconditional love for this wonderful creation that is yours to nurture, and it's very profound and you are changed by it," beamed the mother of two. "In a sense my qualities have changed, my perceptions of the world have changed. I can't look at another child now and think that I have nothing in common with it anymore. This is a compassionate thing. It's a wonderful thing." Family friends who visited the children commented how much they resembled their mother at the same age.

★　★　★

During Annie's absence *Diva* continued to perform well, coming a close second to Simply Red's *Stars* as Britain's best selling album of 1992. The

LP returned to number one in the UK on March 1, 1993, the same week that Annie was voted Best Female Singer by *Rolling Stone* in their Music Awards Readers' Picks. The first single, 'Why', triumphed with the Best Song Musically And Lyrically at the Ivor Novello Awards on May 26.

Dave Stewart had not enjoyed a similarly successful run. While the ex-Eurythmics had not maintained contact, apparently Annie had kept one eye on her former partner's career. "Perhaps they didn't sell so well in England," she said of his last three albums, "but in Europe they did. I didn't allow myself to think about any of that when I was making *Diva* – to be honest, I was too busy thinking about myself." After the failure of both The Spiritual Cowboys and Vegas, the more crass interviewers found it too tempting not to suggest that Eurythmics should reform, if only for Dave's sake.

In November 1993 Dave answered that very question in *Vox*, stating firmly that Eurythmics would not collaborate again. The journalists could be forgiven for jumping to conclusions, as Dave had recently worked closely with former Eurythmics drummer Olle Romo, tracking down previously unreleased live recordings to produce a new double Eurythmics CD, under the resourceful title *Eurythmics Live 1983–1989*.[49] Originally containing two CDs of material from a mix of tours including Touch, Revenge and Revival, the album was later repackaged with a bonus disc containing the acoustic medley from the Revival show in Rome.

Supposedly Dave had not dug up the old material with the intention of seeing his name gracing the charts once more, but rather to finalise the end of Eurythmics.

"This album is Eurythmics RIP. We want to put it to sleep now. We never really wanted to make an announcement that it was finished because we really didn't know," he declared, omitting the impact of Annie's phenomenally successful solo album and the Greatest Hits package of 1991. "It's like putting a full stop on a relationship."

Although many critics were of the opinion that Eurythmics excelled more in the studio and on video than in their stage performances, the release was an interesting catalogue of a decade of touring and recording. It was also exceptionally well-timed to appear in the mournful Eurythmics fans' Christmas stockings.

The simplistic artwork on the cover was blown away by the stunning inside photograph by Laurie Lewis of Annie performing in front of an endless crowd, clapping in unison. As the tracks are ordered by date of the performance it is surprising to hear such a smooth and confident version of

[49] The working title of *Eurythmics Live 1983–1989* had previously been publicised as *Untouched*.

'Never Gonna Cry Again' dating back to March 1983 as the opener. The backbone beat pounds along, allowing the flute to float beautifully over the top in an extended solo.

Jumping forward to July and across the pond to America, the second track is a disappointingly unsure and bitty rendition of 'Love Is A Stranger'. No performance of 'Sweet Dreams (Are Made Of This)' is ever going to be as powerful as the original recording, and while this attempt in front of a German audience is faithful, it can never compare.

'This City Never Sleeps' however is perfectly moody and jerky, sending chills through the cold October air in Manchester. Dave's guitar solo is atmospheric and The Croquettes provide that little extra eeriness to the song's insistence. 'Somebody Told Me' is equally powerful with immense energy and squealing electric guitar. Annie simply drips with hatred and she builds up a good rapport with The Croquettes in the question and answer phrases, building to a gospel-styled finale.

Moving into April 1984 Eurythmics perform 'Who's That Girl?' in Chicago, which, taken slightly too fast, loses the elegance of the original. Moving to Austin in the same month, it is painfully obvious that Annie is feeling the strain of touring on her throat, as she barely struggles through 'Right By Your Side', allowing the band and backing singers to shoulder the bulk of the song. One wonders why anyone would choose this positively hoarse version of such a bright number over others, and can only assume that Annie was absent from the decision making.

Annie had taken a year off before touring again, and the break paid dividends, as her voice is smooth and refreshed in the understated rendition of 'Here Comes The Rain Again' in October 1986. The same month also heard a remarkably upbeat interpretation of *1984*'s 'Sexcrime (nineteen eighty-four)' in Nuremberg.

The appreciative crowd in Rome were treated to an exquisitely intense introduction for 'I Love You Like A Ball And Chain', which had always worked well in a live setting. The track continues to build from the powerful opening, successfully blending Annie's lead with Joniece Jamison's backing. The audience in Houston earlier in 1986 are no less enthusiastic about Clem Burke's infectious drumming throughout the jumpy 'Would I Lie To You?'

By the time the tour rolled into London in November 1986 the group were working well together, and Annie and Joniece shared the vocals on 'There Must Be An Angel (Playing With My Heart)' almost equally. Although it is refreshing to hear the band members each receiving their moment of glory, Jimmy Zavala's harmonica solo was extended a little too much.

'Thorn In My Side' opens with a gleeful spoken introduction before launching into the rigorous workout. Jimmy again steals the show, this time with his saxophone solo, distracting a little from the duo essence of Eurythmics. It is Joniece's turn to shine on 'Let's Go', recorded in Christchurch in the new year. The backing vocalist owns a distinctive voice which sometimes stands out rather than blends in with Annie's, and here she is afforded a substantial role at the end. 'Missionary Man' never fails to impress as a stadium rock number. The heavily reverbed guitar and pristine keyboards entice the Australian fans into this powerful version of the semi-religious classic. 'The Last Time' is a disappointingly standard edition, but the audience, again Australian, find something unheard on the CD to scream about wildly.

A moving piano introduction begins the soft accompaniment for 'The Miracle Of Love'. Recorded during the Revival Tour's stint in Paris, it is given added feeling with the freedom of live tempo, and highlights good use of musical dynamics. Dave's strutting guitar says it all as Annie launches into a rousing version of the swaggering 'I Need A Man'; again the fans in Rome display their enjoyment of Annie's particularly raunchy interpretation.

'We Two Are One', the title song from the 1989 album, provides a fast-paced crowd pleaser in Dublin. '(My My) Baby's Gonna Cry' in Edinburgh puts Dave on the vocal spotlight alongside Annie and Joniece, the whispers of "Tonight – oh yeah" becoming the highlight. Rome's ever vocal audience chant for Annie at the start of 'Don't Ask Me Why', slightly spoils the potency of the song, but Annie soon reclaims hushed attention. Perfectly ending the double CD of live tracks, a rippling piano arpeggio leads into the elegant 'Angel'. This stadium ballad undoubtedly saw flames from thousands of cigarette lighters at Wembley in the autumn of 1989.

In addition, the bonus limited edition six-track CD contains an acoustic medley from the Revival Tour. Accompanied mainly by Dave on guitar Annie sounds a little strained but produces a poignant working of 'You Have Placed A Chill In My Heart', 'Here Comes The Rain Again', 'Would I Lie To You?', 'It's Alright (Baby's Coming Back)' and 'Right By Your Side'. The highlight, 'When Tomorrow Comes', is warm and mellow with an extended acoustic band. Aside from Annie's tell-tale hoarseness creeping in, this is a positive ending to a proficient set.

24

SHE'S INVISIBLE NOW

"Something had to give, and it couldn't be my daughters. They'll only be young once. That's why I made the conscious decision that I did, to go inside and close the door. I came home and began the process of deconstructing the huge thing that had happened to me in becoming famous."

— AL

After the brief dip into the sea of nostalgia, Annie began to re-evaluate her career and home life. As Lola passed her third birthday and Tali approached her first, their mother once again began to yearn for a creative outlet. At the end of 1993 the Lennox Fruchtmanns moved back to England, to new accommodation in Highgate where the foursome settled into a routine as low-key as possible.

"You get stopped by complete strangers on the street. Sometimes people are rude, sometimes friendly – sometimes their timing is just wrong. It has its advantages. You have to be fairly mature to cope well," said Annie of the trials of fame.

The ability to form friendships was stretched to the limit by Annie's unmistakable aura. "The phenomena of being famous and being intro-duced to new people can be very strange, because people already have a preconceived notion of you. They're either intimidated by you, or they're in awe of you, or they want to impress you, or they *don't* want to impress you, or something about the fame which is a kind of barrier between you and them," she stumbled to summarise. "On the other hand, I don't have to prove myself! I get away with going to places without having to dress up overtly to be noticed – I'm usually trying not to be noticed!"

This ability to blend into the crowd was inspired by no less than British soap actress, Joan Collins. One Saturday afternoon Annie was rummaging through an antiques stall when she spotted the famous screen star. Joan's face was uncommonly naked and it was the lack of heavy make-up and stylised hair that provided her disguise. Annie took this lesson to heart and although she had already grown her distinctively dyed short hair into a mousy bob, she went to the extreme of wearing unbecoming clothes and no make-up whatsoever. "With success comes the destruction of your anonymity, which is something I value a great deal," she coldly observed, and clung jealously to the sense of normality she had found within her family.

As Annie contemplated reviving her career again, she carefully considered the impact a surge in publicity and media attention would have on her two children, especially Lola who was reaching an impressionable age.

"The only point at which the implications of what I do will start to concern me somewhat will be in regard to my daughter and her eventual school friends. I don't want her to have to deal with them going, 'Well, your mother's a bit of an old . . . whatever.' I really wouldn't want that to happen, so no doubt I'll get out of it [pop music] before she gets to school age. That's the idea I have in my head, anyway," she justified.

Fortunately, that timetable allowed her to pursue another album in the meantime.

The name was the first thing that came to mind. "When I wrote songs with Dave and then subsequently with *Diva*, there was a title that emerged from the songs. It came right at the very end of the whole process, always. But in this case I had this name sitting around even before the album was put into production. And I liked it. I liked all the implications of it," Annie said. The title was *Medusa*.

The reference was to the hideous mortal woman of Greek mythology whose unsightly appearance of wings, claws, enormous fangs and a head full of snakes turned onlookers to stone. Researching further, Annie drew on her surroundings over the past year and found that 'medusa' in Spanish means 'jellyfish', which is the closest to a creature sprouting snakes in modern times. Hence the cover photo is a naked shot of Annie's head and shoulders while she fixes the camera with Medusa's piercing stare and a stray strand of hair curls down her neck like the slippery reptiles.

The music, however, was not as obvious. Learning from the difficulties she had faced writing *Diva*, and only really experiencing further happiness since then, Annie did not have a lot of angst-inspired stimulus left. So what would be the next direction for the woman who had conquered it all, yet still desired more?

"It has arisen from the need to do something different," she commented of this next project. "To qualify that, from the early Eighties I have been writing and co-writing songs and arrived at the stage where I just wanted to break that pattern for a while." So, instead of creating new songs, Annie set about interpreting other people's. She stressed that this was not a cop-out to avoid the demanding creative side. Her goal lay in the notion of interpretation, not in reconstituting a second-rate version of a ready-made song.

With Steve Lipson's assistance, Annie set about recording an album of covers. Steve in turn brought in an old friend from his days working with the Art of Noise, Anne Dudley.

"People always make a fuss about whether an artist does covers or whether they're doing original material," Dudley states today. "But I can understand why she wanted to do this, because on the best tracks, like 'No More "I Love You's"', she really brought a very fresh approach to it and it doesn't sound like something that's tired and just a cheap idea.

"I think there's just as much creativity gone into producing covers as there is on an original album. I think *Medusa* works as an album . . . I do think it has a unity, although it's all different people's songs. There is continuity about it." One of the musicians on the album, Judd Lander, agrees that Annie succeeded in the venture. "Normally I would think, 'How are they going to bastardise this?' But she gave it a unique flavour. She has done every track justice and if anything, has enhanced the songs with her own delivery."

Again spurred on by Lipson's enthusiasm and determination, Annie embraced the collection as a challenge to alter or enhance old favourites. "It was an album that Annie was pretty much involved with," says Dudley. "She did most of the keyboard parts, she did all the vocal parts, and she and Steve devised the arrangements between them.

"Steve's a real workaholic, and if he doesn't spend at least 12 hours in the studio every day, he thinks he's shirking! He likes to know exactly what's going on, a very detailed approach to everything." The fastidiousness of the pair made them a perfect match, although it is a mystery how either was able to maintain a social life. Working at the same slow pace as *Diva*, Annie and Steve plugged away at the album for the best part of 1994, with the aim of releasing it early the next year. Annie also kept herself busy with family ties and other smaller projects.

Anne Dudley worked closely with both the singer and producer, and was able to observe the way the album progressed. "As the arrangements developed she was always thinking of new vocal ideas and new ways to approach the songs. She was singing better than ever on this album, and she did all the vocal parts. They were very intricate, and extremely well organised and arranged. I think she was really on top of it on this album."

Of course it helped to have such a sturdy partner as Steve Lipson, with whom she now shared years of experience. Harmonica player on the album, Judd Lander, commented on Steve's style, "Steve's a typical producer, he has an idea of what he wants and is brilliant at creating clarity with a big sound, lots of electronic equipment. It's the mass of technology in his production which works." It is hard not to draw comparisons here with Dave and his method of alternately producing and bullying Annie through recording with as many different musical toys as possible.

Medusa introduced Steve to a new way of combining real instruments with his favoured electronics. "Steve hadn't worked with strings or brass before, and he got a bit nervous because this felt like, well these are real people and not machines; they're a little bit outside of his control!" recalls Dudley. "He was kind enough to write me a note afterwards, saying 'Thank you for making my first experience of strings and brass painless!' I think he was a bit nervous about it. Personally, I love the mixture of electronic stuff and orchestras; it's an endlessly fascinating palette of colours."

★   ★   ★

Having passed her 40th birthday Annie entered 1995 with a new lease of life. Contributing to another soundtrack album, she could be heard this year on one of the tracks for Tom Hanks' latest blockbuster movie, *Apollo 13*. Eager collectors were confused when it was announced at an award ceremony that there would be a special edition CD released. Keen to purchase a new product, fans rushed out to buy the limited release at vast expense. Reports of the CD selling for over $200 were not uncommon, but Annie's admirers were only to find that her contribution remained solely the one track despite the listing. Speculation remains as to whether Annie can be heard on 'End Titles', but the song she officially lent her dulcet tones to was 'Dark Side Of The Moon'.

It was Annie's first release from the forthcoming album that caused the real stir; how were the press and fans alike going to react to Annie's compilation of covers?

'No More "I Love You's"' was originally unleashed by The Lover Speaks in 1986, when it achieved a meagre UK number 56. "I think it's a magnificent song, the words, the lyrics were extraordinary, and absolutely the perfect sort of vehicle for me to interpret," Annie bubbled, regardless of its history. Ironically released the day before St. Valentine's Day, this anti-love song soared in at number two in the UK charts.

Annie's promotional performances on chat shows such as *The David Letterman Show* and music programmes like *Top Of The Pops* were remarkable, not least for the surrounding transvestite ballerinas and for her appearance replete with sparkly silver Mickey Mouse ears. One can only assume the fad was inspired by her two small children.

The B-side, not from the album, was also a cover, this time of Annie's heroine Joni Mitchell's intriguing 'Ladies Of The Canyon', about the women of a Californian gorge. Annie altered the 1969 original to retain its charm, but adopting a more modulated and darker element, she also changed the lyrics and annunciation slightly to gain a more rhythmical approach, rather than the conversational style heard from Joni.

For once not receiving an award at the Grammys on March 1, 1995, Annie did not miss out. She backed Carly Simon on a cheeky version of 'You're So Vain' at Arista boss, Clive Davis' pre-ceremony party held at the House of Blues. At the actual award ceremony Annie not only continued to wear the Mickey Mouse ears but added an outrageous element. Her leather pseudo-Minnie Mouse dominatrix outfit and jet black pageboy wig were designed to shock the American public just as she had done back in 1984 with her appearance as Earl. Annie later joined George Michael on stage to present the Song Of The Year trophy to Bruce Springsteen.

★ ★ ★

In March Annie was quoted in *Vanity Fair* as saying of her former Eurythmics partner, "I don't need any association with him any more than he needs it from me." Indeed, David A. Stewart had just launched his first truly solo record, *Greetings From The Gutter*. The 11-song album, containing a mix of hard rock, soul, jazz and even classical music, was released on March 1, beating *Medusa* by two weeks.

The fact that the two were incommunicado was there for all to hear in the lyrics of Dave's album. Dave, like Annie, wrote from personal experience and it is not difficult to find references to his past amongst his work with The Spiritual Cowboys, Vegas or this latest offering. The title track is a pure, unashamed revenge attack at Annie as he sings, "Greetings from the gutter/ I've been here since yesterday/ Sweet dreams in the gutter." He continues by making his backing singer impersonate Annie's style before he utters, "You're a star, you don't talk to me".

'Tragedy Street' is about a character called 'Angie' and is a play on the critics' dubbing of the Eurythmics frontwoman as 'Tragedy Annie'. Furthermore, there is a familiar melody as the backing vocalists sing 'Why'. However, 'Jack Of All Trades' is by far the most autobiographical, and admittedly so. Dave literally tells the story of his life through his relationship with Annie, "Fell in love with a girl on her harmonium stool", the demise of The Tourists, "The band broke up around a pool in Bangkok . . . Our days were numbered like hands on a clock", and the bitterness at the end of Eurythmics, "Me and the serious girl had massive hits all round the world/ We got so big we both became ill".

Promotion for *Greetings From The Gutter* came in the form of an

351

Omnibus documentary. Cameras shadowed Dave in the final preparations for the album and its campaign, as well as visiting his family and friends back in Sunderland. Billed as, "A profile of one of popular music's more complex personalities, drawing on interviews with family, colleagues and even Dave Stewart himself," it became apparent that although Dave and Annie were not speaking, she had in fact contributed to the programme.

But her comments were less than gracious during his hour of glory, hardly surprising if she had so much as glanced at his latest lyrical offerings. "We grew apart and it became impossible for either of us to bear being together. There's still bad blood between us," she said, leading the viewer to question her appearance for any reason other than to gloat about her own success.

★   ★   ★

On March 14, 1995 Annie released her second solo album, *Medusa*. One positive point about the selection of covers meant that it could not be compared to the unforeseen success of *Diva*. Once again she hit the top spot in the UK and peaked one place outside the Top 10 in America, ultimately achieving platinum sales by the year's end.

Interestingly *Medusa* opens with the ultimate declaration of romantic despair on 'No More "I Love You's"' and through the album's course, eventually closes with Annie finally finding 'Something So Right'. 'No More "I Love You's"' commences with pervasive backing vocals of "dobedobedododo-aah" followed by Annie's tormented, high vocals, a quiet calm after a tumultuous storm. This first cover on the album particularly suits Annie's usual lyrical style, displaying pain and torment. Her interpretation is light and clear with minimalist instruments; programmed drums and keyboards. She also makes good use of varying different character voices, from a child's rhetoric mumblings to wild laughing.

Quietly opening Al Green's classic, 'Take Me To The River', with an infectious riff and distant percussive knocking, this R&B classic is given a slightly futuristic sound with warped keyboards and an uneasy mechanical feel. The sparse mix is accentuated with clicks, a fuzz guitar riff and heavy echo where the high notes sound like a computer talking. With Annie's determined vocals, this gritty number retains the original raw blues feel and of all the tracks it ends a little too soon.

Recalling a song with fond links to her childhood, Annie next tackled Procol Harum's 'A Whiter Shade Of Pale'. Introduced on a high tinkling harpsichord sound with childlike leanings, Annie's vocals are respectfully gentle and hazy, much like the original. However exquisite the version, softly mixing a discreet trumpet and harp flourishes with a predominantly electronic background, it cannot escape a certain lifelessness. 'Don't Let It Bring You Down' immediately imbues more life with a solid drumbeat and ongoing synths showcasing a simple song with some exceptionally effective guitar work. Annie handles the persistent vocals well, although the music seems a little middle-heavy in the mix.

'Train In Vain' is one of the highlights of the album. The simple pluck-ing of a string bass exquisitely sets the mood as it lazily plods throughout the song. Smoothly it is joined by a dulcet yet snappy rhythm, filled out with a breathy Annie getting into the groove, and finally a trembling piano. Anne Dudley's bright brass spurts are cleverly introduced halfway through the song and the instruments build thereafter as the number gains momentum, with Annie standing back and soulfully ad libbing. This excel-lently mellow reworking of the Clash's original blends well and shows Annie in one of her most diverse modes.

Maintaining the upbeat rhythm of the last song, 'I Can't Get Next To You', originally by Temptations in 1970, offers a Mediterranean feel with the lush strings appearing in stark contrast to the instantly Spanish guitar. Annie's soft vocals float easily over and above, as again she makes good use of strong backing vocals to effect a snappy ending.

"Funnily enough, one doesn't often get to do an arrangement on the same song twice," laughs Anne Dudley, "but not very long before, I'd done an arrangement on 'Downtown Lights' for Rod Stewart's album. I remember saying to Steve, 'Oh not this song again, I know this song.' He said, 'How do you know this song?' and I said, 'Because Rod Stewart's just done it.' Steve went quiet for a while and then said, 'For God's sake don't tell Annie – because if she knows Rod Stewart's done it, she'll never do it!' So I didn't tell her!

"I think it was probably one of my least favourite songs, especially having waded through it before. It's extremely long and it did need differ-ent colours and different countermelodies all the way through, because otherwise it's a really dull song."

The strong drumbeat at the start of Annie's 'Downtown Lights' remains throughout, as it is augmented with insistent keyboards and Dudley's orchestra. Annie's haunting vocals soar effortlessly over the song as she breezes over the spoken vocal breakdown in the middle. The pizzicato strings work well in an otherwise heavy pop song, but the major downside is the track's length which needs to be cut by at least one and a half minutes where there is a natural fade out – the last section adds nothing apart from an extended confusion of sound.

A mysterious and subdued opening draws the listener curiously into 'Thin Line Between Love And Hate'. Annie tells her friend Chrissie

Hynde's explicit tale, staying close to the mic to give the impression of intimate confession. A plaintive and melancholy harmonica seeps movingly into the story while there is no doubt as to the selfless motives on the wife's behalf. But the gentle arrangement is desperately misleading as the woman, having dutifully taken care of her husband who carelessly came home at five in the morning, violently dishes out the revenge he deserves. Judd Lander's fast and furious harmonica pleads and cries in place of the battered husband, but Annie gives real depth and insight to this paean to a downtrodden housewife's retribution. Annie's version successfully updates the piano-led, funky cover by The Pretenders while simultaneously infusing much more feeling.

"She was very hands-on and knew exactly what she wanted," reminisces Judd. "She talked me through it, put a guide vocal down to give an idea of where to go and what to do – suffice to say it was a tough session but, I think, one that worked, but only because she's a perfectionist. She was a serious sort of person, but very personable – we had a talk, a bit of a laugh, but then on with the work.

"A nice thing about Annie was, when we finished the session I got a little note from her saying, 'Thank you very much'. And that is a little bit unique with artists." It appears that Annie and Steve were both grateful for the additional help.

Annie's version of 'Waiting In Vain' lightens Bob Marley's original and successfully replaces his overriding reggae beat with pleasing guitar work and easy listening. She manages to retain the dramatics of someone waiting through the passing seasons while respectfully transforming the gender from 'girl' to 'boy'.

As was the intention with the album, this cover is different enough to be worth its while yet similar enough to be courteous to Marley's classic. "This was another of my favourite songs," reminisces Dudley. "I was able to use a particularly nice line-up of three French horns and a tuba, maybe some trumpets, which I don't think you can hear very clearly in the final mix. It was a very nice sound."

Paul Simon's simple, elegant love song, 'Something So Right', was another track given due respect. "I remember Steve saying the track felt bare until the strings were on and then the track felt 'fully dressed'. He felt that really completed the track," says Dudley fondly. Indeed the strings provide a refined, understated backdrop to Annie's breathy vocals and this quiet, unassuming number is perfect to finish such an emotional collection.

"This album contains a selection of songs I have been drawn to for all kinds of reasons," Annie summarised on the album sleeve. "They were not chosen with any particular theme or concept in mind – the method was more by instinct than design. The work undertaken was truly a labour of love for me and I feel privileged to have been given this opportunity."

In June 1995, the second single from *Medusa*, 'A Whiter Shade Of Pale', was released, quickly entering the UK Top 20, but halting at 16. This initial enthusiasm, followed by waning interest was indicative of most who heard the song, as the original proved too recognisable to change. "I think the original arrangement of it defines really the ultimate way of doing that song," explained Anne Dudley. "If you don't do it that way, it doesn't seem to be the same song. The arrangement and the song seem very integrated, whereas I thought her approach on many other songs did let you see them in a different light."

Annie typically chose to release the track with several different B-sides, making them all collector's items, including 'Heaven', a cover of Blondie's '(I'm Always Touched By Your) Presence Dear' and various remixes of 'No More "I Love You's"'. Her live performances on music shows were as confusing as her appearance for 'No More "I Love You's"'. Again she was flanked by male ballet dancers on *Top Of The Pops*, where she pretended to play the harpsichord part on a hand-held miniature grand piano.

The skit this bizarre menagerie performed on Steve Wright's daytime show was even stranger. Annie wore sparkly Mickey Mouse ears and a man's suit, and stood in the middle of her drag queen dancers. As the men remove their make-up and tutus, replacing them with dark suits and cartoon character masks, Annie swaps her headpiece for fluffy brown ears and puts on a full teddy bear costume.

An alternative fashion statement was demonstrated at the VH1 Honours ceremony where a bemused Chris Isaak presented an award to Annie dressed in a white clown's outfit. This time the backing band wore the bear costumes. The children's theme made little sense until the release of *Medusa*'s promotional videos, but even then the ideas remained hazy and one can only assume that because she had first heard this particular song at a young age these are the images it conjures up. Perhaps Annie was invoking an ironic dig at the semi-pomp of the serious music world, or maybe the pressures of sustaining a 'normal' life away from the cameras had finally become a little too much . . .

★   ★   ★

Still refusing to tour because of her young children, Annie instead appeared at a selection of one-off events, including the *Donna Sotto Le Stelle* fashion gala in July, on the Spanish Steps in Rome, Italy. The balance between pursuing a career and raising a family proves to be a delicate decision for many women. For Annie, the fine line between being selfish, achieving the ideal of a 'working mum' and stunting her own artistic growth was all too easy to cross, not least because hers was no ordinary profession.

"It's tricky for me because I'm a performer-type person, but being a mother is the paramount thing in my life," she said. "Unfortunately, that can stifle the creativity that gives me identity and it's difficult because I need to stay alive as a creative person. Sometimes I think maybe it would be best not to do anything creative at all and just stay at home, but in a way that narrows me down as a person."

The majority of *Diva* had been recorded at her own home so that she could be with her baby, but equally the working conditions were far from perfect. By *Medusa* she seemed to have the predicament under control, although she admitted, "When I was in the recording studio, I missed my kids. When I was with them, part of me thought I should be back in the studio."

"She's extremely down-to-earth and very normal," says Anne Dudley with admiration. "She's really got her priorities right, because mostly she's very family-orientated and she worked out a way of recording this album while still being able to take her kids to school and pick them up from school. As we all know that's a real juggling act, but she's got it all sorted out."

Judd Lander noticed the connection between the famous mother and her eldest daughter, who was now five. "Lola was sweet, very sensible and mature. It was very warm when they walked in. I think she was pre-occupied by something else, a book or something. She was very studious."

Annie's previous concerns for her children being singled out at school for having a celebrity mum may have been well-founded, but Annie and her new neighbours in Highgate soon managed to overcome their individual prejudices. While most people who bumped into Annie Lennox on the street were probably in awe of her, she in turn was petrified of them.

"I realise now that I used to be very tense and defensive," she revealed to journalist Alan Jackson. "I'd just be waiting for that moment when a stranger came up to me, gave me that look, and said, 'Aren't you . . . ?' And I used to gulp and go, 'Well, sort of, um, er . . .' Whereas now I've managed to turn those encounters into something positive in my head. Instead of approaching it as a horrible ordeal, I embrace it, allow it to be a nice exchange. These days, I just smile and say, 'Yes, I am.'

"I *was* a bit of an item for a while. But credit to everyone, they've been fantastic. One other mum did say to me once, 'Annie, sometimes I feel sorry for you because no one invites you to their parties. They're afraid you'll think they're sucking up to you.' But I thought about that afterwards and I was OK with it. I don't mind not being invited to parties. That kind of social agenda doesn't really interest me at any level . . . I'm just happy that everyone seems to accept me for who I am, just another woman going about her life."

Unfortunately the price of fame meant that her extended family were also called upon by the media and enthusiastic fans. When Tom Lennox passed away Dorothy retreated, remaining in the Scottish countryside of Ellon. Annie's grandparents, Archie and Jean, grew weary of the constant calls for interviews and began to decline them politely using their age as a legitimate excuse. None of the family likes to talk about their famous niece or cousin, as aunt Jean Oates explains, "I don't think Ann really wants publicity, because she has two children and she is very concerned that they have as normal a childhood as possible."

Although Annie's girls were being brought up in another country to their relatives, the Lennox bond remained strong and there were frequent visits to the clan in Scotland. One notable event was Archie and Jean's 70th wedding anniversary when June Smith recalls, "The girls were there for the platinum party. The youngest one was a toddler, but they were all up for the big do. The place was absolutely packed with Lennoxes!"

The major event in promotion for *Medusa* was a free concert in New York's Central Park on September 8, 1995. Six thousand tickets were given away in two local stores in just 15 minutes, partly because it was Annie's first appearance in the city since 1988. Capitalising heavily on this performance, the gig was filmed for a video package and recorded for a limited edition live CD to be paired with copies of *Medusa* worldwide. The day after the free concert, Annie played at a benefit show at Madison Square Garden.

The video of the first gig, simply titled *In The Park*, was released in June, and amusingly aired on the Disney Channel. On face value it appears to just be the concert, but some interesting interview clips and promotional videos are added on the end. The US version notably contains an extra promo for 'Something So Right'.

For the concert, Annie appears in a red tartan trouser suit which is possibly worn to endear her to the Americans, as she has not sported anything so overtly Scottish for a decade or so. The backing singers are dressed as angels in white nighties-cum-dresses with gold wings. The band are fairly uniform in white with furry bear ears on their heads.

Although this was in promotion for *Medusa* there are only three songs from that album performed in the live set, the rest of the music being drawn from *Diva* and Eurythmics' back catalogue. As well as footage of the performance, other clips interspersed throughout the video include songs taped during a soundcheck. These scenes are grainy with Annie wearing a bizarre black crocheted hat, yet while the band are dressed down the singer still looks smart in a masculine suit.

The concert set is an average performance and Annie communicates well with the audience. The climax of the show is 'Train In Vain' until she rolls on the floor as she once used to with Dave. Sadly, as was the case then, the audience are unable to see anything and the song loses substantial impact. For the finale she sings 'Why' before being whisked into a waiting van to leave. The camera follows Annie backstage where she reviews the performance with Steve Lipson. She gives him a big hug as thanks, but he puts it down to "great team work".

Aside from the concert footage, the video offers a rare interview with Annie about *Medusa* and the American TV promotion. With her mousy bob tucked behind her ears, she resembles a typical country lady in a very smart blazer, waistcoat and shirt, particularly seated in such formal sur- roundings. After explaining that she is scared of live broadcasts, Annie moves on to talk about the promotional videos for 'No More "I Love You's"', 'A Whiter Shade Of Pale' and 'Waiting In Vain'. Making a break from the norm, Annie co-directed the videos with Joe Dyer and the overall release came under the umbrella of La Lennoxa Productions, her own company.

The concept for the promo for 'No More "I Love You's"' was unques- tionably bizarre.

"When it came to the video I really wanted the camera to pan up the dancer's dress which was very beautiful, everything that you would expect, very elegant and clichéd. Revealing a man was probably not what you'd expect at the end of the day!"

Indeed the image of a man dressed as a prima ballerina with exaggerated 'draggy' make-up is baffling, but one that works well in the video. Annie took inspiration from an all-male Russian ballet troupe after seeing their version of *Swan Lake* on television. The men used in the video worked hard at their part, even dancing on points which is a painful discipline tra- ditionally left to women. Annie felt that if she could just leave a camera on the men dancing to the song it would be "like having a fantastic palette of colours to paint with".

Nineteenth century impressionist Toulouse-Lautrec's vivid and sympa- thetic paintings of prostitutes and entertainers stimulated the overall story-line for the video, which was filmed in a magnificent old music hall in need of refurbishment on Ensign Street, London. Annie is dressed as a mistress from a Parisian brothel, as per Toulouse-Lautrec's depictions. She flashes her eyes wildly at the camera while singing to portray, as she describes it, her character transforming from a bourgeois lady to express a more natural animalistic love.

The male dancers mock-seriously assume the role of backing singers to great comical effect as they prance around her, removing her cloak and throwing rose petals over her. Halfway through Annie is seen as a little girl in a nightie listening at the door of a prostitute's room in the style of a silent movie. Back at the music hall the audience are all in costume with masks, depicting such diverse characters as Abraham Lincoln and Little Bo Peep.

The video for 'A Whiter Shade Of Pale' is equally eerie and surreal, set in a circus, another of Toulouse-Lautrec's favoured haunts. A horse canters as the camera pans the recognisable circular background. Annie is dressed in a furry bear suit and looks positively wretched, her ghostly face framed by a lank bob held back with kirby grips. She looks alternately schoolgirlish and expressively distraught as she swings on a trapeze, literally turning a whiter shade of pale as she sings the title line.

Members of the circus troupe practise around her including clowns, a tightrope artist, flamenco dancers, the horse and its trainer. Wearing a mask and bear ears Annie imitates the dancers, before reclaiming her position on the trapeze. To climax, all the acts follow Annie in a line round the ring as the camera misses out several frames to give a jerky image reminiscent of early cinema. Just as this becomes too painful to watch the clip ends as it began, with Annie swinging and the horse galloping gracefully.

The video breaks to more of the interview and Annie talks about her experiences working with Steve Lipson, which allowed her the opportunity to explore her own ground and authenticate her own style, as opposed to the partnership with Dave Stewart. While her points are valid, they have already been exorcised before on *Total Diva* and she looks rather uncomfortable talking about her ex-partner.

The video for 'Waiting In Vain' is a much lighter affair as Annie is dressed as a combination of Minnie Mouse and a French maid in a little black puff-ball dress, platform shoes, thigh high socks and Disneyland ears. Filmed solely in a little bedsit, Annie alternately waits by the sash window and performs household chores, ironing, dusting, sweeping. Using several images of herself, she represents the changing seasons, wearing a pink dress for summer and a blue dress for winter with blossom and snow falling outside the window respectively. Describing the headdress as "A little bit of Disney, a little bit of Toulouse-Lautrec", Annie left the fans no clearer as to her obsession with the cartoon ears.

★ ★ ★

The re-release of *Medusa* with the concert CD is credited as being live from Central Park Summerstage, New York City on September 9, 1995. This must be a simple typo however as Annie was playing at Madison Square on the 9th, having performed at Central Park the day before. The striking thing about the bonus CD is that although it is in promotion for *Medusa* and the one-off gig, which contained covers such as 'No More "I Love You's"' and 'Train In Vain', this selection from the Central Park performance concentrates solely on Eurythmics and *Diva*.

The disc immediately sets the scene with audience applause which grows as the crowd recognises one of their favourites from *Diva*, 'Money Can't Buy It'. The song bounces along cheerily enough, though some of the harmonies are perhaps a little hard to reproduce live on stage, but it is powerful nonetheless with a sparkling keyboard accompaniment. This is followed by another track from her first solo album, 'Legend In My Living Room', in standard format.

A gentle piano leads mysteriously into a chillingly slow, soft version of the Eurythmics classic, 'Who's That Girl?' Both the audience and the band appear to enjoy this number as the applause takes a while to die down, offering Annie a little pause for breath, and an opportunity to say "thank you". Staying with passionate Eurythmics songs, a gentle guitar draws the listener into 'You Have Placed A Chill In My Heart', again to the audience's audible delight. Annie breaks away from the original's mould in the vocal breakdown, pleading "I just want someone to hold", before working the ending into a frenzy.

Returning to *Diva* material, Annie tackles the magnificent 'Little Bird', which works well with the aid of tight backing vocals, assuming the lyrics at the end and allowing Annie to ad lib. Maintaining the high spirits, 'Walking On Broken Glass' receives a rapturous response, but it is the exquisitely moving lament of 'Here Comes The Rain Again' that sparks emotional screams from the ecstatic fans. As Annie draws the climax out to the full, the audience show their appreciation before the familiar plinking of 'Why' is heard. Although flawless, it cannot compete with the last outpouring and Annie bids the contented audience goodnight with a kiss.

The final track on the bonus CD is a studio version of 'Something So Right' with the song's creator, Paul Simon. Annie had appeared with Paul for his annual Children's Health Fund benefit concert at New York's Paramount on September 10, and his presence on the recording was intended to return the favour. Annie sticks to the arrangement she did for *Medusa* while Paul adds gentle backing vocals and guitar work.

Continuing the good work, Annie participated in the T.J. Martell Foundation 20th Anniversary Dinner on September 14, to honour Clive

Davis with the 1995 Humanitarian Award. At the end of the month the third single from *Medusa*, 'Waiting In Vain' was released, peaking at UK number 31 despite the various B-side mixes including 'Train In Vain'.

Keeping the fans and collectors on their toes, Annie's next offering was a cover of 'Mama', originally recorded in 1988 by Björk's former band, Sugarcubes. An ominous opening of almost tribal oriented drums gives way to allow Annie's voice to filter through. Her singing is a genuflection to Björk's inimitable style, although occasional streaks of Lennoxia seep into the choruses. The music is sparse and fairly faithful to the original ode to a loving, plump mother. Visions of Dorothy were probably never far away in Annie's personalised rendition of, "Give me a big mother/ Huge and loving one/ I can crawl upon and cling to/ She's a large woman/ Warm and cuddly."

The first version of the song was contributed to an all-female album called *Ain't Nuthin' But A She Thing*, released in America on October 24, 1995. Friend and colleague Marius de Vries was heavily involved in the soundtrack for the 1998 film remake of cult Sixties TV series, *The Avengers*. While he performed the theme song he also produced much of the material and persuaded Annie to record another version of 'Mama' for this album.

The fans had initially been enthusiastic about *Medusa*, but some 10 months later their loyalty for Annie's covers was fading and the final single from the album, 'Something So Right' stalled at UK number 44 in December 1995.

In February 1996 Annie rounded off her success with *Medusa*, picking up her sixth award for Best Female Artist at the BRIT Awards hosted by Chris Evans. Although this was the year that Jarvis Cocker made his spectacular protest against Michael Jackson's Christ-like posturing, it was the Grammy Awards nine days later that would go down in Annie's personal history. On February 28, she collected the Best Pop Vocal, Female for 'No More "I Love You's" ', celebrating with a performance of 'Train In Vain', before joining Seal in a duet of Marvin Gaye's 'What's Going On?' as a tribute to his posthumous Lifetime Achievement Award.

Annie lost her nomination for Best Pop Album, but was undeterred as she was beaten by Joni Mitchell with *Turbulent Indigo*, finally giving the Scotswoman the opportunity to meet her heroine. "I really feel very honoured to be among so many fantastic female performers here tonight," said Annie, finishing her unscripted acceptance speech with, "This is very nice. It's a little cherry on the cake."

In March 1996, with a hearty pat on the back for her second, quite different solo album, Annie once again bowed out of the limelight. She had reached that point where her children were old enough to understand the concept of fame, and although she had not toured either LPs, she felt that she needed to devote more time to her family. "Something had to give, and it couldn't be my daughters," she reasoned practically. "They'll only be young once. That's why I made the conscious decision that I did, to go inside and close the door.

"I came home and began the process of deconstructing the huge thing that had happened to me in becoming famous. Always, it was double-edged for me – music has been a huge part of my life and of who I am, yet I've never been comfortable with all the things that result from being successful at it."

One of those consequences was scrutiny into her worth as a musician as much as delving into her personal life. Harsh critics suggested that she had resorted to covers as she had run out of natural inspiration. In the same way she retaliated when Eurythmics were criticised for selling-out almost exactly a decade previously, Annie fought for her creative integrity. "I've got more to say than ever – too much, really," she said in retrospect two years later. "I disappeared for one very good reason. Well, two actually. My children."

*   *   *

1996 was a quiet year for Mrs Lennox Fruchtmann who preferred to stay at home, organising her life around the family. Living a very ordinary exis-tence Annie tried to do what any other householder should do for environmental harmony, rather than what a pop star might be pressured into. "I recycle our bottles, paper, etc.," she said simply. "The very least we could have is an intelligent recycling system. In Switzerland and Germany you have bins for bottles everywhere, even in little villages. You don't think twice about it. I'd hoped to see that happening in England. I hate the fact that the word 'recycling' has such an 'alternative' ring about it."

Annie went out of her way to stop one project from emerging. Demi Moore's raunchy film *Striptease* was released this year and as the title sug-gests, Moore's character was that of a stripper. In an attempt to make the audience empathise with her plight of custody of her child against her abusive husband, Moore preferred to dance to 'classier' music, namely that of Annie Lennox and Eurythmics.

Reportedly stunned by the erotic scenes, and no doubt mindful of the rumours such a film might spread in her children's school, Annie appar-ently banned three of her songs from being used in the film. The final cut still maintained a large portion of music by the singer who had herself stripped off on stage a decade before. Clearly Annie's point of view had changed in many respects since the mid-Eighties, not least with the additional responsibility of a family to look after.

Her final musical output of 1996 was 'Step By Step', which she donated to Whitney Houston for her film, *Preacher's Wife*. Annie had originally recorded the song and released it as a B-side to the single 'Precious', but as she and Whitney were both signed to Arista, Clive Davis put the two divas and the song together, with Annie on backing vocals.

★　★　★

After a blissfully peaceful year, 1997 brought a startling wake-up call for the happily married star. Having not spoken to Dave Stewart properly since the break-up of Eurythmics seven years previously, Annie was shocked, as were fans and onlookers, to learn that he had split from Siobhan.

"When you're in a relationship that is going wrong you tend to be more restrained, you can't express yourself very well because you're a bit jumbled up about yourself," Dave said a couple of years later. "You put a lot of weight on what the other person thinks about you because you've chosen to be with them, and if that goes slightly off kilter it's a bit confusing. I'm sure the same thing happened to her . . . " Indeed, Siobhan suffered a nervous breakdown after their decision to part.

Dave was particularly conscious of how his two sons would be affected by the marital separation, especially bearing in mind that his own parents divorced when he was a teenager, causing him immense trauma. Sam and Django went to live with their mother, while Dave moved near to Seven Dials in London's Covent Garden and was able to see them regularly at weekends. Having recently dealt with reports of his confused sexuality, Dave was more adamant than ever that he loved his wife and refused to give up easily.

"I went to therapy for a bit, six weeks in a place called Bowden House to help me sort out my marriage. That didn't work out either," he lamented of everything he tried.

Fans and critics alike have been quick to point the finger of blame, but Dave is the one who ultimately knows what went wrong. He openly expanded on his own personal theory, starting with his relationship with Annie. "Basically, we took eight years to untangle something . . . we were eight years in psychotherapy with journalists . . . we spent eight years talking about our relationship when we were both having relationships with other people who were important to us. It caused a disorientation in my marriage camp – one foot over here and the other foot over there."

Although Annie cited Siobhan as a pillar of strength throughout her tragic experience of stillbirth, it is not surprising that Dave's former lover and musical partner of some 14 years unknowingly caused problems between the Stewarts. It was reciprocal of most of Annie's previous relationships, where boyfriends were compared to Dave. Those close to Siobhan however suggest that it was Dave's infamous hypochondria that was the root of the problem. Either way, Dave found himself aged 45 and alone again. Taking a leaf from Annie's book he immersed himself in work, appearing in a cameo role in the 1997 film *Hackers*.

It was then Uri's turn to sink into his career as he not only launched his own production company, Fragile (formed with Barnaby Thompson), but its debut film *Spiceworld, The Movie* was released in 1998. It featured such unlikely cameos as Stephen Fry and Bob Hoskins alongside pop sensations Spice Girls, the latter group then managed by Simon Fuller.

Annie was willing to come out of the woodwork when something of merit caught her attention. In April 1997 an impressive selection of top international stars were brought together by husband and wife team Sting and Trudie Styler to perform songs for a benefit CD, *Carnival*. Among the diverse artists that joined Annie on this effort to raise money and awareness for the Rainforest Foundation International were Bette Midler, Luciano Pavarotti, Elton John, Madonna, Paul Simon and Tina Turner. Annie contributed her rendition of the Scottish lullaby, 'Dream Angus', accompanied solely by piano, a number which she claimed, "belongs in my bones".

Remaining true to her statements of the previous year and returning to her reclusive family life, Annie kept a low profile for the rest of the year. In August 1997 a Joni Mitchell tribute album was supposedly in the pipeline. Naturally numerous female artists wanted to be involved in the project including Chaka Khan, Sarah McLachlan, Etta James, and k.d. lang, but none more so than Annie. There where also whispers of a Fleetwood Mac tribute album named after their most famous album, *Rumours*. Annie was pencilled in to cover the track 'Songbird', while other artists were to include Sarah McLachlan, No Doubt, Jewel and The Cranberries. Neither of these projects materialised this year with any input from Annie.[50]

In December 1997 Annie submitted 'Angel' as her contribution to the tribute album for Diana, Princess Of Wales whose death in a car crash had occurred in Paris the previous summer. Along with Elton John's touching reworking of 'Candle In The Wind', all proceeds of the singles and albums were donated to the memorial fund in Princess Diana's name.

★　★　★

---

[50] The Joni Mitchell tribute album *A Case Of Joni* was due to be released by Reprise late in 2000, with Annie singing 'Ladies Of The Canyon'.

The biggest impact for Annie during 1997 was the death of The Tourists' former singer and songwriter, Peet Coombes. Annie's last memory of Peet had been at the start of his self-destructive path in Bangkok, 17 years previously. Since then, unable to overcome his drink and drug addictions, Peet's life had tragically followed a downward spiral into poverty and he had ended up living rough, busking for money on the streets of London.

Geoff Hannington from Logo Records had cause to see Peet one last time in the Nineties and was saddened by his state.

"He was a good songwriter, and he could have gone on had the demon drink not got hold of him," says Geoff today. "Many years later I met Peet – there was some money owing to him, which had come to us through PRS [Performing Rights Society]. He was living in some squalor in an Islington squat with his girlfriend. When we went round to see him with the money, his girlfriend said, 'Please don't give it to him, because he'll go straight down to the off-licence.' It was a substantial amount. At the end of the day of course, I couldn't *not* give him the dough, so I did. Not long after that he died."

The cause of Peet's death was sclerosis of the liver as a result of his continual substance abuse. Annie was horrified that someone her age, to whom she had once been so close, had died, but it was hardly a surprise. "Peet's death was tragic, but inevitable," she concluded. "He was so greedy with drink and drugs he once downed a whole bottle of brandy in one go while we were on tour in Bangkok. He did it because he couldn't get any heroin or cocaine. Drug addiction is a sad thing to watch."

Aware that an era had ended and forgetting bad blood, Annie instinctively telephoned the one person who had shared that entire period of her life.

"I was at my house above St. Ann's Bay in Jamaica when somebody shouted, 'Telephone!'" remembers Dave Stewart. "Out of the blue, it was Annie. She was very emotional because Peet Coombes, from our previous group The Tourists, had died. She'd got really upset. We talked for nearly two hours."

With Peet's death having brought about communication for the first time since their split in 1990, Annie and Dave were not sure what the next step should be. Although they appeared to talk comfortably for hours, there was still a lot of unresolved animosity between the pair. Out of politeness they maintained distant, but amiable contact over the rest of the year, but made no plans for anything more substantial.

25

I SAVED THE WORLD TODAY

"I myself had a good career in the Nineties, and I never felt, career-wise, that I needed a revival."

– AL

"It's been so long that we actually forgot how good it was to write songs together and play together."

– DS

As the first phone call was unplanned, so too was the reunion. "I can't take credit, my wife takes credit really," said John Preston, managing director of RCA. "I decided I was going to leave [the company] and Ros, my wife, secretly spoke to Dave and said, 'Would you play at John's leaving do?' He said, 'Yeah I would.'"

Apparently Ros wanted to make sure John had a fitting send-off and pushed Dave a little further, asking whether his former Eurythmics partner would consider joining him for the special occasion. As the pair had recently opened the lines of communication, Dave knew that Annie was enjoying her well-earned break from the spotlight. He suggested that Ros should call her to ask directly, but was not sure what the response would be.

"So she called Annie and Annie initially said, 'I don't know, it's terribly difficult – we haven't played together in nearly eight years and you don't just head out on stage and hope it's going to be alright,'" John recalls of his wife's attempts. Fortunately, as he continues, "A couple of weeks later she called back and Ros realised that actually Annie quite wanted to do it, but wanted to feel that she *had* to do it – and she did feel that she had to do it, which was flattering for me."

As the winter of 1997 turned into 1998, Dave and Annie met up to discuss the set they should play at John's surprise gig. Dave went round to Annie's Highgate home, where they shared some soup, talked, played guitar and sang a little. There they decided that their set should be as simple as possible; an acoustic live performance with Annie's vocals backed by Dave's guitar. Without the pressure of organising a band, this was all the preparation they needed and at the end of January Eurythmics movingly performed eight songs at the party. John was so touched by the gesture and the careful planning by his wife and secretary, that he openly broke down and cried.

Annie, on the other hand, was remarkably calm, commenting on how painless the reunion had been. "Performing has never been easy for me because I so want to achieve my high expectations of the situation, and my nerves always, always get in the way," she said of her anticipation of the gig, but added, "It was funny how automatic it was though, being back up there alongside Dave. Like slipping on a favourite old suit, almost. You wouldn't choose to start wearing it all the time again, and you were pleased to take it off afterwards . . . But it felt very comfortable while you had it on."

Having enjoyed a tentative reformation for this special event, Annie surprised herself and others when she offered Eurythmics' services for another occasion. The singer had often read and been inspired by Ruth Picardie's column in the *Observer*. The journalist, wife and mother of two children, had sadly died of breast cancer the previous September, and Annie, who had been a friend and correspondent of the writer, contacted the family to suggest a benefit concert celebrating what would have been Ruth's 34th birthday.

Ruth's sister, Justine, and brother-in-law, Neill MacColl, loved the idea and ran away with it, planning a concert for May 2, 1998 at the Institute of Contemporary Arts in London for 300 people, with big-name musicians performing acoustically. Needless to say the tickets sold out within 10 minutes. The event also marked the launch of the breast cancer awareness charity they founded in Ruth's memory, The Lavender Trust, which aimed to offer "Help, advice and support for younger women with breast cancer".

The evening was opened by Annie, in a pinstripe suit for old times' sake, singing solo on the cheerful 'Mama' to lift spirits on such a sad day. There was then an interlude during which the MacColl brothers sang 'The First Time Ever I Saw Your Face' and their sister Kirsty performed solo, before introducing the night's *pièce de résistance*, the second Eurythmics reunion. After the rousing applause acknowledging the duo's first public outing since their split, Dave and Annie played a selection of Eurythmics classics: 'This City Never Sleeps', 'You Have Placed A Chill In My Heart', 'There Must Be An Angel (Playing With My Heart)', 'Here

Comes The Rain Again', 'When Tomorrow Comes' and 'The Miracle Of Love'. David Gilmour of Pink Floyd did his best to follow in their footsteps, but the evening was stolen once again by Annie who aptly sang the farewell song, 'Wild Mountain Thyme'.

As Annie had taken a lead role in organising the event, it did not take long for rumours to spread that she would come out of her domestic haven to begin work on a follow-up to *Medusa*. Her record label confirmed that she was indeed working on a new album, the working title of which was *Venus*. It was originally intended for release in June, but that date was moved back to the autumn of 1998.

Arguably more exciting was the wild speculation that Eurythmics would now reform properly. Two weeks after The Lavender Trust benefit, reports were surfacing in Germany stating: "Eurythmics reunited seven years after split. Dave Stewart and Annie Lennox have already secretly been writing new material and are currently preparing for a new album." These hopeful signs were picked up by the English press, particularly as it would have been in keeping with the current trend of Eighties revival bands including Blondie, Culture Club and Madness. But Dave was adamant that whatever they were doing, they were not to be lumped in with this prevalent nostalgia trip.

"I think we're pretty timeless," he retorted. "If you played 'Sweet Dreams', it would sound like a record from now. Nothing we did is stuck in one period. We could play acoustically, or we could play with an orchestra like Ray Charles and sing 'Here Comes The Rain Again'. Let's hear Culture Club try that." Along with fashions and music hailing the Eighties, a film was due out early in 1999 called *Edge Of Seventeen*. It was a coming-of-age comedy about a youth who worshipped Annie Lennox, and simply brimmed with memorabilia from the era.

Throwing her fans off kilter, Annie appeared on her own back in Scotland to participate in the Spring Promenade at Haddo House on May 22. The Haddo House Hall Arts Trust was formed in 1988 to co-ordinate and extend their range of cultural activities, and the weekend of events in May raised money for the foundation. Annie joined other celebrities such as Esther Rantzen as patrons of the Trust, with royal representation by Prince Edward. The family fun included a treasure hunt featuring TV star Anneka Rice and a grand raffle which was billed to be drawn by "Annie Lennox of the Eurythmics". She was also credited in the brochure as being a donor of a silent auction lot.

While Annie was toying with opportunities, her husband was making a name for himself as a producer of worth. His project for 1998 was a romantic and sentimental comedy called *An Ideal Husband*, set at the turn of the 19th century. Starring Rupert Everett, Minnie Driver and Cate Blanchett, the film is an amusing tale of lies, temptations, and secret liaisons.

As the record company was continually being called upon to confirm or deny the rumours of a Eurythmics reformation, they released a press statement in June dismissing the claims. Nevertheless they used the opportunity to promote a planned Eurythmics *Greatest Hits* package due out in November which would contain at least two new songs.

Interestingly the renewed fervour surrounding Dave and Annie as a band and individuals spawned a new type of fan club which relied on modern computer technology. The internet had been developing rapidly since the Eighties, and by the mid-Nineties was considered an integral way of life by many. Chat rooms and mailing lists were a convenient way for like-minded people worldwide to share thoughts and participate in discussions. In this vein Eurythmics fans gathered at one such community, 'Onelist' (now 'e-groups'), and formed several mailing lists devoted to their heroes.

One of the most popular and informed websites is 'Eurythmistan', created and maintained by super-fan Vibber, which earned itself a link on the official site when it was set up the following year. Vibber was personally congratulated by Dave, who joked that he often visited Eurythmistan to find out the details of his own schedule.

Dave himself was no stranger to the internet, publicising his numerous projects online. Over the summer he teamed up with Microsoft's founder, Paul Allen, in a scheme to redevelop the derelict St. Paul's Hospital in Covent Garden, into an "Artists' Village"; a multi-use complex for international film and music professionals incorporating studios, offices, restaurants, and screening rooms, while retaining sensitivity to the needs of the local area.

Dave was also heavily committed to many musical ventures including composing film soundtracks for *Cookie's Fortune* and *Nails*, and writing and producing for artists as diverse as Natalie Imbruglia, Brian Eno and Sinéad O'Connor. His own material was not to be passed by – his second album as a solo artist was called *Sly Fi* and was initially released exclusively on the internet on September 15 in a deal with N2K Encoded Music, making its way into the shops a few weeks later. The album's online launch coincided with that of a new website which became the venue for a string of events, among them a 24 hour live 'web cast' from Dave's studio.

Annie's undertaking for the rest of 1998 was a vocal pledge to aid awareness and raise funds to free Tibet from Chinese rule. She financed a self-directed 30-minute documentary film of her interview with Palden

Gyatso, a Tibetan monk who was tortured and imprisoned in China. His plight is one of the many cases that proves the power of organisations like Amnesty International, and the film was used around the world.

"In 1984 I was adopted as a prisoner by Amnesty International and they started a letter-writing campaign," Gyatso told Annie. "The Chinese began to treat us very differently, and even during the interrogation they were much more gentle." Annie took the opportunity to praise the organisation, "Which really goes to prove that if (people) join campaigns like Amnesty International there can be results."

After hearing the exiled Dalai Lama speak in Alexandra Palace, North London in November 1996, Annie had slowly become involved in the Free Tibet campaign. "As a result of that, I ended up going to see him personally in Dharamsala to ask about ways in which I could help support the cause," explained Annie to the *Sunday Times* magazine. "My first instinct was to embark on a series of charity concerts to raise both money and awareness, but that would have taken up a whole year of my life at a time when I wanted to be here, taking my kids to school, picking them up again, putting them to bed at night. So when that idea didn't work, I had to look for other ways in which to be useful. And though I've been active at a kind of underground level, not using my face overtly, I've known that there had to be a way in which I could make a bigger contribution."

The opportunity for greater involvement was presented by Alison Reynolds of the Free Tibet campaign. Alison asked Annie if she would like to meet Sonam Deckyi, the mother of musician Ngawang Choephel who had been sentenced to 18 years in prison in 1996 on doubtful espionage charges.

Annie was initially sceptical about her use to the traumatised family, but over time an idea formulated in her mind to make the most of the publicity opportunity without promoting herself as a martyr or trivialising the cause. "I want to help, not hinder, the Tibetan cause through my being seen to be involved with it," she considered. "And I know that there's a danger some people will think I'm just another bored celebrity dabbling in a trendy cause. Ultimately, though, you have to stop prevaricating and act as you see fit. Feeling as strongly as I do about this, there's no option but for me to raise my hand and be counted."

At the end of the year, as the Lennox Fruchtmanns prepared to enjoy a safe and peaceful Christmas, Annie launched herself into promoting Choephel's cause. Personally she delivered a petition to the Chinese Embassy in London in support of the prisoner's release, signed by others including Paul McCartney, David Bowie and Robbie Williams. Their case insisted Choephel had merely been recording local music and dance rather than taping political secrets. To her frustration, the embassy officials threw the document in the rubbish bin in front of her. But like other dedicated helpers, Annie was not defeated and continued her hard work.

Early in 1999 she joined a host of celebrities including actors Richard Gere and Goldie Hawn, and cultural satirist Mark Thomas, to take part in a public reading at Westminster Central Hall to mark the 40th anniversary of the Tibetan uprising against Chinese rule.

Interestingly, Annie did not support causes closer to home as she remained noticeably absent from the 1998 campaign for Scottish Independence. "I see myself as British rather than Scottish. The more you travel, the less the differences are. They just shrink," she said, a view which pleased her English fans, but saddened nationalists who felt she should be proud of her Scottish heritage.

"I look back on my past with misgivings," she had justified. "I know people who are quite rooted in their home town, and they never seem to experience any sense of isolation from the people and circumstances around them. Sometimes I'm envious of that, because I never felt, in my heart of hearts, that I could fit in somehow." This attitude illustrates why she has not directly helped organisations like her old school, as is a popular gesture from many pop stars. Music teacher Neil Meldrum confirms the institution's general opinion, "I've never asked her because I've always thought that if she wanted to keep up contact then she would come and make the move. But she never has and so we have respected her privacy."

Ironically, Annie inadvertently assisted the school financially, as head teacher John Murray tells, "A few years ago we were raising money for the school library and there was a raffle and someone came up with Annie Lennox's text book with her name in it. So this became one of the sought-after prizes in the raffle."

★   ★   ★

As promised by the record company in July 1998, Dave and Annie did indeed meet up with the intention of recording one or two new songs for inclusion on another greatest hits package. Encouraged by the response they had received at the two one-off gigs earlier in the year, the pair discovered they still worked well together and were surprised when they realised that they had in fact written four or five songs in just a few days. "It's been so long that we actually forgot how good it was to write songs together and play together," said Dave sweetly. "We had a great time playing the songs. It's a great feeling."

They had certainly not intended to create anything as drastic as a new album, but as the quantity of new material grew, it rather took them by surprise. Annie admitted, "After we'd written about six or seven songs, we thought, 'Are we making an album?' We didn't tell the record company what we were doing because we didn't want to make it a big issue." Even so, the secretive pair could not deny rumours forever, as costs were mounting and those accountable at Arista were getting curious.

As 1998 drew to a close Arista were informed that Dave and Annie were due to be presented with the Outstanding Contribution To Music award at the following year's BRITs. When the label approached Eurythmics to perform together for the third time, they were forced to own up to an official reformation.

Celebrating her 44th birthday at Christmas 1998, Annie launched into the final year of the millennium, happy in the security of both her family and exciting work prospects ahead.

The BRIT Awards were undoubtedly a highlight of 1999, if not her career as a whole. On February 16, she joined Dave on stage to receive their 11th combined award, the most won by members of a group. Basking in the prestige of being honoured with the once-in-a-lifetime accolade, Annie and Dave graciously accepted the statuette, which was presented by Stevie Wonder.[51]

Stevie had flown in especially from America for the night's appearance. "It was just the fact that Annie and David are really good friends and I just enjoyed the honour of having a chance to see them again and do this," he said humbly. The audience were unaware of his plans and rose to their feet in appreciation as he walked out to present the award to the duo, whom he described as "wonderful people". Exercising her recently found political voice, Annie said in her acceptance speech, "I would just like to say that music has given us the opportunity to communicate with everybody in the world, no matter what race, culture or creed, and this is why we would like you to keep standing and show your respect for the families of Stephen Lawrence and Michael Menson.[52]

"You have to use your intelligence. You can't just let the opportunity slip by you. If you think you can affect some changes, great. If you think you're going to do some damage – shut up."

Proclaiming that, "We're not a revival band, we're a survival band", Eurythmics launched into a selection of their best known songs. They performed 'Sweet Dreams (Are Made Of This)' before being joined for

---

[51] The Outstanding Contribution To Music award lost its credibility somewhat the following year when it went to Spice Girls who had been around for only six years, producing two formulaic albums in that time.
[52] Lawrence and Menson were both recent casualties of racism in London.

'There Must Be An Angel' by Stevie who stayed on to play piano accompaniment for 'Here Comes The Rain Again'. Annie marked the reunion by adopting a short auburn crop, and clad in designer Union Jack outfits in appreciation of the patriotism of the ceremony, Eurythmics continued with a five-song acoustic medley.

After the event Annie commented to BBC Radio 1, "What really blows my mind is the fact that we performed with Stevie – that's more important to me than any award." To which Stevie passionately reciprocated with, "[They are] people who not only have a feeling about music but about life, and we are becoming, in a very fast way, very good friends and I know that these kind of relationships last for a lifetime."

The award ceremony seemed a suitable time for Eurythmics to reveal their special announcement. Said Dave, "Annie and I had been playing together a little bit in these secret little gigs and we'd also started writing together. [The BRITs] came at a very natural opportune time, y'know – if they'd asked us to appear two years ago we probably would have both said, 'No'."

As he and Annie admitted they were heavily involved in the throes of a new project together, speculation rose as to the motives behind burying the hatchet, and the media were far from kind. Critics suggested that one or both were in need of a cash injection to maintain their lifestyle, but as they were cautiously estimated by *Q* magazine as having an amassed wealth of some $69 million this view did not seem to hold much weight. Some said that neither artist had been successful on his or her own and so needed to join forces to enter the charts. In Dave's case this cut a little close to the bone, but for Annie the accusation was far from fair. "I myself had a good career in the Nineties, and I never felt, career-wise, that I needed a revival," she protested. "I never even toured with *Medusa* and *Diva*, and they were stunningly successful records in a commercial sense."

She continued, jumping to defend her musical integrity: "I want to live an authentic life, true to my own beliefs. The legitimacy of the album is in the bond of creativity between Dave and me." Dave backed her up, insisting that it was probably the most natural recording session they had ever undertaken, relying on their inexplicable, almost psychic method of writing and recording.

By February Eurythmics had returned to The Church to record properly and Annie offered a frank explanation for the smoothness of the pair's altered relationship in the recording studio. "I'm less volatile. Our relationship is less angst-ridden. I don't need to burden Dave with my anxieties, and we don't go down those roads which inevitably lead to bad-mouthing and upsetting each other."

They enlisted the services of Andy Wright, who states that the majority of the album was recorded by just Dave, Annie, himself, and their engineer Nick Addison. Annie arranged the string parts on a keyboard, before printing out the scores for an orchestrator, who arranged and recorded them with real instruments.

One difference about the songs was that they were all credited to Lennox/Stewart, whereas previously they always alternated their names track by track. While Annie perhaps aimed to show that she was more than just the face and voice of Eurythmics, the alphabetical order did not jeopardise their fine balancing act. In fact the friends had rekindled their bond to the extent that in April 1999 Dave, Annie and their respective families were reported to be sailing around Spain's Balearic Islands on a chartered ship to "capture the right vibes" for their album.

Rejuvenated and raring to go after their trip, Eurythmics were proud to be Capital Radio's voters' choice at the 1999 concert in Hyde Park on July 4. Party In The Park, now an annual event held in aid of The Prince's Trust, boasted numerous stars old and new, including Boyzone, Corrs, Ricky Martin, Blondie, Shania Twain and Madness. This was the first time that Dave and Annie had performed together in public since their reunion announcement and predictably they found themselves under close scrutiny. They played four songs in front of the crowd of 100,000, including two premières from their forthcoming album.

Although it was summer, the heavens opened as ex-Spice Girl Geri Halliwell performed her solo hit 'Look At Me'. When Eurythmics came on Annie joked, "I'll see if I can keep the rain away", before launching into a reworked version of 'Sweet Dreams (Are Made Of This)'. Wearing army combats Annie and Dave introduced what was to become their look for the foreseeable future, topped off with ever-present sunglasses. They then introduced a new song, 'I Want It All', a rousing number not dissimilar to 'I Need A Man', before returning to the familiarity of 'There Must Be An Angel (Playing With My Heart)'. The final number of the set was 'Peace Is Just A Word', an emotive anthem which was to become the lead single from the album. Keeping up with modern technology, the day's celebrations were 'cyber-cast' on the internet as well as the usual broadcasts on Capital Radio and recording for TV.

While this was the debut performance of the eagerly awaited reunion songs, the following day's concert acted as a more appropriate launch. Back-tracking on her comments made to Phil Sutcliffe in 1992 which denounced pop stars expending their celebrity for charity, Annie and Dave wanted their ninth studio album, aptly entitled *Peace*, to be more meaningful. They approached both Amnesty International and Greenpeace, with whom they had both worked as individuals, and asked how best they could help. The phenomenal results were announced in a poignant setting.

The original Greenpeace campaign vessel, Rainbow Warrior, had been blown up in New Zealand on its way to protest against nuclear testing in the Pacific, but its replacement, launched in 1989, had been successful in assisting the implementation of a worldwide ban on such experiments. Rainbow Warrior II was then relocated from Norway to Butler's Wharf on the River Thames, London, to provide a venue for the special concert held on July 5, 1999 in front of fans and journalists alike.

The performance was slightly delayed waiting for the backing singers whose taxi driver had unfortunately taken them to the wrong pier, but eventually Annie and Dave boarded the ship to treat the crowds to songs from the new album and details of their forthcoming tour that autumn. Annie declared, "We are so proud to be here – this is a very noble boat," before explaining that all proceeds from the album and tour for *Peace* would be divided equally between Greenpeace and Amnesty International. Outlining their additional efforts to aid the charities, Annie said later, "We want to strengthen the membership of the organisations, because it's only with strong membership that they can really be effective. So we're trying to do that, trying to raise the profile. It was a kind of campaigning run, as well as a concert tour."

The group then performed a set of five songs comprising classics alongside the new numbers, 'Beautiful Child' and 'Peace Is Just A Word'. That evening Annie was seen on the television show *Entertainment Tonight* saying, "What really thrills me about it is the fact that we are so privileged, and we so often feel that we have no power, but actually, if we join organisations like this, we can affect people from all around the globe, and I feel that is so incredibly potent."

Having made their staggering pledges public, the following week Dave and Annie flew to the Isle of Capri to visit Clive Davis and play him the new album. The record label boss was just as enthusiastic as his reformed Eighties band, but they were all keen not to be compared to other, variably successful reunions of recent years. Dave was quick to say, "The last thing we wanted to do was jump aboard some fashionable bandwagon. There's been no attempt to deliberately modernise our sound by using just a drum machine and a Ping-Pong ball. It's got all the classic elements of our best work together. I don't think anyone who liked Eurythmics will be let down." To which Annie firmly stated, "On the contrary, it's the best record we've ever made."

★   ★   ★

On the surface, the first album release in a decade comes across as a little too 'samey', soft and even righteous. Delve a little deeper and there, amongst the overbearing sound of electronics thrust abruptly against orchestras, are some real gems. 'I Saved The World Today' is beautifully crafted, 'Anything But Strong' and 'My True Love' are deeply personal, 'Lifted' is indeed uplifting and 'I Want It All' is pure, unadulterated fun. *Peace* may sound bland on the first hearing, but is increasingly intriguing on repeated playing.

'17 Again' opens the set with a gentle introduction of growing synths and guitar which is instantly recognisable as Eurythmics. In this blatant autobiography Annie laments the couple's early years, blindly stumbling through the abrasive world of fame with their own individual crosses to bear. With phrases like "Who couldn't be together and who could not be apart" and "My bleeding heart" it appears that Annie is once again inviting scrutiny of her private life.

Wandering interest is recaptured with a musical change on "Hey hey, I'm a million miles away", leading into an outright bitch about life in the celebrity circuit. The song builds to an emotional ending of synths, guitars and multi-tracked vocals. As a cute close, Annie sings the famous lines from 'Sweet Dreams (Are Made Of This)' reminding listeners of their past glory, but admits that sweet dreams are made of "anything that gets you in the scene".

The clarity offered in the next track, 'I Saved The World Today', is refreshing as a muted horn line, oboe and elegant strings draw the listener in. Pacifying percussion lends a persistent beat, pushing the song forward. Annie's vocals are tender as she deals with powerful lyrics examining global injustice inflicting some countries with war and famine while allowing others to escape. Halfway through the horn returns for an exquisitely intricate solo accompanied by swooping strings. Annie softly and engagingly harmonises in layers with herself as the track draws to a close, mirroring the introduction. "It was the first thing she sang and she wasn't really warmed up at all – but her first performance was magical," recalls Andy Wright. Amply achieving its goal, the song is peaceful and pleasing, with an ironic feel-good factor.

Shattering the accord of the last number, Dave and Annie joyfully combine electronics and echoed vocals to produce a raw rock feel on 'Power To The Meek'. Catchy, but not necessarily congenial, Annie railroads through the song including particularly abrasive "woo hoo"s over Dave's psychedelic guitar solo. It is interesting to note that the lyrics show Annie's development through her past trauma and torment to the calm state of girl power when she can confidently laugh, "I'm just a girl with my head screwed on".

'Beautiful Child' was intended as a reassuring lullaby for Annie's children, and her maternal development comes across in the increased maturity of her voice. Starting with a gentle acoustic guitar introduction, the track builds up to a relaxed pace. With the benefit of hindsight Annie urges her offspring to believe that the world is a pleasant place, yet at the same time offers the same unconditional love and support she received from her parents. Annie's cloying tenderness aside, interest is aroused with a shift of key provoking an edgy feeling, but is sadly lost as the music becomes swamped by its own making.

A wall of escalating electronic sound almost suffocates the poignant first verse of 'Anything But Strong', but as Annie branches out into the chorus, the music sharpens and pleasantly swings around her soaring vocals. Dancing delightfully back and forth, this beautiful number conceals a darker secret. As 'Anything But Strong' poetically dissects a partnership to demonstrate how the lovers have drifted apart, it is hard not to speculate about possible cracks in Annie's own marriage at this time, "But wanting is not the same thing as needing . . . And loving is so different to keeping".

As the story continues the couple are described as weary, and rather than forcing a stale relationship to continue, Annie suggests that they should part, regain their inner strength and reassess their own goals, asking the potent question "Where do you belong?" This puissant message is sadly submerged on such a mild album, but remove it from the deluge and reap the rewards.

Noting the intensely personal lyrics, Annie admitted of the next track, "The song 'Peace Is Just A Word' is not about Kosovo but about inner peace. Which is something I have a hard time reaching because I become so terrified and overwhelmed by all sorts of things." She barely whispers her impassioned vocal over a warped keyboard blanket for the first minute and a half.

The minimalist instrumentation is then augmented with Dave's strumming electric guitar and 'Peace Is Just A Word' swiftly becomes anthemic in its persistence. Undoubtedly rousing in live performances, this long and cluttered song, surprisingly fails to marry an orchestra of strings and brass with Eurythmics' electronics. However, the all-consuming crazed feeling of the music is rather appropriate, as the song sums up the times when Annie has felt choked by the outside world during her lowest depressions.

The brass and string sections added a certain grandeur to the song. Dave Whitson, who by coincidence had been in the same year as Ann at the Royal Academy of Music and married her friend Norma, played trombone on these sessions. "I remember Dave was there, just sitting in. He was filming the session on a little hand-held video recorder. It was just for his personal use, but otherwise he sat back and let the musical director take charge."

Moving through the album, 'I've Tried Everything' once again utilises treated keyboards and Annie's soft harmonies, but it is an uninspiring track. Slow and rather simplistic, all the themes and sounds have been explored with more proficiency on other tracks, leaving this offering as somewhat superfluous.

Instantly instilling the fight and spite of former Eurythmics tracks, 'I Want It All' superbly combines an aggressive, pushy number with a more mature attitude, not dissimilar in style to the Queen song of the same name. Opening simply with a forceful guitar, Annie's trademark "hey hey" and solid drumming, the track is heightened by mechanical, echoing backing vocals. The music breaks to swirl psychedelically around the "yeah yeah"s before Annie is able to clear her head and rejuvenate her chant of "I don't know what it is/ But I want it now". These occasional changes in direction keep the song relevant to the overall album, but the snap back to the rock thrashing is ultimately satisfying for those tiring of the urbanity thus far.

Annie had divulged many years before that she enjoys a harder sound occasionally. "Sometimes I think I'd like to make the most frenzied angry club music you'd ever heard – what I think heavy metal could be but never is. Heavy metal is very clichéd and sexist, with a chauvinistic swagger. Well I would like to have a chauvinistic swagger too. I think I could do it better than any of 'em!" Proving her point, here she is on fine form, obviously enjoying herself. Reaching a searing climax, the singer clearly relishes the stunning breathy end.

'My True Love' is another possible indication that the Lennox-Fruchtmann marriage was in trouble as it appears Annie mourns the loss of her partner. The lyrics again expose the pain in the relationship, "He's sorry for it all/ And for the hurt we've done". Both 'My True Love' and 'Anything But Strong' contain phrases berating the couple for not learning from their previous mistakes, but it is painfully obvious in these numbers that the damage is beyond repair; "Where is your hope?/ It's all gone up in smoke" and "All the broken pieces/ that cannot be picked up".

As Annie emotes such open pain and sorrow, it is too easy to feel a little intrusive. Dave remains respectfully in the background with subtle guitar work and delicate pizzicato, while the percussion quietly notes the passing of time, allowing Annie free rein to grieve.

Lifting the mood with a confusing introduction of tinkling piano, electric guitar and chords borrowing heavily from the Sixties, 'Forever' is an odd mixture of influences. The mellow brass, striking strings and vocal style are ultimately rooted in The Beatles' *Sgt. Pepper*. Annie bravely attempts to come to terms with losing an old friend 'forever', who has since been identified as Peet Coombes, but her voice belies the strain. This strong and interesting track is not necessarily indicative of Eurythmics, but is stimulating nonetheless.

'Lifted', an unusually moody ending to the album, opens sedately with guitar, drums and synthesised strings. Annie is multi-tracked, offering a promise of hope for her loved ones, whether she is bidding a final farewell to her one true love, or advising her young children on their future. The simile of the freedom of a bird in flight is notably adapted from her own emancipation in 'Little Bird' from *Diva*. 'Lifted' is well-paced, providing renewed interest throughout with pauses, a delicate guitar solo, unusual vocal layering and a fluttering flute solo, all building to a powerful close. With the song's final verse Annie utters a prayer and a proclamation, "Now you can find peace at last."

★   ★   ★

Before commencing on the first Eurythmics tour in almost 10 years, Dave and Annie finished some individual projects. Dave continued his involvement with Paul Allen and set about launching a new television channel dubbed Innergy, aimed to tap into the growing volume of professional British adults seeking a more spiritual dimension to their lives.[53]

This was not Dave's only foray onto the screen. His other project was his directorial debut for the film *Honest*, starring three members of the phenomenally successful girl group, All Saints. "It's about two people who shouldn't be together, but whose relationship somehow works well," he described of the movie's plot. When it was posed to him that this sounded reminiscent of his on-going partnership with Annie, he responded, "You can't help but write from your own personal experiences." The lady in question was present at the film completion party on September 8, and the movie was to be launched at the Cannes film festival the following May.

Annie meanwhile had also been busy, recording her part on The Rolling Stones' classic 'It's Only Rock'n'Roll' in aid of the charity, Children's Promise, which helps children in need. The track featured snippets of vocals from artists as diverse as Natalie Imbruglia, James Brown, Goldie, Robin Williams, John Lee Hooker, Spice Girls, Lionel Richie, Ozzy Ozbourne and Eric Idle. The single was produced by the BBC in the rousing singalong style of 'Do They Know It's Christmas?' and released in time for Christmas 1999 with four tracks; three mixes of the song and an uplifting video.

---

[53] This channel did not see the light of day until UPCtv took up the option in spring 2000.

To support their own album, Eurythmics undertook a short, 17-date world tour, commencing in Cologne on September 18, and moving on to France, Italy, the US, Australia, Sweden and Denmark, before closing in their native UK in December. The Peace Tour was far from comprehensive, and American fans in particular were frustrated to learn that there were only two gigs on either side of their enormous country, one in Los Angeles and the other in New York City, while Canada was bypassed completely. The fans rallied together and put pressure on Simon Fuller, whose services Annie had retained from her solo days. Hopes were up for extra dates to be added, but remarkably the only additional concerts were in Europe, which had already received the lion's share.

Although Eurythmics were aware of this imbalance they felt that they had to put their family concerns first. The lack of additional dates further afield came ostensibly from Annie, who had not toured for either of her solo albums due to her maternal ties. The tour was specifically designed in three blocks, Europe, America and Australia, so she could spend sufficient time with Lola and Tali. Both Dave's and Annie's children accompanied them on the road, quickly building on their existing friendships. Fans reported seeing the two boys and two girls running around together in high spirits backstage – the Lennox lasses not bearing as strong a resemblance to their mother as the Stewart lads to their father.

Feeling the pressures of age, the ever-inquisitive Annie sought advice on maintaining her health while on tour from an Indian practitioner. "He takes blood samples, questions you about your lifestyle and, basically, tells you what it is that you have to do. For me, that's meant accepting this really rigorous regime which excludes all tea, coffee, sugar, alcohol and wheat. Oh, and dairy products too," she explained. "As a result, I do find that I'm calmer, less hyper and edgy, than before. We all of us have to take on board the reality that our bodies change as we enter our forties. No longer can you neglect or abuse them without experiencing a downside."

This extra care of her well-being was also to combat the public demand for Annie's time. "Would you believe, I've just had my third letter from the Vatican?" she told journalist Alan Jackson in disbelief. "So I've found myself making breakfast for the girls and deciding, 'No, I don't think I'll have time to meet the Pope this week!' What I came to realise is that, I can't be in a thousand places at once. And anyway, the whole point of retreating in the first place – other than to create some space in which to deconstruct for myself all the changes that fame wreaked upon me – was to be there for Uri and the girls. They have been the important ones in all this."

★   ★   ★

Between the family emphasis and the generous donations to charity, the Peace Tour seemed to be about trying to please everyone. At the start of the trip Dave reiterated their pledge, "We're giving all the tour profits and all the merchandising and everything connected with the tour to the two organisations.[54] We're also going to try and get a million people to join, so hopefully it will mean a lot." On top of that, Dave and Annie both used the stage to convey their ambition, persuading the audience members to each make a personal contribution of at least £10 to Greenpeace and Amnesty International over the internet. Dave's eagerness to keep up with modern technology meant that he oversaw the creation of a website specifically for the album, tour and charitable causes, under the simple address of www.peacetour.net.

"As we look to the millennium and beyond, more and more people are questioning what the 21st century will hold for them," began the message. "Many of us are looking for a positive way where we can act and join together, to create a more peaceful future. A future where we strive to work more in harmony with each other and the planet . . . not in opposition . . . To achieve this, for the first time we have brought together two of the world's most globally influential organisations – Greenpeace and Amnesty International, defenders of the environment and human rights, who offer solutions for the future. Together they embrace the needs of mankind and the environment." They continued to expound on a "why bother – what's the point syndrome" in the tour brochure, hammering home once more, "All you have to do is become a member. There could be nothing more rewarding."

Musically the show consisted of a mixture of new songs from *Peace*, old friends such as 'Missionary Man', 'There Must Be An Angel (Playing With My Heart)' and 'Sweet Dreams (Are Made Of This)', and even a few tracks from *Diva*. Dave was generally perceived as being extremely gracious to let Annie perform her solo material, but the lyrics from *Greetings From The Gutter* would have been inappropriate for her to sing. One astute e-groups contributor amusingly pointed out that while the album begins on the notes B, A and D, the melody was changed for the live version of '17 Again' to B, C# and A, literally proving that the 'bad' thing had truly gone away.

Staying with the green theme for the set and outfits Eurythmics, including their accumulated backing band, wore the camouflage gear first seen in July. The combats did not appeal to many fans and the ever-present

[54] The contribution was considerable as the tour raised over £1 million to be shared between Greenpeace and Amnesty International.

381

sunglasses seemed to do little else than annoy everyone, particularly when the couple explained the reason they had embellished each other's names on the side was because they "love each other madly".

While they were touring, the first single taken from the album, 'I Saved The World Today', charted at number 11 in the UK, just failing to break the Top 10. "It's a beautiful song, but it contains something dark at the centre," said Annie. The video featured Dave and Annie in their now commonplace army fatigues, performing in front of a full orchestra dressed in military uniform. The pair shake hands with what appear to be world leaders, signifying that a peace treaty has been reached, but at the end of the film Annie knocks a bottle of ink over the document, rendering it null and void. As Dave gently touches her arm to alert her, the two stare up from their seats with blank resignation.

In an effort to appease the disappointed American fans, Eurythmics appeared on a number of US television shows including the *Saturday Night Live 25th Anniversary Special* on September 26. Two days later they taped their edition of VH1's regular series, *Storytellers*. Dave and Annie gave an intimate performance in a New York studio, elaborating on the stories behind the songs for the audience. While Dave joked that Annie was nervous because she did not know what stories he might let slip, the Scots-woman herself admitted, "This is my sort-of-nightmare . . . that I'm stand-ing on the stage and I have to talk to people. Actually, I like to communicate through singing rather than talking."

Eurythmics chose a wide selection of songs including 'Who's That Girl?', 'Missionary Man', 'Sweet Dreams (Are Made Of This)', 'Sisters Are Doin' It For Themselves', 'Why', 'Here Comes The Rain Again' and a medley of 'I Love You Like A Ball And Chain' and 'Would I Lie To You?' although the show that was aired on December 12 was heavily edited. This gave rise to rumours that the full concert would be released on CD, but the only album to appear was a compilation from various artists who have appeared on the programme, including Eurythmics' 'Here Comes The Rain Again' in aid of City of Hope, a research and treatment centre for cancer and other fatal diseases.

On September 30, still much in demand, the couple appeared on *Late Night With David Letterman*, after which they played eight songs at an Arista-organised preview for *Peace* at New York's Kit Kat Club.

Continuing the charitable work, Dave and Annie took time out from their world tour to appear at Wembley for NetAid on October 9, 1999. Along the lines of Live Aid before it, NetAid is a long-term organisation aimed at building an online community dedicated to providing basic needs for the world's poorest citizens: food, shelter, legal protection, human rights and health care. The music side of NetAid comprised three concerts to be held in London, New York and Geneva, championing the cancellation of Third World debt.

Eurythmics opened the London concert, followed by Live Aid veterans George Michael and David Bowie. Maintaining their visual statement in army fatigues, Dave and Annie performed four songs from their regular repertoire. The unusual gimmick about this charity event was that it was broadcast live over the internet, with notable world figures Tony Blair, Bill Clinton and Nelson Mandela being among the first to log on.

Although up to one billion people plugged in globally to witness the ambitious experiment, the organisation has since been forced to admit defeat as the event failed to make any money. Two of the three concerts made a loss, on-line donations amounted to only £625,000, and even substantial contributions from two of the key sponsors (some £7.5 million) failed to make the final figure more than a fraction of the £75 million Sir Bob Geldof raised 15 years earlier. A spokeswoman for NetAid shrugged off the accusations, stating, "It was never about making money. It was about raising awareness of poverty."

★   ★   ★

Picking up the pieces of their tour Eurythmics continued through Europe, adding The Tourists' hit 'I Only Want To Be With You' for the Zurich concert. On October 14, 1999 they held a press conference in Paris, their first since the disastrous fiasco announcing *We Too Are One*, and performed an acoustic set before their next gig the following day which was broadcast over the internet.

Peace was finally released worldwide on October 19, 1999, emerging in Europe a few days earlier, and producing the obligatory collector's item as the Japanese version included a bonus track of 'Beautiful Child' recorded live at The Church. The package was completed by promotional videos and a cover sleeve designed by the world famous photographer, Richard Avedon. In his stylish photographs, Avedon portrays Dave and Annie in pure white, without make-up or covering. Their look is simple, uncluttered and clean.

The media reviews were generally favourable with Q offering, "*Peace* may lack some of the old neurotic edge, but it's a consistently strong set that can be bought with confidence." Some writers noted the absence of the biting commentary once synonymous with Eurythmics. "Their first new music in 10 years is confident and classy, and Annie Lennox's voice is untouched by time," reported Sonic Net – but, "play *Peace* next to *Be Yourself Tonight* or *Savage*, though, and it's painfully apparent that something is missing. Eurythmics' old playfulness and wit, their willingness to shock and their creative abrasion are all gone."

Nevertheless the album achieved commercial success, reaching number four in the British charts and 25 in America, shortly being certified gold. Dave, who had not seen sales as good as his counterpart when the two split, remained nervous and reportedly visited local record shops to check the figures.

Progressing on to America, the dynamic duo gave a concert in Los Angeles and appeared on the *Tonight Show* and *Good Morning America*. Their second and final concert in the USA was at New York's Madison Square Garden on November 9, and a slot on the *Rosie O'Donnell Show* two days later before moving on to Australia.

The tour culminated in England and the 10 musicians including a trio of backing singers had bonded well, particularly when they gathered in close quarters around the piano for an intimate medley. Annie had not lost her touch, captivating her audience by roaming the stage and pounding the floor with her fist. The final gig at Docklands on December 6 was filmed for television, first to be shown on ITV2 and then re-broadcast on ITV on Boxing Day, with an audio recording for BBC Radio 2.

Continuing their successful internet connections, at the end of the tour Eurythmics auctioned off some items including a signed Gibson guitar, two signed T-shirts and Annie's hand-written lyrics to 'Angel' at the online site eBay. Once again proceeds went to Greenpeace and Amnesty International. Rounding off the promotion for *Peace*, Eurythmics performed on ITV's *Friday Night's All Wright* on December 17.

26

REVIVAL

"I'm not concerned with longevity. Making music is my business. Nothing else."
— AL

To round off the century Annie and Dave appeared on Britain's *National Lottery* on December 31, shown on BBC1. There they indicated their unhappiness about not being allowed to play live as Dave pointedly continued to strum his guitar long after the music had finished. Far more impressive was their featured spot at the British millennium celebrations held in Greenwich at the London Royal Observatory. Celebrities included other Eighties survivors Simply Red and Pet Shop Boys, Spice Girls and ex-Royal Academy of Music student Lesley Garrett. Tickets for the concert, which kicked off at 9.00 p.m. were approximately £50 each, and the turnout was excellent in anticipation of a charged night.

Eurythmics' spot took place at the Millennium Dome, and they wore silver jackets over their ubiquitous green trouser suits for extra warmth on the bitterly cold night, yet retained their sunglasses even at midnight. 'Sweet Dreams (Are Made Of This)' opened the set as an acoustic version which was later stunningly augmented by the London Symphony Orchestra with the traditional synth lines played by real strings. Changing tack slightly and bowing to the austere surroundings, Annie and Dave then faithfully covered David Bowie's 1973 hit 'Life On Mars'. 'Miracle Of Love' and 'I Saved The World Today' topped off their last performance of the millennium.

Two acts occurred between theirs and the final countdown at midnight, but then all the star performers returned to the stage. Annie took charge of the microphone, leading the cast and audience in an unforgettable rendition of 'Auld Lang Syne' before ecstatically shouting "congratulations" to everyone at the dawn of a new age.

As she grasped the mic, observant fans noticed an absence of her wedding ring. Combining it with analysis of the lyrics on *Peace*, uneasy questions were posed about the state of the 45-year-old Eurythmics frontwoman's marriage.

On the romantic front, Dave had settled with a new girlfriend since his split with Siobhan three years previously. His new partner was a French photographer called Anoushka Fisz. Curiously her name in Russian translates as 'Little Ann', but the comparisons to Dave's former lover end there, as Anoushka is younger with long, strawberry blonde hair.

Dave was happy to tell the world about his new relationship – as he readily pointed out, he didn't survive well on his own. Looking back over his early marriage to Pam Wilkinson, his four years with Annie Lennox, his nine year relationship and marriage to Siobhan Fahey, it was not surprising therefore when he admitted to needing close company and that he and Anoushka were expecting a child in the spring, his third.

★ ★ ★

Capitalising on Eurythmics fever in Britain after their success with *Peace*, 'I Saved The World Today' and their recent appearance on New Year's Eve, BBC1 aired a documentary called *17 Again* on January 10, 2000. The programme profiled Dave and Annie as a group and individuals through a series of interviews where they talked candidly, together with exclusive footage of their 1999 world tour and a wide range of archive extracts.

The Americans were not to be outdone as *Storytellers* was repeated in January, as was *Revolution* and various late night chat shows with appearances from either Annie or Eurythmics. On January 17 ABC broadcast the American Music Awards live from Los Angeles' Shrine Auditorium, where Eurythmics were playing. Just the two of them, Dave and Annie gave a spectacular performance, segueing together 'I Saved The World Today' and 'Here Comes The Rain Again', before Annie wished everyone a "Happy Martin Luther King Day". One gossip columnist, Liz Smith, later reported that Melissa Etheridge and Julie Cypher were heard sharing child rearing tips with Gloria Estefan and Annie Lennox backstage after the awards.

Their most important promotional event that month in America was to appear on A&E Network's popular programme, *Live By Request* on Wednesday 19, from the Sony Studios in Manhattan. As with the American Awards ceremony the pair were finally found out of their combat gear, and were on exceptional form, providing the fans with a memorable performance. The songs were chosen by fans and celebrities, with David Bowie's call requesting 'There Must Be An Angel (Playing With My Heart)' sparking great conversation with Annie. Old sparring partner Aretha Franklin asked for the classic, 'Sweet Dreams (Are Made Of This)' while the closing number, 'Power To The Meek', was the artists' own choice.

While the television coverage was forced to take commercial breaks, the studio audience saw clips of the *Peace* documentary, Annie's interview with Palden Gyatso and excerpts from Dave's upcoming film, *Honest*. During one such interlude Dave answered some e-mail questions that had been collected, and unofficially announced that he and Annie would be playing at some festivals in the summer. They then kept the audience entertained after the show had finished as Dave made his own request – for a glass of wine – and the duo settled in for a few more songs including Lou Reed's 'Walk On The Wild Side'.

With a new single due out at the end of January, back in Britain Eurythmics were seen on *Top Of The Pops* performing '17 Again'. Somewhat ludicrously, this was the setting for Annie, aged 45, to sing of feeling like a 17-year-old, to an audience who were primarily not only under that age themselves, but who weren't even alive 17 years before to remember 'Sweet Dreams (Are Made Of This)' the first time around!

BBC Radio 2 jumped on the bandwagon and produced a programme called *Sweet Dreams Are Made Of This*, for their interview story series combining songs, narration and chat from the stars. Aired on January 22, this was followed by a recording of a concert at Wembley during the Peace Tour.

Appearing on ITV's early morning show *GMTV* on January 24 and *TFI Friday* later that week, Eurythmics continued the never-ending promotion, this time for the second single from *Peace*, '17 Again'. It emerged on CD format, with B-sides recorded live on the Peace Tour and the accompanying video. The song did not fare terribly well in the UK, reaching no higher than 27, but in America a dance version incredibly reached number one on the dance charts. In a flashback to old times this mix was recalled by Eurythmics as they had not officially approved it.

The video, directed by Eurythmics themselves, caused a certain amount of controversy in America for what were supposedly "graphic battle scenes", thus delaying its release during heavy editing. Featuring the same backdrop and costumes as 'I Saved The World Today', as Annie sings bombs explode near the musicians and bullets are sprayed randomly, forcing the orchestra members to desert their leaders. When the brave pair are the only ones left and Annie recalls the lyrics from 'Sweet Dreams (Are Made Of This)', she too is shot, melodramatically clutching at Dave as she falls to the ground. The video mirrors the theme of the song in its autobiographical sense; suggesting that Annie and Dave have always had to fight their own battles, mainly against the media who fire continuous barbs at them, but ultimately they will remain together.

Ceaseless in their enthusiasm, the duo utilised their current popularity to raise money once again, this time by donating items for a celebrity auction held at the charity screening of cult British film, *Withnail And I*, on February 7, at the Odeon cinema in Leicester Square. The monies collected went to offer academically gifted children in Swaziland the opportunity of attending the Waterford–Kamhlaba school. In their home country at least the pair could do no wrong, and their charitable efforts were lauded by the press on an almost daily basis.

★   ★   ★

While the British were pleased with Eurythmics' success and publicity, the American audience were increasingly discontented, laying the blame on everyone including Clive Davis, Arista and even the record-buying public. They believed that, based on previous poor sales of Eurythmics overseas, the record label felt that the market was not strong enough to support as many singles abroad as in their native country. However, although the Americans were clearly unsatisfied with a few cursory chat show appearances, they missed the fact that there *were* adverts in most magazines, and in-depth documentaries and concerts aired only in the US. If the radio stations were not playing the music it was not necessarily a fault of the label. On the contrary, the Australian fans were worse off, as they had neither singles nor television slots.

Continuing to concentrate their efforts in Europe, Eurythmics performed at what appeared to be the first of the festivals Dave had mentioned at the *Live By Request* show. On February 21, they were introduced to an excitable audience at the San Remo festival in Italy by opera star Luciano Pavarotti, who offered his congratulations on their reunion. Eurythmics then lip-synched to a short version of '17 Again' before being ushered offstage.

On February 28, 2000 Dave was tickled pink to become a father for the third time as Anoushka gave birth to a healthy baby girl. The Eurythmics star gushed to the press, "I'm really pleased because the baby's gorgeous and my sons are crazy about her." Opting for an unusual name in true Eurythmics tradition, Dave and his girlfriend named their baby girl Kaya.

While Dave was allowed to take a break for a new family addition, Eurythmics' promotion was not. A pre-recorded documentary, not dissimilar to *17 Again*, was shown on Dutch television on March 3, swiftly followed by an appearance by Annie alone on the German show *SKL Millionaire*. The official excuse given for Dave's absence was that he was ill and could not fly, but whatever the reason it made for an awkward performance by Annie, with just the tour band backing her.

388

As is always the case in reunions or anniversaries, the *Greatest Hits* package was re-released, along with *Sweet Dreams (The Video Album)*. Unfortunately the critics disapproved of these easy cash-ins.

"There was something grimly inevitable about the Eurythmics' recent reunion," wrote a non-fan at Q magazine. "It tacitly acknowledged that the solo careers had failed, culminating in Dave Stewart's increasingly hysterical attempts to seek attention[55] and Annie Lennox's version of 'A Whiter Shade Of Pale', which seemed to have been the result of a bet. Together though, they had their moments. Her lyrics were anodyne and she seemed to spend most of her waking hours polishing up her unsexiness, but he was a master of the layered soundscape."

Whatever comments Eurythmics were receiving in the press, nothing was to be as damaging as the attacks suffered by Clive Davis, Arista Records and the parent company, BMG. At the end of January 2000, BMG's dark past had been revealed in *The Times*: "Crippled with embarrassment, the huge Bertelsmann Media Group has been forced to admit that it actively profited from its role in Hitler's Third Reich." If that wasn't enough, in February's *Vanity Fair* magazine Clive Davis' past 30 years were hauled under the microscope, climaxing in the humiliating announcement that BMG no longer had need of his services. Among allegations that the executives simply couldn't stand him, there were also accusations that Davis used company funds of up to $6,000 to pay for liposuction on Faith Evans' legs. Davis retaliated with a straightforward denial, claiming that he was being fired because he was too old.

Throughout this public haranguing, Arista continued plans to celebrate their 25th anniversary with an all-star concert in Clive Davis' honour. The event was held at the Shrine Auditorium in Los Angeles on April 10, and was first televised on May 15. The night's revelry applauded Arista Records for its phenomenal rise, endless number one hits and spectacular roster of performers. Davis had founded the company back in 1975, naming it after his high school honor society, and by 2000 the label boasted a core of artists who had stayed with the company for more than a decade; Whitney Houston, Barry Manilow, Patti Smith, Aretha Franklin, Carly Simon and Eurythmics.

Many of these singers paid tribute to the man who had made it all possible, but while Aretha excused herself on the grounds that she was afraid of flying, Annie simply stole the show. Introduced by Melissa

---

[55] In 1999 reports were rife that Dave had succumbed to celebrity disorder 'Paradise Syndrome'. The irony was that Dave had merely invented this disease to illustrate a lecture given at the Royal Geographical Society.

Etheridge, Annie came on to rapturous applause and said a few kind words about Clive Davis before sitting down at a grand piano. Dressed in a long black and silver sequinned gown, a small feather boa, long black boots, and sunglasses she not only looked arresting, but she also took the audience's breath away with her performance of 'Why'. Annie fully deserved the standing ovation she received as she rounded off the last note.

Davis had been equally praising about Annie as both a solo artist and within a group on his label, remarking that some acts need nurturing and some are fully formed – Eurythmics were obviously in the latter category. It will be interesting therefore to see where loyalties lie as his position was filled by Antonio Reid on July 1. Reid had been partners with Kenneth 'Babyface' Edmonds at LaFace Records, also owned by BMG, while Davis was made an offer he perhaps could not refuse. Allegedly BMG put forward a $180 million deal whereby he would create Davis Entertainment, whose primary directive would be an as yet un-named label component that would instantly have the status of a major. If he accepts it, Whitney Houston is expected to follow. It remains to be seen whether Eurythmics will also jump ship.

★　　★　　★

While the Eurythmic treadmill turned, Annie's personal life hit the headlines with a bang. On the weekend of April 22, 2000 the news broke that Annie and Uri had split up after 12 years of marriage. In a desperate bid to play down the trauma, friends rallied round, telling the press that the break was amicable and their two children would stay with their mother at her home in Highgate.

What had seemed to be one of the strongest relationships in the business had apparently fallen foul to the pressures of both parents being active professionals. Reports suggested that they had simply drifted apart, not least because they had barely seen each other since Eurythmics reformed. One close friend told the *Sun* exclusively, "It has come as a shock to a lot of us, but things just weren't working. Uri is extremely busy with his film career and last year was a big one for Annie with the band getting back together."

This turn of events was particularly distressing considering the lengths to which both Annie and Dave had gone in ensuring that their respective partners and families were involved and not left behind during the promotion. No matter how hard she tried, perhaps it was inevitable that Annie could only really sustain one relationship with a male at any one time – after all, it had been Uri who had helped her break away from the suffocating ties to her ex-lover in the late Eighties. Was it really possible for him to stand back and watch Dave re-enter her life?

Annie jetted off with the girls, now aged 10 and seven, on a Caribbean holiday to escape the prying eyes of well-meaning fans and intrusive media. She appeared confident, if a little tight-lipped, and still excited about the success of Eurythmics' reunion.

Meanwhile Uri buried his head firmly in his work. Having set up Fragile three years previously, he had seen success with *Spiceworld, The Movie, An Ideal Husband* and his latest humorous offering, *Kevin And Perry Go Large*. The company prepared to shoot their next project, *Our Lucky Break*, later in 2000; an Ealing-style comedy about a group of prisoners who stage a musical as cover for an escape attempt.

★   ★   ★

During Annie's marital split, the third single from *Peace*, 'Beautiful Child', was due to be released at the end of April. While it is pleasant enough as an album filler it was an unusual and perhaps unwise choice as a single, when a rousing chant such as 'I Want It All' might have been more appropriate for a summer hit. In the event it was not released.

Returning dutifully to work, Annie finally agreed to her previous invitations to see Pope John Paul II, playing at the Rome University on May 1, 2000. Eurythmics joined artists including Lou Reed, Alanis Morissette and Andrea Bocelli for the Great Jubilee Concert for a Debt-Free World. The bizarre spectacle of the Pope sharing a stage with Lou Reed, a founding member of the Velvet Underground whose songs extolled the virtues of sex and drugs, drew a crowd of some half a million people, while more watched the event on national television. As the Pope addressed the rock concert audience standing next to the former wild child, representatives of the religion were keen to point out that they did not look at people's history, but to the future millennium.

Annie was not the only one to perform under strained personal circumstances as Bocelli's father had passed away just a few hours before he went on stage, but professionalism ruled the day and both artists coped admirably.

While coming to terms with the split from her husband, Annie was thrown once again into the limelight with Eurythmics. On May 14, 2000 the *Sunday Times* belatedly released an exclusive interview with the duo along with a limited edition CD. The disc contained three standard tracks from the album, two live performances of songs from *Peace* in The Church and one on Rainbow Warrior, and a selection of interviews. There was nothing of any news to fans and the CD's only worth had been to promote the launch of the *Peacetour* video the following day, except the latter was delayed almost two months for no apparent reason.

Instead, another single was cloned from the album, this time the title track, 'Peace Is Just A Word', in a limited edition format. The CD contained a video of a performance originally aired on a European documentary the previous year. To promote this collector's item Annie and Dave appeared together once again on *GMTV* on May 17. They both seemed relaxed and happy, discussing future Eurythmics moves including the summer festivals that Dave had hinted at before. Annie explained that they were looking to "minimise" their set, playing 12 festivals as a simple acoustic combo. "It's quite ambitious to do this," she said. "Just to have two people on the stage and nothing else is a little exposing to say the least."

Although her personal life was under close guard at the time, Annie was happy to talk about her children's reaction to seeing their mother on stage for the first time in a totally different incarnation. She thought they were a little surprised at first although they approved once they got used to the idea. Ultimately, she sighed, they were both huge fans of bubblegum pop group, Aqua.

Dave in turn spoke about his new film, *Honest*, claiming that the idea had originated from Annie, who had written the synopsis on the back of her boarding pass some time earlier when they were bored on a flight from Birmingham to Glasgow. As Dave is the perennial joker it is hard to know whether to believe this or not. Annie played along, but either way she would have done better to deny it as the film received terrible reviews after going on general release in the UK on May 26. The edgy black comedy was given an 18 rating for content which prevented the majority of potential viewers from seeing it as All Saints fans were typically in their early teens. It was not long before *Honest* was withdrawn from cinemas as a financial disaster.

Undeterred by this failure Dave was already working on his next film and writing a screenplay with Deepak Chopra, the New Age guru to Hollywood stars. The movie's working title was *Juggernaut* and it follows an American hit man in India. However, Dave had unwittingly proved once again that his projects are largely successful only when they include his undeniable soulmate, Annie Lennox. It came as no great surprise, after his solo failure and Annie's marital split, that the two announced in June that they would be returning to the studio later in the year. Before that they planned to take their children on holiday together as a group.

★ ★ ★

Powering ahead with the summer of festivals as promised, Dave and Annie surfaced at the year's charity concert known as Pavarotti & Friends on

June 6. Performing alongside many other famous pop acts such as George Michael, Skunk Anansie, Westlife and once again Lou Reed, Eurythmics played their favoured acoustic version of 'I Saved The World Today'. But one thing was startlingly different – their physical appearance. Literally washing that man out of her hair, Annie wore a slinky dress and returned to an image of yesteryear, completing her look with shocking blonde hair. She also took the opportunity to relax while in Italy, walking around Bologna and showing her children the sites.

Eurythmics' next move was to Germany to take part in the joint Rock Am Ring/Rock Im Park festival between June 9 and 11. The two three-day festivals are held on the same weekend at two different venues in Germany, with the same artists performing at both. Eurythmics played first at Rock Im Park in Nuremberg on June 9, and then at Rock Am Ring in Nurburging on June 10. These dates were followed by the Heineken Jammin festival at Imola, Italy on June 17, and Jam 2000 in Prague, Czechoslovakia the following day. There was no let-up.

At the end of the month the tireless pair flew to America for Microsoft founder Paul Allen's launch of the rock museum, Experience Music Project, in Seattle on June 24, 2000. The city whispers were wild about the opening of architect Frank O Gehry's controversial building, and a crowd of 28,000 bought tickets which ranged up to $150 for the celebrity show. Allen strolled on stage with Gena Gershon to announce the opening performers, his very good friends, Eurythmics.

In contrast to their combats, Eurythmics turned up in glittery silver outfits. Amusingly they matched the décor as the stage involved a revolving platform featuring two stainless steel arches and a silver backdrop. While one band played on one side, the next group set up on the other so as to have a continuous performance. But apparently not everything had been properly planned for the smooth running of the event.

Eurythmics blasted on stage with a powerful version of 'Missionary Man', always a crowd pleaser. But as they continued into 'Here Comes The Rain Again', the helicopters flying above to record the gig for VH1 began to drown out the sound. Dave in particular became disgruntled and stopped playing twice.

Annie went over to him and diplomatically asked him to keep playing, joking to the audience, "I guess we're just *so* famous!" But they were genuinely upset and stopped the song, explaining to the angry fans that they only wanted the music to be good for them. Before they walked off Dave had stuck a defiant middle finger up to the helicopter, which was quickly followed by 28,000 copy-cat gestures. The fans started chanting "Go away" and, on seeing Paul Allen in the wings, "Paul make the call!"

The helicopter did eventually fly off and five minutes later Eurythmics returned to finish their set. They picked up where they left off and completed 'Here Comes The Rain Again' with a vengeance, followed by 'I Saved The World Today', 'I Love You Like A Ball And Chain', 'Sisters Are Doin' It For Themselves' and 'Why'. After a wild finale of 'Sweet Dreams (Are Made Of This)' Eurythmics were offered an encore but politely declined, despite the screaming throng in front of them. Annie was later taken around the museum and enthused, "I think it's going to be lovely for Seattle. I wish I lived in Seattle."

A week later on June 30, Eurythmics were due to receive a coveted Silver Clef Award at the music charity event's 25th ceremony in London. The honour is given in recognition of charitable work, and with *Peace* the previous year Eurythmics had amply secured the vote. Annie was unable to attend due to an ongoing back injury which was triggered by anxiety, and so it was Dave's turn to appear alone. He distracted everyone's attention from Annie's absence in a loud red-checked shirt, but Simon Fuller was forced to make a telling statement on her behalf: "It is a stressful time for her, especially because she is going through a divorce."

Although they had managed to make the Libro Music Festival in Vienna on June 27, Annie's recurring back problem prevented Eurythmics from fulfilling three more festival dates already booked for the Werchter Festival in Belgium, the Eurockeennes Belfort gig in France and the Midtfyns Festival in Denmark. One Danish concert they must have been glad to have avoided was the Roskilde Festival near Copenhagen, as in the frenzy during Pearl Jam's set nine people were crushed to death having fallen on the slippery mud underfoot. Despite Glastonbury donating a large portion of their proceeds to Greenpeace Eurythmics had not been booked to play there.

Concerned fans enquired as to the welfare of Annie, but were reassured that her back had simply been a little overworked and that she just needed some rest. She had planned to spend the summer holidays with her children after the festivals and so this setback just brought that time forward a little. Annie chose to recuperate and spend some much needed time alone with her daughters.

★   ★   ★

For once in Annie's life the future was uncertain. The video album for *Peace* was released, featuring the final concert from the reunion tour, shot at London Docklands Arena on December 6, 1999. The DVD version also contained promotional videos and interview segments.

As Annie Lennox took a breather from the whirlwind that had been the

Eurythmics reformation, speculation grew concerning a few choice comments about the group "returning to the studio in September." Whether this was concerning a new album, a film soundtrack or some form of tribute contribution remained nebulous.

In the past Annie has always successfully balanced family life with her career. Now forced into single motherhood it is unclear how she will amalgamate the demands of her brood with a brilliantly revived career. But Annie Lennox has never failed her public yet.

Epilogue

WHEN THE DAY GOES DOWN

"I've loved Dave from the day I first met him, and I'll love him for the rest of my life. To a certain extent, we are twinned together for all eternity."
— Annie Lennox, May 12, 2000

As the latest chapter in Annie Lennox's life draws to a close, the one thing that stands out is her remarkable bravery. She is admirable in her resilience, championing the modern mother in the wake of her second divorce with a maturity few others could match. Her children have only over the last year or so had the pleasure of seeing her perform on stage, and as Annie prepares to re-enter the studio with Dave Stewart, it looks like Lola and Tali will be watching their mother recommence the battle for chart positions alongside the very pop groups that are plastered across their bedroom walls.

This does not mean by any stretch of the imagination that Annie's coveted personal life will suffer. As close friend Barry Maguire defines, "She is a fantastic person to sit down and chat to, really unassuming, very *real*. The life she's got now I think she always wanted — children and a home, rather than just a house or a hotel room."

But the truth may lie closer to her children than even she suspects. Perhaps with her new lease of Eurythmic life Annie has been granted the opportunity for a second childhood; a chance to banish those lost years before Dave Stewart proposed marriage on first sight.

The icy greyness of Aberdeen, the stifling rigidity of the Royal Academy of Music, the desperation of bedsit land and a handful of failed romances have all provided excellent fodder for lyrical inspiration, but now it is time to bury her ghosts. "I think Annie probably was a mature woman when she was in her teens somehow, there are people who are just old and wise before their years," aptly summarises one-time companion, Peter Ashworth.

"If you're a sensitive person, and I am, it's not an easy life, not an easy cop-out," Annie said in 1988. "It is a charmed life to some extent. I've

396

travelled all over the world and I have some money for the first time in my life and I enjoy it. I'd be a hypocrite to say I don't, but it all has its price. You have to live with what you do and to be able to deal with some very awkward situations."

Within Annie's very ability to deal with such situations there lies the key to her survival. Since recklessly marrying a man with whom she shared no background, religion or long-lasting affection, her biting cynicism rarely lets her down, at least in public. While the magazines are full of precocious divas demanding miles of red carpet, colour co-ordinated puppies and acres of media footage, Annie Lennox quite simply does not believe the hype.

"Most pop stars believe in their own hype, the fantasy world that's created for them. I've never believed in it. I've always known it's a kind of monster. In the end it's all a huge fiction . . .

"The thing is that I so much don't believe in the hype that, if it all means a lot to someone else, I'm kind of embarrassed for both of us. Even if I'm touched by what they say, I find it hard to accept the compliment." The fact that the star admits to being uncomfortable with her most ardent admirers goes a long way to explaining her reluctance to open up, except within her music. Old friends consequently find it hard to recognise the woman behind the performer's mask.

"I was quite disappointed in the way that Annie became brittle and cold, to the outside world anyway, because when I knew her she was a warm person," says the man who introduced her to the music industry, Rob Gold. "But she presents this rather cold persona."

Since the lines of communication have been reopened between Annie and the man with whom she shared a lifetime of success and bitterness, it remains to be seen how long the partnership will last. Undeniably there is now no significant other to distract Annie from her first loves; music and Dave.

Radha Raman once revealingly outlined the unique bond between Annie Lennox and Dave Stewart thus: "Annie gets pessimistic at times. She draws premature conclusions . . . She does really funny things real quick. So other people have to say, 'Hey, look at the pink sky out there, everything's fine.' Dave is expert at that, and I think that's why their relationship works."

Unquestionably, Annie would continue to persevere without her friend's presence, but whether she would ever again consider hoisting herself back into the public gaze alone is debatable. For the moment it doesn't really matter – no other reunited group from the Eighties has struck such a chord with fans and non-fans alike. The sheer lack of any commercial greed from any of the promotion surrounding *Peace* remains unprecedented in the musical world. It's a long, long time since Annie had to cobble together a recipe composed of a piece of broccoli and a carrot for herself and her lover, and now she has more global issues to attend to.

Outside Annie's kitchen window, there is no doubt about it. The sky is currently turning a subtle shade of pink.

Discography

CATCH

| Borderline / Black Blood | Logo GO 103 | Oct 77 |

THE TOURISTS

Singles

Blind Among The Flowers	Logo GO 350	May 79
Golden Lamp / Wrecked (free with above)		
The Loneliest Man In The World	Logo GO 360	Jul 79
I Only Want To Be With You	Logo GO 370	Oct 79
So Good To Be Back Home	Logo TOUR 1	Jan 80
Don't Say I Told You So	RCA TOUR 2	Sept 80

Albums

The Tourists	Logo GO 831148	Jun 79
Reality Effect	Logo GO 1019	Oct 79
Luminous Basement	RCA RCALP 5001	Oct 80
Should Have Been Greatest Hits	Epic	1984
Greatest Hits	Camden74321523812	1997

EURYTHMICS

Singles

Never Gonna Cry Again	RCA 68	May 81
Belinda	RCA 115	Aug 81
This Is The House	RCA 199	Mar 82
The Walk	RCA 230	Jun 82
Love Is A Stranger	RCA DA 1	Sep 82
Sweet Dreams (Are Made Of This)	RCA DA 2	Jan 83
Love Is A Stranger (Re-issue)	RCA DA 1	Apr 82
Who's That Girl?	RCA DA 3	Jun 83
Right By Your Side	RCA DA 4	Oct 83
Here Comes The Rain Again	RCA DA 5	Jan 84
Sexcrime (nineteen eighty-four)	Virgin VS 728	Nov 84
Julia	Virgin VS 734	Jan 85
Would I Lie To You?	RCA PB 40101	April 85

There Must Be An Angel	RCA PB 40247	Jun 85
(Playing With My Heart)		
Sisters Are Doin' It For Themselves	RCA PB 40339	Oct 85
It's Alright (Baby's Coming Back)	RCA PB 403775	Dec 85
When Tomorrow Comes	RCA DA 7	May 86
Thorn In My Side	RCA DA 8	Aug 86
The Miracle Of Love	RCA DA 9	Nov 86
Missionary Man	RCA DA 10	Feb 87
Beethoven (I Love To Listen To)	RCA DA 11	Oct 87
Shame	RCA DA 14	Dec 87
I Need A Man	RCA DA 15 CD	Mar 88
You Have Placed A Chill In My Heart	RCA DA 16	May 88
Sexcrime (nineteen eighty-four)	Virgin CDT 22	Nov 88
Revival	RCA DACD 17	Aug 89
Don't Ask Me Why	RCA DACD 19	Oct 89
The King And Queen Of America	RCA DACD 23	Jan 90
Angel	RCA DACD 21	Apr 90
Love Is A Stranger (Re-issue)	RCA PD 44266	Feb 91
Sweet Dreams (Are Made Of This) (Re-mix)	RCA PD 45032	Nov 91
I Saved The World Today	BMG 69563	Oct 99
17 Again	BMG 72626	Mar 00
Sexcrime	EMI 891913	Apr 00
Peace Is Just A Word	BMG 76575	Jul 00

Albums

In The Garden	RCA ND 75036	Oct 81
Sweet Dreams (Are Made Of This)	RCA ND 71471	Jan 83
Touch	RCA ND 90369	Nov 83
Touch Dance	RCA ND 75151	May 84
1984 (For The Love Of Big Brother)	Virgin CDV 1984	Nov 84
Be Yourself Tonight	RCA ND 74602	Apr 85
Revenge	RCA PD 74251	Jun 86
Savage	RCA/BMG 74321	Nov 87
We Too Are One	RCA PD 74261	Sep 89
Greatest Hits	RCA PD 74856	Mar 91
Remix Collection	Alex 2439	Feb 92
Live 1983–1989	RCA 743211711452	Nov 93
Touch Dance: Remix Collection	BMG 75151	Jun 98
Peace	Arista 14617	Oct 99

Miscellaneous (Compilations, Box Sets, Soundtracks)

Chris and Cosey	RTT148	1984
('Sweet Surprise')		
Who's Zoomin' Who? – Aretha Franklin	Arista ARCD8286	1985
('Sisters Are Doin' It For Themselves')		

Greenpeace	A&M SP-5091	1985
('No Fear No Hate No Pain (No Broken Hearts)')		
Nine And A Half Weeks (S/T)	Capitol C2-46722	1988
('This City Never Sleeps')		
Interview Disc	Baktabak 2128	1988
Rooftops Soundtrack	Capitol C2-91736	1989
('Revenge Part II')		
Greenpeace: Rainbow Warriors	Geffen 2-24236	1989
('When Tomorrow Comes')		
Very Special Christmas	A&M 75021 3911 2	1989
('Winter Wonderland')		
Lily Was Here Soundtrack	Arista ARCD8670	1991
('Here Comes The Rain Again')		
Striptease	EMI 52498	1996
('Sweet Dreams (Are Made Of This)')		

Videos

Sweet Dreams	RCA Columbia	1984
Live	Polygram 080221	May 88
Savage	Atlantic 50125	Jun 88
We Two Are One Too	Pioneer 312	Apr 90
Greatest Hits	BMG 5712	Apr 91
Peacetour	Arista 15749	Jun 00

SOLO

Singles

Put A Little Love In Your Heart	A&M AM 484	Oct 88
(with Al Green)		
Why	RCA PD 45320	Mar 92
Precious	RCA 74321 100252	May 92
Walking On Broken Glass	RCA 74321 107222	Aug 92
Cold	RCA 74321 116902	Oct 92
Little Bird	RCA 74321 133832	Feb 93
No More 'I Love You's	Arista 12804	Feb 95
A Whiter Shade Of Pale	Arista 12850	Jun 95
Waiting In Vain	BMG 74321	Sept 95
Something So Right	BMG 46662	Dec 95

Albums

Diva	RCA PD 75326	Apr 92
Medusa	Arista	1995

Miscellaneous (Compilations, Box Sets, Soundtracks)

Robert Görl – Robert Görl		1981
(Annie contributes vocals)		

Latin Lover – Gianna Nannini	Ricordi 6297	1982
(Annie contributes keyboards)		
Radio Silence – Boris Grebenshikov	Columbia CK44364	1989
(Annie contributes vocals)		
Red Hot + Blue: A Tribute To Cole Porter	Chrysalis CHR21799	1990
('Ev'rytime We Say Goodbye')		
Prelude To A Kiss		1992
('Ev'rytime We Say Goodbye')		
Freddie Mercury Tribute CD		1992
('Under Pressure' with David Bowie)		
The Mermaid – Christa Fast		1992
('Octopi Song', 'The Lovely Seashell')		
House Of Groove		1993
Alternative NRG (Greenpeace)		1993
Unplugged Collection Vol 1	Warner Bros 45774	1994
('Why')		
Melrose Place: The Music		1994
Apollo 13 Soundtrack		1995
Boys On The Side		1995
Ain't Nuthin' But A She Thing		Oct 95
('Mama')		
The Avengers Soundtrack		1995
('Mama')		
Great White Hype		1996
Every Nation		1997
Step By Step – Whitney Houston		1997
Carnival!		Apr 1997
('Dream Angus')		
Diana Princess Of Wales		Dec 1997
('Angel')		
It's Only Rock'n'Roll – Children's Promise	1565982	Dec 99

Videos

Diva	Arista 15719	Apr 92
Live In Central Park	Arista 15734	Jun 96

Eurythmics Bibliography

Books:

Eurythmics In Their Own Words (Omnibus Press, 1984)

Waller J., and Rapport S., Sweet Dreams – The Definitive Biography Of Eurythmics (Virgin, 1985)

Jasper T., Eurythmics (Zomba, 1985)

Martin N., Everything You Needed To Know About Eurythmics (Ballantine, 1984)

O'Brien L., Annie Lennox – Sweet Dreams Are Made Of This (Sidgwick & Jackson, 1991)

Roland P., Eurythmics (Proteus, 1984)

Bright, S., Peter Gabriel An Authorised Biography (Sidgwick & Jackson, 1988)

Geldof, B., Is That It?: The Autobiography (Sidgwick & Jackson, 1986)

George, Boy., with Bright, S., Take It Like A Man The Autobiography Of Boy George (Sidgwick & Jackson, 1995)

Halliwell, G., If Only (Bantam, 1999)

Jackson, J., A Cure For Gravity (Anchor, 1999)

Jones, L., Freddie Mercury The Definitive Biography (Hodder And Stoughton, 1997)

Yates, P., The Autobiography (Harper Collins, 1995)

Reference Books:

British Hit Singles (Guinness, 1999)

Concise Encyclopedia – A Quick Reference Guide (Grandreams, 1996)

Concise Encyclopedia Of World History (Parragon, 1994)

Encyclopedia Of Albums (Dempsey Parr, 1998)

Encyclopedia Of Rock Obituaries, The (Omnibus Press, 1999)

Faber Companion To Twentieth Century Popular Music, The (Faber and Faber, 1990)

Guinness World Records 2000 Millennium Edition

Halliwells Film And Video Guide 1999 Edition (Harper Collins, 1999)

Halliwells Who's Who In The Movies (Harper Collins, 1999)

Hutchinson Encyclopedia 1997 Edition, The (Helicon, 1997)

Q – Encyclopedia Of Rock Stars (Dorling Kindersley, 1996)

Warner Guide To UK And US Hit Singles, The (Carlton / Little, Brown, 1996)

Who's Who In The Twentieth Century (Oxford University Press, 1999)

Reports:

The Aberdeen Typhoid Outbreak 1964 Report of the Departmental Committee of
  Enquiry, December 1964

Periodicals:

*Aberdeen Evening Express, Aberdeen People's Journal, Aberdeen Sunday Post Billboard,
Boston Rock, Daily Express, Daily Mirror, Daily Mirror Video Special, Daily Record, Daily
Telegraph, Eurythmics – A Disco Hotpop Special, The Express Magazine, The Face, Filter,
Goldmine, Graffiti, Guardian, Look-In, Melody Maker, Metro, Mirror Woman, Musician,
New Hi-Fi Sound, NME, News Of The World, No 1, Nuggets, The Observer, The People,
Politiken, Q, Radio Times, Record Mirror, Rolling Stone, Select, Smash Hits, Sounds, Spin,
Spiral Scratch, The Sport, Sunday Express, Sunday Telegraph Magazine, The Sunday
Times, Superstars Of Rock, Time Out, The Times, Tracks, TV Guide, Vox, Weekend,
What's On TV, You Magazine, Zig Zag*

Film Appearances:

Edward II, Revolution, The Room, The Long Way Home

Documentaries:

Diva, Peace, 17 Again

Radio Interviews:

BBC Radio 1 (Paul Gambaccini), BBC Radio 2 (Richard Allinson)

Index